# PSYCHOLOG
# OF SOCI

## Developing a Progressive Vision for Society

Mick Cooper

P

First published in Great Britain in 2023 by

Policy Press, an imprint of
Bristol University Press
University of Bristol
1–9 Old Park Hill
Bristol
BS2 8BB
UK
t: +44 (0)117 374 6645
e: bup-info@bristol.ac.uk

Details of international sales and distribution partners are available at
policy.bristoluniversitypress.co.uk



British Library Cataloguing in Publication Data
A catalogue record for this book is available from the British Library

ISBN 978-1-4473-6102-2 hardcover
ISBN 978-1-4473-6103-9 paperback
ISBN 978-1-4473-6104-6 ePub
ISBN 978-1-4473-6105-3 ePdf



Cover design: River Design Books
Image credit: Shutterstock/Radu Bercan

To my brilliant, beautiful Zac, who I love with everything.

# Contents

# Acknowledgements

I am enormously grateful to Rebecca Tomlinson, Freya Trand, and colleagues at Policy Press for bringing this book to fruition, and to Dawn Preston at Newgen Publishing. To my partner, Julie Allan, for her loving, patient, and generous support and guidance. As ever, I want to express my love and thanks to my four children – Zac, Shula, Ruby, and Maya – who mean the world to me and make all of this meaningful; and to their mum, Helen Cruthers. My passion for politics and for social justice would not have been possible without my dad (an old-school communist), my mum (who always said she would have been a Buddhist), and my elder sisters.

Very special thanks to the following colleagues who gave invaluable feedback on earlier drafts of this manuscript: Peter Baker, Gavin Butt, Rachel Connor, Sue Cooper, Christabel Harley, and Hanne Oddli, along with two anonymous reviewers. Thanks also to colleagues in the Synergy Process Research Group – Ioan Fazey, Gideon Baffoe, Esther Carmen, Suzanne Om, and Lee Eyre – for the rich and stimulating discussions on synergistic processes. Finally, I would like to thank my friends and colleagues in the pluralistic community; and in the School of Psychology at the University of Roehampton – both past and present – for their support, encouragement, and guidance over many years.

1

# Introduction: Progressive politics needs therapy

To be progressive is to believe in the possibility of a better, fairer, and more compassionate world. It is to believe that we can create a society in which people, working cooperatively, can thrive and make the most of our lives. Progressivism is also about the thriving of the organic and non-organic world around us. Whether we are referring to green politics, feminism, or socialism, the focus is on making things better for us *all*: on sharing out what we have, and working together, so that wellbeing and fulfilment are not just in the hands of a privileged few. A progressive vision – the capacity to see beyond ourselves, towards cooperative and caring forms of social organisation – is, perhaps, one of humankind's greatest achievements. It gives us hope that we can create a better world: one in which oppression, suffering, and emotional pain are at a minimum and life is fullest and greatest for all.

## The challenge for progressives

Yet, as progressives know all too well, such a worldview does not always succeed. The Russian invasion of Ukraine, for instance, has shown, horrifically, how progressive and democratic forces can be assaulted by totalitarianism. Authoritarian 'populism' has become pervasive – the Brothers of Italy, Marine Le Pen in France, Trump and Bolsonaro in the Americas – with its hostility to progress, fairness, and justice for all.[1] In the UK, we have the depressing familiarity of rule by a right-wing elite. Across the globe, progressive voices seem to be struggling to garner popular support, and to be in a position where they can take forward an agenda of equality, social justice, and environmental protection. Neoliberalism rules across the global North and, like the Comeback Kid, seems to stay in favour however much it fails and is seen to fail.

The challenges to progressivism, however, do not just lie outside of our field. Inside it too, fragmentations and bitter divisions can be rife. Read the manifestos of the progressive parties, like the Greens and Labour, for instance, and you will find as much contempt towards each other as you will towards the right. Or take the arguments between trans rights activists and gender-critical feminists, which, on social media platform such as Twitter, can descend into name-calling, abuse, and even threats of violence. 'Terfs aren't feminists', states one post, 'terfs are misogynistic'.[2] On the other side, a gender-critical feminist is reported as tweeting: 'People can just fuck off really. Cut their dicks off and be more feminist than me. Good for them.'[3] The sad thing here is that, to a great extent, what both trans rights activists and gender-critical feminists want is something very similar: to support, and achieve equality for, minoritised groups (trans people and cis women, respectively). But somehow, when it descends into antagonism and abuse, two very progressive sets of views become something far from caring and cooperative.

The aim of this book is to show how we can create a progressive vision that can help to overcome such problems: a progressivism that is comprehensive, internally coherent, and compelling to the external world as well as ourselves. More specifically, I want to show how we can develop such a progressive vision through the integration of ideas and practices from psychology, counselling, and psychotherapy (henceforth I'll just use the term 'psychology' to mean all three). Imagine a cake without sugar; or one of those worthy, wholefood, English curries that is entirely bland. That, for me, is what progressivism is like if we do not have psychology as a key ingredient. In other words, I want to show how ideas from psychology can deepen, strengthen, and extend a progressive vision. And, on the other side of this, I want to show how a progressive vision is supported, powerfully, by the field of psychology. Because when you look at 'what works' in psychological interventions, it is amazingly similar to what progressives say 'works' at the societal level (for instance, cooperation, fairness, and prizing otherness). What this reveals is that there are some fundamental, 'system-wide' principles – operative both within people and between them – as to how you can make things better, and progressives are absolutely on the right tracks here. But there is also much more that we, as progressives, can learn, and teasing this out is one of the key aims of the book.

## Plan for the book

So, as the title suggests, this book is about creating a vision for a progressive society that has psychological understandings and practices at its heart. To try and achieve this, the book starts, in this chapter, by explaining why psychology may have such potential, the particular psychological position I am going to take, and by defining key terms. After that, the book looks at one very specific attempt to develop a progressive vision that had psychology at its core: *socialist humanism* (Chapter 2). I want to describe this approach in detail because it was one very compelling attempt to combine the progressive (in this case an anti-totalitarian Marxism) with the kind of psychological perspective that is adopted in this book (humanism). Understanding socialist humanism's strengths, as well as its limitations, will provide the basis for establishing a more contemporary, psychologically informed progressivism. The development of this perspective then commences, in earnest, in Chapter 3. This presents a framework for understanding human existence – drawing together understandings from across the psychological field – that can be smoothly, coherently, and constructively integrated with progressive thinking and political activity. This framework is then extended in Chapter 4, with an account of psychological wellbeing and distress. Again, the focus is on showing how we can understand people in a way that integrates the psychological into a progressive political understanding. Chapter 5 then shows how this psychological framework reveals parallels between optimal functioning at the *intrapersonal* level (i.e., 'within' the person) and at the *interpersonal* level (i.e., between people). This is, as far as I know, an original contribution; and of considerable value to progressives because it establishes common, 'system-wide' principles of what is 'good' (and what is 'bad').

The second half of the book focuses more on what we can do to create a better society, and what this 'better' would concretely look like. Chapter 6 begins by examining how we can get to the 'good', as defined in Chapter 5. Some of these common principles of positive change discussed here will be familiar to progressives – such as being fair, democratic, and prizing diversity – but there are other principles here that add, significantly, to progressive thought and practice. This includes, for instance, developing a capacity to see the bigger picture, trusting, and being assertive. By the end of Chapter 6, a unified set of principles for progressive thought and action have been described; and, in Chapter 7, their potential application in five practical domains is detailed: positive parenting, social and emotional learning, developing a wellbeing economy, emotionally literate politics, and nonviolent communication for all. The aim of this chapter is to show, concretely, how progressives – whether at the level of the individual or of progressive political parties – can roll out a psychology-informed progressive agenda. The next two chapters then take a series of steps further into the future. They ask, 'What kind of world would we, as progressives, ultimately want to see?' Chapter 8 looks at progressive attitudes (and resistances) towards such utopian thinking; and then goes on to try and describe the features of a progressive utopia, based on the psychological framework and practices developed earlier in the book. Chapter 9 then switches into fictional format, and tries to describe what it might actually be like to experience such a world. This chapter is somewhat experimental. However, these utopian chapters have a serious intent: if, as will be argued in this book, where we are going (our goals, purposes, and directions) is integral to who we are; then, as progressives, it is essential to explore, discuss, and articulate our visions for the future. Chapter 10 concludes the book by discussing implications for political strategy and drawing the themes together.

## A psychology-informed progressive vision

Previously, we had planned to call this book something like 'The politics of understanding'. 'Politics', however, turned out not be quite the right word because, as the description of the chapters suggests, the book is more than just about political strategy or tactics (for a book specifically on progressive political strategy see Amiel and Emelien's *The new progressivism*[4]). This book is about building up a particular image of how we, as humans, are; and, more importantly, how we can be – together, with each other, and with our planet. Such a *vision* has practical components (and the term 'vision' is not used to mean some supernatural or grandiose apparition); but it is also more holistic, longer-term, and conceptual. It is a description of what our being together might look like if we can move towards a better future.

The value of developing such visions is emphasised by Dutch historian Rutger Bregman, in his bestselling *Utopia for realists*.[5] Bregman argues that people are hungry for real, radical alternatives to free market, neoliberal capitalism. They have lived, he writes, through the financial crash of 2008; and are acutely aware of the looming environmental catastrophe, fuelled by untamed consumerism. The COVID-19 pandemic, too, has revealed the fragility of our current economic setup, and its dependence on such state-sponsored supports as the UK's National Health Service (NHS). Now, as I write this, we also have surging inflation, an energy crisis, and a military assault in Ukraine. Yet, Bregman argues, progressives suffer from being too reactive and 'anti-': clear about what they are against but not what they are for. What progressives need to do, he writes, is to tell a story of hope and progress, a compelling vision of a future that is more just, democratic, ecologically sustainable, and subjectively satisfying. Ideally, this can also be a common vision for different progressive voices: a shared hope for the future around which we can coalesce.[6]

So where might such a vision come from? Bregman's own utopia starts with the principal of a universal basic income, around which more equitable and humane social practices can emerge. Another contemporary progressive vision comes from Aaron Bastani in *Fully Automated Luxury Communism*,[7] which begins with the assumption of exponential technological advancement: a 'post-scarcity world'. Yanis Varoufakis, the Left-wing Greek economist and politician, lays out the economic foundations for a progressive world in his 2020 book, *Another now*.[8] More concretely, social movements like Black Lives Matter, Extinction Rebellion, and veganism have all inspired millions to believe that we can live in a world without racism, or without environmental or animal destruction, respectively. Inspiration also come from the growing numbers of young female leaders in the world today, among them Jacinda Ardern, Alexandria Ocasio-Cortez, Sanna Marin, and Greta Thunberg.

This book takes inspiration from a very different source, albeit one that is entirely compatible with the perspectives discussed. That source is *psychology*: the systematic study of mind, emotions, and behaviour. To date, psychology has been pretty much absent from contemporary progressive discourses (although, as we will discuss in Chapter 7, the field of *wellbeing economics* is moving rapidly in that direction; and organisations like Compassion in Politics are beginning to emerge). *The alternative: Towards a new progressive politics*,[9] for instance, is one of the most inspiring texts to come out of UK progressive politics for several years. Edited by a Green MP (Caroline Lucas), a Labour MP (Lisa Nandy), and a Liberal Democrat candidate (Chris Bowers), the book laid out a collaborative progressive agenda, with contributions from such fields as economics, social policy, and environmental studies. What was missing from the book, however, was any input from psychology, or any consideration of people's psychological make-up and functioning. There is a similar gap in the political manifestos of the Labour, Green, or Liberal Democrat parties; in their rhetoric; or in other contemporary writings from these, and related, perspectives. Psychology – compared with economics, sociology, history, or other social science perspectives – is notable only by its absence. As Michael Lerner, an American-based political activist, psychotherapist, and rabbi writes: 'Historically, socialist and communist movements (and their remnants in some contemporary movements like the British Labour Party) focused almost entirely on the external realities of life, the economic and political arrangements, ignoring the inner realities.'[10]

This is not to say that the subject of mental health problems, and mental health treatments, has been off the political agenda. Indeed, in recent years, there has been a very welcome recognition of the need for accessible and effective psychological interventions for both adults and children, across the political spectrum. However, such a focus on treating psychological problems – akin to the treatment of other health problems, like diabetes or cancer – is very different to the development of a politics that has psychological understandings at its very heart.

No doubt there are very good reasons why progressives have been wary of psychology. Psychology, to a great extent, individualises. Its very nature means that it tends to focus on processes and dynamics within the person – the 'inner realities' – rather than between people, communities, or classes. Consequently, it can tend to attribute suffering to individual factors – for instance, genetic predispositions, mental processes, or traumatic childhood experiences – rather than to the social and political inequities that progressives have wanted to emphasise. As a consequence of this, psychology has tended to focus on strategies for the amelioration of suffering at the individual level – through, for instance, counselling, psychotherapy, and psychoeducation – rather than through social and economic change.[11] Here, then, 'Ideas of social welfare and community had been pushed aside for individualised notions of resilience, wellness and self-improvement, promoted through a ballooning "self care" industry which relegates care to something we are supposed to buy for ourselves on a personal basis.'[12]

'Self care', the mantra of the personal development industry can, indeed, mean a move away from caring for others.[13] For my undergraduate dissertation I researched the history of the anti-sexist men's movement in the UK. What struck me was that the more that the men got into personal development and therapeutic activities during the 1970s and 1980s, the more they moved away from overtly pro-feminist work, like running crèches for feminist conferences or raising money for women's causes.[14] When this psychological, self-care industry starts to promote 'positive thinking' as the cure to our problems – based on the oft-quoted Hamlet premise that, 'there is nothing either good or bad, but thinking makes it so' – it can be seen as moving further to the right. Happiness, now, is something we can all just choose by changing the way we think.[15] As progressives, however, we know this is not true, and the research backs this up. Inequality – and associated socioeconomic factors like racism, homophobia, and oppression – are all well-established, identifiable antecedents of psychological distress.[16]

What is more, at worst, psychological interventions and theories have been used, at times, to paper over real social injustices: complicit in creating, maintaining, and supporting oppressive practices.[17] One recent example in the UK is the recruitment of psychologists into monitoring, modifying, and 'punishing' people who claim social security benefits.[18] Psychology's sordid history of collusion with reactionary and fascist ideologies – from the use of IQ tests to underpin eugenicist policies through to the American Psychological Association's collusion with the interrogation and torture of post-9/11 prisoners – has, quite understandably, done little to endear psychology to progressives' hearts.[19] Psychology, as American Associate Professor Rakhshanda Saleem and colleagues write, has 'immense potential for harm in the absence of a political, transnational, and decolonial analysis'.[20]

## Beyond social determinism

Yet, in this book, I want to argue that a progressive politics would greatly benefit from the integration of psychological insights and understandings. Why? A first reason is simply because, as the research shows, wellbeing can be strongly influenced by psychological factors.[21] Therefore, if we want to create a society in which people are happier and more thriving, we need to know what those psychological factors are. This is in no way to deny the evidence that social factors can also have a massive effect on people's wellbeing. But, within that, there is always some room for manoeuvre – some 'surplus repression' (see Chapter 2) – which means that, within the same set of circumstances, people can still have more or less wellbeing than would otherwise be the case. That means that, to maximise wellbeing, we need to focus on psychological factors as well as socioeconomic ones. More than that, we need to focus on the interaction between psychological and socioeconomic factors: the way, for instance, that poverty can lead parents to feel more stressed, which can then lead to less sensitive parenting styles, leading to poorer child mental health, and thereby lower levels of social and economic achievement as children grow up (see Chapter 7). Here, what we need is an integrated sociopsychological model of functioning and wellbeing that can allow us to see how both factors contribute to distress and interact. Describing a framework for this is one of the principal aims of this book.

## Understanding human needs and wants

Second, psychology can help us understand what it is that people really, deeply need and want, and therefore what a 'better' world would actually be. In *The alternative*, the Scottish social philosopher Jonathan Rowson, quoting political theorist Roberto Unger, writes that, 'A progressive is someone who wants to see society reorganized … so that ordinary men and women have a better chance to live a larger life.'[22] Yes, absolutely – but what do we mean by 'larger'? What is the inner texture of this way of being? Similarly, when the manifesto of the Labour Party advocates 'richer' lives for all,[23] or the political programme of the Green Party holds that 'wellbeing' should be a measure of progress[24] … yes, yes, and yes. But what is 'richer', and what do we mean by 'wellbeing'? Is it about being happier, or more creative, or greater autonomy? Or all these things and many more? And while advocates of the newly emerging wellbeing economics have done some fantastic work in beginning to address such questions, little of this is linked up to established psychological research, theories, or practices.

So to develop a world in which all people have access to more satisfying and fulfilling lives, we need to understand, deeply, what that satisfaction and fulfilment looks like – at the individual level, as well as in terms of well-functioning communities and societies. Johan Galtung, a Norwegian sociologist and founder of peace studies, used the analogy of a house. He wrote that to assume human beings are developing positively within positive social structures (such as democracy), 'is like assuming that inside a beautiful house there must by necessity be beautiful people'.[25] In other words, we could create a world with highly equitable social structures but still end up with citizens who are miserable, dysfunctional, and devoid of a sense of meaning and fulfilment in their lives.

This is not to say that progressives have ignored human needs and wants. As we will see in Chapter 2, for instance, these are intrinsic to much socialist thinking. But the focus, at least explicitly, has tended to be on material needs – like food, security, and welfare – rather than those non-material needs that are likely to be part of a 'larger' existence too.[26] This might include, for instance, experiencing intimacy with others, finding meaning in life, or being more genuine and authentic. In our day-to-day lives, these are often the things that matter most to us: that make life worth living. So if we are going to create a more equal society, we need to work out what it is that we want all people to have a fair share of. That way, we can develop policies and practices that not only help to create a fairer society at the material level, but at the non-material too. How do we make a world, for instance, in which everyone has access to feeling loved, or to expressing themselves creatively, or to feeling valued and of worth? Lerner describes this as the provision of *subjective caring*, and argues that it needs to supplement *objective caring*, in which we focus on people's material needs. He writes: 'The Left must recognise that suffering is not only based on material lack, but is also based on social, psychological, and spiritual deprivations.'[27]

In fact, to a great extent, progressives *have* probably been aware of the need for all beings to be able to realise non-material needs and wants. At the heart of feminist or postcolonial theories, for instance, is a belief that women, colonised people, or other marginalised groups have a right to experience autonomy and a sense of self-worth. Similarly, veganism is based on the assumption that animals have a right to live without suffering. Indeed, many of us – perhaps all of us – have come towards a progressive viewpoint because we believe passionately that all people should have the right to such non-material needs and wants as freedom, happiness, fulfilment, and the experience of meaning and community. So a desire for equality at the non-material level is there in progressives; it is just that such an understanding is often not made explicit, systematised, or discussed at any level of depth. This means that introducing psychology into progressive politics is less about adding something new, and more about developing tools and a language that can help us articulate – and discuss in greater critical depth – our pre-existing, implicit beliefs and assumptions. What do you think, for instance, makes a genuinely fulfilling life? What do you want all people to have access to? Is it, for instance, relationships, self-worth, or freedom – or all these needs and wants and many more? This book does propose a set of provisional answers to these questions but, more than anything else, my hope is that this book will stimulate progressives to be asking and answering these questions for themselves. In this respect, psychology can help us bring these questions to light, to see our differences and similarities, and to talk together to develop a more compelling and coherent progressive vision.

To say something of my own journey here: I was born, in the mid-1960s, into a family that had progressive politics at its core. Both my parents were members of the Communist Party and, as a child, I eagerly absorbed – and, to a great extent, regurgitated – their communist views. For me, Lenin and Mao were like kindly uncles – something that my children, studying the realities of 20th-century communism at school, found utterly bizarre. A coach trip to the Soviet Union in my late teens, however, started to shift my perspective. One image I remember, in particular, was going to a supermarket near Odessa and looking out over rows and rows of one type of jam. That was it: a single, Soviet-approved preserve. And I remember thinking, 'Where's the variety, where's the opportunity for discovery, for difference?' Communism, it seemed to me, had provided for people's most basic food and shelter needs (although, of course, I was to learn that even that was wrong), but something fundamental to human thriving seemed to be missing: diversity, challenge, growth, excitement.

To the disappointment of my parents, then (and it is not often that parents are disappointed by their children's lack of radicalism), I came to feel that capitalism – for all its flaws – did seem to address (or, rather, promised to address) some very real human needs and wants. This was something about an excitement, a colourfulness, a promise of the new. For me, for instance, it is that excitement of wandering around a farmers' market and tasting dozens of different types of cheese, or browsing online for new books. And while, as a progressive, I find it shameful to admit this; such pleasures are real and a genuine part of what gives my life its 'ups' – just as some people love mooching around vintage clothes shops, or watching tennis, or playing poker. In my family of origin, we tended to dismiss such desires as superficial and mindless: things that would just naturally disappear in the new socialist dawn (my father had a particular vitriol for football, the 'opium of the people'). Such an attitude, however, is not only patronising, it ignores some very real things about what makes people genuinely fulfilled and satisfied. And, by doing so, it means that progressives leave the glitz and the glamour and the promise to satisfy such needs and wants to the right.

Understanding human needs and wants, then, can help us develop a progressive vision that can – genuinely – create larger and richer lives for all. And it is something that we need to take time to consider: because the question of what human beings really need and want is by no means easy to answer. Is it, for instance, about being as happy as possible; or are suffering and challenge also important to a richer life? And what about the need for relatedness – how does this weigh up against a need for freedom? There are also questions about whether needs and wants vary across cultures and individuals? Indeed, can people ever be truly satisfied and, if not, what are the implications of this for progressive thought and political activity? That is why, in this book, the first four chapters are primarily devoted to building up a rich, deep, and rigorously grounded understanding of how people function – individually and together. That way, psychology can genuinely add something of value to a progressive vision, rather than just a superficial gloss. This is not, of course, in isolation from other understandings – including social, economic, anthropological, cultural, and environmental ones – but as part of a joined-up, holistic attempt to understand what it means to thrive within our social, political, and cultural contexts.

## A radical acceptance of the other: the principle of *psychological equality*

A psychological perspective, however, is also important in a third sense. This is in terms of developing a more empathic, compassionate, and radically accepting view of the other – of all others. Bregman, in his recent book *Humankind: a hopeful history*,[28] makes a similar argument, but drawing primarily from the historical and social data. The present book suggests that, to deepen and advance progressive thinking and practice, we need to move from a *politics of blame* to a *politics of understanding*: one in which even our political opponents are engaged with in respectful, valuing, and caring ways (as also advocated by the UK campaigning organisation, Compassion in Politics).[29] The American author and social activist bell hooks describes this as a 'love ethic', and she writes that such an ethic has been strongly emphasised by 'all the great movements for social justice in our society'.[30] Lerner describes this is a stance of 'revolutionary love': a 'socialism of the heart'. It is 'The love of life and all beings, embracing this world with all its complexities, heartaches, and joys. It is an approach that is caring toward everyone on the planet, even those whose behaviors we hope will change, and towards the Earth in all its magnificent diversity as well.'[31]

This stance of radically accepting the other is, I am sure, controversial in the progressive domain; but I believe it is essential to a progressive vision. I see it as a commitment to *psychological equality*, running alongside a commitment to economic, political, or social equality. What I mean by this is that it is a willingness to view the other – every other – as a human being like ourselves, with needs, wants, and experiences that are 'intelligible' and legitimate. It is an openness to putting ourselves in the shoes of the other, and to taking their perceptions seriously, just as we would want them to take ours. 'At its core', writes Bhaskar Sunkara, author of *The socialist manifesto*, 'to be a socialist is to assert the moral worth of every person, no matter who they are, where they're from, or what they did'.[32] In other words, when we engage with others with the assumption that we are 'right' or 'good' and they are 'wrong' or 'bad', we betray, I believe, a core principle of progressive thinking: that all people are of equal worth. Charles Taylor, the Canadian philosopher and social democrat, writes, 'one absolute requirement of ethical thinking is that we respect other human agents as subjects of practical reasoning on the same footing as ourselves'.[33]

For many progressives, the problem with such a perspective is that it can sound horribly naïve. What about homophobes, White supremacists, Putin? Is this saying we should just tolerate their views or turn a blind eye to their deadly practices? Absolutely not. Without doubt, people can do things that have enormously destructive impacts on others and, when they do, they need to be stopped. But what I am suggesting is that, if we start with a commitment to equality, we have to start with an understanding of the other *as* a fellow human being. *Nihil humani a me alienum puto* – Karl Marx's favourite maxim was 'nothing human is alien to me',[34] and this needs to apply from 'us' to 'them', from left to right, as well as from them to us. The principle of psychological equality, then, means moving beyond a demonisation of the other: beyond seeing our political enemies as inherently evil, manipulative, or deceitful; beyond a James Bond-type world of 'baddies' and 'goodies'. It does not mean we cannot oppose them, challenge them, or even use force to stop them hurting others if we have to. But, in all this, it does mean not turning them into monsters: holding on to their humanity with the care, compassion, and the egalitarian spirit that is at the heart of a progressive vision—bell hook's 'love ethic'. In Chapter 3 of this book, which goes deeply into psychological theory, I hope to show how we can make sense of destructive human behaviours, without viewing human beings – or some human beings – as inherently destructive or bad. Bregman, in *Humankind: A hopeful history*, presents an extensive historical and social analysis to show that 'most people, deep down, are pretty decent',[35] and I hope to show how and why, from a psychological perspective, this is the case. Chapter 6 (this volume) onwards looks at how we can try and draw out this human decency to make the best possible world for us all.

This belief in the 'goodness' and capability of human beings, again, is rooted in my own personal journey. When I was a child, and proudly told my schoolmates that I was a communist, the first thing most people would say is 'So you don't believe in money?' 'Nope.' 'Well that wouldn't work. Because everyone would just take whatever they want.' I imagined people going to the local grocery store and stripping the shelves bare of packets of Frosties cereal. My sister and I had, however, a pre-prepared answer. 'They won't do that. People will just take what they need: *people are basically good*. It's just money and society that makes them act bad.'

That conception of people as basically 'good' is still with me – albeit, I hope, in much more sophisticated and nuanced form. In part, it comes from that commitment to psychological equality: it has always seemed to me arrogant, patronising, and anti-progressive to assume that other human beings are less moral, thoughtful, or capable than I am. If I am looking down at someone reading *The Sun*, for instance, or a white van driver speeding through traffic, then what kind of egalitarian does that make me? Yet, at the same time, I know that that position of psychological equality can be incredibly difficult and challenging to hold: because when I see someone reading *The Sun*, or even 'worse' *The Daily Mail*, I do think, 'Oh, for goodness' sake …' Prejudices, assumptions, demonisations are all there – at least in me. That means that holding on to that position of basic valuing and respect can be a constant challenge. I hope, in this book, to show some of the ways that we can get there, without losing any of the challenge and radicalism that is progressivism's core.

The second reason a belief in the essential 'goodness' of others seems, to me, essential to a progressive vision is because, if the other is not 'good', or does not have the potential to be 'good', then what hope do we have for a positive, progressive society? State-enforced equality? Anti-discriminatory practices at the endpoint of a gun? If egalitarian social arrangements need to be imposed on people – against some 'inherent' selfishness or greed – then it seems inevitable that dystopias, rather than utopias, will come to dominate. Kate Raworth, Oxford academic and author of the highly influential *Doughnut economics*, says something similar when she bases her proposals for a socially just and sustainable economics on 'a new portrait of humanity': as social, interdependent, fluid, and embedded in a social and ecological nexus.[36] For her, an understanding of human beings as self-interested, isolated, and calculating is not a 'fact' but an ideology particularly suited to justifying 20th-century capitalist ideology. In this respect, a progressive commitment to equality, compassion, and caring for the other – and for the planet – is not a turning away from our 'natural' humanity, but an expression of our humanity at its very deepest.

Third, if we want to change people – as progressives do – we need to know what is fundamentally motivating them: what they really need and want. So simply demonising people and labelling them as 'bad', ultimately, does not get us anywhere. Rather, if we can understand what is behind their behaviour – an envy, for instance, behind homophobia; or a vulnerability behind antisemitism – then we can find more constructive, prosocial, and 'synergetic' (see Chapter 4) ways of meeting those fundamental needs and wants. If some people are homophobic, for instance, out of a deep-seated envy for the sexual freedom that they perceive lesbian, gay, and bisexual people as having, then helping them to feel freer in their own sexual possibilities may be a means of addressing their homophobia at its root.

## A *humanistic* psychological perspective

Of course, there are many different approaches to psychology, and each of them would have different things to say about human beings and what it is that we most fundamentally need and want. The approach I have taken in this book is an 'integrative' one, which tries to draw together a number of different perspectives and research findings – particularly from the field of psychotherapy and counselling – to present a general theory of human psychological functioning (see Chapter 3). As a psychologist and clinician, however, my own background is in *humanistic* psychology; and the vision developed in this book has been particularly informed by that perspective.

Humanistic psychology developed on the west coast of the United States in the 1940s and 1950s – with such figures as Carl Rogers and Abraham Maslow – and remains popular today. If, for instance, you went to see a counsellor in the UK or US, it is likely that they would have a humanistic orientation or be influenced by these ideas in some way. Humanistic psychology, as with the principle of psychological equality, holds a relatively positive and optimistic view of human beings: that they are 'resourceful and naturally inclined to grow and develop their potential'.[37] Moreover, it sees human beings as essentially prosocial and trustworthy when freed from social constraints.[38] Unlike many psychologies, the humanistic approach rejects an understanding of people in wholly 'mechanistic', 'cause-and-effect' terms, and instead emphasises the human capacity for choice and free will (albeit within social, political, and economic constraints). It is also *holistic*, in that it tries to understand people and their worlds in an integrated way, rather than reducing people down to separable, individual elements. Clinically, in alignment with its theory, humanistic psychotherapy puts particular emphasis on empathically understanding clients and providing them with 'unconditional positive regard'.[39] This is synonymous with the stance of radical acceptance, detailed in the previous section.

Humanistic psychology, itself, is rooted in *humanism*: a philosophical stance that reaches across the arts, ethics, and many other disciplines. Today, humanism is experiencing something of a comeback, in works such as Paul Mason's *Clear bright future: A radical defense of the human being*, in which he advocates a radical, post-capitalist humanism, of persons over machines. Humanism can be defined, in the broadest sense, as 'the yearning to show regard for *all* that is human'.[40] It stretches back to the Hebrew philosophers and Greek sages, and is encapsulated in the statement by the Roman African playwright, Terence, that 'nothing human is alien to me'.[41] This, as noted earlier, was Marx's favourite maxim; and, to a great extent, illustrates the considerable overlap between humanist and progressive perspectives. Both standpoints, for instance, view human lives as equal; emphasise collaboration, solidarity, and democracy across peoples; and encourage a postcolonial openness to multiple cultures, traditions, and differences.[42] Robert Spencer, a cultural theorist, defines humanism as 'a practical refusal to tolerate distant suffering',[43] and this can also be considered the essence of progressive thought and action. Progressivism and humanism are also united in their use of critique: a critical scrutiny, for instance, of the current state of affairs and a revealing of the human labour, energies, understandings, and misunderstandings behind it.[44] 'The humanist's customary mode', writes Spencer, is '[a] biting distrust of received wisdom'.[45] In these respects, humanism can be considered consistent with such contemporary perspectives as postmodernism, feminism, and queer theory. Humanism is, above all else, an ethic, a position of care. It is a desire to show regard to *all* beings, just as feminism or queer theory are fundamentally based in advocating regard for 'the other'.

No doubt, as a budding counsellor and psychologist, I was drawn towards humanistic psychology because I saw it as an expression – within a clinical context – of my own progressive thought and values. And, over time, the progressive perspective that I developed – and will articulate in this book – has been heavily influenced by humanistic psychological ideas. It is important to recognise, however, that this is just one reading of what it means to be progressive; and that there are ways in which humanism can be seen as quite divergent from progressive principles and ideas.

Humanists, for instance, have tended to emphasise the 'universal attributes' of human beings – our 'essential' natures[46] – and this differs from progressives who have emphasised the socially constructed nature of the 'self'. Judith Butler, for instance, the influential American philosopher and gender theorist, has argued that even sex – our 'biological' being as male or female – is not innate but constructed through social interactions.[47] The humanist emphasis on 'will and agency'[48] also contrasts with progressive perspectives that emphasise the determining role that social, economic, or unconscious forces can play.[49] Even the name, *human*-ism, can be seen as problematic today – what about animals, plants, and the environment? Yet if humanism is understood, most fundamentally, as 'a practical refusal to tolerate distant suffering', then such challenges do not undermine a humanistic standpoint, but rather provide opportunities to develop and expand it. Should humanism, for instance, view human beings as interconnected? Yes, absolutely, because it can help us see our bonds with – and responsibilities for – each other. Should humanism care about animal welfare? Yes, absolutely, because distant suffering is distant suffering, whatever the organism. In these ways, then, humanism only tends to be misaligned with other forms of progressivism if it is taken in a narrow sense. Understood more broadly, as an ethic of care, the two perspectives are deeply aligned.

## Understanding the other 'from the inside out'

A key element of humanistic psychology that runs throughout this book, an expression of the principle of psychological equality, is the desire to try and understand people *subjectively*, rather than *objectively*. Let me try and explain what I mean by this. When we look out onto the world we inevitably see it through our eyes. We stand in our shoes and see things and people around us. Right now, for instance, I am looking out onto our family cat Bonnie, curled and asleep; and my habanero chilli pepper plant by the window sill that, I am sure, is slowly dying. And I am trying to think out these sentences on to my Word document – slightly anxious that I cannot quite get it right.

Now suppose that you came into my office and you were trying to understand me, psychologically. There are two somewhat different angles you could do that from. One is that you could try and understand me 'objectively'. So, for instance, you might observe me typing away at the keyboard and infer from that something about how motivated I am. Or you might notice the printed off graph of Scrabble letter values on my noticeboard and think, 'Ah, here is someone with obsessive compulsive issues.' Or you could wire me up to a heart rate machine to assess my stress levels. In all this, you would be looking at me from the outside, as an object, to be measured, examined, and analysed. Martin Buber, the great 20th-century relational philosopher, called this the *I–It* stance, because essentially I am an 'it' for you: a thing to be studied.[50]

If you were to try and understand me subjectively, on the other hand, you would be less looking *at* me, and more looking *with* me. This means that you would be trying to put yourself in my shoes and getting some sense of how I am experiencing my world: an empathic perspective. So, for instance, you might come to sense that I am experiencing some anxiety towards my writing, or towards my chilli plant. And you might be interested in how I am feeling towards Bonnie (scared, she's an absolute killer), or the day ahead; and what gives me a sense of meaning and purpose. The subjective stance is less analytical, then, and more descriptive: it is not asking *why* things are, but *what* they are. Buber calls this the *I–Thou* stance because, when we stand alongside others in this way, we experience them in their humanness. They are not a thing but a purposeful stream of human experiences, thoughts, and feelings.

Much psychology tends towards the objective, outside–in approach. It measures, analyses, and interprets: the 'science' of human mind and behaviour, as psychology is often defined. Here, the human being is like a machine or a computer that we can take apart to discover its inner working. We can find out, for instance, the external 'stimuli' that trigger specific behavioural responses, the unconscious mechanisms that cause particular actions, or the parts of the brain that are associated with particular memories or emotions.

This objective way of understanding people can be enormously informative. In recent years, for instance, neuropsychologists have made major strides in understanding how the brain works: how it responds, for example, to such experiences as trauma and abuse. But, from a progressive perspective, an objective, I–It psychology also has some significant limitations. When we view people as thing-like entities, they become something less than us – less than the subjective, agentic person who is doing the studying. We are the observer and they become the observed. There is a dehumanisation here: not necessarily consciously or malevolently, but one in which the other becomes something 'beneath' our gaze. By contrast, a subjective understanding of the other embodies that principle of psychological equality. It treats the psychological 'subject' as a human being, like ourselves, with perceptions, experiences, and desires that stretch out into the world. When we view the other subjectively we are looking *with* them, not *at* them, valuing and respecting their experiencing as fellow human beings who, like ourselves, have agency and choice.

This focus on the subjective means that a humanistic perspective places less emphasis on what is 'true' or 'right' than a more objective perspective. From a subjective standpoint, different people may experience a similar phenomenon in very different ways, and there is no assumption that there is ever any one objective truth. Supposing, for instance, we ask a question like 'Is social media harmful for young people's mental health?' From a subjective perspective, it may be that for some young people it is, but for others it may not be, and others may experience it as positively beneficial. From this standpoint, it is not that there is no reality, but that 'reality' – including such experiences as distress, oppression, and suffering – lies in our experiencing of things: in how we feel and encounter our worlds.

Philosophically and psychologically, this subjective approach is sometimes termed a *phenomenological* perspective,[51] and is one that has been associated with radical political practices.[52] Foremost here is the work of the Brazilian educator, philosopher, and social activist Paulo Freire.[53] For Freire, minoritised groups can challenge oppressive circumstances by voicing – and dialoguing in communities – their experiences of oppression. Phenomenological enquiry, then, becomes a tool of the oppressed to 'speak their truth', and to challenge the dominant narratives that may be suppressing or distorting their experiences. R.D.

Laing, the Scottish psychiatrist, is another prominent figure who saw the radical potential of phenomenological enquiry, albeit on the more micro scale of the family.[54] For Laing, families silenced their members (particularly their daughters) by imposing on them narratives about what they were experiencing. This can be so severe and distorting that, for Laing, it could lead to psychosis.[55] For Laing, as with Freire, it is when oppressed people go back to the truth of their subjective experiencing that they can begin to dismantle systems of oppression: systems that disguise their interests under the claim of being 'objective realities'.

As with Freire and Laing, this book emphasises the radical potential of a subjective perspective; and, as with these predecessors, it does so without denying the massive impact that external realities can have on people. Poverty, as we know, can massively reduce people's psychological wellbeing; as can poor housing, food poverty, or homophobia. These things are real, and focusing on people's experiencing of them does not make them any less substantive. Most accurately, then, we can say this book takes an 'intersubjective'[56] or 'inter-worldly'[57] perspective: it takes people's experiences as central to their being but, as we will see in Chapter 3, always understands this in relation to their particular 'world'. Subjective experiences, then, are never understood in isolation from others or from the wider social, political, and cultural contexts.

## Across the intrapersonal and interpersonal

To this point, I have laid out in this chapter some of the basic principles on which I will be developing a progressive vision: that we need to take progressive thinking and action forward; that psychology can help us in that; and that a humanistic, phenomenological psychology can be of particular value in that venture. I have suggested that this psychological understanding can be useful to progressivism, first, because it can help us understand the psychological causes of wellbeing; second, because it can help us understand what people genuinely need and want; and third because it can help us be radically accepting and understanding of others – a key principle of progressivism, as well as the humanist tradition. Now I want to briefly say some more about a fourth reason why psychological insights may be of particular value to progressivism – developed in much more detail in Chapters 5 and 6.

As my career in psychological research and practice has developed, I have become more and more struck by the parallels between healthy functioning at the *intrapersonal* level (that is, 'within' the person), and what I, as a progressive, would see as healthy functioning at the *interpersonal* level (that is, between people, communities, and nations). Much of this starts with the idea that we can think of the self as consisting of multiple 'parts', 'voices', or 'subpersonalities' – that we are all a community of 'sub-selves'.[58] So, for instance, right now I have a 'child part' that would like to go and sit in the sun, and an 'insistent parent part' that is telling me I need to work until at least 8pm (and then just have one small glass of wine). As a psychotherapy practitioner and researcher, what I (and many others) have learnt is that good psychological health is not about the existence or non-existence of such parts, per se, but about how they get along with each other. For instance, if the parts are in conflict, or if one of the parts is totally dominant (and that could be either the child part or the parent part), then the person is likely to be in psychological difficulties. Here, the therapeutic work is about bringing the parts back together to talk to each other, and to find mutually satisfying solutions that suit each part's needs and wants. Sometimes – and it is a well-evidenced technique[59] – we even invite people to sit in different chairs and talk *as* these different parts, so that they can listen to, and develop empathy for, each other. So what has struck me here is the amazing parallels between this, and what we, as progressives, might see as happening on the interpersonal or intercommunity level. For instance, if one community is dominating another community, and not respecting its needs and wants, then we would see things as going badly wrong. And, as at the intrapersonal level, we would see the way forward in terms of challenging the dominant voices, and through trying to create the conditions in which each community felt empowered and that it had an equal say.

Why should such parallels be of importance to progressives, beyond an academic interest? First, by looking across these different 'levels of organisation' (Chapter 4), we can establish common, system-wide principles of positive change. And, in doing so, progressives can learn from the psychological field about how to create better forms of social organisation, just as psychologists can learn from the progressive field about supporting individual change. Second, it helps to create smoother transitions between psychological and socioeconomic understandings, and brings these fields together, so that we can develop more comprehensive progressive programmes. Third, when you look at the parallels between what psychologists say 'works', and what progressives envision as more functional ways of relating, it just lends so much support to a progressive perspective. You see why progressive principles such as cooperation and respecting difference and diversity are so beneficial: because they are not just specific to a socioeconomic context, but are general, system-wide principles for how 'better' can be brought about.

## Who is the book for?

As should be clear by now, this book is specifically aimed at a *progressive* readership. Of course, my hope is that the arguments developed here will be of interest to those on the centre and right of the political spectrum too; but my principal aim is to elucidate, and help develop, the meaning and practice of progressivism. This means that I am assuming that the reader already believes passionately in the value of social equality and justice, and that they want to see people – of all communities and cultures – thrive.

But what actually does *progressive* mean? In *The alternative*, Labour MP Lisa Nandy and colleagues give the following, very helpful, definition:

> Progressives want to move beyond the current system and create a better one. … Progressives believe in cooperation. We want a supportive and responsive state that brings the best out of people's instinct to share success and support each other in hard times, and which offers genuine equality to all citizens, together with social justice, civil liberties, human rights and responsibilities, without discrimination on grounds of gender, age, physical ability, race or sexual orientation. … [Progressives] share a rejection of the politics of

> fear and division, and wish to move towards a more inclusive society in which every citizen not only has the opportunity to develop themselves to their full potential but has as much control as possible over their own destiny and the chance to shape the society in which they live. This way we believe we will build a society that both empowers people and allows us to love within environmental limits.[60]

Progressivism, as the name suggests, is a belief in the possibility of progress: that society can move forward to a better, fairer, and more socially just state.[61] Progressives strive to be active creators of progress: 'progressors' as Amiel and Emelien term it.[62] Such progressivism can be contrasted against *conservatism*, which strives to conserve how things are, based on the perceived wisdom of custom, tradition, and 'the natural course of things'.[63] Edmund Burke, considered the philosophical founder of conservatism, writes, 'it is with infinite caution that any man ought to venture upon pulling down an edifice which has answered in any tolerable degree for ages the common purposes of society'.[64] And he goes on to state, 'When ancient opinions and rules of life are taken away, the loss cannot possibly be estimated. From that moment we have no compass to govern us, nor can we know distinctly what port to steer.'[65] By contrast, progressives believe that past tradition is no indicator of future success; and that we can, and should, guide ourselves to a better world. Today, progressivism can also be contrasted against authoritarian *populism* and the 'alt right': reactionary, anti-establishment ideologies, which strive to roll back progress on equal rights and social justice.[66] While progressives seek to forge a better, fairer, more inclusive world; right-wing populists seek a return to a fantasised world of safety, predictability, and homogeneity. Interestingly, in the psychological field, this maps on to the differences between an 'approach' mindset and a more problematic 'avoidance' mindset, respectively, which we will explore in Chapter 4 of this book.

By *progressives*, then, I mean a broad spectrum of left-leaning people, including those who would identify with socialist, feminist, postcolonial, anarchist, green, vegan, and, to some extent, liberal democrat and anarchist perspectives. Probably, as a 'rejection of the politics of fear and division', this definition rules out some of the more extreme left-wing and anarchistic views: those, for instance, that see class, race, or gender violence as necessary and desirable elements of political change. It would also tend to exclude those on the right and centre-right of liberal democracy: who put particular emphasis on individual freedom over all other values, or who would choose coalition with the Conservatives over Labour.

Of course, there are many differences in views and emphases across these progressive perspectives, and some might question what is, and is not, part of this spectrum. However, for the purposes of this book, what is seen as making progressive progressive is some commitment to genuine social equality – to developing a political system that is inclusive, empowering, and welcoming to all[67] – and to cooperative ways of working.

This book is written for those without any specialist knowledge of psychology, counselling, or psychotherapy. A more complex presentation of the psychological perspective articulated here (primarily in Chapter 3) can be found in my 2019 book, *Integrating counselling and psychotherapy: Directionality, synergy, and social change*.[68]

Although I hope this book will be of interest to counsellors, psychotherapists, and other mental health practitioners – my own professional community – it is not specifically targeted at this audience. This is not a book about how politics should inform therapeutic theory and practice. No doubt, as already discussed, there is much here for us to learn. Fortunately, there are now some very good texts that show how this might be achieved.[69] Most recently, UK clinical psychologist Lucy Johnstone and colleagues have developed the *Power threat meaning framework*, which offers a radical, social justice-based approach to psychological assessment and intervention.[70] There is also a professional network, with its own journal, that focuses in this area (Psychotherapists and Counsellors for Social Responsibility), with emerging research.[71] Interestingly, too, about two-thirds of clients say that they have spoken to their therapists about politics, and around half would like to do so more frequently.[72] Clearly, the role of politics in therapeutic practice is a critical one, but the focus of this book is on the other side of the coin: how psychology can inform political thought and practice.

As this book is primarily targeted at a progressive readership, I have tended to focus on the psychological processes and principles underlying this progressive vision, rather than the political ones. As indicated, the aim of this book is not to argue for equality, just as it is not to convince readers of the need for human rights or ecological awareness – I am assuming that such beliefs and values are already there. So, for instance, when I map out a psychologically informed progressive utopia in Chapters 8 and 9, I mainly focus on what this would mean psychologically and relationally, rather than the kind of equality that would exist and how this would be achieved. This should not be taken to mean, however, that these macro-level political, social, cultural, and environmental issues are of any less importance.

## My positioning

A question that confronted me as I came to the final drafting of this book, and probably should have emerged much earlier, is this: What can a White, heterosexually identified, middle-aged, able-bodied, global North, male academic contribute to an understanding of social change? Do we really need another White man's 'grand vision for how everything works'? Of course, I would hope the answer to this question, at least in part, is 'yes' but then, given my demographic, that is what I would tend to say!

Perhaps one way to answer this question is to reflect on what my limitations in writing this book might be, as well as my strengths. As someone largely identified with privileged groups, I do not have extensive experience of marginalisation. I have not faced severe discrimination, violence, or oppression because of my identity; and I have not lived in poverty or with other severe social, political, or economic restrictions. That means, inevitably, I cannot fully understand the experiences of those who have; and, in trying to envision a progressive future, I will inevitably fall short of fully understanding what such people might need or want. In particular, I may come across as too willing to respect, and engage in dialogue with, more reactionary and oppressive forces.

On the other side, my years of working as a psychological therapist, researcher, and teacher – across a range of clients, participants, and students – have given me some deep insights into how people experience their worlds, and their fundamental needs and wants. I have sat with people in all their vulnerability, stripped of any sense of meaning or possibility, and been with them as they have clamoured towards something more hopeful. I have seen what works in people, and what does not; and although I have not come away from this with easy answers, it has given me a powerful sense of how human beings tend to function best – both individually and with others. At a personal level, I should also say that I have struggled with mental health challenges, specifically severe anxiety, throughout my life, so that I have a lived sense of what it means to not thrive as well as thrive. My Jewish heritage also gives me some indirect sense of what it means to experience violent oppression. My mother narrowly escaped the Nazis, leaving Berlin in 1939; my father was a second generation immigrant from the pogroms of Ukraine. I am sure, for both of them, those experiences of persecution shaped their progressive ideologies; and their passions for social justice – as well as their transgenerational anxieties – have shaped me too.

So I think I have something to say, and I hope what I say will have some relevance to others. But I fully appreciate that it is just one way of envisioning a more progressive world, and no doubt it will be the interplay between multiple progressive visions – from multiple perspectives – that may, one day, help us to achieve a society that is fairer, more socially just, and more thriving for all.

## Summing up

'What is the object of Revolution?' asks William Morris, in the utopian novel *News from nowhere*.[73] He answers, 'Surely to make people happy'. The aim of this book is to outline an approach to politics that, by integrating an understanding of human wellbeing and suffering, hopes to contribute to that revolutionary goal.

There is no doubt that we live in troubled times. Police racism, climate emergency, the Russian invasion of Ukraine, pandemics … these are just some of the challenges that we currently face. Never before, perhaps, has there been such a need for a new political vision – nor such an opportunity for one. Yet to be compelling, as Bregman argues, this new perspective needs to be more than just critical and cynical.[74] It needs to be about what we want, what we believe in, what we are passionate for. This book aims to develop such a vision: a world in which all individuals can live deeply satisfying and fulfilling lives, oriented around loving relationships with others, and engaged in creative and meaningful pursuits. This is a world, as we will see, in which diversity is prized, and in which each human being is encouraged to find their own, unique way of being. In this book, I hope to lay out the psychological foundations for such a world, and to show that it is within our grasp.

# 2

# A psychology-informed progressivism v1.0: socialist humanism

The aim of this book, as described the Introduction, is to develop a psychologically informed progressive vision. I want to show how we can envision society, and the people and relationships within it, if we integrate psychology into a progressive commitment to equality and social justice.

To begin this journey, I want to discuss the development of the *socialist humanist* tradition. *Socialist humanism* was an international movement of intellectual thought – and, to some extent, activism – that advocated a psychological, humanistic reading of the works of the German philosopher and social activist, Karl Marx. The current book is by no means just for Marxists, and there are several ways in which the analysis to be developed in this book will differ from a classic socialist humanist stance. Nevertheless, I wanted to begin with a critical presentation of socialist humanism. This is for several reasons. First, it shows the depth, richness, and complexity of analysis that can be achieved by integrating humanistic psychology ideas into a progressive political base. It paints a powerful and compelling – albeit, at times, problematic – picture of how society, and the people within it, can be seen to function. Second, and closely related, it shows how a progressive perspective as radical as Marxism can, in fact, be understood in a way that is highly compatible with humanistic ideals and psychological beliefs. Third, a discussion of socialist humanism provides a means of introducing, and showing the radical foundations for, several of the key principles in the present text. Indeed, the perspective developed in this book could be considered a modified, contemporary version of socialist humanism. Fourth, a discussion of the limitations of socialist humanism helps to identify some of the pitfalls that a psychology-informed progressivism can fall into, signposting ways towards a more genuinely egalitarian and humanistic vision. Fifth, along the lines of Mason,[1] I have a desire to show the ongoing relevance of Marx's writings to contemporary progressive philosophy and politics. Maybe it is my father's bust of Marx on my bookshelves, but I am continually astounded by the depth and far-sightedness of his insights – psychologically as well as philosophically. Finally, my hope is that this chapter will whet the reader's appetite for the rest of this book by stimulating reflection on a range of key issues at the psychology–politics interface. For instance, what is our understanding of human beings, and how does that fit with a progressive political analysis? And, are the things that people need and want, in a capitalist society, what they really need and want? This chapter will, I hope, open up these questions and many more.

## A humane Marxism

Socialist humanism, also known as 'Marxist humanism'[2] or 'radical humanism',[3] held that the very essence of Marxist thought lay in a set of humanistic principles, values, and objectives.[4] It drew primarily from Marx's earliest works: in particular, Marx's writings in his 20s published as the *Economic and philosophical manuscripts of 1844*, where Marx explicitly states that communism 'equals humanism'.[5] Probably the best known proponent of socialist humanism was Erich Fromm, the German-Jewish psychologist closely associated with the 'Frankfurt School' of social and critical theory.[6] For the socialist humanists, Marxism was not primarily a form of economic or historical analysis,[7] but a political movement aimed at the liberation of human beings.[8] Its aim, wrote its American founder, Raya Dunayevskaya, was the creation of a society in which the full and free development of every individual is the ruling principle.[9]

Socialist humanism appeared in the 1940s and 1950s, reached its zenith in the late 1950s and 1960s, and waned from the late

1960s.[10] Its decline was partly due to its denunciation by the French Marxist philosopher Louis Althusser. Althusser's 1965 book, *For Marx*, argued for a more 'macro-level' understanding of Marxism: away from a focus on individual subjective experiences towards social structures and systems. Despite this, considerable interest still exists in the approach, as advocated by such authors as Paul Mason and the contributors to the 2017 book *For humanism.*[11]

Socialist humanists defined themselves in opposition to the 'totalitarian Communists' of the Soviet Union,[12] which they saw as having a 'brutal contempt for individual dignity'.[13] For them, the Soviet system was essentially a form of 'state capitalism'[14] betraying and tarnishing the meaning of 'socialism'.[15] Indeed, Dunayevskaya wrote that Soviet-style communism – as 'a theory and practice of enslavement' that mobilises itself with 'murderous vigilance' – was directly opposed to Marxism as a theory of liberation. For E.P. Thompson, the British social historian and political activist, socialist humanism placed 'real men and women at the centre of socialist theory and aspiration', rather than 'resounding abstractions' such as 'the Party' or 'the Vanguard of the Working Class'.[16] 'By what vile alchemy', writes E.P. Thompson, 'do some communists, who spring from the common people … become transformed into monsters of iniquity like Beria and Rakosi – lying, slandering and perjuring, destroying their own comrades, incarcerating hundreds of thousands, deporting whole nations?'[17] Closely related, socialist humanists critiqued the dogmatism that they felt could permeate the left. Leszek Kołakowski, for instance, a Polish philosopher and historian of ideas, described Stalinism as a self-perpetuating, ideological sect, akin to a church doctrine. He wrote:

> Every petrification of doctrine leads necessarily to its transformation into a mythology, an object of worship, surrounded by a ritualistic cult and immune to criticism. In this situation theoretical progress becomes impossible; and new dogmas that appear are monopolized and served up, with no reason given, as articles of faith.[18]

## What does it mean to be human?

'If I could rescue only one of his [Marx's] achievements', writes Mason, 'it would have to be his first: a clear definition of human nature'.[19] For the early Marx, 'communism meant simply the realization of human nature'.[20] Hence, to understand what Marx meant by an ideal progressive society, we need to understand how he made sense of human existence.

When I revised for my final exams at the University of Sussex in 1988, there was one Marx quote that I rehearsed over and over again: 'It is not consciousness that determines life, but life that determines consciousness.'[21] What Marx means by this, as emphasised by the socialist humanists, is that an understanding of people needs to be rooted in an understanding of our real, concrete, embodied activities; immersed in particular social and historical context.[22] In other words, Marx's understanding of human being does not start from some abstract, idealised conceptualisation of a person: as, for instance, Stalinist iconography tends to do.[23] Rather, it starts from human beings in their concrete, 'in-the-world' *doing*: producing, reproducing, and relating. This is an insight from Marx that was, psychologically, years ahead of his time: it suggests that human being is, first and foremost, neither 'inside' ourselves nor exclusively shaped by our environments, but something that emerges through our 'in-the-world' activities – at the person–environment interface.

For Marx, then, our lives are not simply a product of something 'inner', like a genetic predisposition or personality traits. But, equally, this Marxist perspective rejects the idea that human beings are simply 'blank pieces of paper',[24] 'lumps of clay',[25] or 'puppets': moved and manipulated without any will of our own.[26] Rather, socialist humanists emphasised the active, 'agentic' side of human beings: that we come to 'meet' – and act towards – our environments. In the British horror film *His house* (dir. Remi Weekes, 2020), for instance, we see how a refugee couple from South Sudan face all kinds of economic and social challenges when they come to the UK, such as treacherous seas, appalling housing, and racism. These forces are structural and societal: not something that the couple have control of or create. In all of this, however, the couple never *become* these forces: they consistently meet, and strive to meet, their circumstances in particular ways. In this respect, we can say that the couple have some degree of freedom (within severe limitations); and, for the socialist humanists, as well as the early Marx, there was a view of human beings as essentially free.[27] Again, this did not mean that human beings could do whatever they wanted – Marx's whole theory, as is well known, is based on the assumption that we cannot – but that, at an *ontological* level (that is, in terms of the nature of our existence), there is always the possibility for choosing between options. This was a view particularly emphasised by the more existentially oriented socialist humanists, such as Jean-Paul Sartre and Simone de Beauvoir.[28] It is also a view shared by progressive writers on race, such as Cornel West, the American philosopher and social activist. West writes, for instance, of holding the tension between recognising that Black people have been victimised, while also acknowledging that they 'have never simply been victims': 'wallowing in self-pity or begging for white giveaways'.[29] Black people for West, like all marginalised groups, are never reducible to their oppression alone. There is courage, resistance, and there is a real human being who is striving to meet their circumstances in the best way they know how. To ignore that – albeit out of a desire to recognise the magnitude of the oppression – is to risk dehumanising marginalised individuals even further.

If human beings are understood as acting towards their worlds, then there must also be some 'inner' directions or forces guiding our choices. And, indeed, the socialist humanists, as with the early Marx, did see people as having certain innate needs and wants, such as a desire for social cooperation, support, and freedom.[30] Galtung suggests that 'Marx's entire theory is actually based on thinking about needs';[31] and, from this perspective, social progress can be understood as the increased satisfaction of such needs.[32] For Marx and the socialist humanists, this inner nature also included certain inherent abilities, such as the potential for collective effort, creativity, and language.[33] In this respect, then, the socialist humanists saw human nature as less of a 'thing' and more as a direction or *potentiality*; and, as a theory at the person–environment interaction, they saw the unfolding of this potentiality as dependent on social, cultural, and economic circumstances. Noam Chomsky, the great linguist and progressive political thinker, describes something similar when he writes:

> People want to explore, we want to press our capacities to their limits, we want to appreciate what we can. But the joy of creation is something very few people get the opportunity to have in our society: artists get to have it, craftspeople have it, scientists. … I think people should be able to live in a society where they can exercise these kinds of internal drives and develop their capacities freely – instead of being forced into the narrow range of options that are available to most people in the world now.[34]

## Alienation

The socialist humanists, then, believed that human beings had innate agency, freedom, desires, and potentialities; but the heart of their political analysis was the assertion that, under capitalism, these became lost. That is, as human beings we have become *alienated*: estranged from our true possibilities. This perspective, again, can be traced back to Marx. He writes:

> All means for the development of production transform themselves into means of domination over, and exploitation of, the producers; they mutilate the laborer into a fragment of a man, degrade him to the level of an appendage of a machine, destroy every remnant of charm in his work and turn it into a hated toil; they estrange from him the intellectual potentialities of the labor process in the same proportion as science is incorporated in it as an independent power, they distort the conditions under which he works, subject him during the labor process to a despotism the more hateful for its meanness; they transform his life-time into working time, and drag his wife and child beneath the wheels of the Juggernaut of capital.[35]

For Marx, as we have seen, the essence of human being is in our productive activity.[36] So, to the extent that this production is owned by forces outside of ourselves (that is, by the capitalist) – in other words, to the extent that the product of our labour becomes alien to us – so we become fundamentally estranged from ourselves. I work, for instance, delivering pizzas, and my life energies go into delivering food that I have no ownership of, or identity, with: it takes me yet has nothing of me. This contrasts with, for instance, a crafts- or arts-based mode of production where the creator is *in* their work: it remains *my* painting (even if sold), or the beautiful pot that *I* have made (see Chapters 8 and 9, this volume).

Furthermore, for Marx and the socialist humanists, under capitalism, the worker 'sinks to the level of a commodity'.[37] In the terms of Buber, as introduced in Chapter 1, we became an *It* (that is, an object, a thing), rather than a *Thou* (that is, a human subjectivity). Indeed, for Marx, we become 'the most wretched of commodities': 'living capital', bought and sold by the capitalist as a means towards accumulation, with our labour costs treated, on the balance sheet, as essentially 'pilfered sales'.[38] Here, in the mechanics of the assembly line or in the routine of the office, any potential for human creativity, meaning, or growth is lost. Marx writes that the living, breathing human 'has sunk to the level of a machine'[39] – indeed, we are 'confronted by the machine as a competitor', For Marx, we become a '*spiritually* and physically *dehumanized* being', a 'crippled monstrosity'.[40] In the words of the existential humanist psychiatrist R.D. Laing, the worker becomes 'a shrivelled, desiccated fragment of what a person can be'.[41] And, as the division of labour proceeds – with increasing abstraction, rationalisation, and specialisation of operations – so there is a progressive elimination of any human, individual, and 'qualitative' attributes of the worker.[42] Fragmentation of the production process gives fragmentation of the producer, while 'the personality can do no more than look on helplessly while its own existence is reduced to an isolated particle and fed into an alien system'.[43]

Furthermore, for the socialist humanists, capitalism not only alienates workers from themselves, but from our relationships with others.[44] Marx writes, 'An immediate consequence of the fact that man is estranged from the product of his labor, from his life-activity, from his species being is the *estrangement of man* from *man*.'[45] Human beings, fragmented by the division of labour, split along the assembly line, can no longer associate naturally and closely with each other. In this respect capitalism, from a socialist humanist perspective, also undermines human beings' natural tendencies towards cooperation, instead pitting worker against worker (or unemployed people against workers and each other). In the competition to find employment, or in the jostling for promotion, workers come to see other workers as foe rather than friend. Capitalism, then, fragments both outside and in. We are lost to others as well as ourselves: isolated from the intimacy and web of relatedness that would be our true home.

### *False needs*

Developing this concept of alienation further, a core assertion within the Frankfurt School was that capitalism not only alienates people from their real selves and needs – it also works to create *false needs*.[46] Such a distinction between real and false needs goes all the way back to Aristotle.[47] It is also evident in Marx, who distinguishes between *constant* needs (or 'fixed', that is, real needs), and needs that are *relative*: 'which owe their origin to certain social structures and social conditions of production and communication'.[48] Marcuse writes:

> 'False' are those [needs] which are superimposed upon the individual by particular social interests in his repression: the needs which perpetuate toil, aggressiveness, misery, and injustice. Their satisfaction may be most gratifying to the individual, but this happiness is not a condition which has to be maintained and protected if it serves to arrest the development of his ability (his own and others) to recognize the disease of the whole and grasp the chance of curing the disease. The result then is euphoria in unhappiness. Most of the prevailing needs to relax, to have fun, to behave and consume in accordance with the advertisements, to love and hate when others love and hate, belong to this category of false needs.[49]

For Marcuse, any needs beyond our most 'vital' ones (such as for nourishment, clothing, and lodging) are false.[50] Fromm, on the other hand, defines *genuine* needs as those that make the human being more alive and sensitive; while *synthetic* (that is, false) are those needs which tend to weaken us, that make a person 'more passive and bored, a slave to his greed for things'.[51] For Fromm, the synthetic needs are also characterised by a prioritising of 'having' over 'being': so, for instance, owning the latest mobile phone, trainers, or bread maker, rather than a genuine immersion in life. In fact, Fromm goes on to argue that the essence of capitalism is not the need to *own* things, but the need to endlessly *consume*. Here the person becomes a '*homo consumens*', who devours endlessly to 'compensate for his inner vacuity, passivity, loneliness and anxiety'.[52] Fromm writes:

> [T]he need for profit of the big consumer industries, through the medium of advertising, transforms him into a voracious man, an eternal suckling who wants to consume more and more, and for whom everything becomes an article of consumption: cigarettes, liquor, sex, movies, television, travel, and even education, books and lectures. New artificial needs are created, and man's tastes are manipulated. … *Homo consumens* is under the illusion of happiness, while unconsciously he suffers from his boredom and passivity. … He mistakes thrill and excitement for joy and happiness, and material comfort for aliveness; satisfied greed becomes the meaning of life, the striving for it a new religion.[53]

Chomsky argues something similar when he writes that neoliberalism, and its philosophy of 'the market *über alles*', produces 'consumers' rather than 'citizens': disengaged, demoralised, and socially powerless.[54] And, he adds, other people in this consumerist world becomes means rather than ends: channels towards fulfilling particular needs of the self (that is, Buber's 'its'), rather than recipients of care and regard. In this sense others, too, becomes things we consume: the delivery driver, the builder, the waiter, all become devoured in our quest for more.

### *False consciousness*

From a socialist humanist perspective, it is not just that people have false needs, it is that we become blinded to the falsity of these needs. Human beings, from this perspective, *internalise* external demands, but we come to believe that these false, synthetic needs are actually our own. So I come to see myself as someone, for instance, who must have the latest trainers, or that I cannot survive without an upgrade to my phone; and that these desires – for having and consuming – are the deepest, most fundamental expressions of my existence. Fromm writes: 'we can have thoughts, feelings, wishes, and even sensual sensations which we subjectively feel to be ours, and yet that, although we experience these thoughts and feelings, they have been put into us from the outside, are basically alien, and are not what we think, feel, and so on'.[55]

More broadly, socialist humanists have argued that human beings blind themselves to the reality of the social, economic, and political structures around them, a 'false consciousness'. So we take what is most salient – neoliberal, capitalist consumerism – and see it as the 'natural' state of affairs, not recognising, or questioning, its social and historical specificity.[56] 'It is easier to imagine the end of the world', writes Bastani, 'than the end of capitalism'.[57] Neoliberal consumerism is so evident to us, so all-consuming (quite literally), that we just cannot imagine a world otherwise. And, it is argued, capitalism, as a system that, in reality, serves only the interests of a minority, needs such powerful deception to survive.[58] It is like the Wizard of Oz who hides the mechanisms of his magic behind a curtain: if we saw what was really going on, none of us would be very impressed. But more than that, from a socialist humanist perspective, we are like hypnotised fools: inured and unwilling to even believe that a curtain is there.

For Marcuse, this false consciousness is sustained by a subtle and nuanced web of deceits and manipulations.[59] Forces of domination and alienation, for instance, are presented to us as 'administration'. In other words, capitalism controls us today, not through distanced owners sitting above the factory floor, but by bureaucrats and officiates at the end of a webchat. Here, 'the tangible source of exploitation disappears behind the façade of objective rationality.

Hatred and frustration are deprived of their specific targets, and the technological veil conceals the reproduction of inequality and enslavement'.[60] Now, I vent my frustration at my erratic Wi-Fi network speed at a call centre worker in India – equally exploited – while the multimillionaire shareowners continue, unabated, in their accumulation of profit.

Then there is the media, and Marcuse suggests that people have become so dependent on it that they would no longer be able to think and function without it. He writes:

> [T]he mere absence of all advertising and of all indoctrinating media of information and entertainment would plunge the individual into a traumatic void where he would have the chance to wonder and to think, to know himself (or rather the negative of himself) and his society. Deprived of his false fathers, leaders, friends, and representatives, he would have to learn his ABC's again. But the words and sentences which he would form might come out very differently, and so might his aspirations and fears.[61]

Marcuse goes on to say:

> To be sure, such a situation would be an unbearable nightmare. While the people can support the continuous creation of nuclear weapons, radioactive fallout, and questionable foodstuffs, they cannot (for this very reason!) tolerate being deprived of the entertainment and education which make them capable of reproducing the arrangements for their defense and/or destruction. The non-functioning of television and the allied media might thus begin to achieve what the inherent contradictions of capitalism did not achieve – the disintegration of the system.[62]

What Marcuse is suggesting here is that, if our broadband did fail, and if our media did all stop, we might start to see the reality of capitalism for what it is. The curtain would be drawn back. We could look at our lives and ask where the mad rush for ownership and consumerism is taking us. Do we really need the next iPhone model? Or is it our relationships with loved ones, or our sense of excitement and pleasure in nature, that really matter?

Marcuse describes a range of other deceits and manipulations through which capitalism keeps us from seeing beyond its veil of illusion.[63] There is, for instance, the way that it uses personalised language – telling you of *your* member of parliament, *your* Google account, and *your* Amazon shopping basket – to make us feel that we are individualised, and not one of millions of other 'individualised' souls at the end of a computer algorithm. Then there is the focus on the concrete and functional – the tasks of everyday living, such as working, shopping, and leisure – which stops us from taking a critical perspective and seeing things in their historical, social, and political context. 'Head down', we just focus on how things *are*, rather than how things might be. For Marcuse, too, the frantic pace of modern living stops us from ever considering alternatives. We rush, manically and seamlessly, from meetings to emails to public transport to reserving a table for an evening meal (and sometimes all four at once). Like the magician who 'misdirects' the audience's attention from what they are really up to, capitalism presents us with understandings, questions, and concerns that are tangential to the real issues at hand.

## A return to full humanity

In contrast to such alienation, the socialist humanists envisaged a *full* human being: free to act in accordance with their own needs, abilities, and proclivities; free to express and affirm their unique individuality.[64] This was, in Marx's term, the 'real *appropriation of the human* essence by and for man'.[65] Unfragmented by the division of labour, this full human being might, as Marx famously wrote, 'do one thing today and another tomorrow, to hunt in the morning, fish in the afternoon, rear cattle in the evening, criticise after dinner … without ever becoming hunter, fisherman, herdsman or critic'.[66] For the full human being, there was no need to pick up and choose between these activities: they could coexist as part of a homogenous, integrated whole.

Furthermore, from a socialist humanist standpoint, such full human beings would not only refrain from objectifying themselves, but also from objectifying others.[67] Relationships, for this full human being, would no longer be mediated by the forces and values of objects – in particular, money – but would, instead, be direct and im-mediate. The primary modes of human relating, then, would become closeness, connection, and caring. This human being loves, and 'feels the welfare of others as his very own':[68] Buber's 'I–Thou' stance.

## Critical reflections

So, what do you think? To what extent do you agree, and disagree, with this socialist humanist analysis of social and individual functioning? What aspects of it make sense to you – such as its image of human being, alienation, and false consciousness – and which aspects do you find more problematic?

For me, some key strengths are that socialist humanism presents a progressive political analysis with an understanding of human needs, potentialities, and experiencing at its heart. Without minimising, in any way, the devastating impacts of macro-level economic and social factors; it manages to focus on micro-, psychological-level experiencing: what social forces – in particular capitalism – do to real human lives. In this respect, it provides a powerful and compelling framework for integrating interpersonal and intrapersonal processes. At a 'gut' level, much of what the socialist humanists have claimed may also feel right: when we look, for instance, at consumerism and the way that it seems to create 'needs' in people; or the way that, in neoliberalism, massive disparities in wealth and freedoms are shrouded by illusions of happiness and individualisation. Yet, in terms of developing a coherent, credible, and genuinely equitable progressive vision, there are also some important limitations.

### *The a-humanism of socialist humanism*

First, and paradoxically, there is something somewhat dehumanising and patronising – verging even on misanthropic – to some of Fromm and Marcuse's writings. While this perspective does, indeed, start from an understanding of people as active agents with some degree of freedom; its essential premise is that people are weak, liable to manipulation, and passive in introjecting their external environments. Fromm, for instance, states that man 'is one of the most pliable natural forces; he can be made to serve almost any purpose; he can be made to hate or to cooperate, to submit or to stand up, to enjoy suffering or happiness'.[69] But is that really us? Or is that how we see others; reserving for ourselves the qualities of agency, insight, and choice? Rollo May, one of the founders of existential psychotherapy, writes:

> If you conclude that the troubles lies in the fact that human beings are so susceptible to influence by their culture, so obedient to orders that they are given, so pliable to their environment, then you are making the most devastating of all judgment … in human beings. In such case we are all sheep, dependent on whoever is the shepherd.[70]

The question here, then, is whether the socialist humanists really hold on to a position of psychological equality (see Chapter 1), or whether they tend towards a more arrogant, condescending, and patronising perspective. David Ingleby, in his critical introduction to Fromm's *The sane society*, suggests that Fromm's 'man in the street' expresses something of Fromm's own cultural elitism, whereby 'Only the culture of his own class … is true culture: the rest is scathingly dismissed by Fromm as an "opiate".'[71] From this standpoint, Fromm's *homo consumens* – suckling away at their cigarettes, television, and liquor – are more middle-class characterisation and demonisation of the working class (as, for instance, also described by Owen Jones in *Chavs*[72]), than a respectful and valuing acknowledgement of the other. Ingleby goes on to state, '"Modern man" appears to Fromm as a robot, but one suspects that this is because he has not gone to the trouble of getting to know him well enough.'[73]

From a progressive standpoint, not only does such a view of 'modern man' contradict the principle of psychological equality, but it legitimises exactly the kind of elite-driven, authoritarian 'guardianship' that the socialist humanists so vehemently opposed.[74] This contrasts with democratic rule which, for the influential American political theorist Robert Dahl, is based on the principle that 'each adult person is in general the best judge of his or her good or interests'.[75] Furthermore, if human beings are seen as infinitely malleable then, as Chomsky writes, they become 'a fit subject for the "shaping of behaviour" by the state authority, the corporate manager, the technocrat, or the central committee'.[76] In addition, without some understanding of human beings as proactive and agentic, it becomes impossible to understand the emergence of revolutionary strivings and activities.

A closely related problem for Fromm and Marcuse is the positing of 'true' and 'false' needs. Ágnes Heller, a Hungarian philosopher, writes that it 'places the judge (the theoretician) outside the world to be judged'.[77] It is as if, somehow, Fromm and Marcuse have escaped the fog of false consciousness that the rest of society is trapped within, and are able to report on how things 'really' are. Yet, as Heller writes, 'How does the theoretician known that his consciousness is "the" correct one? If the theoretician assumes that society is being objectively fetishized, he disqualifies his own knowledge as being "the" correct one since his consciousness, too, is a product of society.'[78]

This critique of Fromm and Marcuse's socialist humanism links to important contemporary debates about the 'third face of power'. This is the assertion that power is not just exercised publicly and through agenda setting, but also ideologically: by influencing, shaping, or determining the needs and wants of the other.[79] On the one hand, such an analysis allows us to see how power can operate – sometimes most effectively and troublingly – 'unobserved and behind our backs'.[80] It is hard to deny, for instance, the role that ultra-rich media barons play in shaping voting patterns. As *The Sun* themselves wrote after the 1992 Conservative Party election victory, 'It's *The SUN* Wot Won It.' Again, however, the problem with such a stance:

> [I]s the deeply condescending conception of the social subject as an ideological dupe that is conjures up. Not only is this wretched individual incapable of perceiving his/her true interests … but rising above the ideological mists is the enlightened academic who from his/her perch in the ivory tower may look

> down to discern the genuine interests of those not similarly blessed.[81]

This critical analysis of socialist humanism, then, leaves us with a challenge. How can we develop a psychologically informed progressive vision of people and society that recognises the multiple – and, at times, insidious – ways that power can act; while at the same time holding that people are, ultimately, the best judges of their own good or interests? The next chapter provides a model of psychological functioning that hopes to address this challenge.

### *A missing model*

A second important limitation of the socialist humanist tradition is that it lacks a comprehensive, in-depth model of human being. The socialist humanists drew on ideas from humanistic and existential psychology and from psychoanalysis, but their range of sources are limited and, inevitably, uninformed by contemporary psychological research or theory. As a consequence, the approach cannot explain many basic psychological processes, including those that are central to their analysis. Where, for instance, does the human desire to consume come from? The socialist humanists suggest that this is a product of capitalism but, psychologically, such powerful forces cannot simply be 'implanted' by the external world. Some process of internalisation must take place here; some encounter and interaction with the person's pre-existing needs and wants.[82]

Along similar lines, the distinction between 'false' and 'true' needs can be seen as simplistic and lacking psychological depth and complexity.[83] Where, for instance, is the line between them? If we take Marcuse's definition that the only true needs are those that have an 'unqualified need for satisfaction', then it is fairly clear that hunger is a true need, or the desire for shelter. Equally, it is fairly self-evident that the 'need' for a multimillion-pound mansion is a false need, on the grounds that the person could live without it. But what about a person's need for a moderate-sized terraced house, or for a bathroom, or for self-esteem, or for friendships? How do we develop an 'objective standard for judging the relative authenticity of felt needs'?[84] Humanistic psychology has tried to address this issue by distinguishing between *intrinsic* (that is, emerging from the person) and *extrinsic* (that is, emerging from the environment) needs;[85] but all needs, from a person–environment interactive standpoint, can be seen as having some external component. Hunger needs food, friendship needs people, consumerism needs goods – so which of these needs, then, are truly outside or in? Moreover, as discussed in the previous subsection, we are left with the problem of explaining how external needs get inside a person, without invoking some highly passive model of humankind. We are also left with the problem of understanding how people can move from intrinsic to extrinsic needs, and vice versa. For instance, how can *homo consumens* transition to the authentic, ideal human being that Fromm and Marcuse describe?

This critical analysis of socialist humanism, then, gives us a second challenge: to develop a more complex understanding of human functioning that can underpin a progressive, psychologically informed vision of people and society. Again, this challenge will be taken up in the next chapter and throughout this book.

### *Is socialist humanism still relevant?*

A third question that can be asked of socialist humanist is whether it is still relevant to our contemporary world. For a start, the workplace has changed massively over the last century, and even more so since Marx's time. The factory is no longer the principal place of employment for most working people: in the UK, for instance, just 9 per cent of workers are in the manufacturing sector, compared with 30.2 per cent in 'public administration, education, and health', and 18.2 per cent in 'distribution, hotels, and restaurants'.[86] Employer–employee relationships have also transformed into a much more complex set of roles, functions, and classes.

In addition, as Barbara Epstein, a leading contemporary socialist humanist writes, the socialist humanist approach also did not have a 'great deal to say about issues that have since become priorities for movements for social change: environmental crisis, race, gender, sexuality, technology and its social impact'.[87] Epstein also makes the point that there is now a need to consider the rights of other inhabitants on the planet: that is animals, plants, and the environment as a whole.

Socialist humanists, I am sure, would be open to all of these challenges. On the issue of anthropocentrism, for instance, Epstein states, 'An expansion of human concern to include the welfare of other living creatures, and the planet, is clearly compatible with socialist humanism.'[88] Yet there comes a point where such great expansion is needed that, perhaps, a Marxist approach is no longer the most useful theoretical frame. That is, when taking into account issues like climate catastrophe, transphobia, and animal welfare, while one could start with Marx and the alienating effects of capitalism, there are multiple other legitimate ways in. For instance, in the classic radical feminist text, *The dialectics of sex*, Shulamith Firestone argues that the division between sexes lies at the roots of oppression;[89] and the same case might be made for race, human–animal relationships, or the way that people have come to objectify and exploit their natural worlds.

There is also, perhaps unfortunately, an issue of terminology. However much the socialist humanists have attempted to reclaim the word 'socialism', it may be that it is so tarnished with the spectre of totalitarianism that it is beyond redemption. In fact, the first working title for the present book was 'Socialist humanism: A progressive politics for the 21st century'; and I would still, personally, identify as a 'socialist'. But it soon became apparent that, for many progressives, the term 'socialist' did not fit. Whether this is because the term is misunderstood, perceived as too authoritarian, or as too narrowly focused on class; it is clear that there are many people with a commitment to equality, cooperation, and social justice who do not consider themselves, first and foremost, as 'socialists'.

## Summing up

Despite these limitations, Kevin Anderson, Professor of Sociology, Political Science and Feminist Studies at the University of California, suggests that the conditions may be ripe for a revival of socialist humanism. He writes:

> [W]e may be on the eve of a revival of radical humanism at a time when the hopes and aspirations of a new generation are being articulated in a way that

> brooks no compromise with an utterly dehumanised global capitalist system that has plunged the whole generation into depths of despair out of which revolutionary challenges are beginning to emerge.[90]

Epstein and Mason hold very similar hopes[91] and, personally, I hope that they are right. If nothing else, the environmental catastrophe that global capitalism has unleashed makes it absolutely evident that something must change. Yet whether socialist humanism, as a post-Marxist tradition, is quite the right vehicle for this transformation remain unclear.

On the one hand, as I hope to have demonstrated in this chapter, socialist humanism shows how we can develop a progressive political stance that integrates a rich and considered understanding of human being. Socialist humanism shows that the psychological sphere and the socioeconomic sphere are not distinctive entities, but that the very essence of human experiencing is at their interface. In this respect, it also shows that even the most radical progressive perspectives have a place for – and can incorporate – psychological understandings. Indeed, it is psychology that take such radical perspectives from a place of abstract and conceptual analysis to a real understanding of real people's lives, in their concrete and tangible actuality. It is also psychology that can help to ensure that such perspectives do not segue into much more brutal, authoritarian, and depersonalising dogmatisms.

In addition, the socialist humanist analysis presented here introduces, and shows the radical foundations for, a range of concepts that can be key to a psychologically informed progressivism. First, there is an understanding of human being as emerging from a person–environment interaction: structured and limited by social and economic forces; yet also agentic, volitional, and with the potential to realise our needs and wants. Second, however, is an understanding that we can become estranged from this potential: living isolated, fragmented lives; away from cooperation, community, creativity, and meaning. Third, and making matters worse, is the suggestion that we can then become blind to this estrangement. We become so caught up in the drive for economic and social achievement that we do not see the bigger picture: a world of alienation, inequity, and frustration. Yet, fourth, there is the potential for us to reclaim our humanity. By seeing our world for what it is, and ourselves for what we are, we can begin the process of moving towards a society in which we can find genuine community and fulfilment, within our environmental and planetary limitations.

Through this analysis, I hope to have shown the continuing relevance of the socialist humanist approach, and Marx's thinking, to a progressive worldview. If nothing else, I hope it has whetted the reader's appetite for issues at the psychology–politics interface. Yet, as already indicated, there are also limits to what socialist humanism, as developed to date, can contribute to a contemporary progressivism. There are paternalistic elements to Fromm and Marcuse's writings that do not sit well with a progressive value base; the theory of psychological functioning is not well-specified or informed by current psychological theory and research; and there are many other contemporary issues for progressives that lie outside of a socialist humanist, Marxist frame.

In the following chapters, a framework for understanding individual and social functioning will be developed which builds on the insights of the socialist humanists, while also striving to overcome some of their key limitations. This is a framework that starts with an understanding of people as agentic and acting towards their worlds; but struggling, at times, to realise their most fundamental needs and wants. In this framework, such difficulties may be due to socioeconomic factors, psychological factors, or a complex combination of the two; with people taken over by 'rogue goals' that blind them to the totality of their human potential. Later chapters in this book then look at how this humanity can be reclaimed: first conceptually (Chapter 6), then in real concrete terms (Chapter 7), and finally in terms of a far future utopia (Chapters 8 and 9).

# 3

# Understanding people: a contemporary framework

Our review of socialist humanism has shown how a progressive approach can be developed with psychological understandings at its heart, and it introduced concepts that can be valuable to such an analysis. The aim of this chapter is to develop these starting points into a fully fleshed out psychological framework that can serve as the basis for a contemporary progressive vision for society. This framework, therefore, retains several key elements of a socialist humanist approach – for instance, conceptualising people as agentic but with unrealised needs and wants – but it is also integrative of a wider range of contemporary psychological theories, practices, and findings.

Why might it be important to spell out such a psychological framework to a progressive audience? Could we not, for instance, just skip to the practical applications of a psychology-informed progressivism? In this chapter, psychological theory is, deliberately, presented at a level of depth, detail, and complexity. This is because the kind of progressive perspective being proposed in this book is not just about how we behave. Rather, it is also about how we think, feel, and relate to each other – at the deepest possible level. The principle of radical acceptance, for instance, is not so much a way of acting towards another as a particular stance or understanding. So, to develop such a foundation, we need to go into the psychological theory and consider the very nature of human being. By the end of this chapter, then, readers should have an understanding of people that can underpin and support a psychology-informed progressive vision. My hope is also that this chapter will encourage progressives to think psychologically: to deeply ask, for themselves and for others, what might be going on at the level of thinking, feeling, and experiencing.

This framework is based on an analysis developed in my book *Integrating counselling and psychotherapy: Directionality, synergy, and social change.*[1] That book is specifically for therapists but, if you are interested in the framework and its clinical application, you can find out more there. The framework is not a radically 'alternative' or new way of thinking about mind and behaviour. Rather, what the framework does is to try and find a way of drawing together, and articulating, the basic principles underlying many different psychological and therapeutic perspectives and research findings. It is, of course, just one way of drawing these principles together; but it is a way that is founded in decades of research, theory, and clinical practice. This means that, at the very least, it is a relatively robust starting point for a psychology-informed progressivism.

The basis for this framework is the principle of psychological equality (see Chapter 1): that we should try to understand others as human beings like ourselves, with needs and wants that are understandable within that person's context. This means an 'inside–out' approach (Chapter 1), and that leads on to a series of basic propositions. The first of these, developing socialist humanist principles, is that human beings are always actively striving to fulfil certain needs and wants, however psychologically 'damaged' they might be. The second proposition is that these needs and wants can be conceptualised as existing in a hierarchy, from the things that we are most fundamentally striving for (like love) down to the more context-dependent means through which we might try to get there. This analysis can help us understand 'false' needs in a respectful, humanising way. The third proposition, following on from this, is that we can conceptualise all human beings as having certain needs and wants – such as relatedness, safety, and self-worth – though we must always be wary of seeing these outside of particular cultural and individual contexts. Understanding these fundamental needs and wants will be particularly important when we consider the nature of an ideal, progressive society (Chapters 8 and 9).

Just to note, while the focus of this, and the next, chapter are on processes and experiences at the individual, micro level, Chapter 5 onwards then broaden this exploration out to more macro level, social concerns. As a psychologist, I do tend to start with the individual: How they function (this chapter), and then how they become distressed (the next chapter). However, as I make clear in Chapter 6, this is just one starting point for a psychology-informed progressivism: interindividual, intercommunity, and international processes could all equally well serve as a starting point for the whole.

## The *agentic* human being

At the heart of nearly all contemporary psychological and psychotherapeutic perspectives is an understanding of human beings as actively and dynamically engaged with their worlds. That is, as Marx and the socialist humanists argued (Chapter 2), we are do-ers and act-ers, engaging proactively with the contexts around us. An understanding of people in this way stands in contrast to more traditional models of human being that view the person as passive, sponge-like, or solely conditioned by their environment. While some early psychologists did, indeed, see people in this way,[2] there is now general agreement that human beings, at least to some extent, act towards – and construct – their worlds. Albert Bandura, for instance, one of the world's most influential psychologists, stated that people do not just act like 'weathervanes', 'constantly shifting in radically different directions to conform to the whims of others'.[3] He added, 'Anyone who attempted to change a Bircher [a far-right winger] into a Communist, or a Catholic into an atheist, would quickly come to appreciate the existence of potent internal sources of behaviour control.'[4]

There are many different terms that can be, and have been, used to describe this active quality of human being. We might talk about human beings, for instance, as being 'agentic', 'intentional', 'motivated', 'purposeful', or 'goal-directed'. Philosophers, from fields such as existentialism, has written of the 'forward-pressing', 'not-yet-determined' nature of human being.[5] In my 2019 book, I used the term 'directional' to describe this agentic quality. All these words try to convey the way that human beings are always oriented to something: always striving to move along particular paths. We may be trying, for instance, to finish our work, or to be close to others, or to give friends and family more support and care. This does not deny, in any way, the massive impacts that our worlds can have on us. But it suggests that, within that, there is always a person coming to meet those worlds in particular ways.

Such a directional understanding puts people's needs and wants centre stage in terms of making sense of why we do what we do. Needs and wants are the engine of that directionality: the force that leads people to reach forward. Again, there are many different terms that have been used here – for instance, 'desires', 'motives', 'intentions', 'purposes', 'goals', 'drives', and 'directions' – but these are all different ways of expressing that basic dynamism within human beings: of wanting to get from A to B. For the purposes of this book, I will tend to use the terms 'needs and wants' or 'directions' to describe, synonymously, such forces.

Putting needs and wants centre stage is, perhaps, more commonly associated with a 'me-first' neoliberalism. However, in this and the following chapter, I hope to show how such a foci can also be closely aligned to progressive and, indeed, Marxist perspectives. A focus on human needs for relatedness, freedom, and self-worth is, for instance, highly consistent with progressive, egalitarian values. Moreover, in Chapter 5, we will look at how the concept of directionality can be transposed to societal- and community-levels, such that it is, in no way, inherently individualistic.

This agentic, directional quality has been described by philosophers as the 'hallmark' of living, organic systems.[6] It is what, for instance, differentiates our cat Bonnie – who *wants* to get outside my door, who *wants* to snuggle down with my daughter (and not with me!) – from my chair, which wants nothing. Similarly, my computer can process information far more quickly than I can: it can, for instance, easily beat me in a game of Scrabble. But in all of this, it cannot *want* to beat me, it does not *care* if it wins or loses. I, by contrast, do care – and even against a computer (and probably because I project on to it a human desire to beat me, which is not, actually, there). Directionality, then, is what distinguishes us from machines as well as from other inorganic objects, and this point is of particular importance to Mason, whose *human*-ism concerns itself with the rise, and potential dominance, of robots and other thinking machines.[7]

Psychological research shows that people's intentions are, indeed, at the roots of their behaviours.[8] If we want something, we are far more likely to do it. Of course, we do not always do what we want, but this is often because other needs and wants come into play. I want another cup of coffee, for example, but I know that I have already had two this morning, and I do not want to be shaking with nerves all day. And I also do not want to be going out to the shop for milk. So, as we will see, needs and wants can run up against other needs and wants. Psychological research also shows that needs and wants are among the earliest ways in which human infants make sense of themselves and others.[9] Indeed, 'I *want* …' is among the most basic human statements.

This agentic understanding of human beings emerges, particularly, when we understand people in an inside–out way. If we viewed you from the outside, from an objective perspective, we might say that there are certain external stimuli (for instance, your children shouting at you for dinner) that make you behave in certain ways (for instance, putting this book down and starting to cook). But if we tried to stand in your shoes and experience how you experience your world, we would have a much stronger sense of your needs and wants and how they shape your behaviours. So it might still be that your children are shouting at you, and that then you feel you should cook the dinner; but that whole processes is mediated by your own needs and wants: for instance, to care for them or to stop them complaining. So there's no, direct, mechanistic 'children shouting→cook dinner' cause–effect relationship. Rather, it is fundamentally mediated by your own directions. Take a minute to ask yourself, 'What do I need and want right now? What am I aiming towards?' Perhaps you are wanting to finish this chapter. Perhaps, at the back of your mind, you are also wanting to go out for a walk; or perhaps you are thinking about having a bath. Most likely, there will be multiple – and, potentially, conflicting – needs and wants. But, from this inside–out perspective, you are never entirely without directions. Indeed, even if you are wanting to be in a meditative, 'non-wanting' state, this is still something you are *aiming* towards.

From this perspective, then, behind every action there will always be something that you are striving to do. Try acting without any direction at all: it is impossible. Even moving a finger cannot be done without some kind of aim or intention behind it.

Importantly, in terms of psychological equality, an understanding of human beings as agentic means that our behaviours are always understood as *intelligible*. This means that those behaviours are 'a meaningful and comprehensible response towards the world: there "for a reason", and not something that is simply irrational, ad hoc or meaningless'.[10] As we will see, this does not mean that human beings are always acting in ways that are best for others or for themselves; but it does mean that, whatever we do, there is always some purpose and rationality behind it: something that we are striving for.

Of course, the needs or wants that drive our behaviour can be unconscious as well as conscious. So we may have a consciously set goal (for instance, finishing this book), but there may also be unconscious, bodily-based desires (such as yearning to stand outside and breathe the fresh air). The existence of unconscious desires is supported by numerous psychological studies, which show that goals can be triggered, selected, and pursued without people being consciously aware of these processes.[11] In a classic psychological experiment, for instance, people who were exposed to the scent of a citrus all-purpose cleaner were more likely to clean their environment, but had no idea that the scent was affecting their behaviour.[12] 'Needs and wants', then, covers our most basic, embodied urges, driven by the more primitive parts of the brain, as well as our longer-term goals.[13] I hear a loud scream, for instance, from my 14-year-old son's bedroom, and rush over to check what is going on (he's fine, the Wi-Fi just went down). Here, there is no conscious planning – or even awareness – of what I am doing; my body just jumps up and responds instinctively.

### *Needs and wants as 'in-the-world'*

From a progressive perspective, this emphasis on needs and wants might seem too 'internal': not focused enough on the external, socioeconomic forces that shape our lives. However, as with the person–environment model of human being discussed in Chapter 2, our needs and wants are not just rattling around inside of us, but are always 'reaching out' to something in our environment. Every desire has something desired; every goal has a 'goal object', and these things that we intend towards are an essential component of the need or want itself. In the conflict resolution field, these external elements are termed *satisfiers* (see Chapter 5), defined as 'the means by which the organism re-establishes the desired state'.[14] Satisfiers may be 'active', in the sense that they are something we actively seek, or 'passive', in the sense that we only notice them when they are not there. For instance, when I think about having a biscuit with my tea, that is an active satisfier; but the oxygen around me is a passive satisfier in that it is only something I would notice if it were gone.

This 'in-the-world-ness' of our directions is very consistent with Marx's understanding of human being, as discussed in Chapter 2. Marx writes: '[T]he *objects* of [man's] impulses exist outside him, as *objects* independent of him; yet these objects are *objects* of his *need* – essential *objects*, indispensable to the manifestation and confirmation of his essential powers. [Man can] only *express* his life in real sensuous objects.'[15] This recognition of an external component to needs and wants is particularly important when we consider wellbeing and distress; because it means that these states – and their causes – are not just inside us, but linked to our external, socioeconomic world.

Our needs and wants are also in-the-world in the sense that the directions we adopt are often – and, perhaps, always – infused with the values and meanings of our external environment: our relationships, communities, and cultures. For Marx, as we have seen, it is our concrete, social being – including our use of language and our means of productive activity – that determines our consciousness.[16] Similarly, for Marx, our needs and wants, 'from the very beginning', can be considered 'a social product, and remains so as long as men exist at all'. One of my current desires, for instance, is to vacuum my carpet so that it looks more presentable when my partner comes to visit. But is that an 'internal' direction, or something that is also shaped by cultural norms?

## *Higher-order* and *lower-order* needs and wants

A basic assumption among many theorists and researchers in the philosophical, psychological, and psychotherapeutic fields is that our needs and wants can be conceptualised as existing in a hierarchy.[17] Here, there are a small number of fundamental (or what we can call 'highest-order') needs and wants (for instance, for pleasure), beneath which are less fundamental, 'lower-order' needs and wants (for instance, for tea). These lower order needs and wants, themselves, have further lower-order needs and wants (for instance, to boil the kettle); cascading down to the lowest-order needs and wants (for instance, to move my hand so that it reaches the kettle). This multilevelled, hierarchical system is a bit like an upside-down tree. At the top (the trunk) are a small number of fundamental directions; and as you move downwards the needs and wants branch out, becoming more numerous, but also expressing more peripheral directions.

A vastly oversimplified example of such a hierarchy is given in Figure 3.1. At the most fundamental, highest-order level, for instance, you might want pleasure and relatedness. But how do you get there? With pleasure, let us say, you try and do this through exercise, as well as through having sex, and no doubt through numerous other activities. And if we look at your desire to exercise, it might be through playing tennis, going to the gym, and through running. Again, we can then go down the hierarchy: if we ask how you fulfil your desire to run, maybe you do that through trying to get good shoes, and also trying to find time away from children. Equally, we can ask how you go about getting relatedness in your life, and that might also be through sex, and through friendships, the latter of which you achieve by spending time with your best friend as well as new people that you have met. Note, as you can see in Figure 3.1, a lower-order desire (for example, sex) can be *multibeneficial*: helping to achieve more than one higher-order desire (for example, pleasure and relatedness).

Within this inverted tree, lower-order needs and wants are the means by which we try to reach our higher-order needs and wants. Conversely, higher-order needs and wants form the reference point for lower-order directions: the reason why they are undertaken. Hence, as we go up the hierarchy, we ask 'why'

**Figure 3.1**: An example hierarchy of needs and wants

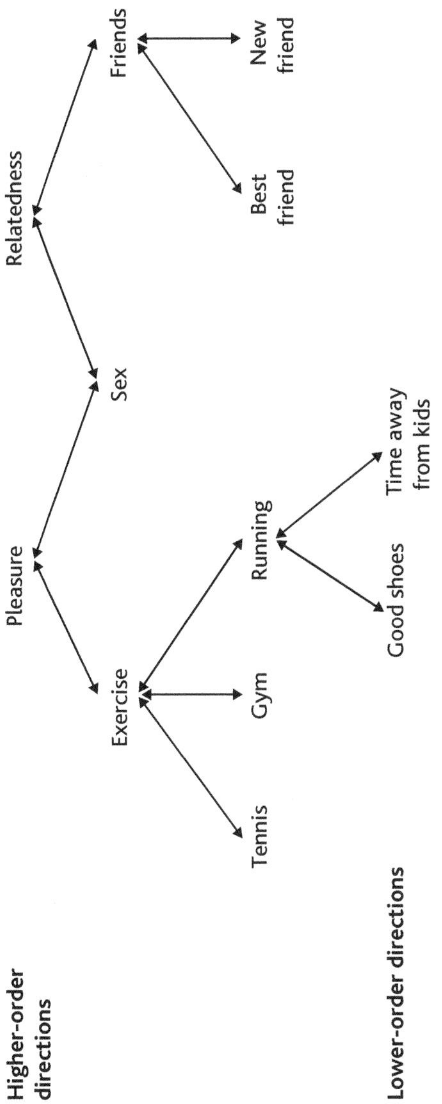

**Higher-order directions**

Pleasure

Relatedness

Exercise

Sex

Friends

Tennis

Gym

Running

Best friend

New friend

Good shoes

Time away from kids

**Lower-order directions**

something is done.[18] By contrast, when we go down the hierarchy, we ask 'how' something is done. Highest-order needs and wants are similar to Marx's 'constant' needs – or the 'real' needs of Fromm and Marcuse – in that they are the ones most fundamental to the person. However, as suggested in the previous section, no need or want can be considered entirely free of social forces, particularly given the mediating role of language. Equally, while lower-order needs and wants are likely to be more socially mediated and context-dependent – as with Marx's 'relative appetites' or Fromm and Marcuse's 'false needs' – they are always understood, in this framework, as intelligible means by which the individual strives to achieve higher-order ends. In these respects, this framework allows us to conceptualise different levels of needs and wants – with greater or lesser levels of social mediation – without labelling some as 'truer' than others.

This means that, in contrast to the socialist humanist approach discussed in Chapter 2, this framework does not conceptualise consumerism as a 'false' need – nor the desire to watch Netflix, or to read the *Daily Mail*. Rather, these can be considered lower-order means by which a person strives towards some higher-order end. That fundamental goal might be pleasure, or a reduction in anxiety: for instance, a person wants to read the *Daily Mail* to relax or to have their views of the world confirmed. And, from this perspective, these desires are always understood as intelligible: a wish to read the *Daily Mail*, for instance, is understood as a comprehensible means towards some goal; not some random, bizarre, or crazed act (however much it might seem that way from the outside). Importantly, though, as we will see, this does not mean that it is 'right', in the sense that it contributes something positive for society or even for that person. Needs and wants, both within people and between people, can run against each other; such that what is intelligible can also be deeply destructive to both self and other.

This hierarchical framework suggests that our attention, and our actions, can be driven by very different orders of things: from the most fundamental, highest-order needs to much more peripheral, lower-order desires. At one point in the day, for instance, you might be reflecting on the meaning of your life; at the next, whether you are going to have peas or beans for dinner. A useful means for understanding how we move up and down these levels was developed by William T. Powers, an independent American scholar and psychologist, who founded 'perceptual control theory'. This is a well-respected psychological model that has also been directly applied in clinical practice.[19] Powers suggests that, at each level in the hierarchy, there are a series of 'Test–Operate–Test–Exit' (TOTE) sequences. A TOTE sequence begins with the person testing their perception of how things are against their desired standard (consciously or unconsciously). For instance, I am experiencing my office as somewhat airless, and would like more fresh air. If a discrepancy is found (as in this case it is), this then leads to behaviour at a lower level in an attempt to bring the perception back in line with the reference standard (I aim to open my door). There is then a further test phase at the higher level, as the person checks the new situation against their reference standard ('Does the air feel any fresher now?'). If the discrepancy has been overcome, the loop is exited; and, if not, there are further behaviours, at lower levels, to try and address it. Using this theory, then, we can see how discrepancies at the highest, most fundamental orders (for instance, 'I don't have enough relatedness in my life') link to behaviours at the very lowest, most peripheral orders (for instance, 'press the letters on my keyboard so I can write an email to a friend').

Why should such a theory matter to progressives, beyond a purely academic interest? When we start to understand people in this way, we can begin to see how it is possible to recognise the value and legitimacy of what people are striving to do, while also feeling able to challenge the way that they are doing this. Take environmental pollution, for instance. Someone drives to work because going in a car makes them feel safer than going in public transport. Great, we can appreciate their desire to feel safe. But, at the same time, we can challenge them to consider whether, overall, the pollution that they create by driving is actually going to lead to more safety in the long run, or less. In this way, then, we can hold a progressive respect for the intelligibility of others – a stance of psychological equality; a radical acceptance for them as an agentic, directional being – while at the same time feeling able to question their lower-order means of doing things. And they (and we) can also challenge us. Here, no one is a fool, no one is unintelligible; but, equally, levers are available that can help us challenge each other in terms of getting to where we most fundamentally need and want to be.

## What do people most fundamentally need and want?

This hierarchical framework is also of considerable value to a progressive vision because it brings to the fore a key question for developing a more fulfilling, thriving, and equal society: 'What is it that human beings most fundamentally need and want?' That is, 'What is at the top of this hierarchy of directions, and is it the same for every person, community, or culture?' Examining this question is essential to progressivism – yet has rarely been discussed, to date – because, without understanding what people really need and want, we cannot know what sort of society would be best for us all. In addition, understanding these highest-order needs and wants, as we shall see, provides empirical support for a number of key progressive assumptions; and can help to underpin a progressive, humanistic understanding of people: as inherently 'good', but also with the propensity to behave in very destructive and asocial ways.

Within the psychological theory and research, there are inordinate answers, or sets of answers, to the question of what people most fundamentally need and want.[20] Some of these posit one highest-order direction (for example, pleasure, control, or growth); other, more contemporary theories, tend to suggest a range of highest-order needs and wants.[21] Across these different theories, however, there are a number of directions that are consistently posited as being highest-order (albeit with somewhat different terminology).[22] In the following sections, I will take some time to review and discuss these.

### *Physiological needs*

At the most basic level, human beings are seen as having some essential *physiological* needs. These include such needs as for air, food, water, warmth, excretion, and sleep.[23] Such needs often operate at unconscious and automatic levels: for instance, the cycle of breathing that maintains appropriate oxygen levels in my blood, or turning my radiator up or down to maintain a comfortable body temperature. It is only when something goes wrong – for instance, my boiler stops working – that I become more conscious of these basic needs and my means of trying to achieve them.

### *Safety*

Closely related to physiological needs is the need for *safety*.[24] This can be physical safety: for instance, from the elements or from organic threats such as COVID-19. At a psychological level, it is also the need for safety from others, including the need not to be hurt, traumatised, or abused in emotional, physical, or sexual ways. In the field of peace and conflict studies, Galtung referred to these as 'security needs', and considered their realisation central to the resolution of armed conflict.[25] Ukrainians, for instance, need to feel safe from Russian invasion; Palestinians need to feel safe from the threat of Israeli attacks, and vice versa. Destructive behaviours, however, may also be underpinned by a need for safety. The UK journalist Reni Eddo-Lodge, for instance, in her bestselling *Why I'm no longer talking to white people about race*,[26] shows the fears for safety – psychologically and nationally – that underlie the far right views of British National Party leader, Nick Griffin. Equally, underneath the misogyny, resentment, and self-loathing of the contemporary 'incel' (involuntary celibates) movement, we might see a fundamental insecurity in the face of women's sexual autonomy and power. This does not, in any way, excuse these behaviours, but it does give progressives a way in to understanding (and tackling) them in humanising, rather than dehumanising, ways. A fundamental human need for safety is also evident across psychotherapy. A client, for instance, may be fearful of leaving a critical partner because, at some level, there may also be a sense of security and familiarity in that relationship. Again, that does not in any way justify the partner's behaviour, nor minimise the control that the partner may be exerting; but it can help us to understand why people sometimes stay with things that, at a surface level, may not seem to be in their best interests.

### *Pleasure*

From the earliest days of civilisation, the pursuit of *pleasure* – and the avoidance of pain – have been considered, by many, the most fundamental human direction. This 'hedonic' tradition has continued through such philosophical movement as utilitarianism, with Bentham stating that, 'Nature has placed mankind under the governance of two sovereign masters, *pain* and *pleasure*.'[27] In the 20th century, many of the dominant psychologies continued to assume that pleasure and pain were the ultimate drivers of human behaviour: Sigmund Freud, for instance, with his pleasure principle;[28] and B.F. Skinner, a highly influential American 'behaviourist', with his emphasis on the shaping role of rewards and punishments.[29]

Throughout history, however, there have also been challenges to the assumption that pleasure is the single, highest-order direction.[30] How does it explain, for instance, the martyr, who is willing to sacrifice all their earthly pleasures – and endure untold pains – for something they believe in? Could it be, here, that values or meanings are actually more fundamental than pleasure itself? And why is it that so many people, when given a hypothetical choice between an authentic human life of ups and downs and a stimulated state of constant pleasure (in *The matrix* terms, the 'red pill/blue pill choice', respectively), would actually choose the former?[31] If only pleasure mattered, would we not all be willing to forgo reality and an awareness of our 'selves' to be able to experience it? While pleasure, then, might be an important direction to consider in developing a better future society for all, it may be essential not to prioritise it above all.

### *Growth*

Historically, a hedonic, pleasure-focused understanding of our most fundamental needs has been contrasted against a 'eudaimonic', *growth*-based view.[32] This perspective, widely embraced within the humanistic psychology field (as well as by the young Marx), holds that the highest-order human desire is towards the 'actualisation of potential': achieving the best that is within us.[33] This growth tendency can also be described as a direction towards increased differentiation and complexity: *heterostasis* (a drive towards growth and change), as opposed to *homeostatis* (a drive towards balance, consistency, and the status quo).[34]

Desires for creativity and learning can be seen as part of this movement towards growth – for Marx, creativity was a unique expression of humankind.[35] More controversially, perhaps, consumerism might also be considered an expression of this growth tendency. When someone drools over the textures and colours of a vintage jacket on eBay, for instance, there is, perhaps, some underlying drive towards learning, experimentation, and expansion. It is a tendency towards something new: to explore and discover, for instance, the different sides of ourselves that such a jacket brings out. Or if a child walks into a sweet shop and sees a glorious, multicoloured abundance of confectionery: Is there not some desire for experimentation and discovery here (as well as pleasure) that underpins that child's excitement? Again, this is not to justify consumerism in any way. There is no doubt that consumerism can have a profoundly destructive effect on both ourselves and our planet. But, as progressives, if we can understand the highest-order needs and wants behind even the most destructive behaviours, we may be best able to forge a society that can satisfy those directions, but in much less destructive ways.

### Relatedness

Across a wide variety of theories, as with Marx and the socialist humanists (Chapter 2), human beings are consistently considered to have a highest-order desire for interpersonal *relatedness*: that is, for attachment, connectedness, affiliation, intimacy, and love.[36] Research suggests that this desire for relatedness is, indeed, one of the most powerful human directions:[37] rooted in our evolutionary need for belonging, community, and social bonding.[38] An abundance of research shows that the achievement of relatedness is closely associated with feeling happier and more fulfilled in life.[39]

Importantly, this direction towards relatedness can also be considered inclusive of a desire for altruism and fairness: the egalitarian strivings at the heart of progressive politics.[40] This is a highest-order direction to give as well as to receive, to love as well as to be loved. Along these lines, research shows that a desire for fairness stretches back to the very beginnings of humankind, and is evident in many closely related animal species.[41] 'Biologically', writes Mary E. Clark, American Professor of Conflict Resolution, 'we are *obligatory* social animals'; and she – like Bregman in *Humankind* – challenges the widely accepted 'Hobbesian' viewpoint that, without society, we 'would be at each other's throats in a grand free-for-all'.[42] Similarly, Marshall Rosenberg, founder of *nonviolent communication* (see Chapter 7, this volume), writes that it is 'our nature to enjoy giving and receiving in a compassionate manner'.[43] Indeed, based on an extensive review of the evidence, 'give' – for instance, through volunteering, small acts of kindness, or expressing gratitude to others – was identified as one of the five key ways to mental wellbeing.[44]

The contemporary evidence that human beings have a fundamental need, want, and propensity for relatedness is some of the most powerful psychological support for a progressive vision. It shows that we have a deep desire, and capacity, to relate to others in cooperative, supportive, and non-discriminatory ways; and this points towards the possibility of forging a society in which people work with each other, rather than against each other. Moreover, it shows that such a mode of relating has the propensity to be deeply fulfilling for us as human beings: not against our human nature, but an expression of the very heart of it.

### *Autonomy*

A desire for *autonomy* features alongside relatedness as a highest-order desire in many taxonomies, and is viewed as *the* highest-order direction in several theoretical models.[45] This desire for autonomy is sometimes expressed as a desire for control (over self, not others), or for freedom: 'the ability to make choices; to move around; to be independent; to feel unrestrained and unconfined'.[46] This fundamental desire to be free is also widely recognised in progressive thinking and activism: indeed, it could be considered its raison d'être, and is defined by the young Marx as 'the essence of man'.[47] This might include freedom from oppressive state control; the freedom to live, work, and love as we want; the freedom to define ourselves and our communities in our own ways.[48] A highest-order direction towards autonomy means that we have a basic desire to feel in charge of our lives – not to be dominated and determined by others or things (like technology, even if they may bring us immediate pleasure). Research provides support for the importance of autonomy to wellbeing, showing that the two are closely associated.[49] However, contrary to a neoliberal perspective, the theory and evidence presented in this section suggests that freedom is just one of several highest-order directions. While, therefore, it is an essential consideration in the development of a better society, it cannot be held as the single guiding light by which such a society should be judged.

### *Self-worth*

Self-worth is posited as a powerful highest-order desire in a range of models[50] – feeling good about one's self, pride, and self-esteem – and its association with wellbeing is well-established in the literature.[51] Self-worth is closely linked to feelings of *competence*, defined as 'feeling effective in one's ongoing interactions with the social environment and experiencing opportunities to exercise and express one's capacities'.[52] This shows that a progressive desire to help different individuals and communities feel dignity, pride, and honour in themselves is well-founded in psychological theory and research.[53] However, a highest-order direction towards self-worth can also help progressives to understand more destructive behaviours, and the humanity of the needs and wants ultimately underlying them. Another way of understanding incel activity, for instance, along with many other forms of prejudice, is that it is an attempt by members of a dominant group to maintain their sense of self-worth. The reality is, for instance, men – like, for instance, White people, able-bodied people, and heterosexual people – do feel shame, vulnerability, and self-hatred. In psychotherapy, we see this all the time. And one means of defending against such feelings may be by putting other groups down: 'If you are worse than me, then I am not so bad.' This, to repeat, does not excuse such behaviours, and it also does not mean that the suffering of the 'majority' should be given precedence over the suffering of those minoritised. But, for progressives, it does mean that we can understand the fundamental directions behind such behaviours and, rather than simply demonising or dehumanising them, can consider alternative ways in which such needs and wants may be met.

## *Meaning and values*

A highest-order drive towards *meaning* is considered by some therapists, particularly of the 'existential approach', to be among the most fundamental human directions.[54] From this perspective, what we strive for most in our lives is to have a reason for why we are here and doing the things that we do. Other needs and wants, like happiness, may be important but, from this standpoint, they are a means towards meaning, rather than highest-order direction in themselves. In other words, people strive towards happiness because they believe that that is what makes a meaningful life, rather than happiness being an ultimate, highest-order goal in itself. Support for this perspective can be seen in cases where 'people are quite willing to endure pain, deprivation, and other adverse events if there is some meaning such as a purpose or justification or an increase in self-worth'.[55] In the words of Nietzsche, 'He who has a *why* to live can bear with almost any *how*.'[56]

Closely related to meaning and purpose is the suggestion that, at the highest order, are *values*: principles, standards, morals, or preferences that people believe are of ultimate worth.[57] Such values might be 'fairness', 'environmental protection', or 'faith': deep set commitments that can override other, more 'innate' needs and wants. This explains the behaviour of, for instance, environmental or animal rights campaigners, who are willing to sacrifice their pleasure for what they perceive as a greater good. Indeed, as stated earlier, values may be pursued 'even at the expense of life itself'.[58]

Understanding the fundamental role that meaning and values can play in our lives is important for progressives because it means that, as human beings, we have the capacity to 'stand above' our more inherent needs and wants and put ethical and moral principles first. Moreover, it means that these principles – like care for the environment or for animal rights – are not secondary or 'superficial' directions, but can be at the very heart of our being. Even if, then, we did not have an innate human direction towards relatedness, prosociality, and equality, such values could still play an intrinsic part in who we are.

## *Critical reflections*

***How do these highest-order needs and wants relate to each other?***

Across the theory and research, then, there are several needs and wants that are commonly posited as being most fundamental to people: physiological needs, safety, pleasure, growth, relatedness, autonomy, competence, and meaning and values. And while some early 20th-century theorists, such as Frankl, have argued that one of these is *the* most fundamental – to which all others point – there is increasing acceptance that multiple highest-order needs and wants are likely to exist.[59]

In some cases, these directions have then been further grouped together. For instance, physiological needs and safety have been grouped together as 'material needs', while the other directions can be termed 'non-material needs'.[60] Along these lines, Maslow distinguishes between the more basic *deficiency needs* (physiological, safety, relatedness, and self-esteem), so-called because they are intended to make up for something lacking; and then the *being need* of growth (or 'self-actualisation'), which takes us forward into new and uncharted territories.[61]

Famously, in his *hierarchy of needs*, Maslow suggests that we must fulfil the more basic needs before we can attend to those at a higher level (note, Maslow's use of the term 'hierarchy' here is different to how it is used in the present book).[62] This hypothesis has been widely criticised and bears limited empirical support.[63] Indeed, Galtung argues that such a hierarchy can serve the interest of powerful Western elites: justifying a focus on 'the masses' basic material needs, rather than their more sophisticated, complex, and creative wants.[64] West states something similar when he writes, 'people, especially degraded and oppressed people, are also hungry for identity, meaning, and self-worth'.[65] Nevertheless, it seems likely that there is some truth to Maslow's claim that our material, 'deficiency'-based directions can feel more urgent – and can exert more of a 'press' – than our non-material, growth-oriented ones. This gives good justification for the tendency of progressives to focus on equalities at the material level: such as housing, food, and physical safety. Yet it also suggests that we should not focus exclusively on this plane, but should also be mindful of non-material directions – like creativity, love, and self-development – and the need for their equal realisation too. The specifics of how we might do this is the subject of Chapter 8 (this volume).

### *A 'web' of highest-order needs and wants*

Although, as argued earlier, it is helpful for progressives to explore human beings' highest-order needs and wants, there are several reasons why we should be cautious in creating any definitive list. First, we need to be wary of being too 'atomistic': any of these needs and wants are not discrete, isolated forces; but interwoven elements of a complex, seamless, multi-overlapping web. A desire to feel competent, for instance, could be seen as closely overlapping a desire for growth, as well as directions towards relatedness and meaning.

### *A tentative list*

Second, and closely related, we are still a long way from identifying, and finding the right terms for, the key dimensions in this directional web. What about other potentially highest-order directions, for instance, such as a need to be authentic, or to see reality as it is? And where would such directions as the desires for recognition, personal integrity, authenticity, or tolerance fit: are these about relatedness, or autonomy, or values; or should these all be subsumed under one overarching want? The fact that innumerable taxonomies of highest-order wants and needs have been posited highlights the distance we are from finding any definitive 'truth'. Indeed, from a progressive position, it could be argued that we are only going to see the genuine nature of human beings' highest-order needs and wants when we can finally pull back the veil of capitalism's false consciousness.[66] In this respect, the set of highest-order directions presented in this section must be treated as preliminary and indicative only.

### *Cultural and social factors*

Third, and perhaps more fundamentally, we may never get to a point where we are able to identify a fixed set of highest-order needs and wants, because these directions will always be affected by the particular social and cultural contexts in which a person is embedded. In other words, while some have claimed that there are a set of biologically based highest-order needs and wants common to all; it has also been argued, as already discussed, that our directions – right up to the most fundamental – are always infused with the meanings and values of our social environment.[67] From the latter standpoint, then, 'highest-order' wants like autonomy, self-esteem, and growth may bear a strong Western imprint – what Galtung refers to as 'need imperialism'[68] – and may not be generalisable to other cultures. Equally, non-Western cultures may have their own, non-generalisable highest-order needs and wants. For instance, some nomadic communities have a powerful need to relocate themselves at least twice a year – something few of us have a powerful need for in the West.[69] Cultures may also differ in the relative strength of different desires: for instance, research suggests that interpersonal contact is more strongly needed in Japan than in Western Europe or the US.[70] There may also be differences in highest-order needs and wants related to sociocultural factors such as gender: for instance, research suggests that men place more emphasis on autonomy than women, while women place more emphasis on relatedness.[71] A supposedly 'ungendered' list of highest-order needs and wants, then, is at risk of hiding the workings of masculinity, femininity, and power in in our culture; resulting in a taxonomy that, actually, 'suspiciously mirror male needs'.[72]

As Galtung argues, however, the issue around cultural relativity of highest-order needs and wants is complex, as human beings are not 'infinitely malleable' – and nor are their rights.[73] What if a culture, for instance, claims that its highest-order desire is for female genital mutilation – surely these needs do not then become legitimate? Indeed, by its very nature, the United Nations' Universal Declaration of Human Rights asserts that there are certain cross-cultural needs and wants that must be respected: such as the desire for freedom of thought (Article 18), education (Article 26), and rest and leisure (Article 24).

### *Individual variations and freedom to choose*

A fourth limitation of any taxonomy is that considerable variations in highest-order needs and wants may exist at the individual level.[74] As the psychologist Henry A. Murray and anthropologist Clyde Kluckholn famously put it, 'Every man is in certain respects (a) like all other men, (b) like some other men, (c) like no other men.'[75] For one person, then, the desire for safety may be foremost; another person may primarily strive for autonomy and growth; and a third person may have a particular, relatively idiosyncratic set of meanings – such as supporting a local charity organisation – as their highest-order direction. 'People aiming to live a good life', writes the American philosopher John Kekes, 'are no more aiming at the same goal than artists aiming to create a work of art are aiming at the same goal'.[76] The assumption, then, that 'we all have the same basic needs' can be a denial of the uniqueness and 'difference' of the other – based on the mistaken assumption, perhaps, that everybody else needs and wants what we need and want. More importantly, perhaps, 20th-century philosophers such as Isaiah Berlin, John Kekes, and John Rawls[77] have argued that the very definition of a democratic society is that it allows for a 'plurality of conceptions of the good (within the limits of justice) between which citizens are at liberty to choose'.[78] That is, by its very nature, a democratic society allows people to define, in their own way, what it is that they most fundamentally need and want: it does not impose on them particular, fundamental directions.[79] And, more than that, such a plurality of values – even if in conflict – is not 'a regrettable feature of our life' but, rather, 'a positive value' in itself.[80] The plurality of our pursuits is 'worthy of celebration', writes Kekes, 'because it makes life interesting, rich, full of possibilities, and provides one of the strongest motives why we should be interested in each other'.[81] Such a belief – that a plurality of fundamental directions should be allowed to flourish – is, I think, shared by most progressives; and something that may differentiate us from more totalitarian left-wing positions, where a universal, highest-order value (such as social unity) may be insisted upon.

### *What does this all mean for progressives?*

In this section, we have reviewed, and critically discussed, what human beings' highest-order needs and wants might be. The conclusion is that we can tentatively posit some common, highest-order directions; but that we need to be sensitive to individual and cultural variations, and that a definitive taxonomy is neither likely nor, necessarily, desirable. So what does this all mean for progressives?

First, as I will discuss in much more detail in Chapter 8, it gives us some very valuable clues as to what might make a better society: one in which more people feel more fulfilled more of the time. Because to know what makes people feel fulfilled, we need to know what it is that they most fundamentally need and want. While the list here, as clearly acknowledged, is by no means the 'right' one, simply asking and exploring this question can help us develop a sharper and more refined understanding of the world we are trying to create.

Second, the psychological evidence on what people most fundamentally need and want provides some valuable support for some key progressive principles. In particular, that human beings have the desire, and capacity, to live cooperatively with each other; that we need to feel safe and secure; and that meanings and values can be an important part of our lives.

Third, and related to this, such an analysis can help to underpin a progressive, humanistic understanding of people as basically prosocial, while also recognising that we have the propensity to act in incredibly destructive and asocial ways. Because when we look across the many different theories of highest-order directions, there is hardly ever the positing, or the evidencing, of inherently malign, destructive, or anti-social highest-order needs and wants. That is, there is no widely agreed assumption – or evidence – that, at the most fundamental level, people want to hurt others, discriminate, or act in oppressive ways. 'No living creature', said the 15th-century English social philosopher Thomas More, 'is naturally greedy, except from fear of want'.[82] This, then, underpins an attitude of *radical acceptance*, as introduced in Chapter 1 (this volume). Here, people are seen as having the capacity to act in highly destructive ways but, ultimately, those behaviours are understood as lower-order means towards some higher-order need or want that is not, in itself, inherently malevolent. So, for instance, as we have seen, racist bullying might be understood as a means by which someone strives towards self-worth; or the accumulation of vast wealth by the ultra-rich might be understood as a means towards pleasure, self-esteem, and autonomy. Again, to emphasise, such an understanding does not in any way justify or condone such behaviours or standpoints, but it does challenge the assumption that the person 'behind' these acts is inherently evil, malevolent, or oppressive. Rather, ultimately, they are a person, like ourselves, striving to realise a set of highest-order directions, albeit through lower-order means that can be deeply destructive to others. In this way, as discussed in the Introduction, we can maintain a position of psychological equality; we can hold hope for a society built on cooperation and caring; and we can look towards developing a society in which people might be able to get such highest-order needs and wants met in less destructive ways.

To a great extent, then, this psychological framework moves us away from moral judgements of other human beings. Indeed, Rosenberg argues that the whole notion of morality serves the interests of powerful social elites, who can control people by dictating what is 'good' and 'bad'.[83] Yet, as we have seen, the present framework does allow for judgements about behaviours that are more or less destructive (both to self and others); and some highest-order needs and wants (for example, relatedness) may be more socially constructive than others (for example, pleasure) (to be discussed further in Chapter 8, this volume). In addition, the inclusion of 'values' at the highest order allows for the possibility that some people may be more other-oriented than others. Hence, while this psychological framework challenges the assumption that all of us, or some of us, are inherently 'bad'; it also recognises that some people may be more oriented to the needs and wants of other people than others.

## Summing up

This chapter has introduced a psychological framework that can underpin a psychology-informed progressive vision for society. It conceptualises people in a way that is aligned to progressive thinking; provides theoretical and empirical support for a progressive analysis; and lays the groundwork, at a psychological level, for developing a progressive vision further. Building on insights from the socialist humanists, it has shown how we can conceptualise people in respectful, agentic ways – as striving and choice-making – yet also embedded within, and influenced by, their particular contexts. It also provides a means of recognising the reality of destructive, asocial behaviours; while still retaining a sense of others as equal to us, and as having an intrinsic capacity to be prosocial.

In developing a progressive vision of society, this chapter has also helped us consider what it is that people might most fundamentally need and want. What it has not done, however, is to discuss the implications of this for an understanding of wellbeing and distress? Is psychological thriving, for instance, having all our needs and wants met? Is distress the frustration of our directions? In considering the nature of a society in which all people can thrive, understanding what it means to function well – or to suffer, psychologically – is essential; as well as the means by which such states may come about. This is the subject matter for the next chapter.

# 4

# Wellbeing and distress: a directional account

This chapter follows on closely from Chapter 3. Having introduced a basic framework for understanding psychological functioning, I want to show how this framework can be extended to a conceptualisation of psychological wellbeing and distress. As with Chapter 3, I want to spend some time describing this theory, because the kind of progressive society we envision is so deeply rooted in how we think about others and ourselves. Indeed, the question of what we mean by human wellbeing – implicitly or explicitly – is right at the very core of progressive concerns: we cannot help to create a society that is better for people unless we know what 'better' is.

The aim of this chapter, then, is to show how we can conceptualise wellbeing and distress in a way that can underpin a progressive vision for society. This is, first, by providing theoretical and empirical support for the view that distress, and its amelioration, is dependent on social and economic factors (like poverty and oppression), as well as psychological ones (like experiencing a traumatic childhood). This means that, to create a world in which more people thrive more of the time, we need to address socioeconomic inequalities. However, contra to a classical Marxist analysis, I also want to show that there can be other, more psychological, ways of understanding and addressing distress; and that, actually, socioeconomic and psychological understandings do not need to be opposed, but can be part of a single, integrated framework. Second, I want to develop a conceptualisation of psychological wellbeing and distress that, as we will see in

Chapters 5 and 6, allows for the identification of common, system-wide principles of optimal and suboptimal functioning – whether at the level of the individual, the community, or the planet. That these principles – such as cooperation, taking responsibility, and openness to diversity – are strikingly similar to currently existing progressive values offers strong support for a progressive standpoint, and its capacity to form the basis for a better society.

Chapter 3 outlined three basic propositions from my book *Integrating counselling and psychotherapy*, and this chapter is based around a further four. First, that psychological wellbeing – the 'richer' and 'fuller' life – is the realisation of our fundamental needs and wants, while psychological distress is the failure to realise them. Second, that such failures can come about for both 'internal' (that is, psychological) and 'external' (that is, socioeconomic) reasons, and generally a complex combination of the two. Third, that the internal generation of difficulties is often to do with conflicts between a person's different needs and wants, as well as ineffective ways of striving towards them, and unrealistic expectations. Fourth, and following on from this all, that greater wellbeing can be brought about by changes in our external environment; by more cooperative, effective, and realistic internal configurations; and, again, through a complex combination of the two.

## Wellbeing and the realisation of needs and wants

If we understand human beings as oriented towards their highest-order needs and wants, then wellbeing (at the individual level) can be understood as the optimal realisation of these directions. This is similar to what Marx, Chomsky, and many of the socialist humanists proposed (see Chapter 2). However, following our analysis of highest-order needs and wants (Chapter 3), we can be somewhat more specific and say that a good life is likely to be one in which we have our physical needs met; feel safe, free, and of worth; and experience pleasure, relatedness, growth, and a sense of meaning. From a progressive standpoint, defining wellbeing in terms of such *highest-order* needs and wants (and not just needs and wants, per se) is important because it allows for the possibility that actualising some of our lower-order directions – for instance, for wealth, power, or consumer goods – may not actually be of overall benefit for the individual (as, indeed, the research demonstrates[1]). Rather, it will primarily be dependent on whether or not these lower-order directions actually help us towards our highest-order needs and wants; and also whether, in doing so, we end up realising, or undermining, other highest-order directions (we will explore these two issues further in this chapter).

The hypothesis that wellbeing comes from getting the things we most fundamentally need and want is well supported by the research.[2] However, what the research also shows is that it is not just the *achievement* of these highest-order directions that is associated with wellbeing. In addition, it is also about having *a sense of direction*, feeling that our highest-order needs and wants are *attainable*, *approaching* them, and being able to *appreciate* what we have achieved.

### *A sense of direction*

Research shows that it feels good to have *a sense of direction* in life: knowing where we want to go and what is most important to us.[3] This 'sense' of direction does not need to be a conscious, explicitly articulated goal; it can be some inner feeling of orientation or pointedness towards something of worth. It may be an intuitive knowing, for instance, that we thrive through close relationships; or that life feels meaningful to us when we contribute to our communities. The converse of this is that, as an abundance of research shows, a lack of direction can be experienced as deeply disorientating and upsetting, and is associated with a range of psychological difficulties.[4]

### *Attainability*

Research also suggests that it feels good when we perceive our highest-order needs and wants as *attainable*: that we can get to where we want to be. So, for instance, this might be a feeling that we can develop intimacy with others, or that we have the potential to make a meaningful contribution to my community. Attainability is closely related to feelings of competence; and is shown in the psychological research to be among the most important predictors of what people actually do.[5] So, for instance, if I feel that I am good at developing intimacy with others, not only is that likely to enhance my wellbeing – as feelings of hope and optimism – but it also means that I am more likely to try and achieve that goal (which then enhances my feeling of competence). By contrast, if I feel that my highest-order needs and wants are unattainable, then I may be left with feelings of hopelessness, despair, and futility – and, with that, less motivation to try and achieve my goals: a self-perpetuating downward spiral.

### *Approaching*

Making progress towards our highest-order needs and wants is also key to feelings of wellbeing. With this comes excitement, expectation, and empowerment – indeed, getting closer to our goals can sometimes generate more positive affect than their actual attainment. The converse of this is that failing to progress towards our goals – or moving further away from them – can evoke such feelings as sadness, demoralisation, and anxiety (when we are uncertain of whether progress is possible).

### *Appreciation*

Finally, appreciation is about savouring what we have done: being mindful of our successes. It is closely linked to an attitude of 'gratitude': taking time to recognise that we have the things that we want, rather than rushing on to more and more. Through appreciating the achievement of our needs and wants, we can experience such positive feelings as satisfaction, pride, and accomplishment. Conversely, if we do not – or cannot – we may be left with feelings of dissatisfaction, anger, and low self-worth.

### *Discussion*

Viewed in this way, wellbeing can be understood as having two interrelated components. First, as discussed in the previous chapter, is the experiencing of particular highest-order needs or wants: feeling, for instance, safe, autonomous, or of self-worth.

Second, though, is the sense of wellbeing that comes from the directional process, itself: that is, having a sense of direction, feeling our directions are attainable, approaching our goals, achieving our goals, and appreciating our achievements. Together, we can refer to these two components as the *realisation* of our needs and wants. So this two-fold perspective suggests that we do not just feel good when we experience, for instance, relatedness; but also when we feel we are moving towards the relatedness that we want, or when we reflect, appreciatively, on the relatedness that we have. In other words, wellbeing is not just about achieving an outcome but also about the process itself – if all our highest-order needs and wants were permanently satisfied, ironically, it would probably not be that satisfying.[6]

Understanding wellbeing in terms of the directional process, itself, is important to progressives because it can help to explain why directions, *in themselves*, can become so compelling and self-perpetuating. Why, for instance, a person strives to accumulate wealth even if, the richer they become, the more miserable they get. This does not make much sense in terms of the satisfaction of highest-order needs and wants, per se; but it does if we see the striving, itself, as a source of reward: for instance, the fighting, the battling, the sense of direction, the groping towards something. Have you ever played a board game like Monopoly or Risk and wondered, 'Why am I getting so competitive about this?' Or been stuck in an argument where you are trying to prove you are right, all the time knowing that it is pointless to keep going? Such feelings show the power and compelling nature of directionality, per se: we do not just want something, we want to want something because it can make us feel vibrant and alive.

This, second, source of reward is, I think, an element of capitalism that progressives have often overlooked. Why is capitalism so compelling when it clearly creates so much misery, suffering, and hardship? As discussed in Chapter 2, we can explain it in terms of the creation of false needs and a false consciousness, but that moves dangerously close to an elitist and dehumanising view of 'the masses'. Alternatively, we can see the attraction of capitalism in terms of the hope and possibility it creates for people: the way that it provides people with a sense of direction and a feeling that their goals can be attainable. 'You, too, can have this amazing lifestyle. You can have the beautiful house, the swimming pool, the luxury that you always dreamed of. And you can be *someone* in this world: someone who is admired and respected, who has significance.' Even if, as most people know, such goals are chimera; the orientation and hope they provide – and the momentary feelings of 'success' that can be experienced as one takes a small step in their direction – can be enough to sustain belief in, and commitment to, this worldview. In other words, capitalism taps deep into our directional, goal-oriented nature, such that we can become blind to other possible ways of living.[7] In *Doughnut economics*, Raworth recounts a discussion with a leading figure in economics who, when asked why gross domestic product (GDP) growth was seen as an obvious necessity in high income countries, replied, 'We have a deep-seated desire for growth. … People need something to aspire to'.[8] Recognising this human need to aspire – and harnessing it to prosocial effect – is, I believe, the difference between a progressive politics that will genuinely motivate, energise, and excite people; and one that is psychologically unsustainable.

'In America, you can be whatever you want to be' – the American Dream. From a progressive perspective, we know how wrong such a claim is. Around 15 per cent of the US population live in poverty;[9] millions more spend their lives in frustration and disappointment, striving for something they will never achieve. And yet, unless a progressive politics can, in some way, recognise this need for direction – providing people with a sense of challenge, hope, and striving – it may always be in danger of losing out to the right. Traditionally, and quite rightly, progressives have tended to focus on the need, for all, to have their highest-order needs and wants met (in particular, material physiological needs and safety); while achievement-focused desires (for instance, to strive, endeavour, and compete) have often been denounced and attributed to the right. This makes absolute sense: for every 'winner' (glorified by the right) there is a loser (that the left cares about); for every success there is someone who fails. And yet, in terms of a holistic understanding of human beings, there is something that progressives are missing here. Human beings are not, naturally, lotus-eaters. Or, at the very least, we are not *only* lotus-eaters – we are also fighters, strivers, and do-ers. So, from this perspective, the question is not how we shun or repress this side of our being, but how we can harness it? That is, what kind of progressive society can we create in which people can strive, hope, and struggle – but in which everyone also has their basic needs met? This is the challenge taken up in the latter part of the book.

★★★

If psychological wellbeing can be conceptualised as the realisation of our highest-order needs and wants, psychological distress can be seen as the failure to realise those directions. That is, we experience distress when we do not have our most fundamental needs and wants met; and also when we do not feel that we have a sense of direction, we do not feel we can achieve our goals, we are not progressing towards anything, and/or there is no appreciation of what we have done. But why might this failure to realise our most fundamental needs and wants happen? The following sections suggest four key explanations, each of them pervasive throughout the psychological literature: limited external resources, inner conflicts, ineffective ways of doing things, and unrealistic expectations.

## Limited external resources

The most obvious and immediate reason why people do not realise their highest-order needs and wants – and one that progressives are acutely aware of – is due to limits in our external satisfiers. Poverty, insecure housing, back-breaking working conditions, for instance, are all examples of socioeconomic conditions that create misery by limiting people's abilities to realise their fundamental physiological needs. Similarly, misery can be the consequence of safety needs being violated: for instance, through homophobia, domestic violence, or war. External factors can also play a critical role in obstructing the realisation of non-material highest-order directions. For instance, homophobia not only threatens someone's physical safety, but also a highest-order direction for self-esteem or relatedness. Marginalised social groups suffer because they are denied the dignity, pride, and honour that they strive for (and have a right to); and because they are denied the capacity for autonomy and self-determination.[10] From this perspective, anti-governmental acts, such as protests and riots, can be seen as an expression of that need for freedom, respect, and self-worth. Similarly, neoliberalism's creation of an urbanised, anonymised world – in which social bonding and community is often absent – causes suffering as people fail to realise their higher-order desires for relatedness.[11] Galtung states, 'A society that systematically counteracts [the need for togetherness] will be punished sooner or later.'[12] Yet socialist societies, too, may have impeded their citizens from achieving such fundamental desires as autonomy, meaning, and direction itself (as suggested in the previous section) – in some cases by focusing too exclusively on the satisfaction of basic physiological and safety needs.[13] An overwhelming body of research supports this claim that external factors – social, economic, political, and interpersonal – can all significantly impact a person's psychological wellbeing and adjustment.[14]

For Marcuse, the existence of limited external resources can be conceptualised as a state of *scarcity*. By this, he means that 'the struggle for existence takes place in a world too poor for the satisfaction of human needs without constant restraint, renunciation, delay'.[15] Marcuse goes on to argue that the conquering of want, in the future, will allow for these highest-order directions to be realised. Bastani, too, emphasises the possibility of a *post-scarcity* world, in which all fundamental needs and wants can be met.[16] Here, writes Bastani, labour will be reduced to a minimum and people will live in abundance and luxury. Yet, as both these authors recognise, it is not simply the case that a lack of resources, at the individual level, is a result of limited resources, more globally. Rather, there is *surplus repression*, whereby things are more restricted than, given external circumstances, they actually need to be.[17] This is the case with respect to non-material needs and wants and well as material ones: social limitations – such as racism, homophobia, or bullying – simply do not need to be there. Rather, here is the possibility of creating a more 'resource-rich' world: one, for instance, in which people can be accepted and valued whatever their sexuality. In Chapters 6 to 9 (this volume), we will examine this in much more detail.

Recognising the problem as surplus repression is particularly important because, in some instances, it is essential to acknowledge, and respect, the real limitations of our world. The key case in point here is the environment, and Raworth's *Doughnut economics* focuses on the essential issue of living within our limited planetary means. Attempting to live beyond this, as Raworth writes, lies 'critical planetary degradation such as climate change and biodiversity loss'.[18]

Of course, what progressives also recognise is that different individuals, and different communities, are limited by external factors to very different degrees. As a White, middle-class, global North male, for instance, I have far greater access to certain resources than many people of colour, women, or those who live in the global South. Again, this is not just in terms of material resources but also non-material ones. For instance, my privilege means that I am more likely to feel of worth in the world, and to have the freedom to act as I want. From a progressive standpoint, then, a better society is not just about becoming more resource-rich (within our planetary limits), but about making more resources available to more people more of the time. While we all cannot have all of what we want, the sine qua non of a progressive vision is that society's resources are distributed in such a way that everyone, as far as possible, can realise their highest-order needs and wants.

## Inner conflicts: when what we want is not what we want

As progressives emphasise, then, external limitations can restrict our abilities to experience and realise the things we need and want. Yet such an account of human distress, in itself, is insufficient; and this is for two related reasons. First, it risks falling back into a social determinism, whereby the individual's wellbeing is understood solely in terms of external, causal forces. Certainly, when we hit a roadblock, we do sometimes just stop and give up; but the reality of concrete human activity is that we will often try multiple creative and ingenious methods before we do so. To overlook this is to risk losing the essence of a progressive view of humanity: that people are directional, resourceful, intelligible human beings who are striving to make things happen in their world (Chapter 3). Second, such an understanding cannot explain variations in wellbeing at the individual level. Why is it, for instance, that two people with seemingly equal levels of external resources can experience such different levels of psychological wellbeing? Research confirms, for instance, that poverty is a major risk factor for social, behavioural, and emotional problems in early development. But, it is 'just' a *risk* factor – about a 30 per cent increase in risk – with psychological and relational factors, such as quality of parental attachment and the child's temperament, also playing an important role. Indeed, research suggests that attachment relationships may be even more important to wellbeing among chronically impoverished children. Similarly, as we know from the media every day, people with access to every possible resource can still be profoundly miserable.

As progressives, we cannot just ignore these individual-level variations. They may not suit our theories, but to disregard them means closing our eyes to some very real source of psychological distress. If we want to create a world in which more people can experience more wellbeing more of the time, we need to know what that wellbeing, and distress, is *really* founded on – in all its multiple sources. And if we are able to recognise, and develop policies to address, the real causes of distress, then we are more likely to have an approach that is attractive and compelling to others.

A concept that can help here to make sense of psychological distress at the individual level, pervasive across the counselling and psychotherapy literature, is that of *inner conflicts*.[19] 'Inner' means conflicts 'within' the person – although, as stated earlier, needs and wants always have an in-the-world correlate. Of course, conflicts can be constructive as well as destructive.[20] They can instigate positive change (as in Marx's theory of the dialectic[21]); they can be fun (as in playing a game of Risk); and, to some degree, are unavoidable in life.[22] But for the purposes of this book, the term 'conflict' is used to refer specifically to destructive conflicts. These can be defined as conflicts where one direction prevents, obstructs, interferes, injures, or in some way makes the realisation of another direction less likely, to the detriment of the whole.[23] This can also be described as the opposite of a cooperative, *synergetic* relationship: a 'negative synergy'[24] or what I have termed a 'dysergy'.[25]

Such inner conflicts can involve two different needs or wants pulling the person in different directions at the same point in time. For instance, a person may want to go dating to experience greater relatedness in their lives, but they may also be scared of going dating because the prospect of being intimate with another person makes them feel unsafe (perhaps due to insecure childhood attachments). So the person experiences anxiety; and because they are torn between two competing directions, neither is realised to any satisfying extent. Another example: a person wants to relax, take life easy, enjoy time with friends; but then there is another part of them that wants to achieve things, and is very critical of the 'take life easy' part. 'C'mon', that critical part shouts, 'don't lie there in bed, get up, get moving. There's so much to be done'. Here, as with all conflicts, both parts are legitimate expressions of needs and wants, but the problem is the way they relate to each other. They shout, defend, counteract: so that the person feels torn, and then either stressed (when doing what the critical part wants), or guilty (when doing what the 'take life easy' part wants).

Alternatively, conflicts can exist over time, in the sense that first one, and then another, direction dominates. For example, a person may become consumed with a desire for relatedness – 'I must have people close to me', 'I cannot cope on my own' – act on it, and only subsequently shift into the opposing position: 'This feels really unsafe to be so close to others', 'I need to be on my own'. When a person becomes 'taken over' by one particular need or want, to the exclusion of the greater whole, we can describe that direction as going *rogue*.[26] That is what happens when you miss your stop on the train because you are so engrossed in Candy Crush Saga. Rogue goals may be particularly driven by primitive, biological forces: for instance, our 'fight, flight, or freeze' stress response.[27] We find ourselves, for instance, shouting at a partner, or avoiding contact with our line manager, all the time knowing that it is an 'irrational' thing to do. At a physiological level, however, our bodies are urging us in a direction that feels impossible to resist. Psychological research supports this clinical observation that we can be taken over by rogue goals. Indeed, John Bargh, a Yale University-based professor of social psychology who has led research in this area, argues that the 'self' essentially consists of 'many, often-conflicting goals', and that these will selfishly and single-mindedly 'pursue their agenda independently of whether doing so is in the overall good of the individual person'.[28]

Why is it that we can lose the 'bigger picture': that directions can pull against each other or go rogue in a way that is destructive to the greater whole? One answer lies in the fact that, as we saw earlier, realising our directions, in itself, can be rewarding. So, for instance, when we match three candies on Candy Crush Saga, it is not just that completing that level is a means towards highest-order wants (for instance, to feel self-worth). Rather, the achievement of that particular goal (completing the Candy Crush Saga level) – that 'Test–Operate–Test–Exit' (TOTE) cycle – becomes compelling in itself. This means that, as human beings, we can get caught up in pretty much any need or want, lower- or higher-order; because the achievement of that direction, in itself, can come to take precedence over the greater whole. Stamp collecting, macramé, competitive chilli pepper eating … millions of activities exist that, from an objective perspective, might seem absurd; but from the 'inside' can become important – even obsessive – goals in themselves. And when it is a lower-order direction that comes to dominate, it may get in the way of many other higher-order, more fundamental needs and wants being realised.

Needs and wants such as these can become especially compelling because, as we become immersed in a particular direction, so our attention becomes narrowed down to it, and we come to see and define ourselves in that way. Hence, it takes on ever-greater perceived importance. If we get into competitive chilli pepper eating, for instance, then the goal of eating the most hot chilli peppers takes on increasing salience, and we come to see ourselves as a 'chilli head'. The world becomes a world of chilli pepper-oriented needs and wants: 'What's the best preparation for a chilli pepper-eating contest?' 'Do we prefer chocolate habaneros or orange habaneros?' And through mingling with other chilli heads and reading websites like *Chilli Magazine*, our chilli pepper-oriented directions become reinforced by the community around us. Such narrowed foci, in themselves, are by no means a bad thing. Indeed, in Chapters 8 and 9, I will suggest that they can be an element of a more thriving society. But, again, the problem is if and where they come to dominate over all other needs and wants.

One of the most pervasive forms of internal conflict is between short-term, immediate goals and longer-term objectives. Walter Mischel, author of *The marshmallow test* and a leading American psychologist, wrote: 'Human behavior is often governed by a competition between lower level, automatic processes that may reflect evolutionary adaptations to particular environments, and the more recently evolved, uniquely human capacity for abstract, domain-general reasoning and future planning.'[29] So, for instance, part of us may want another glass of red wine while a second part is looking towards our longer-term health; or part of us may want to rant at our partner in an argument while a second part urges caution, knowing that such behaviour would be counterproductive.

As with all other needs and wants, both short-term and long-term directions can be considered intelligible (sometimes, the best thing *is* another glass of wine, just as sometimes it *is not*); but, generally across the psychological therapies, there is a tendency to emphasise the value of longer-term directions. Windy Dryden, a leading UK-based cognitive behaviour therapist, for instance, writes:

> Frequently … we defeat ourselves by attempting to satisfy our short-term goals while at the same time sabotaging our long-term goals. Thus, for example we often strive to avoid discomfort when it would be advisable for us to experience discomfort because doing so would help us to achieve our long-term goals.[30]

This is consistent with empirical evidence from psychology. Famously, for instance, in Mischel's Marshmallow Test, children who delayed gratification as preschoolers (choosing to wait for a larger reward of two marshmallows, as opposed to a more immediate reward of one marshmallow) were more likely to do well mentally, physically, and intellectually as they grew older.[31] Similarly, in adulthood itself, research shows that a preference for smaller, more immediate rewards over larger, delayed ones is associated with a wide range of mental health problems, such as depression and obsessive-compulsive disorder.[32]

For Mischel, the immediate rush to snaffle a marshmallow is an expression of our brain's 'hot emotional system' – designed to respond immediately and impulsively to pleasure- or pain-inducing stimuli – as opposed to the 'cool cognitive system', which is capable of slower and more complex reflection.[33] In this respect, we could see the problem with short-term directions as not their existence, per se, but with their greater tendency to go rogue and take over the system as a whole. Put conversely, the capacity to prioritise longer-term goals can be seen as closely associated with the capacity to 'stand back' and consider a wider range of needs and wants. In fact, if we only prioritised longer-term goals, life would 'become stifling, a joyless driven life of postponed pleasures, happy diversions not taken, emotions not experienced, possible lives unlived'.[34] Good psychological functioning, then, is likely to involve a balance between short-term and long-term – hot and cold – needs and wants: working together rather than any one part dominating.

By understanding distress in terms of inner conflicts, progressives can maintain a view of human beings as active, agentic, and intelligible; but also with the capacity to get things wrong and contribute to our own suffering by undermining our own best intentions. It is a view of human beings as trying to do our best, but also recognising that doing our best is not always the best thing we could be doing – for ourselves or for others. Here, we can become 'alienated' from many of our own highest-order needs and wants, but it is not because we are weak, passive, or pliable (see Fromm, Chapter 2). Rather, it is because, in intelligibly striving for one thing, we can impede or undermine some other intelligible striving. And, while we may lose sight of what we most fundamentally need and want – a false consciousness – it is not out of gullibility or stupidity but because, as human beings, we have a tendency to get caught up in things and lose a sense of the greater whole. In this way, then, the humanism and psychological equality of a progressive perspective is maintained; but also the capacity to identify points of leverage in forging a better society, on the 'inner' as well as 'outer' planes.

### *Inner conflicts and limited external resources*

From a psychological perspective, then, it is not just that limited external resources impede the realisation of our directions; it is also that we can come to impede them ourselves. However, to 'roll back' a little, there is a complex relationship between the two, because the more limited our external resources, the more likely we are to experience inner conflicts. As I have written previously:

> A person in a context of limited financial resources, for example, might only be able to achieve their desire for financial security by suppressing their desire for excitement and stimulation: for instance, by taking a job in a fast food restaurant. Alternatively, in that environment, the person may be able to actualise their desire for stimulation by forming a musical group with their friends, but then they might have to compromise their desire for financial security.[35]

Such a perspective does not lose the notion of a choice-making, active, intelligible human being who is constantly striving to realise their directions. However, what it suggests is that, the more restrictive a person's social and economic circumstances, the more that those directions gets turned against each other. It is as if, as the social 'space' gets smaller and smaller, so the person bounces up against themselves more and more: like molecules of air in an ever-tightening balloon. Given a resource-rich environment, the person can do 'A' and 'B' and neither need be sacrificed in this process. But where resources are limited, a choice to do A means choosing against B, and vice versa. In support of this, research shows that, when people report on conflicting goals, a great majority are due to limited resources.[36]

Bregman articulates exactly such a conflict when he writes about the *scarcity mentality* of people living in poverty, in which the 'long-term perspective goes out of the window' because the person is so consumed by short-term challenges.[37] 'Scarcity narrows your focus to your immediate lack, to the meeting that's starting in five minutes or the bills that need to be paid tomorrow.'[38] Here, then, people are less able to actualise longer-term needs and wants because they have to be so focused on the immediate now. Marx, too, described the way that 19th-century poverty forced workers to sacrifice all but their most 'animalian' drives. 'The Irishman no longer knows any need now', he wrote, 'but the need to eat, and indeed only the need to eat *potatoes* – and scabby *potatoes* at that, the worst kind of potatoes'.[39] For Bregman, such a scarcity mentality is like a computer running multiple programs at once: slowing down, making more and more errors, and eventually freezing. And, indeed, he presents research showing that our cognitive abilities are impaired under conditions of scarcity. To some extent, this analysis also corresponds to Maslow's concept of a 'hierarchy of needs', introduced in Chapter 3: that if we have urgent material, physiological needs we are less able to actualise our more growthful, non-material directions.[40]

This understanding of the relationship between inner conflicts and limited external resources can be applied to non-material needs and wants as well as material ones. Conditional parental love, for instance, has been described as 'a case in which the social world has essentially pitted the need for relatedness against the need for autonomy. The children are thus in the uncomfortable position of being controlled, of having to relinquish autonomy (and thus not be who they really are) in order to gain parental love'.[41] This is a description, then, of how children may sacrifice their freedom to maintain relatedness to their parents, under conditions in which they can only have one or the other, but not both. Again, though, it is not simply the case that the child's environment *makes them* feel and act a particular way. Rather, the child – as a creative, resourceful, intelligible being – adopts a particular stance (albeit one against themselves) as the best means of dealing with restrictive circumstances.

This is how we can understand the devastating impact of adverse childhood experiences (ACEs), such as trauma and abuse.[42] It is not that the ACE *makes* the child one thing or another: it is not a direct causal relationship in which the child, themselves, is an inert target. Rather, experiences like abuse lead children, as intelligible and creative beings, to respond to their worlds in ways that, while self-protective, can end up having negative consequences in their lives. For instance, a child who experienced physical abuse may grow up to always expect the worse, and that leads to feelings of hopelessness and depression as an adult. For the child, those negative expectations developed as a meaningful and intelligible way of coping with the real world around them; but the problem is, as an adult, they may no longer be 'fit for purpose'. That is, the person's world has changed (or, at least, there is the possibility for a better world), but their expectations and way of being in the world have not: these patterns of seeing and behaving have become chronic.[43] Here, improvement is not simply a matter of choosing to see the world in a more positive way: once we come to particular mindsets and behaviours, they can be incredibly difficult and frightening to change. But, ultimately, the work of therapy is in helping clients to see what their patterns of thinking and behaviour are, and helping them reflect on whether these are, indeed, the most useful ways of engaging with their worlds. Where it is recognised that they are not, the work can then begin on gradually revising them.

From a progressive standpoint, recognising that even inner conflicts are shaped by the availability of external resources is important because it supports the view, presented in the last section, that socioeconomic factors are central to psychological wellbeing. While, as argued in this section, not everything can be reduced down to social and economic forces; this analysis shows that even the most micro and seemingly 'psychological' problems have important external components. And, as we have also seen in this section, the external factors that can shape a person's inner conflicts can be non-material as well as material: like the degree of love and acceptance available to a person, or the presence or absence of traumatic hurts. This means that, in developing a society in which more people can experience more wellbeing more of the time, we cannot just focus on material resources. The availability of love, acceptance, and the potential to be creative, for instance, are also issues that progressives must attend to if we want to create a world in which inner conflicts are minimised.

### *Developing cooperative solutions*

As the last subsection has argued, then, even the most 'internal' sources of distress have an external dimension. And yet, within any set of external resources, there is also an internal dimension that may lead to more or less levels of conflict. For instance, under conditions of limited income, one person may feel that they have to choose either pleasure (for instance, by drinking alcohol) or health; while another may find ways of experiencing both pleasure and health (for instance, through focusing on close friendships). Resolving such conflicts, at the individual level, is the realm of therapy, and each of the principal psychotherapeutic approaches has an understanding of conflicts at its heart.[44] Classic 'psychoanalytic' therapies, for instance, try to help clients mediate the conflict between their sexual and aggressive desires (the 'id'), and their socially mandated conscience (the 'superego'). 'Humanistic' therapies, on the other hand, aim to help clients overcome their desire for social approval, and instead realise their growthful, creative, and relational tendencies. The cognitive-behavioural therapies (CBT) tend to focus on helping the client control their tendency towards short-term thinking and rewards; and instead develop their capacity for longer-term, 'cool brain' processing and planning. The focus of the therapeutic work in all these approaches, then, is on helping clients lessen inner conflicts, so that they can do more of what is good for the person as an overall whole.

For example, Jade, a secondary school teacher, comes to counselling to try and address her alcohol dependency. She is drinking about a bottle of white wine every evening: sometimes with her girlfriend, sometimes on her own. 'I just need to blank things out', she says. 'I get to the end of the day, and I just want to kill off everything I feel.' Jade and her counsellor explore more of her day-to-day life: in particular, the stress and anxiety that she feels as a teacher. 'It's a constant need to be in 100 per cent control', says Jade. 'I feel like a policewoman, always on edge.' With her counsellor, Jade starts to see how her drinking is an attempt to get relief from the intense pressure she experiences. Jade and her counsellor (implicitly, rather than using these actual terms) acknowledge the intelligibility of this desire, but they also recognise that it is a rogue goal. That is, the drunkenness is a desire that is achieved at the expense of other important needs and wants, such as Jade's desire for health, or a desire for genuine relatedness with her partner. On this basis, Jade and her counsellor explore ways of being in which the relationship between her needs and wants are less conflictual and more cooperative: for instance, helping Jade to find healthier ways of managing stress at work. Such actions may not necessarily change Jade's external circumstances, but by creating more cooperation between her needs and wants, there is greater realisation overall.

This cooperative relationship between different directions – of working together in support of each other – can also be referred to as *synergies*. This is the opposite of (destructive) conflicts: it is when two or more sets of needs and wants support and bolster each other, so that they create greater overall benefit. If Jade, for instance, manages her stress by going running rather than drinking alcohol, then this multibeneficial activity means that the more she reduces her anxiety, the more healthy she also becomes. So there is now a synergy between her striving for calm and her striving for health.

Peter Corning, an American social scientist, described synergies as 'nature's magic' and, in many ways they are magical.[45] Synergetic, cooperative relationships allow for more to be created within the same set of external resources: they create something out of nothing, making 1 + 1 > 2. Stephen Covey, the bestselling American author on leadership, described the capacity to synergise as one of the '7 habits of highly effective people'. He wrote, 'Synergy is the highest activity in all life.'[46] Covey goes on to state, 'What results is almost miraculous. We create new alternatives – something that wasn't there before.'[47] For both Corning and Covey, synergies are not just something 'good' that happens within people, but are the very essence of positive growth, change, and evolution across many different systems. Covey, for instance, points out that 'Synergies are everywhere in nature': from people coming together to make a child, to 'mutualistic' animal relationships – such as between clownfish and anemones.[48] Synergies are also prevalent in the inorganic world: for instance, chrome, nickel, and steel coming together to form an alloy that is much stronger than the separate parts combined.[49] As we will see in Chapter 5, then, whether we are thinking at the psychological, interpersonal, or intercommunity level, the development of cooperative, synergetic relationships seems to be a key element of making things better – and one already at the heart of much progressive thinking.

## *Discussion*

For progressives, the psychological framework being developed here is a way of bringing together two things that most of us would consider to be true. First, that psychological wellbeing and distress is massively influenced by a person's social and economic circumstances; and second that, within that, there is some scope for things to be better or worse, depending on how someone meets those circumstances. In this section, I have suggested that what makes a difference here is the degree to which a person encounters their circumstances synergistically – with their different needs and wants supporting each other and acting cooperatively – as opposed to being in internal conflict. Bringing together these two understandings into a single, integrated framework is helpful for progressives because it gives us a richer, deeper, and more comprehensive understanding of wellbeing and distress, which can then serve as the basis for our political thinking and activity (to be developed later in this book). For instance, if we know that wellbeing is about cooperative relationships on the internal plane as well as the external one, then helping children develop skills in self-awareness and self-management (see Chapter 7, this volume) may take on greater priority. More than that, it means that we are not switching between socioeconomic and psychological frameworks when we consider the development of better ways of being, but are able to look at both sets of impacts and effects in tandem and as an integrated whole – a synergetic relationship, in itself. Say, for instance, a progressive political party was looking to develop its agenda around tackling obesity. Bringing psychologists together with other health and social policy specialists could help to develop an integrated policy initiative. This would be one that aimed to tackle the social and economic circumstances that pushed people into unhealthy eating choices; but also one that helped people, within their circumstances, weigh up their choices in more helpful and healthy ways. Moreover, by considering such issues as an integrated whole, it could also consider – and strive to address – the complex interactions between socioeconomic and psychological factors: for instance, that as healthy choices become cheaper and more available, so people need to be encouraged to adopt these choices. That is, on their own, neither socioeconomic nor psychological policy initiatives may be enough.

This section has also introduced the concept of cooperative, or synergetic, relationships, and argued that they are essential to wellbeing on the intrapsychic plane. As already indicated, however, later chapters of this book will develop this concept further: arguing that cooperative relationships are a more general property of well-functioning systems – whether on the individual, interpersonal, or collective 'levels of organisation'. This is a key insight in support of progressivism, because it suggests that our belief in cooperation is not just a hypothesis specific to politics, but an expression of a more general 'law' about how things work well. This is particularly explored in Chapter 5, which follows shortly.

## Ineffectiveness: when we are not good at getting what we want

In this book, the principal focus – at both the intrapersonal, and wider systemic, level – is on difficulties that arise due to conflictual, dysergetic relationships. However, across the therapeutic fields, there is also an understanding that sometimes people fail to realise their most fundamental needs and wants because the ways that they try and get there are just not very effective. In some instance, this may be because, with the best will in the world, the person has not been able to work out effective ways for themselves; they may not have been taught effective ways; or they may be modelling their behaviour on significant others who were not, in fact, behaving in effective ways themselves ('social leaning theory'[50], see Chapter 7, this volume).

Take the example of a person who is desperate to rid themselves of debilitating anxiety attacks. As they start to feel panic, the person grits their teeth and says to themselves, 'I mustn't panic, I mustn't panic.' That is a totally intelligible strategy: they are trying to ward off the feelings of anxiety in the best way they know how. Unfortunately, however, such a response often has the opposite effect: the person becomes more afraid that they will panic, and so their symptoms (such as trembling and light-headedness) intensify. Consequently, their panic attack worsens in an escalating, vicious spiral. In fact, as 'behavioural therapies' teach us, when people are starting to panic, they are generally better off saying to themselves something like, 'If I have a panic attack, it is not the end of the world, I know I will survive.'[51] Such self-talk has more chance of defusing the panic cycle, but it is not something we are born with an innate knowledge of how to do. In other words, and again with the best will in the world, we do not always know how to realise our most fundamental needs and wants (in this case, to feel free of anxiety). And, sometimes, this is not to do with limited socioeconomic resources or even internal conflicts – it is just that we do not know.

As with inner conflicts, in many instances, ineffective strategies arise because we have learnt ways of doing things in the past that are no longer fit for purpose. This is, de facto, the basis for much psychotherapeutic work: helping clients trace back dysfunctional responses to their childhoods, and finding ways of acting that may be more effective in their current circumstances. Faffy, for instance, feels quickly overwhelmed when her partner, Boz, talks about his fears and vulnerabilities. Faffy feels unhappy with herself for lashing out at Boz at these times, but she also feels that she cannot stop herself feeling angry and irritated (a rogue goal). With her therapist, Faffy comes to see that this is related to having overly disclosing parents who were always talking about their fears and worries and leaving little space for Faffy, herself, to feel safe or cared for. In this way, Faffy comes to see that her fear of being overwhelmed by Boz, and her anger, are strategies of self-protection: ways of trying to stop Boz 'devouring' her emotional space, just as her parents tended to do. But what Faffy also comes to see through this exploration, is that Boz *is not* her parents: that, actually, Boz can talk about his fears while also leaving space for Faffy to do so. Faffy, then, can start developing effective strategies for her actual present (for instance, telling Boz that she feels scared when she opens up, but also that she wants to listen and support Boz), rather than carrying over strategies that were fit for earlier times. Here, then, Faffy learns to do things in a 'better' way: more suited to getting more of what they actually want more of the time.

Another common example here is that clients may have developed very critical inner voices, as a way of pre-empting the criticism that they knew they would receive from their parents or carers.[52] Essentially, if you know someone is going to attack, demean, or shame you for doing something, you are better off 'getting in there first' – at least it can give you a feeling of control over things. But the problem is, that form of self-talk can become automatic and chronic, so you carry on beating yourself up for things even when there is no one outside who is now going to do that. Again, then, a means towards a higher-order direction that emerged for intelligible reasons is no longer fit for purpose. It is 'surplus repression': things are more limited than they actually need to be.

Within many therapies – whether for individuals, couples, or families – education around relationship and communication skills may play a particularly important role in helping people find better means to get to their ends.[53] For instance, in couples therapy, partners may be taught about essential ways of talking to each other than can build a strong relationship, such as sharing their fondness and admiration for each other, or 'nonviolent communication' (see Chapter 7, this volume). Alternatively, they may be taught specific techniques for solving relationship problems, such as defining the problem, proposing different solutions, and weighing the pros and cons of each solution (see Chapter 6, this volume). Therapists may also demonstrate to their clients different relationship and communication skills through role play.[54]

As with the previous section on internal conflicts, what this section says to progressives is that we cannot understand distress and wellbeing in terms of external factors alone. Rather, within the same set of limitations, people can do things that are more or less effective in improving their own psychological wellbeing. That means, again, that in striving to create a more thriving society, we need to take into account psychological as well as socioeconomic factors, as well as the interactions between them. Chapter 7 applies this directly by detailing skills training in three important areas: parenting, social and emotional learning, and communication – key issues, as argued in this book, for a progressive agenda. In addition, as with previous parts of this framework, the analysis presented in this section allows us to retain a position of psychological equality, while still recognising levers for change. People are not idiots, nor do they need others to tell them what they most fundamentally need and want; yet, at the same time, there is more that all of us can learn in terms of how to realise our highest-order directions.

## Unrealistic expectations

If distress is understood, to a great extent, as the distance between the objectives we set for ourselves and what we have actually achieved, then we can also consider the role that expectations might have in shaping our levels of satisfaction. More specifically, if we have very high standards for what we 'should' achieve then, however much we do actually achieve, we may still end up experiencing feelings of failure, misery, and hopelessness. At its extreme, such high standards can take the form of perfectionism, whereby our expectations are way beyond our, or anyone else's, reach. In support of this, research suggests that having modest expectations is generally better for our happiness;[55] and that people who are unrealistically optimistic about what they can achieve end up having higher levels of disappointment.[56]

Expectations are a psychological factor but, like conflict and ineffective strategies, have a strongly socioeconomic element. As stated in Chapter 3, our needs and wants are infused with the values and meanings of our external environment; and in our current, consumerist world, we are constantly bombarded with messages about what we should have and who and how we should be: the latest smartphone, the fastest Wi-Fi, the fittest and tautest beach-ready body. Against such standards, we will almost inevitably fail. No surprise, then, that, for instance, around 60 per cent of adults, and an even higher percentage of children, said that they feel 'negative or very negative about their body image most of the time'.[57]

Perhaps the most problematic reference standard that we internalise from our consumerist world is with respect to happiness, itself.[58] Advertising consistently presents us with images of people who are smiling, satisfied, and enjoying life – rarely do we see the realities of people struggling, unhappy, and worried (that would not do much for sales). Social media can be the same: on Facebook or LinkedIn, for instance, people (including, I know, myself) are far more likely to post about their life highlights – a brilliant night out, a new relationship, a career achievement – than the lowlights that inevitably also occur. So that can leave us feeling that we are not as happy as everyone else; and that, in itself, can then evoke feelings of failure and misery. There is some research to support this. For instance, a study found that those with high expectations and plans for the millennium celebrations were less happy on the night than those with lower level expectations and plans.[59]

So when, as progressives, we think about creating a better world, we also need to consider the standards and expectations that are communicated to people. It seems important, for instance, to create a culture in which people feel that it is OK to fail; and that dissatisfaction, anxiety, and misery are all parts of a 'normal' life. Moreover, we also need to consider the expectations that we communicate and 'model' to people through how we, ourselves, behave. For instance, if progressive politicians consistently hide their vulnerabilities – putting on a strong front – then what does this communicate to others about how they should be (see Chapter 7)? Creating realistic expectations for people is also important because, at a planetary level, there are some very real environmental limitations that we have to live within: Raworth's doughnut.[60] The consumerist, neoliberal myth of unbounded expectations, then, is not just bad for people directly, but also indirectly because we inhabit a world that just cannot sustain such fantasies.

## Summing up

This chapter has presented a framework for understanding psychological wellbeing and distress that smoothly integrates psychological and socioeconomic understandings. Here, psychological distress is conceptualised as the failure to realise highest-order needs and wants, and four reasons have been given as to why this might happen: limited socioeconomic resources, conflicting internal directions, ineffective means towards our highest-order needs and wants, and unrealistic expectations of what we can achieve. In this way, psychological and socioeconomic understandings of wellbeing and distress run alongside each other and interact: they are not opposed or mutually exclusive explanations, but overlapping parts of a coherent psycho-socio-economic whole. To put this otherwise, this framework suggests that we cannot understand wellbeing and distress either in socioeconomic or psychological terms alone. Rather, we need both; and recognising that is a way that progressivism can help to develop a genuinely more thriving society.

This framework is relatively consistent with the model of human being articulated by the young Marx and the socialist humanists (Chapter 2). However, the present framework provides an understanding in which the agency and intelligibility of the other is always maintained. As presented in this chapter, human beings can be massively restricted: forced into 'crevices' in which people are desperately pitted against themselves and each other. Yet in all of this, contra Marx, the human being never becomes a 'machine', 'idiot', or 'cretin'. Rather, the other is always still another intelligible, sense-making human: the psychological equality that states 'nothing human is alien to me'. In addition, in contrast to the classic socialist humanist approach, the present framework allows for a richer, more complex, and more nuanced understanding of human being; and one that is consistent with a broad range of contemporary psychological and psychotherapeutic theories and evidence.

For progressives, this analysis is useful because it helps us to think about strategies for social betterment in psychological as well as socioeconomic terms. In Chapter 7, I will look particularly at the kind of psychological agenda that may be developed from it. Before doing so, however, I want to develop another set of concepts that were introduced in this chapter: that of cooperative action, or synergies. As already mentioned, what is fascinating about synergies is that they are not just a feature of wellbeing at the intrapersonal level, but also at higher 'levels of organisation': between people, communities, and nations. Exploring this can be useful in developing a psychologically informed progressivism, because it can help us to identify some general, system-wide principles of what is 'good' and how we get there. It is to the former question we now turn (Chapter 5), with Chapter 6 then going on to establish some common principles of positive change. This will then feed in to the articulation of a concrete agenda for a psychologically informed progressivism (Chapter 7), as well as envisioning a longer-term progressive utopia (Chapters 8 and 9).

# 5

# Conflict and cooperation, inside and out

Long before I studied psychology I was captivated by the idea of 'multiple personalities'. *Sybil*, *The Three Faces of Eve*, *The Minds of Billy Milligan*: I found it fascinating to imagine a world 'inside' the human being that mirrored the world 'outside', with different personalities collaborating, fighting, and scheming against each other. Was it really possible, for instance, that the party girl 'Eve Black' could be doing all those things behind the prim Eve White's back? Perhaps my fascination came from my desire to play with my own identity. By the age of six, I had decided to change my name from 'Michael' (my first name) to 'Barry' (my second name), on the grounds that the former seemed unbelievably dull. Then, in my late teens, I changed it again to 'Mick' ('The most working class variant of "Michael" you could find', a friend sneered).

I never went on to study 'dissociative identity disorder' – the current term for multiple personality as a clinical condition. I did, however, co-edit a book on 'multiplicity in everyday life' (*The plural self*), and wrote a thesis on how facial masks could bring out the different sides of ourselves.[1] And, indeed, the idea that the each of us have different 'parts', 'voices', or 'subpersonalities' is now well-established across the psychological and psychotherapeutic literature.[2] As introduced in Chapter 1, for instance, one of the most common – and best evidenced[3] – psychotherapy techniques is to invite clients to talk 'as' different parts of themselves as they sit in different chairs (*two-chair work*). In one chair, for instance, the client might be asked to express their self-critical part ('You're so stupid, why do you always do what your boyfriend tells you to?') and then to sit in another chair as the part that is being berated and respond ('I just can't help it, I feel so little and small'). The idea is then to develop the dialogue between these two parts, such that more cooperative forms of relating can be found. Such a 'pluralistic' conception of the self sits very closely to the model of human being described in Chapter 3, with different needs and wants 'within' the person having the capacity to pull in different directions, acting as semi-autonomous agencies within a more encompassing whole.

What particularly fascinated me about this pluralistic conception of self was the parallels that seemed to exist between structures and processes at this intrapersonal level and those on more interpersonal planes. For instance, just as healthy psychological functioning, as we have seen, seemed to be characterised by cooperative relationships between different internal parts, so a well-functioning couple, or a well-functioning nation, seemed also to be characterised by such cooperative relationships. Here, what was also apparent is that healthy intrapersonal relationships seemed to map, specifically, on to a progressive view of how things worked well at the interpersonal level. That is, as a therapist, I was trained to encourage my client towards collaborative, democratic, egalitarian forms of inner relating – exactly the kind of relating that, as a progressive, I would hope to see on the interpersonal plane.

The aim of this chapter is to show how these two worlds, the intrapersonal and interpersonal, align. More specifically, I want to show how the core concepts introduced in Chapters 3 and 4 – directionality, wellbeing as the realisation of directions, conflict as problematic relating, and cooperation as healthy relating – can be mapped from the intrapersonal to the interpersonal plane. Along the way, I will be introducing some well-established interpersonal theories – Basic Human Needs theory, preference utilitarianism, and game theory – that evidence and support these parallels. Such an analysis, I hope, will be of considerable value to progressives, and this is for two reasons. First, it provides compelling support for a progressive perspective, because it shows that the values and modes of relating we propose are not just limited to the socioeconomic domain, but are of a more universal, system-wide nature. Second, because it provides a framework in which learning can be shared across levels of analysis. For instance, we can use therapeutic understandings to help make sense of conflicts between nations; or draw from the political domain to help understand what a well-functioning, 'democratic' psyche might look like. Such learnings are set out, in more detail, in Chapter 6. Exploring such parallels is also important for this book because it moves us on from the individual focus of Chapters 3 and 4 towards an acknowledgement of more macro levels of functioning: communities, cultures, and society. This is consistent with a progressivism that, while acknowledging the individual, is not individualistic.[4] Rather, the individual, the community, and the socioeconomic context are all understood as mutually functioning, mutually embedded wholes.

## Levels of organisation

The work of Arthur Koestler,[5] the Hungarian British author and journalist, provides a useful starting point for exploring structures and processes across intrapersonal and interpersonal levels. In *The ghost in the machine*, Koestler suggests the existence of multiple *levels of organisation* within a *holarchy*. An example of such a holarchy is presented in Figure 5.1, which ranges from intrapersonal levels of organisation to the planet. Here, as with the hierarchical model of individual functioning presented in Chapter 3, higher-level organising units are 'made up' of lower-level organising units. So, for instance, the individual is made up of intrapersonal 'parts', the family is made up of individuals, and the community is made up of families. However, because the higher-level organising units are formed through the *relationships* between the lower-level organising units, they are never simply reducible to them. For instance, you could not fully understand a family by focusing on the individual characteristics of each family member alone, because something 'more than' is created when those family members come together: a 'more than' which, indeed, then influences those individual characteristics in reciprocal ways. Hence, at each level of organisation, the parts can be considered as functioning wholes – self-regulating and semi-autonomous – with none more real or significant than the others.

**Figure 5.1:** An illustrative holarchy

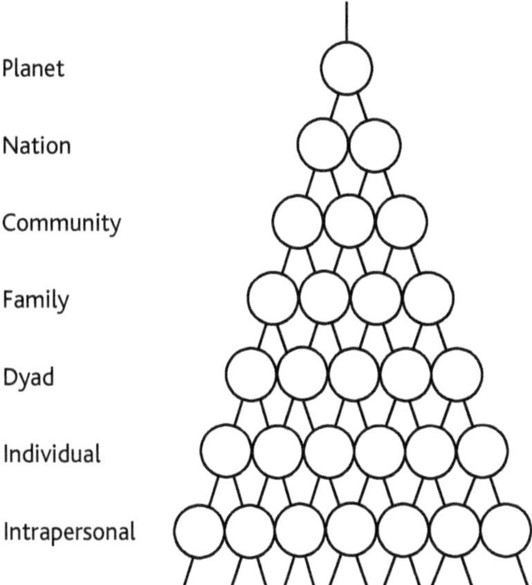


Koestler's theory is highly consistent with contemporary *systems thinking*, which strives to understand social and environmental processes in terms of 'interacting or interdependent elements forming an integrated whole'.[6] Systems thinking, as with Koestler, holds that the whole is more than the sum of its parts. It focuses on relationships and patterns across parts, and the contexts within which parts are embedded; rather than reductively focus on the parts, per se. Systems thinking terms the 'more than' at each level of organisation *emergent properties*. These are 'the novel properties that arise when a higher level of complexity is reached by putting together components of lower complexity'.[7]

To note, this concept of 'more than' can also be seen in contemporary *intersectionality* theory, which hold that marginalisation by such factors as race, class, and gender cannot be understood separately. Rather, intersectionality theory emphasises the way that these different forms of oppression build on each other, work together, and interact.[8] So, for instance, Black women do not just suffer the marginalisation experienced by Blacks, and then the marginalisation experienced by women. There are also distinctive forms of marginalisation of Black women, per se, that they must contend with (termed 'misogynoir'): for instance, the stereotype of the 'angry Black woman', or of the hyper-sexualised, twerking 'Jezebel'.

This concept of a holarchy becomes a way of extending the intrapersonal framework introduced in Chapters 3 and 4. This looked at how intrapersonal needs and wants functioned within the individual; but we can also look, for instance, at how individuals function within a family, or families within a community, or communities within a nature. In this chapter, we will focus, in particular, on structures and processes between individuals (in a dyad), between communities (in a nation), and between nations (on the planet). What I hope to show is the striking parallels between structures and processes at these interpersonal levels of organisation with those at the intrapersonal level of organisation, as discussed in Chapters 3 and 4. Most importantly, I hope to show that greatest benefit, at any level, comes from cooperative relationships between the parts. The last section of this chapter draws *game theory* into this discussion, which can help us in a more formal analysis of the structures and processes associated with positive change.

## Directionality across levels of organisation

In Chapter 3, the concept of directionality was introduced as a core characteristic of individuals and their internal parts: that we are agentic, intentional, oriented towards some end. This is a quality that can be seen as existing at other levels of organisation too. At the heart of Marxist theory, for instance, is the assertion that each social class has particular interests; and we can see such social phenomena as 'structural racism' as the expression of a collective will or set of beliefs of oppressive groups.[9] A couple, family, or community, too, can be seen as having particular goals, desires, and hopes: from consciously stated objectives or 'mission statements' (for example, 'We will build a loving family together') to implicit aspirations (for example, 'We will be there for each other whatever happens'). Similarly, in the conflict resolution field, nations can be considered directional agents: striving for goals like security or expansion.[10] Such higher-level directionality has been termed a 'we-intentionality'[11] and, as with all aspects of these organising units, cannot just be reduced down to the directionality of its constituent units. That is, like two people dancing together, the overall direction of an interpersonal unit is not simply the additive sum of individual sets of actions. Rather, like a dance, it 'co-evolves' in a highly interactive way. The directions of a couple, community, or nation, then, are emergent: they have a life of their own.

As at the intrapersonal level of organisation, these interpersonal directions can be seen as playing a central role in shaping actions. Within an organisation, for instance, the 'mission statement', 'purpose', 'vision', or 'objectives' tends to act as the keystone around which subsequent strategies, choices, or behaviours are then derived. It is the starting point, the 'where-we-are-going', from which the 'how-we-will-get-there' is then defined. Of course, as at other levels of organisation, the explicitly stated directions are not always the same as the implicit ones. The vision statement of Pizza Hut, for instance, is 'to improve the well-being of our customers, community, and people connected to our enterprise'.[12] In reality, making profit is probably a much more central direction. But the fact that a set of directions are implicit does not mean they are any less central to driving behaviour. Companies overtake other companies, nations go to war, couples have children ... all the time following directions that may never be explicitly stated.

Linked to the realisation or not of these higher-level directions, Lynne Segal, the eminent UK-based feminist socialist, suggests that emotions can also exist at more social and collective levels of organisation.[13] For instance, when the supporters of a nation's football team erupt in joy together at scoring a goal, it is not just a set of isolated, individual experiences. Rather, there is a collective joy, a 'radical happiness' in which each person's emotions are part of a greater whole. I look across the pub and I see other people celebrating and I celebrate together with them. As any football fan knows, watching a match, alone, on one's own television, is just not the same thing: we go to the pub to experience that communal joy (or despair). Similarly, Segal writes about festivals in which there is a collective celebration of music and dancing and being together. Again, it is a very different experience from dancing around one's own living room. At these moments, Segal writes, we are released from individualism, egoism, and self-importance: we become part of a 'transindividual subject'.[14] And it is a transindividual subject that moves in waves: celebrating or mourning as it realises, or fails to realise, its collective directions.

One of the best examples of directionality at the interpersonal level, of particular relevance to a progressive worldview and this book, is the United Nations' (UN) Sustainable Development Goals (SDGs).[15] These are 17 goals, agreed by the UN in 2015, that have the overall aim to 'promote human dignity and prosperity while safeguarding the Earth's vital biopsychical processes and ecosystem services'.[16] Examples of these goals are 'no poverty', 'gender equality', and 'reduce inequality'. Each goal is then broken down into a series of more concrete targets (169 in total). For instance, the SDG of 'reduce inequality' has ten targets, such as 'By 2030, progressively achieve and sustain income growth of the bottom 40 per cent of the population at a rate higher than the national average.' Here, then, we can see a hierarchy of directions very similar to the intrapersonal one we saw in Chapter 3. At the highest order are a small number of relatively conceptual objectives – in this case, 'a supremely ambitious and transformational vision [of] a world free of poverty, hunger, disease and want'[17] – which is then achieved through a larger number of lower level, more practical and context-dependent means. Indeed, in recent years, a set of 'Inner Development Goals' have been articulated to translate the SDGs back to the level of individual abilities, skills, and qualities.[18]

### *Basic Human Needs theory*

Before discussing how concepts of wellbeing, at interpersonal levels of organisation, parallel intrapersonal conceptualisations, I want to introduce Basic Human Needs (BHN) theory. This is a theoretical framework and set of practices that emerged in the conflict resolution field – addressing clashes between communities and nations – but has striking similarities to the model of individual functioning developed in Chapter 3. BHN theory is a great example of how a directional framework can be applied to understanding, and addressing, problems at social and political levels of organisation. It also shows how we can move, fluently, between the needs and wants of an individual and those of a community or nation – thus enhancing our capacity to think in integrated psychosocial ways.

BHN was established primarily by the Australian academic and diplomat John Burton, and emerged in the early 1980s.[19] BHN theory was applied in a range of conflict resolution situations with Israelis and Palestinians, and in Cyprus and Darfur. Although it is not credited with any major breakthroughs, it did prepare for negotiations as a form of early 'Track Two' diplomacy[20] serving a 'valuable pre- or para-negotiation function in the context of an overall peace process'.[21] Although the approach is less prevalent today, its core ideas continue to be strongly reflected in the contemporary human rights and human security field, such as the UN's Responsibility to Protect (R2P), a global political commitment to preventing mass atrocity crimes and human rights violations.[22]

The BHN approach drew from the work of Maslow as well as other humanistic psychologists, but extended that work much more broadly and politically. Its basic premise was that conflict, disorder, and civil unrest arose, not because of 'lawlessness' or 'character deformities', but because people's basic needs and values – their 'highest-order directions' (Chapter 3) – were being suppressed, disregarded, or otherwise unfulfilled. 'All social groups have fundamental needs for recognition, identity, security and participation', wrote American Professor of International Peace and Conflict Resolution, Ronald J. Fisher, 'which, when frustrated, result in an inexorable push for redress and satisfaction'.[23] For instance, the Arab Spring uprisings in the early 2010s can be understood as the demands of oppressed citizens for dignity, pride, and self-determination; the Palestinian–Israeli conflict can be understood as a struggle between two peoples who each want security, freedom, and self-worth.[24] In this BHN model, power is understood as the attempts, by authorities, to suppress the basic needs of marginalised groups.[25] Yet such suppression is seen as being, ultimately, doomed to fail, because those basic needs are non-negotiable, ineradicable elements of human being.[26]

BHN theorists developed various taxonomies of human beings' basic needs, understood as emerging from both biological and cultural processes.[27] As with the set of highest-order needs and wants discussed in Chapter 3, they emphasised non-material needs and satisfiers as well as material ones. That is, they believed that human conflicts were not just driven by such needs as for food, land, or security; but also by such non-material needs as for identity, recognition, and control. Victoria Rader, for instance, who worked with homeless people in America, wrote:

> People need food and shelter for biological survival, but they need dignity and love to remain human beings. Physical needs can be very cheaply provided; the shelter does it every day. Yet, in a society driven by material success, men and women who have lost everything material must struggle fiercely to retain their pride. … It is my experience that when individuals are forced to choose their dignity over shelter or food, they will often choose the former even at some risk to their lives.[28]

For BHN theorists, threats to the very right to exist – as a physical or social entity – could be seen as driving the most intense conflicts.[29] If, for instance, a people's land or language are taken away, they may feel that their very essence is under threat of annihilation. At these points, BHN theorists argue, people may act to re-establish their core needs no matter how much power is exerted against them.[30] It is a fight, literally, to the death.

BHN theory was applied, in practice, through 'problem-solving workshops'. These brought conflicting groups together, for instance Palestinians and Israelis, to try and help them find constructive ways of moving forward.[31] The basic process here was one of 'controlled communication', in which the groups would share their perceptions, understandings, and experiences of the situation. The basic aim was to try and correct misperceptions across groups and, importantly, for each group to articulate something of their basic needs to each other. As with the psychological framework introduced in Chapter 3, BHN theory holds that, ultimately, these highest-order needs and wants are essentially prosocial.[32] Hence, if groups can communicate to each other what they most fundamentally need and want – for instance, security, identity, or freedom – they can begin to connect with the other side's humanity. In addition, through expressing their basic needs and wants, both groups can then work together to generate strategies, solutions, and agreements that can allow for more, mutual satisfaction. In Chapter 6 (this volume), we shall see how such processes are common to many synergy-building frameworks.

## Wellbeing across levels of organisation

If organising units, across different levels, are understood as directional, then we can define wellbeing – at any level of organisation – as the maximum realisation of highest-order needs and wants. That is, just as a well-functioning person realises their needs and wants to the maximum extent, so a well-functioning family is one in which each member's highest-order needs and wants are most fully realised. In such a family, for instance, everyone feels nourished, secure, loved, and of value; and the family members' own idiosyncratic highest-order directions – for instance, Child A's need for creative expression, or Parent B's need to have a sense of meaning – are also maximally realised. Moving up the levels, a well-functioning nation can be conceptualised as one in which its individuals and communities realise their highest-order needs and wants to the fullest extent; with a well-functioning planet seeing the maximal realisation of its nations' directions (that is, our SDGs). In systems theory terms, such a well-functioning system can be described as *regenerative*: one in which the output is greater than the input. This compares with a *degenerative system*, in which the system devours its own sustenance such that there is less going out than in.

### *Preference utilitarianism*

The idea that a 'good' society can be defined in terms of its citizens' maximal realisation of needs and wants is similar to the philosophical position of *preference utilitarianism*. This perspective is closely connected to contemporary economic philosophy and principles, best exemplified in the work of the Hungarian-American economist John Harsanyi.[33] As with BHN theory, I will spend a little time introducing this philosophical approach. As a well-respected theory with a long-standing history – and from an entirely different field – preference utilitarianism provides good support for the transposition of the directional framework to the social and political level.

Utilitarianism, in its classic form, was a social and moral philosophy associated with such 18th- and 19th-century reformists as Jeremy Bentham. It held that the rightness of an action should be judged by the contribution it made to an increase in human pleasures and a reduction in human pain.[34] A good society, therefore, was defined as one in which the levels of 'social utility' (that is, pleasure minus pain) were maximised. And because, radically for its time, each person in society was considered to 'count as one'; it was not enough for just a small ruling elite to have high levels of pleasure. Rather, this pleasure needed to be maximised across the entire population: the 'greatest good of the greatest number'.[35]

An important limitation of classical utilitarianism, however, is that it assumed pleasure as the sole definition of human good, and that this was consistent across all individuals. As we saw in Chapter 3, however, human beings' most fundamental needs and wants – both at the general and individual level – may be far broader than that. That means that it may not be particularly optimal to focus on maximising people's pleasure when, in fact, they might want other things: such as autonomy, growth, or meaning. At worst, as raised in Chapter 3, this can lead to the kind of dystopias presented in *Brave new world* or *The matrix*, where people are sedated into 'pleasure' irrespective of their volition and choice.

A contemporary alternative to a pleasure-based utilitarianism, then, is one based on people's preferences or desires. Such an approach assumes *preference autonomy*, that, 'in deciding what is good and what is bad for a given individual, the ultimate criterion can only be his own wants and preferences'.[36] Here, then, a 'good' society is not defined in terms of the maximisation of pleasure and the minimisation of pain, per se, but in terms of maximising people's attainment of their preferences.

For American professor of philosophy, Nicholas Rescher, this preference utilitarianism can be described as the *Principle of Benevolence*: 'A world in which people have what they want is a better world than one in which they do not, provided there is no harm to what they [or others] want.'[37] Kekes, the pluralist philosopher, says something similar when he defined morality as 'a bargaining process whose aim it is to achieve a condition in which most individuals could realize most of their preferences'.[38] In lay terms, we can also equate preference utilitarianism with the *Platinum Rule.* This is a step on from the *Golden Rule* ('Do unto others as you would have them do unto you'); and instead simply states, 'Do unto others as they want you to do unto them.'[39]

Preference utilitarianism, however, is not simply about people getting whatever they want at any one point in time. Here, Harsanyi distinguishes between *manifest* and *true* preferences. A person's true preferences 'are the preferences he *would* have if he had all the relevant factual information, always reasoned with the greatest possible care, and were in a state of mind most conducive to rational choice'.[40] This is similar to Dahl's description of a person's 'interest' or 'good' as '*whatever that person would choose with fullest attainable understanding of the experience resulting from that choice and its most relevant alternatives*'.[41] In these ways, true preferences can be considered to take into account consequences at all possible time points, and not just the immediate now. In effect, then, a person's true preferences can be considered equivalent to their highest-order needs and wants (or what the socialist humanists termed 'genuine needs'; Chapter 2, this volume); or means towards these directions that are synergetic, effective, and realistic. Manifest preferences, by contrast, can be considered equivalent to our lower-order, day-to-day needs and wants that may, or may not, be synergetic and effective means towards those things we most fundamentally need and want.

Note, as with directions, true preferences do not need to be conscious to be true. This may be particularly important when we consider the needs and wants of nonhuman species, whose highest-order preferences, perhaps, might also be taken into account when calculating the overall good of a society. Brian Tomasik, at the Centre on Long-Term Risk, writes:

> What shall we do with organisms that don't explicitly recognize what they care about? For instance, what if the universe consisted entirely of a single mouse that

> was in pain? We can suppose for the sake of argument that the mouse doesn't conceive of itself as an abstract organism enduring negative sensations. Presumably the mouse doesn't think, 'I wish this pain would stop.' But the intuition that motivates our concern for the interests of other beings rests not upon the ability of those beings to explicitly state their wishes – rather, it comes from an empathetic recognition that those wishes exist and matter. Clearly the mouse's pain is a real event that matters to the mouse, even if the mouse can't articulate that fact. So preference utilitarianism does give consideration to implicit preferences – whether held by human or non-human animals.[42]

Just as a well-functioning psyche, then, can be understood as the maximal realisation of its different parts' directions, so a well-functioning society can be understood in term of the maximal realisation of its different parts' (that is, its citizens' or communities') needs and wants. For progressives, there are some important limits to this position – in particular, that *maximum* realisation does not mean *equal* realisation (see Chapter 6, this volume) – but this overall definition of 'good' fits well with a progressive stance. Progressivism is founded on the belief that more 'better' is possible: 'Maximizing the possibilities', write Amiel and Emelien, 'is the progressivists' mission'.[43] Furthermore, from a progressive stance, 'better' should be defined in terms of what parties, themselves, want – not defined or imposed from outside. Of course, as at the individual level, maximisation of interpersonal directions must be within environmental and global limits; but this is implicit within the concept of maximisation itself. If, for instance, the realisation of particular needs and wants leads to massive increases in global warming, the realisation of numerous other directions will be fundamentally undermined such that it is no maximisation at all.

### *Enhancing wellbeing across levels of organisation*

Wellbeing at each level of organisation is not independent but fundamentally interrelated. In particular, when we create 'more' at higher levels of organisation (for instance, in a community or in a nation), there is then more to go around for everyone. 'There is no real maximization of individual possibilities', write Amiel and Emelien, 'that does not depend on the maximization of collective possibilities'.[44] This is a key point, because it means that working together creates more for all even if, in the immediate term, it may feel like it is creating less for the individual agent. If, for instance, I pause my daily run to help out a drunken person sprawled over the pavement, it may not serve my short-term directions (to finish my run, get home, and get back to work). However, by acting in caring and cooperative ways I can contribution to the creation of a society that, ultimately, will also benefit me. As progressives have argued, then, if we want to facilitate our own thriving or the thriving of those close to us, we also need to attend to the thriving of higher-level organising units: our communities, nations, or planet. It is hard to thrive alone, or succeed in higher-level systems that are failing.

At the same time, the relationship between the realisation of needs and wants at a lower level of organisation (for example, the individual or community level), and those at a higher level (for example, society as a whole), is complex. For instance, a system that is regenerative, within itself, still has the capacity to be degenerative at a higher level of organisation. In the example of Bolsonaro's government or a fascist political organisation, for instance, the more its members work well together, the more destructive they may be to other communities at higher levels of organisation. Similarly, it is possible that an individual may be well-configured internally – with high levels of cooperation between their internal parts – but then in conflict with other individuals around them. However, there are two points to note here. First, as already raised, cooperative configurations at a higher level of organisation create more overall benefit to the system as a whole: more resources to go around. Hence, each lower-level system, within this configuration, is likely to do better. The intercommunity conflict that a fascist organisation creates, for instance, means that they, too, then have less access to satisfiers, such as feeling safe. Second, as suggested in Chapter 3, one of our most fundamental needs may be for relatedness – and also for fairness. Hence, if people are wholly integrated at an individual level, they are not likely to behave in highly destructive ways towards others. Rather, such behaviour would suggest some degree of fragmentation and the suppression of more relational needs and wants.

Related to this, as we are likely to be aware, people can vary in the level of organisation that they focus on when striving for benefit. That is, some people, some of the time, may focus primarily on benefit for themselves; others may focus on benefit for their families or communities; and others may focus on benefit for the world as a whole: organic as well as non-organic. At the heart of this book, indeed of progressivism, is the belief that focusing on higher levels of organisation is generally a good thing; and, indeed, it is, because it creates more overall benefit for the system as a whole. However, there is no, simple one-to-one relationship between lower level and higher levels benefits. In certain circumstances, a focus on benefits at lower levels of organisation may bring more direct gains to an individual or their community – at least in the short term. This is where, perhaps, values such as progressivism become so important. If our key strivings are towards fairness and social justice, then we can retain that focus on benefits at higher levels of organisation, even when it may not suit our own individual needs and wants. And, by doing so, we can help to create a world which – in the longer term – has more to go around.

## Conflict at different levels of organisation

Across different levels of organisation, then, wellbeing can be understood as the maximum realisation of highest-order needs and wants, and distress as the minimisation of such realisations. But why might such minimisation come about? At the intrapersonal level, this was explained primarily in terms of conflictual relationships between parts (Chapter 3); and a similar analysis can be applied at interpersonal levels of organisation. That is, we can understand interpersonal-level distress in terms of the prevention, obstruction, or interference of one person's or community's directions by another person's or community's, to the detriment of the whole. Research shows, for instance, that lower levels of happiness and stability in couples are predicted by greater degree of defensiveness, contempt, and belligerence.[45] In particular, negative 'start-ups' by wives, followed by a husband's refusal to accept influence and a failure to de-escalate the conflict, were found to lead to subsequent marital difficulties. Similarly, racism can be understood as a form of intercommunity conflict that leads to an overall loss of wellbeing at the societal level. Here, one community may realise certain lower-order directions through discriminatory acts, but at the cost of dramatically reducing another community's capacity to realise its own highest-order needs and wants (for instance, for safety, autonomy, or a sense of competence). This explains why, from a progressive standpoint, we know that such forms of discrimination are a 'bad' thing. Not only does one community badly lose out, but the other community does not actually gain much – or only gains things that they could achieve in less dysergetic ways. Again, we come back to the concept of 'surplus repression' (Chapter 2, this volume): things are more limited, across the whole, than they really need to be.

Capitalism is another form of social configuration that can be considered inherently conflictual, leading to lower overall wellbeing. Here, one class strives to realise its interests at the expense of another; and the ideology of capitalism, with its focus on the individualistic pursuit of goals, means that it is naturally conflictual rather than cooperative.[46] Indeed, for Mason, neoliberalism can be defined as 'competition forced into all aspects of society by a coercive state'.[47] Mason goes on to write, 'The dogma that if everybody competes with everybody else, things can only get better? Disproven in every welfare office, at every food bank, with every sorry doorway filled with a human being huddled in a sleeping bag.'[48]

We might also understand capitalism as a rogue goal, or a set of rogue goals (Chapter 3, this volume), where one class, and one set of directions – to purchase, consume, and expand – takes over to the exclusion of all else.[49] Head down, the company's board of directors and its chief executive officer focus, exclusively, on greater profits or greater market penetration. They watch, obsessively, the statistics going up or down; while other considerations – like community wellbeing or environmental sustainability – are pushed to one side. Capitalism can be considered an interpersonal level equivalent of an obsessive compulsive disorder. People get 'locked in' to one overriding concern – losing the bigger picture of what is best for themselves and the wider society. Here, then, the problem is not so much that the desire to grow or consume is 'wrong', but that it dominates over all other fundamental needs and wants. As argued in Chapter 3, however, the psychological rewards that can come from striving to realise our needs and wants, per se, can mean that we are always prone to such rogue processes.

War – the social ill that causes an abundance of misery, terror, and loss – might be considered the most macro, and destructive, form of conflict at an interpersonal level.[50] Here, the needs and wants of nations – or of communities within nations – come into direct conflict, with a massive loss of overall wellbeing in the process. This issue remains a critical one. Across the world, from 1945 to 2007, there were approximately four new wars per year (armed conflicts with greater than 1,000 battle-related deaths) – the majority within, rather than between, states (for example, civil wars).[51] As with capitalism, war can be understood in terms of directions 'going rogue': an obsessive, all-consuming drive by one nation, or one community within a nation, to eradicate the other – bolstered by the fantasy of one's own righteousness, importance, and place in history.[52] Nowhere can this be seen more clearly than in Russia's invasion of Ukraine, with thousands of soldiers and civilians killed on both sides; and millions of refugees and homes and lives destroyed. And for what? In attempting to annihilate Ukraine – treating it as an object-like, dehumanised 'it' – Russia has also come to damage itself. No one wins.

As at the psychological level, interpersonal dysergies may be driven – or intensified – by limited external resources (Chapter 3, this volume).[53] This could be material resources such as food, money, or territory; and/or it could be non-material resources, such as autonomy or self-worth. At the heart of the Palestinian–Israeli conflict, for instance, is the desire for the same piece of land. Similarly, intercommunity conflicts may be more likely in nations where there is extreme poverty or high unemployment because the financial safety or health of one group may seem to necessitate the subjugation of another.[54] In social psychology, this has been termed *realistic conflict theory*; and the more limited the external resources, the more that conflictual, chaotic, rogue directions may come to the fore.[55] Edward Bellamy, author of the utopian socialist novel *Looking backwards* (Chapter 6, this volume), uses the analogy of the Black Hole of Calcutta to describe how limited social resources led to intensified interpersonal conflicts in 19th-century society:

> A number of English prisoners were shut up in a room containing not enough air to supply one-tenth of their number. The unfortunates were gallant men, devoted comrades in service, but, as the agonies of suffocation began to take hold on them, each one for himself, and against all others, to force a way to one of the small apertures of the prison at which alone it was possible to get a breath of air. It was a struggle in which men became beasts … the Black Hole of Calcutta, with its press of maddening men tearing and trampling one another in the struggle to win a place at the breathing holes, would seem a striking type [analogy] of the society of their age.[56]

For philosophers like the 18th century Scot David Hume, such conflicts between people were an inevitable consequence of the scant provisions that nature has made to satisfy human needs and wants.[57] However, as at the intrapersonal level, a key premise of this book is that, within the same set of resources, there is nearly always the possibility for more cooperative – and less conflictual – configurations. That is, virtually every system, at every level, has surplus repression that can be reduced through more synergetic, cooperative configurations. So, for instance, while financial poverty may make some White communities more racist towards communities of people of colour ('If I can't feel good about myself by being rich, I can feel good about myself by putting down another community'), that racism is not inevitable. Rather, that White community, within that set of external limitations, can still find more collaborative, supportive, and mutually beneficial ways of relating to communities of people of colour. Of course, that does not obviate the need to also look at means by which the resources of both communities, overall, can be increased.

There is a proverbial story of two children quarrelling over an orange that may help to illustrate this point.[58] After many hours of wrangling over who should have the orange, the children eventually agree to divide it in two. The first child then eats the fruit of their half and throws away the peel, while the second uses the peel of their half for baking and throws away the fruit. Here, both children do get something of what they want. The 'tragedy' of this situation, however, is that, within the same set of external resources (that is, one orange), both children could have had so much more. There is wastage, surplus repression, more is thrown away than needs to be. From an egalitarian perspective, the good part of this story is that both children get half of the orange, and that is very fair. And, ideally, we might hope that the children can have more oranges to share out among themselves. But, even so, what we see is that fairness, by itself, is not enough to maximise what both children can get out of this situation. There is also how they configure things between themselves: and with the same amount of orange, both can either have a lot more, or a lot less. It depends on how things are done.

In recent years, there has been considerable interest in researching conflicts between interpersonal-level directions – as well as synergies – in the SDG's field. This has been done at both the level of goals and targets; and through either expert ratings of different interactions on a 'conflicting–synergetic' scale (for instance, from -3 = 'cancelling' to +3 = 'indivisible'), or by statistically analysing the relationships between target-level indicators.[59] 'Understanding the range of positive and negative interactions among SDGs is key to unlocking their full potential at any scale', writes the International Council for Science, 'as well as to ensuring that progress made in some areas is not made at the expense of progress in others'.[60] Research shows, for instance, that while the conflicts between SDGs (or what are termed here 'trade-offs') are largely outweighed by the synergies; there are some SDGs that are generally synergetic with others (such as 'no poverty' and 'quality education'), and others that have larger numbers of trade-offs (such as 'decent work and economic growth' and 'industry, innovation, and infrastructure').[61] Such knowledge can support policymakers in more effective and coherent decision-making: identifying SDGs and targets that may be particularly valuable to promote, as well as those where more caution may be needed. For interested readers, an SDG Interlinkages Analysis & Visualisation Tool is available online,[62] which digitally represents synergies and trade-offs between SDG targets for a range of nations.

## Cooperation at different levels of organisation

An intrapersonal understanding of distress in terms of conflict, then, can be transposed to interpersonal levels of organisation. Similarly, when we try and understand wellbeing, the concept of cooperative relationships can also be transposed to the interpersonal plane. That is, wellbeing, at any level of organisation, involves cooperative relationships between the parts. Cooperation across individuals, communities, or nations has the capacity to create something out of nothing. It is a way of maximising wellbeing within the same set of resources, of making 1 + 1 > 2. This is a synergetic process, in which two or more organisations, substances, or other agents interact to produce a combined effect greater than the sum of their separate effects.[63]

The value of cooperative interpersonal configurations – and the striving to create them – can be seen as the underlying principle for a wide range of facilitative, interpersonal practices: from couples therapy to mediation to international conflict resolution. The following sections discuss these practices, showing how the development of synergetic relationships is at their heart. Understanding such practices is of value to progressives, because it shows, in multiple ways, how our core belief in cooperation can be seen as a general, system-wide principle for creating more benefit. That is, cooperation is a general principle for how things can be improved. Such an analysis gives a universality and a robustness to progressive thinking. It also provides the basis, as will be discussed in Chapter 6, for identifying general, cross-level principles for developing positive, synergetic changes.

### *Couples therapy*

How do you help a couple who are experiencing problems in their relationship? Research indicates that couples therapy can bring about large and sustained (at least to six months) improvements in relationship satisfaction;[64] and at the heart of couples therapy is the process of finding synergetic, rather than conflictual, relationships between the two partners' wants and needs. Indeed, research shows that problem-solving and communication skills training explain most of the efficacy of couples therapies.[65] 'In the past', writes Marina Williams, author of *Couples counselling*, 'your couple has solved problems where one person would be the winner and the other the loser. You are going to demonstrate to them that there is a way to solve a problem where both people win'.[66] How do couples therapists do that? The first step is to give each person an opportunity to tell their story and to feel that their experiences, perceptions, and emotions are understood and validated. Critically, as part of this, the couples therapist tries to help both partners identify what it is that they really need and want: the higher-order directions behind the more conflictual dynamics.[67] For instance, relationship experts, Julie and John Gottman, propose the *dream catcher exercise*, in which one partner asks the other such questions as:

1. Do you have any core beliefs, ethics, or values that are part of your position on this issue?
2. Tell me why this is so important to you.
3. What would be your ideal dream here?
4. Is there a deeper purpose or goal in this for you?
5. What do you wish for?
6. What do you need?
7. Is there a fear or disaster scenario in not having this dream honored?[68]

Once such highest-order needs and wants are expressed by each partner, the couples therapist then helps the partners to generate ideas about how both sets of directions can be realised together. The best (that is, most synergetic) solution can then be identified, trialled in the real world, and reviewed with the therapist.

Williams gives the example of Sarah, who is upset with her partner Mark, because he avoids going to her family get-togethers.[69] When the therapist asks Mark why he does not want to go, he explains that he likes Sarah's family but feels awkward at the parties not knowing anyone, and he feels that Sarah just leaves him stranded. The synergetic solution: Mark agrees that he will go along, but Sarah agrees to spend more time with him; and they also agree to set a leaving time before they go. The Gottmans give another example.[70] Stephan and Derek have not had sex for a long time. Stephan is particularly upset by a time when Derek came back to find him on his computer and, thinking he might be video-flirting with someone else, became quite aggressive. Through sharing their perceptions and experiences, what becomes clear is that both actually feel very rejected by the other, with neither's need for intimacy and connection met. Through this recognition, they begin to look at ways in which they could give each other what they really need and want: for instance, by saying more about how they were feeling before tensions built up.

Such synergetic solutions may not be perfect for either party, but they lead to an overall increase in wellbeing – greater than what existed before. And, ideally, the couple can work towards the creation – or discovery – of 'shared meanings'.[71] This may involve both partners having similar life goals (providing an ideal opportunity for synergetic functioning); or, as the Gottmans write, 'finding ways to support each other in realizing' their life dreams.[72] For instance, the Gottmans describe a case in which, having unearthed one partner's deepest sense of purpose, they could then work with the other partner to look at ways in which this could be supported. Indeed, even with very different life meanings, the Gottmans suggest that it is still possible for couples to create dovetailing interests whereby one partner's goal actualisation supports that process in the other. As the nursery rhyme tells us: 'Jack Sprat could eat no fat./His wife could eat no lean./But, together both,/They licked the platter clean.' This is the essence of what it means to do things cooperatively and synergetically, rather than through destructive, conflictual relationships.

### Mediation

Mediation is a facilitated, semi-structured process for resolving disputes between conflicting parties, often as an alternative to expensive legal proceedings. This might be two business people who have fallen out and need to agree a division of assets, or two neighbours in dispute over noise at night. Unlike couples therapy, the aim here is not, in most cases, to improve an ongoing relationship, but to bring things to a close in a way that is agreeable to both parties. Nevertheless, at the heart of mediation work is a principle that, as with couples therapy, parallels therapeutic work on the intrapersonal plane: 'Focus on their interests'.[73] In the *Mediator's handbook*, Jennifer Beer and Caroline Packard write, 'Interests are the fulcrum of the whole mediation process. They contain the information that helps systems and relationships learn and grow. They are the basis for problem-solving and making decisions.'[74] And what Beer and Packard mean by *interests* is essentially the same as higher-order directions: 'the needs and wants that motivate someone, the benefits that people are protecting or seeking. … "Interest" is a dry word for passionate matters. Interests are the fire in your belly.'[75] The core questions to both parties in a mediation process, then, is 'What do you need?' and 'How can I help you get there?'[76] Beer and Packard add that, often in mediation, people's core interests are to protect themselves and those that they love: for instance, to ensure that they are not exploited, 'done over', or shamed. This may reflect highest-order directions towards safety and self-worth, as discussed in Chapter 3 (this volume).

Mediation, like individual and couples therapy, aims to bring to the fore the *underlying* interests of both parties: what they really want, need, and care about.[77] They do this in a range of ways: for instance, focusing on concrete instances where conflict has emerged (for example, between two neighbours who are in dispute over night-time noise: 'So let's look at what you were feeling and wanted that night you couldn't sleep'); helping disputants turn problem-based statements, blame, and demands into goal-based statements (for example, from 'He's always playing music late and he's got to stop' into 'I want my children to feel safe and be able to sleep properly'); and encouraging empathy (for example, 'Do you have a sense of how it might feel if you knew your children couldn't sleep'). Often, as in individual and couples therapy, emotions (such as distress and anxiety) are used as windows in to someone's higher-order needs and wants. 'I feel so anxious that my children can't sleep', for instance, becomes, 'It's really important for me, as a father, to protect my children.'

In their classic text on negotiating 'win–win' solutions, *Getting to yes*, Roger Fisher, William Ury, and Bruce Patton make a useful distinction between *positions* and *interests*.[78] Positions are the fixed demands that disputants may enter a negotiation with, for instance, 'The music must be turned off by midnight' or 'I must be free to play my music whenever I want.' Interests, drawing on BHN theory, are defined as a person's 'core concerns' (for example, autonomy, appreciation, affiliation) that is, again, their highest-order needs and wants. A key theme of *Getting to yes* is that positions are generally unhelpful in negotiations. Rather, disputants (and any negotiators) should focus on theirs, and each others', interests, and be flexible and open-minded as to how they will ultimately achieve mutually beneficial solutions. 'Interests', as the disputants' higher-order needs and wants, are considered 'the silent movers behind the hubbub of positions', causing the disputants to take the positions they do.[79] In terms of the hierarchical model discussed in Chapter 3, then, the process of mediation involves 'going up a level' by asking 'Why?' For instance, 'Why do you want the music should be turned off at midnight?' 'Why is it important for you to feel free to play your music?' In doing so, compatible interests are then more likely to be found. 'When you do look behind opposed positions for the motivating interests', they write, 'you can often find an alternative position that meets not only your interests but theirs as well'.[80]

So why is it that disputes between 'positions' (for instance, 'I want the music off by midnight' and 'I want to play my music whenever') becomes that much easier to resolve when it moves to the level of 'interests' (for instance, 'I want my children to feel safe' and 'I want to feel in control of my own life'). First, from a mediation standpoint, people can easily become 'locked' into fixed position, where the focus becomes more about self-esteem and being 'successful' than finding a mutually satisfying compromise (that is, rogue goals).[81] Second, because as you go up the hierarchy, directions become less material and concrete, and therefore more amenable to cooperative solutions. Also, as you move above fixed positions, what you discover is that each side actually has *multiple* interests – and that leads to greater options for synergies.[82] Focusing on underlying interests also makes it more possible that disputants can, as in couples therapy, find common and superordinate goals.[83] Positions, being concrete, are likely to be highly idiosyncratic. Underlying interests, by contrast, are more likely to express common human concerns, which can then support the establishment of shared directions (for instance, 'We want a safe and friendly neighbourhood').

Finding solutions that fit with people's underlying interests is also critical in mediation, or in any other form of negotiation, because that is what people *really* need and want.[84] Having a position conceded to is, ultimately, of little value (aside from feeling of victory) unless it is a means towards realising some higher-order interest. Sometimes, as the saying goes, people would 'rather be right than be happy': but such short-term gains are, by their very definition, only satisfying in the short term. By contrast, if a solution meets a disputant's deeper interests, then the satisfaction, again by definition, is likely to be more profound and long-lasting. The goal of mediation work, therefore, is 'workable, durable solutions that meet the participants' practical, emotional, and social concerns as fully as possible'.[85] As mediation focuses on practical solution, change may not be at the very highest order of directions, but the aim is to find out where 'leverage' is possible.

### *International conflict resolution*

Negotiation, at the most macro level, takes the form of conflict resolution between nations, or between communities within nations. In contrast to mediation, it does not need to include a third party, and may be adversarial as well as more cooperative.[86] However, like mediation, its aims to 'develop a mutually acceptable settlement'.[87] From a BHN perspective, as we have seen, the basis of more macro conflicts can be seen as the denial of particular, 'nonnegotiable' needs and wants, and therefore conflict resolution work involves identifying those fundamental directions and trying to address them.[88] As with dialogue at the intrapersonal or dyadic level, the ideal here is to find a point 'where both parties can get what they want at the same time'.[89] That is, to create '200 per cent of something out of 100 per cent'. Galtung terms such synergetic solutions 'transcendence', but there are other potential outcomes as well: for instance, 'compromises' and 'withdrawals'.[90]

As with mediation, there is a recognition in the international conflict resolution field that progress comes from moving up to higher-order needs and wants. Herbert Kelman, Professor of Social Ethics at Harvard University, states: 'When parties probe beyond their stated positions and presumed interests into their underlying needs, they may find that these needs are in fact not incompatible (or no longer incompatible in the light of changing circumstances) and that an apparently intractable conflict can in fact be resolved.'[91] Kelman, who was involved in Middle East peace negotiations, goes on to write:

> For example, in a conflict over territory, such as the Israeli–Palestinian conflict in its current phase (with its focus on the West Bank and Gaza), the parties would be urged to talk about why each wants the contested territory. At the risk of oversimplifying the issue for the sake of illustration, let us propose that the Palestinians want it primarily to establish and express their national identity, while the Israelis want it primarily to safeguard their national security. Once the conflict is redefined in terms of these underlying needs, the parties may be able to invent solutions that would satisfy Palestinian identity needs and Israeli security needs without threatening the other's existence.[92]

Dialogue between Palestinians and Israelis has helped both groups recognise the other's need for self-determination.[93] Mutual acknowledgement of this can then be part of a cooperative solution. Similarly, dialogue in the Philippines between conflicting Muslims and Catholics helped them realise that both groups had shared needs for security, identity, and recognition.[94] As another example of finding cooperative solutions in the Middle East, negotiations at Camp David in 1976, between President Sadat of Egypt and Prime Minister Begin of Israel, led to the return of the Sinai to Egyptian sovereignty, but demilitarised in large areas.[95] Here, creative dialogue helped identify a synergetic, win–win solution in which both parties' higher-order needs and wants could be met: Egyptian needs for national integrity, and Israeli needs for security. Hence, dialogue allows both groups to go beyond the existing range of satisfiers and find alternatives that would allow for more synergetic solutions.[96]

### *Discussion*

In this section, we have seen, across multiple domains, how the process of conflict resolution at interpersonal levels of organisation parallels that at intrapersonal levels, as practised in therapy (Chapter 3). Essentially, to create something better, find cooperative solutions. That is, reconfigure the relationship between different directions, so that instead of pulling against each other they can pull together. And, across levels, the way that you can do that is by looking 'upwards' to higher-order needs and wants: moving, in negotiation terms, from 'positions' to 'interests'. At lower orders, there is often not much that can be resolved. As Albert Einstein states: 'the significant problems we face cannot be solved at the same level of thinking we were at when we created them'.[97] Nation A and Nation B, for instance, want the same piece of land; or ex-Wife A and ex-Husband B are in dispute over who gets the house; or two 'parts' of a person are struggling over how much to eat. But as you move to higher-order needs and wants, then more cooperative, creative solutions become possible. Nation A and Nation B, for instance, see that what they both, most deeply want is recognition from each other; and to feel their culture and rights to self-determination are being respected. Now, it is no longer an 'either/or' conflict, where one wins and the other loses, but a 'both/and' situation, in which both parties can win. Essentially, you create 'more' by working out, together, what is really needed and wanted, and that opens up possibilities for more synergetic solutions. Why? Because, as we have seen, higher-order needs and wants tend to be less concrete, material, and singular; and therefore more amendable to creative, synergistic, multifacted solutions. They also allow each party to see the common humanity of the other; and, because higher-order needs and wants are, ultimately, what each party are striving for, they are more likely to lead to meaningful, sustainable, genuinely satisfying solutions.

Cooperation, then, can be seen as a general system-wide principle for creating more benefit, and this provides compelling support for a progressive outlook. You do not 'get to yes' in mediation through stoking competition between the parties, or help couples by encouraging them to outdo each other. Nor do you find workable solutions on any plane by supporting the needs and wants of one community against another. In all these fora, progress towards 'better' comes from supporting parties to work together, to share successes, and to engage in egalitarian ways: to recognise that each other's highest-order needs and wants are legitimate and intelligible. And this approach to relating, between individuals or communities, is the *sine qua non* of a progressive perspective.

However, there are three important caveats here. First, what is meant by synergetic, cooperative solutions is a *genuine* coming together of higher-order needs and wants, and not a shoving together of directions into more profitable or 'efficient' arrangements. A business, for instance, may claim that it is making 'synergies' by merging two departments into one, but to the extent that it creates redundancies or stress for its workers, it may actually be more dysergetic than synergetic. Second, synergies, in themselves, do not necessarily take into account issues of power and inequalities. In negotiations between Palestinians and Israelis, for instance, the parties may have very different abilities to impose their wants upon each other. To the extent that, in synergetic arrangements, *both* party's highest-order directions are being met, these issues may be indirectly addressed. However, a more in-depth and nuanced discussion of power and inequality issues – and their relationship to synergies – is covered in the following chapter. Third, the creation of synergies is not a substitute for an overall increase of resources. If a nation has very limited access to food or water, for instance, then the overall wellbeing (that is, the realisation of highest-order needs and wants across individuals) may be very low, whatever the synergies. Indeed, as with conflicts, the level of cooperative possibilities is likely to increase or decrease with greater or lesser resources, respectively. At the same time, the key point here is that, within any specified set of resources, there is always the potential for more or less synergetic configurations. To understand more about what that means, and the nature of collaborative decision-making, we now turn to the field of *game theory*.

## Game theory

Game theory is 'the study of strategic interdependence – that is, situations where my action affect both my welfare and your welfare and vice versa'.[98] This covers pretty much all the intrapersonal and interpersonal processes that we have explored to this point in this book. Game theory was developed in the

1950s, and has been applied across the social sciences, although it is particularly associated with economics and conflict analysis.[99] Game theory adds to the present analysis by using mathematical modelling to describe, analyse, and research the processes and outcomes involved in conflict and cooperation. Because it is based in mathematics, game theory can be quite complicated to understand, and it presents a vastly oversimplified and reductive view of relationships. Nevertheless, the insights its provides on the nature of conflict and cooperation – and particularly the conditions required to facilitate the latter, which we will explore in Chapter 6 – make it well worth the study.

To begin with, a helpful distinction made by game theorists is between *zero-sum* and *non-zero-sum* 'games'. A zero-sum game is one in which the total benefit across parties is always the same. A game of poker between two players, for instance, is zero-sum, because if A wins £50 then B loses £50 and vice versa: there is always the same total amount in the pot: a fixed sum. In *non-zero-sum* games, however, the total amount of benefit is not constant. An example might be making love. Here, both A and B could have a great time (with a high total benefit) or both might have a terrible time (with a low total benefit): so the total amount of benefit could vary considerably. One could, perhaps, imagine 'zero-sum sex' – where, for instance, A's pleasure came at a cost to B and vice versa – but this kind of transactional exchange would have nothing of the relational or companionate qualities of making love. In zero-sum games, the only options are win–lose, lose–win, or draw–draw. But in non-zero-sum games, we also have the possibility of win–win and lose–lose outcomes. A win–win outcome can be considered equivalent to a cooperative, synergetic solution: with more total benefit created than was in the individual parts alone.[100] By contrast, a lose–lose outcome can be considered equivalent to conflict. This is surplus repression, where there is less overall benefit for the two parties than there need be.

A non-zero-sum game, then, is a necessary condition for the formation of cooperative solutions. And because, in reality, most situations are non-zero-sum – where parties are 'interdependent' – there is nearly always some impact that levels of cooperation will have on overall outcomes. This is another way of stating the principle discussed earlier: that within the same set of external resources there is nearly always the possibility for better or worse overall levels of benefit. And, as we see here, the key is the degree of cooperation. This game theory conceptualisation also helps to explain why, as you go up towards higher-order needs and wants, cooperative solutions become more possible. At lower orders, satisfiers tend to be quite material (for example, 'I want an apple', 'I want that house'), and material satisfiers tend to be fixed sum. So, for instance, if you have one apple, you cannot create two apples or no apples. There's a 'fixed pie'. But as you go to higher-order directions, needs and wants become more non-material, softer, and flexible – and this means greater possibilities for overall increases (and decreases) in benefit. There is no fixed sum for feeling valued or loved in a relationship, for instance: two partners can create more love between them, and they can also create less. So when mediators or conflict negotiators focus on interests rather than positions, they are essentially trying to change a zero-sum game into a non-zero-sum one. That is, by focusing on higher-order needs and wants, they are opening up the possibility for cooperative, win–win solutions.

Within game theory, the classic scenario that has been used to explore non-zero-sum games is the *prisoner's dilemma game.*[101] This goes as follows:

> Two criminals, A and B, are arrested and imprisoned. They are in solitary confinement so that they cannot talk to each other. If they both stay silent (i.e., 'cooperate' with each other), the police will not have enough evidence to prosecute them, but they can get them on a lesser charge, and each will go to prison for one year. However, the police offer each criminal the opportunity to 'defect' (i.e., admit the crime), with the promise that if they do so, then they will be set free (and their partner will get three years in prison). However, if both criminals defect – and admit to their crime – then they will both receive a two year sentence. So what should each criminal do?[102]

**Table 5.1**: Payoff matrix for the classic prisoner's dilemma game

| B / A | B cooperates (stays silent) | B defects (admits crime) |
|---|---|---|
| A cooperates (stays silent) | B gets 1 year<br>A gets 1 year | B gets 0 years<br>A gets 3 years |
| A defects (admits crime) | B gets 3 years<br>A gets 0 years | B gets 2 years<br>A gets 2 years |

To help explore such dilemmas, game theorists have developed 'payoff matrices', with different numbers representing different 'wins' or 'losses' for different 'players'. The payoff matrix for the game, in terms of years imprisoned, is shown in Table 5.1. This displays the different combinations of 'moves', and the payoffs for A and B if each makes the choice to cooperate with, or defect on, the other. The 'payoff' for A is in the bottom left of the square cells, and for B in the top right of the cells. So, for instance, in the top left-hand cell, we can see that, if B cooperates with A and A cooperates with B, A will get one year in prison and B will get one year in prison. However, in the top right-hand cell, we see that, if A cooperates with B but B defects on A, A will get three years in prison and B will get no years in prison. What this matrix also shows, as a non-zero-sum game, is that the *total* payoff varies from cell to cell: from two years in total (A and B both cooperate) to four years in total (A and B both defect).

In some instances, the solution with the highest overall benefit may be the one that serves both players' interests. For instance, with the two children quarrelling over an orange described earlier, both get the best possible outcome if all the peel is given to one, and all the fruit is given to the other. However, what is fascinating about the prisoner's dilemma is that if both players act, independently, towards their own self-interests, then the overall benefit is actually the lowest of all outcomes (that is, the bottom right cell, four years imprisoned in total). If A, for instance, considers their best options, then they might think: 'If B stays silent, then I am better off admitting the crime (no years in prison rather than one year); and if B admits the crime, then

I am also better off admitting the crime (two years in prison rather than three years).' The exact, same logic holds for B. However, if both A and B act on such 'rational' self-interest, then the overall outcome (two years in prison each) is worse than if they had chosen to act with regard for the other (one year in prison each).

Such a scenario of non-zero-sum interdependence is important to consider because, across many different levels of organisation, it can be seen as 'an abstract formulation of some very common and interesting situations' in the real world.[103] Take, for instance, the situation where two romantic partners, A and B, are having an argument. Both would much rather the row was over and that they were back, canoodling, in front of the television. But A, by themselves, does not want to apologise and admit that they were wrong, and neither does B – it would feel too awkward and shaming. So both A and B continue the argument, and end up worse off than either needs to be. The arms race can be considered another form of the prisoner's dilemma game, scaled up to national levels.[104] Nation A and Nation B, for instance, have the choice to arm or not arm; and Nation A might think, 'Well, if Nation B is arming, we should arm so that it is not more powerful than us; and if Nation B is not arming, then we should also arm so we can be more powerful than it.' But the problem, of course, is that this also works the other way around: both countries, acting in 'rational' self-interest, feel the need to arm, but the overall outcome (two mutually armed countries) is a poorer overall outcome than if both countries chose, together, not to arm.

As suggested in Chapter 3, many intrapersonal problems can also be understood as lose–lose relationships between different parts of the self. A person who constantly oscillates, for instance, between wanting others and shunning others may experience a pervasive sense of anxiety. When they have the relatedness that one part wants, the other part is trembling with fear; but when they have the separation that the other part craves, the relational part is terrified of isolation. Both parts, then, acting rogue and towards their own interests, bring misery to the whole.

These scenarios beg a critical question: How can people, in such non-zero-sum, interdependent situations come together to find cooperative solutions? Because if they only act in terms of themselves and their immediate self-interests, they are both worse off overall. So how, for instance, can partners A and B stop their argument and get back to canoodling in front of the TV? How can Nation A and Nation B spend their money constructively – for instance, on education, science, or health – rather than arms? How can the individual who wants both relatedness and autonomy find psychological peace? In Chapter 3, we saw how, at the intrapersonal level, therapy could provide some useful answers to this question: implementing strategies that could help bring about cooperative solutions between parts. Equally, in the present chapter, we saw how couples therapists, mediators, and conflict resolution workers help to find cooperative solutions at interpersonal levels of organisation. Game theorists, too, have addressed this question, most famously by setting up a 'round robin' tournament of the prisoner's dilemma game, in which computerised strategies play against each other to see which is the most effective strategy, overall.[105] What is fascinating here is that the answers from all of these different sources triangulate. That is, whether you are looking at what works in therapy, what works between people, or what works in abstract simulated games, the answers all point in similar directions. And, of profound encouragement to progressives, is that these answers are aligned to the kinds of practices, principles, and values that progressivism has promoted for many years. In Chapter 6, we will see what these strategies for promoting win-win solutions are.

## Summing up

The aim of this chapter has been to show how an understanding of wellbeing and distress, in terms of cooperation and conflict, can be extended from intrapersonal levels of organisation (Chapter 4) to interpersonal ones. Wellbeing, at any level of organisation, can be understood as the process of cooperative functioning, so that there is more overall benefit: for more people, or more communities, or more nations – to get more of what they most fundamentally need and want more of the time. This recognition of the value of cooperative relationships is, perhaps, of no great surprise to progressives. Yet, in this chapter, I hope to have shown how this principle reaches across many different levels of organisation. That is, it is not just social-economic wellbeing that benefits from cooperative relationship; but dyadic relationships, international relationships, and, perhaps most strikingly, relationships 'within' the person too (Chapter 3). So the progressive emphasis on cooperation is not just one particular political perspective; rather, it is a system-wide principle for how things work well, whatever level of organisation we are looking at.

In Marxist theory – developed from Hegel – there is a well-known emphasis on the 'dialectic': thesis, antithesis, and synthesis. By contrast, the present text suggests that another process should be considered the heart of progressivism: win–win, cooperative synergies. Dialectical processes, in the synthesis of thesis and antithesis, may lead to synergetic outcomes; but the concept of synergies is broader and suggests that there are other, less oppositional, ways towards greater overall benefit. Synergies puts empathy, care, and a willingness to creatively cooperate at the fore: a desire to 'master the art of "we"'.[106] It is a *politics of understanding*—in contrast to the *politics of blame* that can, so frequently, characterise the left. In dialectics, the other is our antithesis; but in synergies, the other is not inherently against us. In practice, they may be; but if we can understand their higher-order directions, then we can come to stand alongside them as two, equally human, human beings: both with legitimate needs and wants that have the potential of coming together. In the following chapter, we will explore, across multiple levels of organisation, how such synergetic outcomes might be brought about.

# 6

# Common principles of positive change

Chapter 6 moves us into the second half of the book and, with it, a more specific vision for what a psychology-informed progressive world might look like, and the concrete steps that might get us there. In Chapter 5, we saw how, across different levels of organisation, increases in wellbeing were associated with more cooperative relationships. This chapter develops this analysis – building on work presented in my previous book[1] – by looking, more specifically, at how such synergetic relationships can be established. As with Chapter 5, the focus here is on identifying common processes across different levels of organisation: from the intrapersonal focus of therapy to the international conflict resolution domain. My aim, here, is to describe a set of system-wide, generic principles for how we can create 'better'. Some of these principles, as stated earlier, will be familiar to progressives. Here, what I hope to do is to demonstrate support for a progressive perspective by showing how such strategies are underpinned by a wider, more encompassing logic. Some of these principles, however, like being assertive and genuine dialogue, may be newer (and potentially more controversial to progressives). In this way, the aim of the chapter is to lay out a particular, 're-visioned' way of thinking about progressivism. This is an approach to progressivism that is psychological and relational, as well as socioeconomic, in nature. It is a progressivism of how we are with those close to us and ourselves, as well as how we act and think on more macro planes. This is a wider, more encompassing, more integrated progressivism: one in which the personal and the political become closely aligned.

## See the 'bigger picture'

Lose–lose strategies are characterised by 'agencies' (whether parts of a person, people, communities, or nations) thinking individually in interdependent contexts. That is, they ask, 'What is best for me?' rather than 'What is best for us?' and paradoxically, in doing so, fail to find the best solution for themselves. More specifically, lose–lose strategies demonstrate a failure to appreciate the larger whole: that I, and the other, are locked together into an interdependent system (at a higher level of organisation); and that 'there is no best strategy independent of the strategy used by the other player'.[2] That is why, in the prisoner's dilemma game, the tactic of following one's immediate self-interests – repeated over time – nearly always fails. Because it only considers one's immediate payoff, and does not consider the interpersonal context in which that payoff is embedded. More specifically, it treats the other as a non-agentic, passive 'it'; rather than recognising that the other has agency, subjectivity, and directionality of its own.

Anatol Rapoport, a recognised leader in peace and conflict research, puts this another way when he writes that the tragedy of human beings is that we try to 'play' non-zero-sum games *as if they were* zero-sum games.[3] That is, we see situations in terms of us winning and the other losing, or vice versa, rather than recognising that we and the other, together, can determine how much overall 'winning' or 'losing' there is. So a cooperative, win–win strategy involves looking 'up' to higher levels of organisation (for instance, from the individual to the community, or from the community to the nation) and considering what is best for the larger whole. And by creating more for the larger whole, as discussed in Chapter 5, we can then create more for ourselves.

John Lennon said that there are two basic motivating forces, love and fear. If that were true, love might be understood as an embracing up towards higher levels of organisation, while fear is a hunkering down towards what is below. Love moves us towards unity with something larger, where we feel ourselves part of a greater whole. Fear, on the other hand, focuses our attention on what needs doing now to protect ourselves, to maintain our individual integrity. Of course, both are important and intelligible directions; but, as we saw in the previous chapter, it is love and looking upwards – the cooperative action of different parts – that ultimately creates more benefit overall.

### *Mentalisation*

At the intrapsychic level of organisation, this ability to see the bigger picture has been termed the capacity to *mentalise*, and there is growing consensus in the therapy field that this is key to psychological health. Mentalisation has been defined as 'the mental process by which an individual implicitly and explicitly interprets the actions of herself and others as meaningful on the basis of intentional mental states such as personal desires, needs, feelings, beliefs and reasons'.[4] Mentalisation (also termed 'reflective functioning') is the capacity to recognise what we, and others, are doing: to stand 'above' it, at a higher level, and to understand what it is for. Without it, a person can be immersed in such rogue behaviours as raging destructively at others, or obsessively restricting their eating – acting *on* their desires, needs, or feelings – without understanding its meaning.

In many respects, 'mentalisation' is just a contemporary way of describing what every form of therapy has always focused on: helping clients to develop *self-awareness*, to recognise *why* they are doing what they are doing. Self-awareness has the capacity to facilitate wellbeing and cooperation because it can help individuals stand back from what they are thinking, feeling, and doing, and recognise other possibilities. Indeed, in 'the Method of Levels', a form of therapy based on Powers's perceptual control theory (see Chapter 3), therapists specifically work to 'nudge' their clients' attention up to higher levels of directions.[5] A therapist might say, for instance, 'You are really trying to avoid seeing your father. … I wonder, do you have a sense of what that is about?' From a Method of Levels perspective, shifting that attention higher can be helpful because the client can spontaneously begin to find resolutions to their problems: resolutions that cannot exist at the lower orders, as Einstein put it. This is, effectively, the basic principle of finding cooperative solutions that was discussed in Chapter 5 of the book.

As will be evident here, a lack of mentalisation and self-awareness is essentially synonymous with the dominance of rogue goals, as discussed in Chapter 3. Here, where a person cannot recognise their needs and wants *as* needs and wants, they can become taken over by them, to the exclusion of other directions. So the individual rages at their partner – vents the full force of their anger – failing to recognise that this will push their partner away and, in doing so not only harm their partner, but also themselves. A lack of mentalisation, then, is like the scoffing of a marshmallow without any capacity for 'self-distancing' (Chapter 3, this volume),[6] or being consumed in a cloud of false consciousness and losing sight of our genuine needs and wants (Chapter 2, this volume). It can also be considered an intrapersonal equivalent of a prisoner's dilemma strategy that focuses on immediate self-interests, alone. The individual is narrowed down, locked, focused myopically on only how part of it can 'win', rather than seeing the context as a whole. That part is failing to recognise that, over time, a 'winning' strategy needs to take into account needs and wants beyond their immediate own.

Mentalisation, however, is also relevant at the interpersonal level of organisation, because it is not just defined as the capacity to see our own mental states, but also those of the other. It means being able to understand that the other is a subjective, experiencing being like ourselves, who is also acting towards their own needs and wants. Mentalisation, therefore, can be considered akin to a stance of psychological equality and a capacity for empathy: to understand that the other has an experiencing of the world, and that this may be different from our own experiencing and perceptions. This capacity to mentalise the other is critical for relationships – for instance, a parent's capacity for reflective functioning has been shown to be associated with early security in child attachment[7] – and the emergence of any form of win–win solutions. In couples therapy, the Gottmans state that a principal source of conflict in relationships is the belief that there is only one truth, and that we possess it.[8] In the field of negotiation, too, Fisher and colleagues advise, 'It is not enough to study [the other] like beetles under a microscope; you need to know what it feels like to be a beetle.'[9] In other words, we need to be able to realise that the other is not just the *object* of our needs and wants, but also a subject who is also acting towards us. And that means recognising that we are in an interlocking system: our acts affect how they act towards us and vice versa in a complex, integrated, multidirectional chain. For win–win solutions, then, not only do we need to be able to recognise the needs and concerns of the other, but also to respond to them, and shift to a level of 'joint thinking' where we are working together to find solutions that are mutually – rather than unilaterally – satisfying.

Such an analysis has important implications for a progressive approach to political debate and action. If we want to bring about win–win solutions, we cannot engage with our political 'opponents' on the assumption that we are right and they are wrong. Such a mindset fails to fully mentalise the standpoint of the other: that they, like ourselves, are directional beings striving to make sense of their worlds. From this perspective, the radical newspaper seller who sets out to convince others of their politics – disinterested and closed to the views of the other – is not likely to bring about positive, synergetic developments; and neither are they, from the present standpoint, embodying a progressive stance. Certainly, from the present perspective, we can hold particular positions; but the capacity to see above this and recognise the intelligibility and meaning of alternative positions is a key foundation for progressivism in action.

### *A 'universal' moral standpoint*

At the social level of organisation, this capacity to mentalise might be considered similar to the widely held moral principle of 'universalisability', as articulated by the German enlightenment philosopher Emmanuel Kant. This holds that you should 'act only in accordance with that maxim through which you can at the same time will that it become a universal law'.[10] That is, act only in ways that you would be happy for others to also act – *the Golden Rule* – stand above your own point of view, needs, or interests, and assess a situation from the standpoint of an impartial (but sympathetic) observer.[11] John Rawls, one of the most influential moral philosophers of the 20th century, suggests something similar when he writes that we should choose principles of justice from behind a 'veil of ignorance': where we would not know our social status, abilities, or psychological propensities.[12] Now, if we might end up being anyone, what kind of social structures would we choose?

## *Principled negotiation*

For Fisher and colleagues, the capacity to adopt this universal standpoint – to see the bigger picture of which both you and the other are part – is essential to effective negotiation. They write:

> If a negotiation is to be compared with a legal proceeding, the situation resembles that of two judges trying to reach agreement on how to decide a case. Try putting yourself in that role, treating your opposite number as a fellow judge with whom you are attempting to work out a joint opinion. In this context it is clearly unpersuasive to blame the other party for the problem, to engage in name-calling, or to raise your voice. On the contrary, it will help to recognize explicitly that they see the situation differently and to try to go forward as people with a joint problem.[13]

When we get caught up in a quarrel with someone, it is often not just that we are focused on our own self-interests, but that we are focused on only the most immediate, in-the-moment self-interests. For example, our priority becomes to 'save face', to defend ourselves, or to 'prove' to the other that we are right.[14] By contrast, as with a universal moral standpoint, Fisher and colleagues argue that the most effective bargaining strategy – both for self and others – is one of *principled negotiation*. Here, each party strives to set out universal, objective criteria for reaching agreements, independent of the will of either side. For instance, this might be that the parties should exit the agreement with equal financial gains, or that a third party should be asked to decide what is fair, or that both parties' cultural heritages should be prioritised. Only once these principles are established, they suggest, should the parties then decide on who gets what. That way, the decision made is in terms of principles at a higher level of organisation, rather than the individual demands of either party alone. This is like the childhood practice of one person sharing out the portions of a treat, and then the other child deciding who gets which one. Again, we see how the principle of standing back and seeing the bigger picture leads to more synergetic, and fairer, outcomes overall.

### *Capitalism as a rogue goal*

As suggested in Chapter 5, both at intrapersonal and interpersonal levels of organisation, capitalism can be seen as system in which we lose our sense of the bigger picture: where we become dominated by rogue goals. Fromm writes that capitalism creates subservience to 'inhuman, depraved, unnatural, and *imaginary* appetites'.[15] Foremost among these is the need for – and idolisation of – money, described by Marx as a 'bestial barbarization, a complete, unrefined, abstract simplicity of need'.[16] Money becomes our striving, our focal point, our sole satisfier for success: we are good to the extent that we are rich in it, bad to the extent that we are poor in it. Here, then, a natural human tendency to recognise, and progress towards, multiple goals – our heterogeneity, both within people and between people – gets bottled down to one, all-pervasive satisfier.[17] Mason describes neoliberalism as 'an assault on humanism. It enforced the reduction of human nature to economic competition and it suppressed all attempts to experiment with alternatives.'[18] And yet, as the research shows, the striving for financial success does not tend to bring with it happiness.[19] Rather, it may divert people from other, potentially more direct and rewarding sources of wellbeing, such as relatedness or meaning.

### *Fascism as a rogue goal*

In *The fear of freedom*, Fromm conceptualised fascism as an even greater failure to mentalise: to see beyond one specific need or want.[20] Here, he writes, the individual – freed from the traditional bonds of medieval society into isolation and uncertainty – surrenders themselves to fascist and racist ideologies so that they can experience the safety of the collective and submission to authority. 'I do not need to choose for myself' … 'I do not need to think for myself'. Fascism, for Fromm, satisfies a rogue desire for safety: freeing the person from the anxieties of individual responsibility. This 'symbiosis', this relief from the stressors and complexities of modern living, can be compared to the feelings of security we might experience when sinking into a warm bath. But, as Fromm argues, it comes at tremendous cost. For the individual there is a loss of many other needs and wants: for instance, the person's desires for expansiveness, growth, and creativity. More importantly, perhaps, when such imbalanced, one-sided ways of being come together collectively – in the form of mass fascism – then whole swathes of humanity may be threatened. By losing sight of the bigger picture, fascist ideologies, by definition, fail to meet the needs and wants of the whole. And because the victims of fascism can never, entirely, be turned into non-agentic things, then a 'return of the repressed' is almost inevitable. Hence, even fascists do not, ultimately, profit from fascism: it is the ultimate short-sighted strategy that can only ever lead to a massive loss of overall benefit.

The authoritarian populism proliferating today can also be seen as a failure to mentalise: to appreciate a wider range of perspectives both within, and beyond, the self. Mason, for instance, writes that, 'Trump understood that tired people don't want logic or principles. … What they want is a leader who rises above logic and truth and tells them that all their inner prejudices are right.'[21] Here, where people's psychological resources are low, an emotionally charged, black-and-white ideology – aligned to 'intuitively' felt prejudices – can become compelling. Yet in responding to this, progressives need to be careful not to fall into another form of single-sightedness, where populism is, de facto, wrong, and progressivism right. Rather, we need to be able to hold, and argue, our truth, while also being able to stand above it to recognise different perspectives. This is what can make progressivism something truly different than what has gone before.

## *Ecocide as a rogue goal*

The current climate emergency can be seen as another example of what happens when we are overtaken by rogue goals, and fail to look 'up' to see the bigger picture. UK-based psychotherapists Hilary Prentice and Mary-Jayne Rust write that this ecocide shows a 'psychopathological lack of empathy or remorse' towards our planet as a whole.[22] It is, they write, 'behaving with reckless abandon', as though unaware that our behaviours are destroying all that we depend on for life, 'atmosphere, rainforest, clean oceans full of life, weather systems, habitats, biodiversity, social structure, water tables'.[23] At the most macro level of organisation, the actions of states like Bolsonaro's Brazil, in deforesting the Amazon rainforest, seems the very definition of a rogue goal: putting the desire for economic expansion, for one country, before any other global needs or wants. At the more micro, individual level of organisation, behaviours like driving to work (when we can cycle or take public transport) – while entirely intelligible ('Who wants to sit on a dingy train!') – are also rogue, because they fail to take into account impacts at higher levels of organisation. What, again, is needed is the capacity to 'look up', to see the bigger picture, to mentalise the larger whole – not just our small proportion of it. This is the essence of the Golden Rule: not to act from 'I want X' but from, 'X is good (or not good) for all of us to do.' It is moving the locus of decision-making up to a higher level of organisation: from self to self-with-others.

## *Discussion*

Of course, we cannot always spend our time – whether at intrapersonal or interpersonal levels of organisation – looking up towards the greater whole. Our attention, inevitably, moves up and down a system; and sometimes it is essential to focus down on the lower, more individual, and more concrete levels of organisation. However, for cooperative relationships to emerge, we need, at least *sometimes* – and particularly at points of stuckness, crisis, or conflict – to be able to move our attention up: to be able to see our perspective and our actions as part of a wider whole. This, perhaps, should be a key element in defining progressivism: not just that we believe in cooperation, but that we believe in the value of standing back from our own perspective and seeing a larger whole.

Such an openness to multiple perspective can be seen as a key difference between progressivism and more conservative stances. Conservatism, as discussed in Chapter 1, can be understood as a privileging of what we already 'know': a reliance on how we 'intuitively' see and feel about the world, rather than a willingness to revise our worldview by standing back and considering new perspectives. Burke, for instance, writes that 'prejudice':

> [E]ngages the mind in a steady course of wisdom and virtue, and does not leave the man hesitating in the moment of decision, skeptical, puzzled, and unresolved. Prejudice renders a man's virtues his habit, and not a series of unconnected acts. Through just prejudice, his duty becomes part of his nature.[24]

From such a standpoint, Burke counters such philosophies as atheism on the grounds that it is against 'our instincts'. Here, as with populism, what we feel and think is 'right' because we intuitively know it: consideration of further perspectives is unnecessary and can only serve to muddle our minds. What this ignores, of course, is the fact that any so-called 'instinctive knowledge' is inevitably located in a historical and cultural context: what seemed 'intuitively' true in 18th-century Europe – from the legitimacy of slavery to the medical value of tobacco smoke enemas – would not seem true today. Moreover, the 'prejudice' and 'intuition' that Burke so encourages us to rely on is essentially the 'hot emotional system' that Mischel warns us against in the Marshmallow test.[25] As the evidence shows, prejudice does not engage the mind 'in a steady course of wisdom and virtue'. Rather, it leads us – and others – to a whole host of emotional, physical, intellectual, and relational difficulties.

## Take responsibility

As suggested in the previous section, seeing the bigger picture – looking 'upwards' and recognising the possibilities for collaborative solutions – is not something that just naturally happens. In fact, given the challenges and stresses we all face in our everyday lives, our natural human tendency may be to focus 'down': 'What do *I* need, for me and mine, right now?' Moreover, we may all have a natural tendency towards stagnancy and conservatism, even if the situation is a lose–lose one. Change risks short-term security and rewards, and instead requires a faith in longer-term, uncertain possibilities. We also know, from the research, that risks tend to loom larger in the psyche than benefits.[26] As we saw in the prisoner's dilemma game, the attempt to establish more cooperative relationships also risks the worst of all outcomes: that our attempts at working together will be met with the other's defection. So, for cooperation to happen, as Powers states, people must deliberately choose cooperation as a goal.[27]

This need for deliberate action is certainly the case on the intrapersonal plane. People get stuck in ruts – a boring job, a poor relationship – that they know are not good for them, but feel safe and familiar. Therapy can help them reflect on this, and to find the will to do things differently. Ultimately, however, as the research shows, therapists cannot change their clients.[28] The biggest determinant of success, whether in individual or couples therapy, is the client's willingness and motivation to change.[29] Along similar lines, psychological research shows that people's natural thinking can tend towards the prejudicial style that Burke so venerates: simplistic, black-and-white, and error-prone.[30] Thinking in more accurate, realistic, and non-prejudicial ways takes effort. The same is true at the interpersonal level: driving to work or buying a new plastic bag every time we go to the shop are easy routines to fall into, and then to hold onto. They suit our individual needs. Stepping up a level of organisation – to think about the community, the country, or the planet – requires effort, something *more*.

There is a theme here that taking responsibility, as with many other cooperative strategies, requires thinking in the long-term as well as the short-term: beyond the immediate now to also consider what is to come. Capitalism focuses on short-term interests: How can we make the most of what is out there, for us, in the immediate present? How can we exploit this environment to make the most money for our shareholders here and now? But short-term interests bring short-term benefits; if we want a more sustained, more enduring wellbeing for the future, we have to think about the future – there is no way around this.[31]

Taking responsibility is not just about making things happen; it is making things happen when others are unwilling or unable to do so. Len Fisher, from a game theory perspective, writes about the *tragedy of the commons*: when everyone thinks it is OK for them to do their own thing and no one is willing to try and coordinate efforts, with the result that everyone loses out.[32] This, then, points to the issue of *leadership*: that people are needed who are willing to initiate the search for more cooperative solutions, whatever else others might do. In relation to Black Americans, for instance, West writes:

> We need leaders – neither saints nor sparkling television personalities – who can situate themselves within a larger historical narrative of this country and our world, who can grasp the complex dynamics of our peoplehood and imagine a future grounded in the best of our past, yet who are attuned to the frightening obstacles that now perplex us.[33]

Of course, 'leadership' here does not refer to control and the abuse of power, but to serving the greater whole in a facilitative, coordinating, mediating role. Indeed, Covey states that the very essence of leadership is in the development of 'creative cooperation', or synergies.[34] Leadership may be essential to the development of cooperative solutions because agencies, however willing they are, may be limited in the perspectives that they can take. That is, however much we may strive to see the bigger picture, we may need people who can help to identify and establish common principles and standards. Leaders can also work to bring together different viewpoints, both within and across agencies, and to challenge distortions and misperceptions.

This facilitative role is akin to a therapist who helps mediate the client's intrapersonal conflicts; or, on the interpersonal plane, a mediator in negotiations, the therapist in couples therapy, or a 'third party' in international conflict resolution.[35] Such facilitators, by holding a detached, non-partisan position (the impartial but sympathetic observer), have the capacity to see beyond the immediate – and sometimes rogue, biased, and emotionally driven – needs and wants of both parties, to help identify the underlying sources of the conflict, and see mutually beneficial solutions. This means creating a space in which all voices can be heard: a 'calm presence amidst the storm'.[36] To facilitate such processes, leaders can help to establish norms of open, respectful communication (see the section, Communicate, later in this chapter). They can also introduce structured techniques or methods – for instance, giving each person a certain amount of time to talk while the other listens – to help 'steady the process' and contain the volatile swirl of emotions, needs, and wants.[37] Good leaders do not dominate the process of negotiation or discussion, but allow, wherever possible, the other parties to take the lead. But they gently help to keep the process on track, and are ready to step in when there is a sense that things are going rogue. In this way, the function of a leader shares many similarities with the process of mentalisation: standing above any one position to be able to see, and act in the interests of, the greater whole.

Particularly important, in terms of leadership, may be holding open the space for difference: for those parties that may be more marginalised, minoritised, and suppressed.[38] Indeed, a democratic system – at every level – can be defined as one in which all needs and wants can be heard. In couples therapy, for instance, the therapist may ask one partner to hold back if they are speaking or interrupting a lot, so that the other partner can talk.[39] Holding open this space for otherness is important because, at any level of organisation, there are always differences in how much *power* the agencies have: the ability to 'make or to receive any change, or to resist it'.[40] Paradoxically, then, a leaderless space may actually support more unequal power structures: reifying and masking pre-existing power relationships; allowing the implicit, ruling elites to maintain control.[41] The reality is, power differentials between agencies do exist, it is not an equal playing field, and therefore facilitators – with structures and interventions – may be needed to help ensure that power, at least to some extent, is equalised.

Leaders may also be needed to help the group see beyond the immediate now and to take into account future horizons. This, de facto, is the role that many progressives take – as, for instance, environmental or animal rights campaigners. Here, an activist might say something like, 'I know you like driving to work in your car, I know it is quicker and easier for you; but in the longer-term good of us all, it is something that needs to change.' Of course, people do not always want to be reminded of what is in the longer-term good over their short-term self-interests; and there may be a tendency to justify the latter or discredit the former: 'They're just a bunch of hippies trying to spoil my day.' But the role of leadership is not always to be popular. Rogue, short-term goals have a force; and those who stand up against them may be experienced as frustrating and an annoyance.

Leaders also have an important role in helping a group come up with collaborative solutions themselves. In international relations work, for instance:

> The third party's principle task is to look for innovative ways of analyzing the basic need structure on both sides, to try to come up with multiple ideas for partial outcomes that can benefit both sides, or alternatively benefit one side without hurting the other; in any event, to try and bring alternative ideas forward which could leave both sides better off in terms of total need satisfaction.[42]

Within negotiations, a mediator may be the person who encourages both parties to write down an agreement, and then to ensure that they have ways of sticking to it.[43]

Finally, leaders can have a role in making things happen: in initiating action and change.[44] Identifying cooperative solutions is one thing, but the resistance to change may always be strong. Someone is often needed to 'cross the Rubicon': to have the courage to take the first step in doing things differently.

At every level of organisation, then, the development of cooperative solutions requires people to make this happen: to lead and to take responsibility. And, to the extent that progressivism advocates the development of cooperative solutions, we each have a role and a responsibility here to lead. 'Power' has often been a dirty word in progressive circles, associated with dominance and oppression. But if power is most generally understood, as defined earlier in this section (from Steven Lukes, the influential British sociologist), as the capacity to 'make or to receive any change, or to resist it', then progressives also need to enact their power. That is, we need to take responsibility for making changes that can create a more cooperative, satisfying, and socially just world. It will not happen without us.

## Trust

Cooperative relationships, as we have seen, require deliberate effort, but deliberate effort towards what? Research from fields as diverse as conflict resolution and game theory suggest that a key focus needs to be *trust*.[45] Fisher and colleagues write, 'If we could find ways to trust each other, we could then find win–win solutions to many of our most serious problems.'[46] Trust can be defined as the willingness to rely on the other's actions, to forgo attempts to control them.[47]

At the intrapersonal level, therapists are well aware of the importance of trust for positive change. A client comes to therapy, for instance, hating their vulnerable part: the fact that they cry so easily, feel wounded so much of the time. They want to get rid of that part of themselves, throw it away. Through exploration in therapy, however, they come to recognise that that vulnerability comes from painful experiences of rejection in childhood, and that actually it is intelligible and has a right to be there. More than that, they can see that that vulnerability is striving to protect them: a warning signal to try and ensure that they are not hurt so deeply again. Now, slowly, the client comes to trust, respect, and ultimately integrate that vulnerable part. Rather than perceiving it as a source of disturbance, they begin to trust its capacity to guide them in life. As Richard Schwartz, founder of the Internal Family Systems model of therapy puts it, there are 'No bad parts'[48]—just as there are no 'bad' highest-order directions (Chapter 3, this volume). Rather, 'all our parts have valuable qualities and resources to give us'.[49]

At the dyadic level, too, trust would seem a 'crucial requirement for viable, close relationships'[50] – or between communities or nations. If a nation, for instance, does not trust another nation, it becomes so much more difficult to work towards cooperative solutions. Any form of communication or engagement is likely to break down.

Trust, of course, is not something that one side can do alone: it is a fundamentally inter-active process. Community A, for instance, lets go a little, and relies a little more, on the actions of Community B; Community B does no harm, and lets go some control to Community A; Community A feels more trusting to Community B, and so lets go, and relies on its actions a little more; and so on. The development of trust and synergies, in this respect, is like the building of an arch bridge: you have to, carefully, build both sides together – until there is a keystone that can hold the whole structure in place.[51] Nevertheless, even in such a delicate, interactive process, someone has to make the first move: so this comes back to the issue of taking responsibility and leadership.

Despite all its risks, a strategy of trusting the other – of building cooperative solutions – holds the promise for the greatest success. Famously, in the original round robin tournament of the prisoner's dilemma game, the overall winner was a strategy called TIT FOR TAT. This was one of the simplest strategies, and consisted of 'cooperating on the first move and then doing whatever the other player did on the previous move'.[52] So TIT FOR TAT started from a position of 'trust': its default position was goodwill towards the other and, provided that the other cooperated, TIT FOR TAT would also cooperate. TIT FOR TAT was not gullible – if the other player started to defect then TIT FOR TAT would defect too – but TIT FOR TAT would quickly get back on track with a position of 'trust' (that is, cooperation) if the other player started to act, again, in more cooperative ways.

What is interesting here, then, is that TIT FOR TAT also had the quality of 'forgiveness'. It did not bear grudges: if the other party returned to cooperative behaviours, TIT FOR TAT did so too. Indeed, under conditions in which players may be more prone to miscommunication and error, a strategy of 'two tits for a tat' (that is, only defecting if the other player defects twice) seemed most profitable overall. In addition, TIT FOR TAT was not 'envious', in the sense that it did not act 'nasty' if it was defeated by other particular strategies. In fact, remarkably, TIT FOR TAT never once scored better in a single round than its 'opponent'. So 'it won the round robin tournament, not by beating the other player, but by eliciting behaviour from the other player which allowed both to do well'.[53] Hence, overall, it scored highest. This is a fascinating finding because it supports the view that, even if acting cooperatively does not bring about the greatest immediate benefit, it is a way of maximising benefit to ourselves (as well as to others) in the longer term.

The capacity to extend trust to the other is closely linked to our willingness to radically accept them (Chapter 1). As discussed earlier, this does not mean tolerating or accepting whatever the other does; but it does mean holding that, ultimately, they are not 'bad' people: that their highest-order needs and wants are probably similar to our own. If we believe that the other, at the most fundamental level, is out to destroy us, it is unlikely that there is any way we can ever trust them. If, on the other hand, we believe that they can get what they most fundamentally need and want in ways that do not harm us, we are much more likely to believe that cooperative solutions are possible.

An openness to trusting the other, then, means moving beyond blame. Blame is where we attribute problems to someone's negative characteristics: for instance, 'She made that joke because she's an anti-Semitic a********,' 'He voted Tory because he's a selfish git.' Moving beyond blame does not mean that we cannot still challenge someone if they hurt us or act in oppressive or immoral ways, but it does mean refraining from judging the person as a whole. Within couples counselling, blame (or 'criticism'), is considered one of the 'Four Horseman of the Apocalypse'.[54] Another closely related 'Horseman' is *contempt* – an even more corrosive form of blame – which can be manifest as name-calling, put-downs, sarcasm, or mockery. Criticism and contempt are attempts at getting what we need and want from a relationship, and may have some short-term payoffs in terms of relief; but the research shows that they do not work in the long term. Why? Because, as with other conflictual strategies, they ignore the agency and subjectivity of the other: they imagine the other will just absorb our blame, rather than responding in kind. Yet, as the Gottmans write: 'Only someone like the Dalai Lama, who meditates hours a day, can calmly respond to words like "slob" or "What's the matter with you?" And he's not married.'[55] So we may think, for instance, that criticising a partner for being 'selfish' or 'lazy' is going to change them; but actually it is more likely to trigger a defensive response or a counter-attack. It is, again, playing a non-zero-sum game as if it were zero-sum. Moreover, it is unlikely to be productive because it gives the other person little guidance on what to do differently – they cannot just change 'as a person' and be, for instance, less 'arsehole-y'. Hence, while couples therapists may try to help clients express their 'complaints' to each other – what they do not like about the other's behaviour – they are likely to encourage them to do this from a place of trust.[56]

This stance, of valuing the other while challenging their behaviour, is advocated in many other forms of negotiation and interpersonal skills, including nonviolent communication (see Chapter 7, this volume).[57] Fisher and colleagues, for instance, suggest that you should give 'positive support to the human beings on the other side equal in strength to the vigor with which you emphasize the problem'.[58] Here, as with mentalising, the emphasis is on looking for the interests behind the other person's position rather than simply blaming them for holding a particular stance or acting in a particular way.

In creating cooperative solutions, then, we need to trust – and, as progressives, we may have a role and a responsibility to lead on that. Right-wing ideologies, like populism and conservatism, are founded in very low levels of trust: 'Everyone is out for themselves so you need to be too.'[59] But progressivism believes in people and people's potentialities: that is, people's ultimate trustworthiness. Nevertheless, leading on trust – particularly, for instance, when we are engaging with our political 'opponents' – is challenging. It is *really* challenging, because it makes us emotional vulnerable; it opens us up to being hurt, manipulated, and ignored. Here, the temptation may always be to fall back onto a safer, more sceptical position – and, as stated earlier, we do need to be cautious not just to leap, with both feet, into an all-trusting stance. But if we, as progressives, cannot lead on trust, who will? In Chapter 7 (this volume), I discuss in more detail what a politics of trust might look like.

## Be nice

As with TIT FOR TAT, in the prisoner's dilemma round robin tournaments there was, 'a single property which distinguishes the relatively high-scoring entries from the relatively low-scoring entries. This is the property of being *nice*, which is to say never being the first to defect'.[60] Being nice meant avoiding unnecessary conflict for as long as the other does. Axelrod goes on to report that each of the eight top-ranking strategies were nice, and that they did particularly well when playing against other nice strategies. In other words, two nice strategies – cooperatively relating to each other – can gain enough benefit between themselves to make up for more mixed encounters with 'nasty' strategies. Moreover, once in the majority, nice strategies are relatively 'stable': in the sense that they continue to do well in a round robin tournament even if a few nasty strategies 'invade'. This is because, although the nasty strategies may win out in single bouts against the nice strategies, their combined scores are much lower than in nice–nice matches. Interestingly, however, the reverse is not true: that is, just a small number of nice strategies can invade the nasty strategies and start to 'take over'. In other words, although cooperative approaches may be difficult to establish, they also have a certain hardiness. Like weeds pushing up through concrete, 'cooperation can emerge even in a world of unconditional defection'.[61]

Being nice means being kind and generous to the other. It involves recognising the other as a subjective, agentic being. It does not do *to* the other. Rather, as with Buber's I–Thou stance, it strives to stand alongside the other and support them in the realisation of their own needs and wants. Niceness is also more than just accepting or tolerating the other, but positively prizing them and sharing with them positive feedback: helping to create a more general culture of positive regard.[62]

At the intrapersonal level, niceness towards self – in such forms as self-acceptance, self-compassion, and positive self-regard – is a key goal of many therapeutic approaches.[63] These therapies recognise the destructive effects of 'nasty' inner voices (for example, self-criticism, low self-esteem, and shame); and help clients find more positive and prizing ways of relating to themselves. At interpersonal levels, too, kindness, warmth, and respect towards the other would seem a key foundation for collaborative working.[64] For instance, in couples therapy, clients are encouraged to raise problems with each other through 'positive start ups' rather than the harsh ones that are associated with more problematic relationships.[65] And, at an international level, conflict resolution work aims to have both parties 'realize their shared humanity, that is, "humanize the enemy"'.[66]

Why is niceness important at all these levels? Perhaps because acting nicely towards another makes that other feel less threatened, and therefore more trusting to open up. If the other is nasty to us, then how can we trust them to behave in collaborative ways? As the research shows, friendly behaviours to others elicits complementary, friendly responses.[67] So by being nice to the other we are more likely to elicit responses in them which then make us feel more trusting and willing to cooperate. Niceness fuels niceness in a virtuous cycle, just as nastiness can fuel a downward spiral of fear and mistrust.

It is not only, however, that niceness lays the basis for cooperative relating; it is also, perhaps, the quintessentially synergetic act, in itself. This is because it is not just the 'recipient' of niceness that benefits. Rather, niceness – as caring, compassion, and reaching out to the other – is also, in many instances, rewarding for the 'giver', as a means towards the higher-order direction of relatedness.[68] Communal goals – like volunteering work and political activity – can be deeply satisfying to people.[69] Consistent with this, research suggests that there is a 'positive relationship between volunteering and subjective well-being, and altruistic behaviour promotes subjective well-being'.[70] Indeed, as stated earlier, giving to the community was identified as one of five key ways to psychological health and wellbeing.[71] In Chapter 8 (this volume), this synergetic quality of relatedness will be of particular importance when we consider the characteristics of a more thriving society.

For progressives, the principle of niceness provides a valuable description of where our politics may, most effectively, start from. It is a means of welcoming the other, of opening out, of inviting – and offering – cooperative working towards a better, more inclusive system. Niceness, without doubt, has the risk of seguing in to naivety and passivity; but in combination with such principles as 'be assertive', 'take responsibility', and 'see the "bigger picture"', provides a powerful and compelling basis for a contemporary progressivism. This is both in terms of how we act politically (see Chapter 7, this volume), and also in our broader relationship towards the world. Win–win relationships, writes Covey, require both consideration and courage, niceness and toughness.[72] With such an integrated stance, progressivism can move beyond the black-and-white dichotomies of 'strong versus weak' or 'controlling versus controlled' to something that is more genuinely constructive and beneficial to our world.

## Prize diversity and difference

'Let a hundred flowers blossom, let a hundred schools of thought contend.'[73] Prizing diversity and difference is, in many respects, an extension of being nice: valuing the other whatever their otherness. This prizing is essential in allowing cooperative relationships to flourish: if we cannot acknowledge and embrace the other, then it is not going to be possible to find synergetic solutions with them. 'Valuing the differences is the essence of synergy',[74] states Covey; and he goes on to write: 'The person who is truly effective has the humility and reverence to recognize his own perceptual limitations and to appreciate the rich resources available through interactions with the hearts and minds of other human beings.'[75]

The importance and value of prizing difference and diversity is clearly evident in the therapeutic field. A therapist's work is to hear – and provide space for – all the different parts of a client's being: for instance, their shame, their anger, their feelings of hope and possibility.

Therapeutically, we know, as suggested earlier in this chapter, that the repressed return. As Schwarz puts it, 'We often find that the harder we try to get rid of emotions and thoughts, the stronger they become. This is because parts, like people, fight back against being shamed or exiled'.[76] If a person's anger, for instance, is not acknowledged, it shouts louder, demanding 'repatriation'. This, then, can create conflict, anxiety, and feelings of helplessness: 'I am really not an angry person', for instance, 'But at some level I know that I am.' Why do those unwanted voices not just go away? Because, whether at the psychological or interpersonal levels, they are an intelligible, legitimate expression of needs and wants. We see exactly the same thing at a societal level: our marginalised communities – be they disabled, ethnic minorities, or other – cannot just 'disappear' (however much reactionary forces might want them to), and neither can their needs and wants.[77] Suppression, whether internal or external, may 'work' temporarily (for the oppressive group), but ultimately it is doomed to fail.

A prizing of diversity and difference, however, also contributes to wellbeing because it provides opportunities for the 'prizer', themselves, to develop and grow. Through encountering different cultures, different types of people, different ways of being, they all discover different means towards their ends. Indeed, if growth is considered a highest-order need or want (Chapter 3), then the encountering of diversity has the potential to bring with it intense benefit. As with being nice, then, prizing diversity is a quintessentially synergistic act, because it gives to the 'doer' as well as the 'receiver'.

As a counterpoint to this argument, it might be suggested that human beings also have a basic tendency to fear the diverse and different: that, as human beings, we also have a desire for the familiar and known. This might be understood as an expression of our highest-order need for safety (Chapter 3). Yet, as the research shows, an attitude of openness and embracing towards things (an *approach* stance) tends to be associated with greater thriving than an attitude of fear and pushing things away (an *avoidance* stance).[78] Why is that? First and most basically, when we try and push something away, it tends to get scarier. This is the basic principle behind some of the most successful and widely used treatments for anxiety: if you want to get over anxieties, you need to encounter the thing you are afraid of, rather than persist in trying to avoid it.[79] Second, if you are focused on avoiding things, there is no real way of knowing when you have got there. You can never be certain, for instance, that you have, entirely, cocooned yourself off from difference ('Perhaps the next neighbours will be Jews', 'Perhaps they will be my children's teachers'); whereas if you are seeking out difference, you can know – and celebrate – when you have achieved it. Third, and along similar lines, the mean of avoiding something is often much less clear than the means of approaching something. If someone thinks, for instance, 'I want to keep away from Jews', it is not easy to see how they could ensure that will happen. And such a goal is so much more difficult to accomplish than one that involves learning about, and engaging with, the Jewish community. Fourth, the achievement of something positive can give one a sense of pride and buoyancy, whereas the avoidance of something 'negative' only gives a vague and diffuse sense of relief from fear. Finally, trying to avoid things is inherently problematic because it requires us to call to mind the thing we want to avoid: the antisemite, for instance, who hates Jews, is constantly having them in their mind's eye. Hence, for all these reasons—and simply at the level of individual wellbeing—an attitude of embracing difference and diversity tends to do more good for people than an attitude of rejecting it.

A progressive valuing of difference and diversity, then, is not only justified on an ethical basis: it is a system-wide principle for how 'better' can come about. When we are inclusive and accepting of otherness – approach- rather than avoidance-oriented – we do not just support that other, but create a more thriving society that has more to offer for us all. This principle is already at the heart of progressivism and is one that, I hope to show, can form a key lynchpin for envisioning a progressive utopia (Chapters 8 and 9).

## Be assertive

Cooperative functioning require us to see beyond our own, immediate needs and wants and to take into account the directions of an other. At the same time, however, to neglect or sacrifice our own needs and wants to a 'greater good' – 'lose–win' outcomes – is not to create cooperative solutions: our needs and wants, or those of our families and communities, are also part of the larger whole. So the development of synergies requires us to be able to clearly and consistently articulate, and make a case for, our own directions. This is what is meant by *assertiveness*: to be able to calmly, non-aggressively, and non-manipulatively state our own needs and wants, and to hold them as of equal value to others.[80] This is not only what we think we need and want at a cognitive level, but also to 'gut check': to sense, in our bodies, what feels right or wrong for us and to express that.[81] An assertive communication style is typically contrasted against communication styles that are *aggressive* (attacking, blaming, and controlling), *passive* (indirect, inhibited, and apologetic), and *passive-aggressive* (indirect, dishonest, and implicitly conveying anger and blame).

As therapists, much of our work often boils down to helping clients develop their assertiveness. And, indeed, research suggests that this may be the most common goal of clients.[82] Furthermore, there is good evidence for the value of assertiveness training.[83] Ibrahim, for instance, is a client struggling with his marriage: he is frustrated at the lack of contact and engagement he has with his husband, James. James works, sleeps, wants to have sex. Ibrahim wants to talk and do things together: go for walks and plan holidays. By session 4 there's an obvious question brewing. 'Ibrahim, have you talked to James about this at all?' Ibrahim says 'No, not really.' He has hinted at it, hoped that James can see it. But he is worried that, if he raises it directly with James, James will have one of his 'reactions' and push Ibrahim away for good. And so Ibrahim and I talk more about his fears and where they may come from. Ibrahim describes how his father was 'awful' at hearing feedback, how Ibrahim found it so difficult to say anything to his parents. Ibrahim also describes how recognising his gay sexuality at a young age meant that he felt he had to hide himself away. And Ibrahim starts to realise how, in so many other areas of his life, like work, he desperately tries to avoid conflict rather than expressing his own needs and wants. Then we start to think about ways that Ibrahim, perhaps, could address things more directly with James. We talk through different options, try out different opening lines – for instance, 'James, can we talk about some stuff?' – role-play how the conversation might go. Then it is time for Ibrahim to actually try being assertive – with James, and then with others – and we use the therapy to reflect on how it has gone and how Ibrahim can improve these skills further. By the end of the work together, Ibrahim still hates conflict, would still much rather avoid saying what he wants. But he has learnt that he can be assertive, and that his fears of how others will respond are somewhat unfounded. They, like James, are a lot more receptive than he imagines; and by actually, explicitly stating what he needs and wants, he now feels much more enabled to get there.

This principle of assertiveness holds at the intrapersonal level of organisation as well as at interpersonal ones. In the example of two-chair work, for instance, it is when a vulnerable part of the person expresses its experiences and needs to the critical part – 'the more you shout at me, the worse I feel', 'I want you to give me a break sometimes' – that a more cooperative solution 'within' the person can be found.

When needs and wants are assertively expressed, two things happen that make cooperative solutions more likely. First, the other comes to see more clearly what our directions are. This is critical for cooperative outcomes: if we do not say what we want, the other side is unlikely to be able to get there.[84] It is easy to assume that people know what we need and want but, in reality, others may be relatively unaware of it. Ibrahim, for instance, reported that James was genuinely surprised to learn that Ibrahim felt lonely in the relationship and wanted more time together. 'I knew you were annoyed with me', said James to Ibrahim, 'But I thought it was because you felt I wasn't pulling my weight in terms of income.' James, in fact, loves the idea of planning more holidays together, and he is delighted to know that Ibrahim wants that too. So by simply communicating our needs and wants to another, we increase the possibility of finding solutions in which they will be met.

Second, and even if cooperative solutions are not easy to come by, assertively expressing our needs and wants puts them 'into the mix' and means that we cannot be simply sidelined or ignored. It means that we stand up for ourselves, and say that our needs and wants (whether at an intra- or interpersonal level) are important and need to be respected. This, in a sense, is the 'TAT' in the TIT FOR TAT. This winning strategy was not simply gullible or a pushover – it differed from a 'consistently cooperate' strategy that could be easily exploited by another. Drawing these kinds of 'lines in the sand' is important in many different forms of intra- and interpersonal work. For instance, in couples therapy, it is essential to make clear that certain behaviours, like domestic violence or abuse, cannot be tolerated and need immediate action.[85] Equally, we know, at the international level, that appeasing a destructive force is not the route to good outcomes – as the Munich agreement of 1938 so clearly showed.[86] So a successful strategy needs to say something like, 'I want to be nice, I want to cooperate, but if you try and exploit me then you will not get what you want either.' Effectively, it brings to the attention of the other that their rogue goals are, indeed, rogue; and, ideally, it does this as clearly as possible. In TIT FOR TAT's case, this was by switching to defection immediately after it was defected against, and then cooperating again as soon as the other strategy cooperated back. Here, there was no room for ambiguity – its message was crystal clear: 'cooperate and we can work together, act selfishly and you will suffer too'.

For progressives, this question of how we can stand up to oppressive forces is a critical one. When we look around the world – at, for instance, the Putins, the Bolsonaros, and the Trumps – it is clear that principles such as 'trust' and 'be nice', in themselves, are not enough. As Mason writes, 'Living the antifascist life involves putting your body in a place where it can actually stop fascism':[87] progressives need to do all they can to create 'liberated spaces' in which all needs and wants – and not just those of a dominating group – can be realised. Assertiveness, however, is a means that progressives can do this without falling back into the same old politics of blame: reseeding the grounds for resentment, division, and lose–lose outcomes. Assertiveness is a means by which progressives can say 'no' to oppression while also saying 'yes' to the humanity of the other and the possibility of creating cooperative solutions. It is, as West puts it, 'to speak the truth to power with love'.[88] We will explore this dual stance further, and more concretely, when we discuss nonviolent communication in Chapter 7 (this volume).

## Communicate

Across levels of organisation, perhaps the most obvious and important ingredient in the development of cooperative solutions – underpinning, and drawing together, many of the principles already discussed – is communication. Game theory research shows that cooperative choices can be as much as doubled when players are allowed to talk to each other, while misunderstandings increase the levels of defections.[89] Encouraging different agencies, within the person, to communicate with each other is also the basic principle behind most therapies; as it is to couples counselling, mediation, negotiation, and international conflict resolution on the interpersonal plane.[90] 'The way out of conflict', states *The mediator's handbook*, 'is through dialogue, which means talking and listening directly to each other'.[91] Similarly, Williams writes, 'if people could just talk to one another properly, any problem could be solved'.[92] Sometimes, even compelling different parties to communicate may be necessary as a means towards resolving conflicts.[93]

### *Understanding the needs and wants of the other*

So why is communication so critical to the development of cooperative solutions? A first reason, touched on in the previous section, is that it is often essential in helping different agencies to understand what the other actually needs and wants. As we have seen, our 'intuitive' sense of an other's directions is often wrong – and this is no surprise given how common misunderstanding and miscommunication are. Between mothers and infants, for instance, typically one of the strongest bonds, research found that miscommunication occurs about 70 per cent of the time.[94] Here, a 'good' relationship is not so much characterised by getting communication right as the capacity to 'repair' breakdowns in the communication process. The assumption that others know what we are thinking and feeling (and therefore that we do not need to explicitly communicate it) is called the 'myth of mind-reading' or the 'myth of self-transparency', and has been associated with a wide range of psychological and interpersonal problems.[95] If we assume others know what our needs and wants are, then it can end up feeling like they are deliberately trying to obstruct us if we are not getting what we strive for. We can then respond with anger; and if the other also assumes we know what they need and want (which, most likely, includes 'not being faced with anger'), they can respond in kind, creating a vicious, downward spiral.

We may also make the mistake of deducing the other's *intention* from the *effects* that their actions are having. If a person's behaviour makes us feel upset or powerless, for instance, it can be very difficult not to feel that this was their intention to do so. But the reality is that the effects that a person's behaviour may have may be very different from the intention behind it. For instance, Person A might feel vulnerable when their partner, Person B, goes out for the evening with friends: 'Why don't they want me with them?' 'What if they meet someone they are attracted to?' And, on this basis, they might feel angry with Person B: 'Why would they want to hurt me?' But, for Person B, the reason for going out may be entirely different: 'I just want to be able to focus on my best friends some evenings and do things they and I enjoy.'

Miscommunication, in essence, leads to waste: surplus repression. It means we end up acting in ways where there is less overall benefit in a situation than there needs to be. Conversely, communication can help both parties understand what the other, genuinely, needs and wants, and therefore be most enabled to find cooperative ways forward. If the two partners introduced in the previous paragraph, Person A and Person B, never share their actual needs and wants with each other, Person A may simply go on feeling hurt that Person B is 'deliberately' rejecting them, and Person B, likewise, may go on feeling frustrated, controlled, or misunderstood by Person A. But if Person A can say something like, 'It makes me feel scared when you go out, and I really want to know that you love me,' and Person B can say something like, 'I really want to spend time with my friends, AND I really do love you,' then cooperative ways forward become much more possible. That is why, whether in couples counselling, mediation, or international problem-solving workshops, agencies are encouraged to explicitly and specifically tell the other what they need and want rather than relying on mind-reading, 'intuition', or inferring intents from effects.[96] And the hope is that people can express their needs and wants at the highest possible order: so not just the manifest preferences, but what it is that most fundamentally, truly matters to them. Couples counsellor Marina Williams tells her clients, 'You can't expect people to fulfil your needs unless you express them clearly.'[97] Indeed, in practices like mediation and conflict resolution, the other party is often encouraged to reflect back their understanding of what those needs and wants are, just to make sure they have really clearly been understood.[98]

### *Finding cooperative solutions*

So communication helps each party understand what the other genuinely needs and wants, and then it allows them, together, to develop more mutually beneficial cooperative solutions. This, as discussed in Chapter 5, is generally the pattern recommended across a range of contexts: first, let people express their higher-order needs and wants, then, when they have done so, start to look at how these can be brought together.[99] Through the free flow and exchange of information, people can work creatively together to generate synergetic solutions, with a minimum of waste.[100] This is something that can also be seen on the intrapersonal plane: for instance, in two-chair work in therapy. Such a dialogue may go something like this:

| | |
|---|---|
| Critical Part: | You are just so weak, pathetic, you get hurt so easily. I want you to 'man up' and be strong. |
| Vulnerable Part: | I can't. I can't control it. I just get hurt and I want to cry. |
| Critical Part: | Shut up! You're pathetic! |
| Vulnerable Part: | [Cries]. I … you're always picking on me, always telling me I'm no good. |
| Critical Part: | I want you to be stronger. I want you to be strong. I'm ashamed of you. |
| Vulnerable Part: | [Cries]. And the more you shout at me, the worse I feel. |
| Critical Part: | [Pauses]. So what do you want? |
| Vulnerable Part: | I want you to give me a break sometimes. I want you to … just talk to me in a different tone. I'm trying. |
| Critical Part: | Not shouting so much …? |
| Vulnerable Part: | Not shouting, not blaming. |
| Critical Part: | But I need to say when I feel this is too much. When I feel like you just need to get on with it. |
| Vulnerable Part: | Yes, I can see sometimes I can dominate as well. I guess I also need to let go. |

What we see here is that, as these two parts talk together, they start to state their higher-order wants and needs. And, as they do so, they can begin to find mutually beneficial – rather than mutually destructive – ways of relating. If the critical part can talk to the vulnerable part in a less attacking, less blaming way, then the vulnerable part may feel less frightened, and may feel able to respond to the critical part in a way that actually gives the latter more of what it needs and wants.

### *Humanising the other*

Communication can also be invaluable to the development of cooperative solutions because, as agencies start to talk to each other, so they start to get a more humanised sense of the other – and that can be essential in developing trust.[101] When one agency listens to the other, and particularly their higher-order needs and wants, they can begin to sense that the other is like themselves; and not the malevolent, destructive force that they may have built them up to in their minds. Equally, if agencies feel listened to by the other, then they can begin to feel more trusting because they have a sense that the other is genuinely interested in their welfare. This can also help them feel more in control of the situation, and therefore more willing to let go and allow the other to act in their own way. Communication, then, can break down pathological suspicion: through talking personally to the other, agencies are reminded, quite literally, that the other has a human face.

### *Genuine dialogue*

Communication, however, is only going to be as useful in the development of cooperative solutions as the quality of the communication taking place. If agencies, for instance, start being defensive and/or stonewalling the other (the other two 'horsemen' of intimate relationships[102]), then 'communication' can lead to less trust rather than more. That is why, in practices like couples counselling and mediation, it is not enough just to encourage people to talk to each other, but also to teach them good communication skills.[103]

We will explore the specifics of effective communication in Chapter 7 on nonviolent communication. However, the essence of it can be described as *genuine dialogue*.[104] This is not a mechanistic set of rules for how people should talk; but a philosophically informed understanding of what it means for two people to be 'present' to each other – an authentic 'turning towards' the other with interest and concern.[105] Genuine dialogue is characterised by participants being both *receptive* and *expressive* to the other. Receptivity means 'taking in' the other. This is a listening, attentiveness, or curiosity: a putting to one side of assumptions and preconceptions and an openness to the other as something new, different, and unknown.[106] Receptivity means actually listening to the other when they are talking, and not simply planning what we are going to say next.[107] Expressivity, on the other hand, is a willingness to be genuine and transparent in the encounter. It is a commitment to sharing *all* of oneself, including those aspects that might be more withheld in everyday life, such as one's vulnerabilities, hidden qualities, or implicit experiences, the 'wordless depths'.[108] Genuine dialogue is facilitative of cooperative solutions because, by definition, it means both agencies are expressing their deepest, most fundamental needs and wants, and 'taking in' those of the other. It means that they can then work, carefully and thoughtfully, towards mutually beneficial solutions, in an atmosphere of trust and respect. By expressing their genuine humanness – including their vulnerabilities, weaknesses, and anxieties – it can help both parties feel less threatened by the other.[109]

### *Written agreements*

Perhaps the most concrete, explicit, and formalised mode of communication between parties is the development of written agreements, in the form of contracts, joint action plans, or peace agreements. This is common across couples counselling, mediation, and international conflict resolution – as well as more legalistic proceedings – as a means of trying to establish, and ensure the sustainability of, cooperative solutions.[110] At the international level, formal peace agreements, such as the Camp David agreement between Israel and Egypt in 1979, have stood the test of time. They are an integral part of the conflict resolution process and may play a significant part in consolidating and sustaining peace. The development of written agreement between agencies may go through many iterations: from an initial draft, early on in negotiations, to a finalised contract. As such, the process of developing an agreement may be as important as its final content.

There are a number of reasons why establishing a written agreement may support the emergence, and maintenance, of cooperative solutions.[111] First, as discussed, simply the process of working on a written agreement together can encourage agencies to focus on the specific, concrete details of what a cooperative solution might look like: giving 'definition and direction' to win–win outcomes.[112] Second, formal, written agreements make it more likely that everyone understands – explicitly, unambiguously, and in detail – what has been agreed. Third, they reinforce the seriousness of the agreement, and the commitment required to maintain the agreed actions. Fourth, written agreements, once 'in print', serve to remind everyone of what they have signed up to. Fifth, written agreements provide the agencies with tangible evidence that they have achieved something, thus enhancing feelings of self-efficacy and the confidence required to sustain the agreed actions. Against this, it could be argued that written agreements focus too much on the 'letter' of what is to be done, rather than the deeper sentiment and meaning. There is also the danger that they can impose a set of behaviours on both agencies that can feel restrictive. But it is rarely the case that, without written agreements, there are no 'rules'. Rather, the rules are often implicit, and imposed by whoever has the power to do so.[113] Hence, explicitly discussing and agreeing the rules can support a process of democratisation: ensuring that expected standards are transparent and challengeable by all.

### *When communicating makes things worse*

Communication is one powerful means of developing greater wellbeing for systems as wholes. But it is not the only answer, and it is not always appropriate. Eddo-Lodge, for instance, puts forward a powerful and compelling argument for why she, as a Black woman, no longer wants to talk to White people about race.[114] This on the grounds of self-preservation: that trying to explain to White people what it means to be Black is too draining, exhausting, and does not lead to sufficient levels of change. In some instances, it may also be that engagement in communication allows an oppressive agency to justify the continuance of disempowering and domineering acts, on the basis that they are 'trying to talk'.

In situations such as these – where communication serves to maintain oppressive and inequitable structures – it may be that withdrawal from communication is more appropriate than communication. However, this is not inconsistent with the present framework. At any level, wellbeing requires the flourishing of all different parts of a system. Ideally, these are in cooperative relationships with each other. However, if communication undermines the flourishing of any one part, it may be that the overall system is better off with its termination. In these instances, what is needed, rather, is for the more powerful and privileged parts to find ways – between and within themselves – to create more opportunities for those that are marginalised. Racism, for instance, writes Eddo-Lodge, is a 'white problem. … It is a problem in the psyche of whiteness that white people must take responsibility to solve.'[115]

At the same time, it is important to note that, when 'communication' is making things worse, it may be because the kind of communication being carried out is not 'genuine dialogue', as defined earlier in this section. Where White people, for instance, respond to Black people with such dismissive comments as 'Well, we're all different colours', or 'Some of my best friends are Black …', it indicates that there is not a genuine receptivity to Black people's experiences of marginalisation. If White people are genuinely listening to the pain, suffering, and humiliation that centuries of oppression have caused to Black people – and making changes accordingly – it may be that Black people would feel less of a need to withdraw from communication. For White people, as I know in my own experience, it can be painful and shaming to be reminded of White privilege: 'a manipulative, suffocating blanket of power that envelops everything we know, like a snowy day'.[116] And it can be tempting to respond with defensiveness or attempts at distraction: 'white victimhood'.[117] But genuine dialogue, as with the capacity to mentalise, requires us to stand back from those urges and listen to the genuine experiences of others, however much we are implicated in that. For White people, holding in mind that we are not 'malicious monsters driven by ill will'[118] can, I think, reduce a desire to respond defensively; but that needs combining with a willingness to take responsibility for change (see 'Take responsibility', this chapter). Such allyship to Black people can include, for instance, standing up against conscious and unconscious racism in other White people, and contributing financially to Black organisations with a social justice mission.

### *Discussion*

Communication, in most instances, is a key element in the development of cooperative relationships and outcomes. This makes it, therefore, an essential question for progressives: How do we talk to other people, both in political and personal life? In this section, I have suggested that a genuinely dialogic stance is at the heart of a psychology-informed progressivism: a willingness to listen, engage, and establish mutually agreeable solutions with an other. From this perspective, this is not just a corollary to progressivism, but at the very essence of what it means to be in the world in a progressive way. In Chapter 7, the application of this willingness to communicate, and this mode of communication, will be developed further.

## Be fair

The relationship between maximising wellbeing, and its fair distribution, is a complex one, but a critical consideration for progressives. On the one hand, where the bottom 60 per cent of the world's population (approximately 4,250 million people) hold the same wealth as the 1,226 richest billionaires,[119] it seems manifest that greater inequality is associated with less overall wellbeing. But what if, for instance, 99 per cent of the world could fulfil their needs and wants on the basis that the remaining 1 per cent had to endure intense suffering? Here, extreme inequality could, theoretically, be associated with greater overall benefit. This issue is at the heart of debates between radical and more liberal progressive perspectives, with the former placing greater emphasis than the latter on the need for absolute equality across people.

### *Equality: lowering overall good*

In terms of the present framework, there are almost certainly ways in which an emphasis on equality – under certain conditions – could lead to a reduction in overall wellbeing. If people in a society, for instance, felt that 'success' was impossible – that is, that there was no way for them to progress, develop, or achieve something better – then the wellbeing that comes from realising directions might be fundamentally undermined. As argued in Chapter 3, human beings need and want something to aim for, to feel like we are progressing, and to have a sense of achievement. So if a society required us all to be at exactly the same level, in every area of our lives, a key source of wellbeing would be denied. Such as enforced equality would also lower overall benefit by reducing people's capacity to realise such fundamental desires as for autonomy and significance, as well as for uniqueness. As the American political theorist Michael Walzer writes, while we may 'dream of a society where all the members are equally honored and respected … we know that we cannot refuse to recognize – indeed, we want to be able to recognize – the many different sorts and degrees of skill, strength, wisdom, courage, kindness, energy, and grace that distinguish one individual from another'.[120]

Closely related to this, an enforced equality may be problematic because, to some extent, our sense of ourselves and our achievements tends to be in relation to others.[121] This means that, to realise our feelings of self-worth, it may not simply be enough to have, for instance, a large social network or a large house – it may be that it needs to be *larger* than others. This, I know, is a controversial proposition in a book for progressives. We want to emphasise cooperation over competition: so the idea that wellbeing may come from feelings of being 'better' than others is somewhat distasteful. From a progressive perspective, it is also objectionable because supporting some people to be 'better' will, inevitably, mean that others are 'worse'. Of course, the suggestion here is not that being 'better' is the only way to feel good: to a large extent, having friends or somewhere to live may be rewarding in their own right. However, when it comes to such fundamental needs as for self-worth or significance, it may be that there is an unavoidably comparative component. Acknowledging this, rather than denying it, may help us think about how to support these needs in ways that are least damaging to communities and society as a whole (see Chapters 8 and 9, this volume).

### *Equality: increasing overall good*

There are ways, then, in which equality, potentially, could reduce overall good; but there are many more ways in which it is likely to enhance it. *The spirit level*, a bestselling book by British academics Richard Wilkinson and Kate Pickett, presents compelling evidence that equality is not only better for the disadvantaged members of society, but for everyone.[122] Societies with the greatest *income inequality* – that is, the gap between its richest and poorest members (like the US and the UK) – have the greatest physical health problems, mental health problems, and social problems, like violence. Wilkinson and Pickett write: 'The evidence shows that reducing inequality is the best way of improving the quality of the social environment, and so the real quality of life, for us all.'[123]

So why might greater fairness lead to greater overall good? In part, it may be because, as the research shows, inequality reduces trust, which is essential for the development of cooperative solutions (see 'Trust', this chapter).[124] To some extent, this may be because, through the creation of subgroups within a society (for instance, by class, gender, or race), 'in-group' and 'out-group' dynamics are likely to form. It may also be because those that are disadvantaged will feel that the advantaged members of society have got something 'over' on them, while the advantaged members of society may feel that the disadvantaged members are trying to 'take' something from them.

In these respects, greater inequality can also create greater overall stress; compounded by the fact that the disadvantaged are likely to feel hopeless, envious, shamed, and out of control; while the advantaged may feel under threat: desperately trying to protect the resources and social status they do have. Closely related to this, if members of a society sense that they can 'end up in the gutter' at any point – rather than, for instance, feeling that they will be buoyed by a welfare state – then their feelings of safety may be dramatically eroded. Granted, a more unequal society may also give people greater 'highs' to aspire to but, as we know from the psychological research, as human beings we tend to be more sensitised to losses than gains.[125] That is, our fears of failure occupy our minds more than our hopes for success.

In addition, if some members of society feel disadvantaged by others, then their focus is likely to be on their own, individual goals and aspirations, rather than those for the group as a whole. In essence, we might liken this to a game of prisoner's dilemma in which one party – the privileged – has already started off by defecting. The natural move of the disadvantaged, then, may be to defect too, with a consequent spiralling down into conflict. This, then, is likely to create stress for everyone, both 'winners' and 'losers'.

Inequalities may also lower overall wellbeing, because 'most of us share a desire to live in a society where fairness is the operative norm'.[126] G.A. Cohen, in *Why not socialism?*, uses the examples of friends going together on a camping trip. Surely most people, he argues, would want – and expect – cooperation, community, and sharing, rather than each person vigorously asserting their rights over their own equipment and activities. 'You could imagine a camping trip', he writes,

> where bargaining proceeds with respect to who is going to pay what to whom to be allowed, for example, to use a knife to peel the potatoes, and how much he is going to charge others for those now-peeled potatoes that he bought in an unpeeled condition from another camper.[127]

But, Cohen goes on to state, 'most people would hate that'. Developing the analogy, he writes that most people would find it ridiculous if someone kept, to themselves, the rewards from a particular innate skill, like the ability to crack nuts. Equally ridiculous, Cohen suggests, would be the argument, on hereditary grounds, that as a camper's father had been to the site many years ago and created a good fishing pool, so they should have more fish.

This higher level valuing of fairness, equality, and justice is found in virtually every society, stretching back to early hunter-gatherer cultures.[128] Wilkinson and Pickett state, 'for about 95 per cent of the last 200,000–250,000 years of human existence … human societies have been assertively egalitarian'.[129] Here, not only did hunter-gatherers have no dominance hierarchies, but members striving to take up dominant positions were actively opposed. This desire for equality and fairness is still operative today. For instance, a recent UK survey found that around 80 per cent of people thought that the gap between the richest and poorest was too large, with just 1 per cent feeling that it was too small.[130] Indeed, around 90 per cent of British people expressed a preference for reasonable levels of wellbeing for everyone, as compared with higher overall levels of wellbeing but with some people high in wellbeing and others low.[131] Research also suggests that people will, and do, sacrifice self-interest to make things fairer.[132] Consistent with this, in the prisoner's dilemma game, participants seem to experience mutual cooperation as the most personally satisfying outcome; with neuroscientific evidence linking it to the stimulation of reward areas in the brain.[133] Similarly, in 'ultimatum game' experiments, where players propose – and then either accept or reject – shares of a reward, players most commonly come to equitable solutions.[134] 'People all over the world can be and are moved by ideals of justice and equality', writes Edward Said.[135]

What is at the roots of this desire for fairness? Corning suggests that it is probably a mixture of nature and nurture.[136] In terms of the former, a deep desire for fairness may have emerged for evolutionary reasons: those individuals who strove for fairness would have created more cooperative communities and therefore been more fitted to survive. Wilkinson and Pickett make this case, writing that, 'prosocial characteristics were instilled in us during human prehistory by the evolutionary power of social selection in egalitarian societies'.[137] A desire for fairness may also be one expression of our innate needs for relatedness and attachment. If we have an inherent desire to be connected with others – and to empathise and to care for them – then it is likely that we would also have an inherent capacity to experience pain and discomfort at seeing them suffer. In support of this argument, nonhuman primates – such as capuchin monkeys – have been found to display such fairness-related behaviours as sharing (particularly in relation to food), reciprocity, and conflict resolution.[138]

Socially, too, it is evident that the principle of fairness is taught to us at the earliest possible age: adults telling us, for instance, to 'share', 'don't grab', or 'don't be greedy'. Indeed, greed – the belief that we should have, or are justified in having, more than others – is a near-universally condemned characteristic across societies; while generosity is near-universally praised. In the COVID-19 pandemic, for instance, the UK's weekly 'Clap for Heroes' was not for those making millions of pounds from sales of vaccines, but for NHS workers and others who were willing to risk their own wellbeing for the wellbeing of others. Research shows that, by the age of seven or eight, most children prefer for things to be allocated in equal ways, even if that is to their personal disadvantage.[139]

In addition, in terms of maximising overall benefit, greater fairness makes sense because the worth of something is likely to be greater to someone who does not have that thing than someone who does.[140] In technical terms, as English moral philosopher R.M. Hare writes, there is a 'diminishing marginal utility of all commodities and of money, which means that approaches toward equality will tend to increase total utility'.[141] A thousand dollars, for instance, is likely to mean very little to Jeff Bezos, Amazon Executive Chairman: it is less than one millionth of his $182 billion net worth. But for a person from the Democratic Republic of Congo (DRC), the poorest country in the world, it is three times their annual earning. In fact, if we were to share out just half of Jeff Bezos's fortune among the people of the DRC, we could give each DRC citizen that $1,000. In terms of a 'wellbeing calculation', then, such a redistribution could make 84 million people a whole lot happier, at the cost of just one person's small reduction in happiness. Furthermore, as stated earlier, people are more sensitised to losses than gains.[142] That means, for instance, that one person feeling that they *do not have* a thousand pounds is likely to cause more suffering than the gains for another person in *having* a thousand pounds. As Layard writes, then, 'if money is transferred from a richer person to a poorer person, the poor person gains more happiness than the rich person loses'.[143]

## *What kind of fairness?*

In terms of the present framework, then, fairness would seem to have considerable potential to enhance overall benefit but also, potentially, to lower it. To a great extent, however, this depends on how it is defined and operationalised. So what kind of fairness would be most conducive to the creation of synergetic outcomes?

### ***Fairness as an equal start***

A fairness defined strictly by outcomes is probably least likely to contribute to overall benefit. This would be an equality that required people to end up at the same point, whatever they did. Such an equality would make it very difficult for people to realise a direction towards autonomy or other individual meanings, and to have a sense of significance to their individual lives.

By contrast, in terms of the present framework, an equality of opportunity seems a more productive means of defining fairness. This means less that we all end up at the same ending point, and more that we can all strive forward from a similar starting position. Walzer says something similar when he defines equality in the negative, as an 'abolitionist' politics, aimed at eliminating forms of subjugation, domination, and privilege – such as aristocratic privilege, capitalist wealth, and racial or sexual supremacy – so that we all have equal opportunities to move forward.[144] Such an equality does not stop people from realising their unique needs and wants, to feel free, or to achieve meaning and significance in their lives – indeed, it optimises everyone's opportunities to do so. Fairness, here, is not everyone completing the race at the same time. Rather, it is everyone starting at the same time, at the same point, and without anyone taking performance enhancing drugs, so that no one has a 'leg up' which means that they are more likely to win. This, then, is an 'egalitarianism without the Procrustean bed; a lively and open egalitarianism that matches not the literal meaning of the word but the richer furnishings of the vision'.[145]

### *Fairness for the most disadvantaged*

While striving to enforce an equality of outcomes may lead to a range of problems, it is important to recognise that equality of opportunity can lead to a great deal of inequality further down the line. Life is a long race, and there needs to be some degree of fairness across the life course, and not just at the start.[146] In other words, we may not want to make everyone finish the race at the same time, but if someone breaks their ankle halfway down the track, we do not want to simply leave them there. Alongside an equality of opportunity, then, there needs to be some threshold below which no member of society can be allowed to fall. As Galtung puts it, 'tell me how much material and spiritual misery there is at the bottom of society and I will tell you what kind of society you have'.[147] This relates to Rawls's, and related, 'rights-based' critiques of utilitarianism – whether in pleasure- or preference-based forms. For Rawls, 'Each person possesses an inviolability founded on justice that even the welfare of society as a whole cannot override.'[148] Hence, utilitarian attempts to maximise the wellbeing of all individuals in society – as an aggregate – may lead to unjust outcomes, for the needs and wants of the most disadvantaged members of society may be overlooked. As asked earlier in this section, for instance, would we choose a world in which 99 per cent of the people could realise all of their individual needs and wants, if 1 per cent had to endure intense suffering? As a utilitarian calculation of benefit, the answer here may be 'yes', but this would seem morally and politically perverse, and not the kind of social vision that progressives would endorse. There are complex philosophical and moral questions here, beyond the scope of this book, but the key point is that an ideal society – from a progressive standpoint – needs to combine ways of maximising overall benefit with ensuring that no, one individual is below some minimum threshold.

### *A multiplicity of 'goods': complex equality*

One strategy for trying to maintain fairness for all, without imposing restrictions on what people can achieve, is through the concept of multiple 'goods' (that is, things that are of benefit).[149] As argued in Chapter 5, in the neoliberal world, just a few, rogue goods tend to dominate: that is, can control and monopolise access to all other goods, and to which all other goods can be reduced. Foremost here is money: if you have it, you have access to a vast array of other goods in society, such as pleasure, health, and status (although, as Slavoj Žižek, the controversial Slovenian philosopher, quips, 'money can be defined as the means which enables us to have contacts with others without entering into proper relations with them'[150]). Property, closely linked to money, might be considered another dominant good in the neoliberal world. Inevitably, such a limited range of dominant goods are likely to be concentrated within a small section of the population – there is not much to go around. In addition, this narrow range creates a zero-sum situation: if one person has some of these very restricted goods, it means that someone else cannot.[151]

Furthermore, neoliberal goods such as money and property – by being material and relatively finite – are inherently zero-sum.[152]

The same can be said for status and class, two other predominant goods in a neoliberal world.[153] Compare this, however, with non-zero-sum goods such as health, education, or creativity. No one gets less creative if I get more, or sicker if I get healthier (unless access to healthcare is determined by a zero-sum good, such as money). This suggests that, to maximise the goodness of a society, we should focus it on the attainment of non-zero-sum, rather than zero-sum, goods.

The alternative to a small number of dominant, material goods, then, would be to have a multiplicity of highly valued goods in society – ideally as non-material and non-zero-sum as possible – each of which are irreducible to the others. For instance, skills in a range of arts and crafts might be highly valued in a society, alongside wisdom, and personal qualities like integrity or warmth. Here, each good has its own domain: set at a local, community level rather than being universally or monopolistically held. This is what Walzer means by complex equality. It means 'no citizen's standing in one sphere or with regard to one social good can be undercut by his standing in some other sphere, with regard to some other good'.[154] If a society with a singular good, such as money, is like a narrow passageway through which everyone has to squeeze their way; a society with multiple goods is like a wide tunnel, through which everyone can comfortably pass.

This complex equality can also be conceptualised as the availability of multiple satisfiers: that is, multiple means towards fulfilment of our highest-order needs and wants. Take, for example, a need for recognition. If the only appropriate satisfier, within a particular society, is a respected occupational role, then the relative scarcity of such roles – a zero-sum situation – will create conflicts between people.[155] But if the number of respected roles is expanded (for instance, through recognising excellence in friendships, cleaning, or caring), and/or alternative satisfiers are developed for those not feeling recognised (for instance, by paying garbage collectors more than lawyers), then more people should be able to get more of what they want more of the time. In Chapters 8 and 9 (this volume), we will explore further what a future society of multiple goods might look like.

## *Power*

If we assume that each human being has a desire for freedom and autonomy, and that we can never truly know the needs and wants of another, then equality (or, indeed, any other need or want) is not something that can be distributed paternalistically. Rather, each agency must have the ability to decide for themselves how they want to act. This means that, to maximise overall benefit, there must be an even distribution of *power*. This is the capacity to make changes, to have an effect – both directly and indirectly – to turn our needs and wants into realities.[156] Given the unequal playing field that we start from, however, that means some groups will need to relinquish power (for instance, White people, men, ruling classes) – and 'affirmative actions' may be needed[157] – so that others can take up those reins.

For any specific individual, this giving up of power is likely to be disadvantageous in some ways: 'To ask persons with great power to share this power is to ask them to give up the possibility of gratifying needs.'[158] But, as with synergies more generally, a sharing of power is likely to bring about a greater overall benefit, as compared with systems of dominance, oppression, or control. Almost inevitably, and certainly as we have seen in history, efforts to control others are likely to lead to an overall reduction in benefit because they fail to take into account the agentic nature of the other: that they have their own desire to direct their own lives. If the other was an inanimate 'thing', successful subjugation might be possible – just as it might be possible to ignore their directions (Chapter 5, this volume). But, to the extent that the other is a directional organism with its own needs and wants – including, most likely, a desire for freedom – then the desire to control the other is always likely to be doomed. The other, as Powers writes, 'cannot be arbitrarily controlled *by any means* without creating suffering, violence, and revolution'.[159]

This is also true on the intrapersonal level. Dictatorial, repressive, or dominant voices – like 'the inner critic' or 'the inner patriarch'[160] – may give an individual greater short-term clarity and focus; but, as therapists know, they almost always end up invoking inner resistance, opposite, and insurrection.[161] We cannot eradicate intrapersonal agencies, just as we cannot eradicate interpersonal agencies, because those psychological agencies *are* parts of who we are.

## *Democracy*

At all levels of organisation, then, this analysis points towards the value of *deep democracy*. This is a form of power whereby all the different voices within a system are respected, valued, and 'encouraged to express themselves completely'.[162] Here, as in family therapy, there is a recognition that even the most disavowed and feared parts of a system are necessary to making up the whole.[163] In democracy, each agency is considered of equal worth – 'everybody to count for one, nobody more than one', as Bentham put it[164] – and their interests and goods are given equal consideration. More than that, though, in a democracy, each agency has an equal capacity and power to participate in decisions affecting their situation.[165]

For Dahl, at the societal level of organisation, democracy is 'the most reliable means for protecting and advancing the good and interests of all the persons subject to collective decisions'.[166] This is for two reasons. First, because people are likely to be the best judges of what they need and want, with a uniquely privileged insight into their own self-experiences. Second, because people are likely to be most motivated to advocate for, and accurately define, their own interests and goods. In addition, Dahl argues that participating in democratic decision-making can help people develop personally: 'gaining a more mature sense of responsibility for one's actions, a broader awareness of the others affected by one's actions, a greater willingness to reflect on and take into account the consequences of one's actions for others, and so on'.[167] As Dahl points out, democratic decision-making may also increase the likelihood of good choices being made. This is because 'the pooled judgments of many different persons are likely to wiser on the whole, and certainly less subject to gross error, than the judgments of one person or a few'.[168] In all these ways, then, democracy, as an equal sharing of power, enhances benefit for a system as a whole. Both intrapersonally and interpersonally, it is a form of organisation that leads to greater overall good.

### *Discussion*

A belief in genuine equality is, de facto, at the heart of progressivism. This is particularly the case for socialists and others on the left of the progressive spectrum. The analysis presented here shows that egalitarian, democratic structures are not just politics-specific values, but more general principles for how systems work well. When power is shared, when access to resources are equally distributed, and when each agency has the capacity to represent its own interests, then the amount of overall benefit is optimised. This is important fuel for a progressive position, because it shows that advocating equality is not just about 'moral goodness', but about creating a society that has more to offer everyone, overall. However, this discussion of fairness also raises some complex questions: for instance, 'What kind of fairness is best?' And, 'How do we support people to strive and grow while still maintaining opportunities for all?' Drawing psychology into the mix to help answer such questions – along with numerous other disciplines, such as philosophy, sociology, and anthropology – is likely to be of considerable value: giving us a rich, comprehensive, and multifaceted knowledge base with which to answer such critical questions.

## Summing up

The aim of this chapter has been to explore, across different levels of organisation, the principles that are associated with positive change: that is, with the development of cooperative relationships, and thereby greater overall benefit. In doing so, as with Chapter 5, I hope to have shown the striking parallels across different levels of organisation. That is, whether we are talking about what goes on within individuals, between individuals, or between communities and nations, better things happen if agencies communicate with each other; are assertive yet also trust and prize the other; see the bigger picture; take responsibility; and act in fair and democratic ways. This is a process, fundamentally, of taking the other in and trying to respond to their needs and wants without losing sight of our own.

What is striking, too, is that many of these principles are ones that progressives – at societal levels of organisation – have already advocated for many years. Not only the emphasis on fairness but, for instance, on prizing different and diversity, on looking to the long term, and on taking responsibility for creating cooperative solutions. Perhaps this is because, at some implicit level, progressives recognise that these are ways in which greater overall benefit can be achieved. We sense, for instance, that equality between the sexes is 'right', because the benefits it gives to women, and to society overall, more than outweigh any (temporary) disbenefits that men may experience. Even if this is not the case, the analysis presented here gives valuable support for a progressive standpoint. It shows that the principles and practices advocated by progressives are not merely ad hoc; but, rather, deeper, more universal, system-wide principles about how more benefit can come about.

At the same time, the principles developed in this chapter give, I hope, a deepened and extended account of what it means to be progressive. Here, progressivism is not only understood in terms of a particular, socioeconomic or environmental, stance, but also in terms of how we relate to others, and also to ourselves. Progressivism, from this psychology-informed perspective, means a willingness to trust the other, to recognise the intelligibility of the other's position (as well as our own), and a willingness to dialoguing across difference. In other words, it is not just a commitment to social, political, and economic equality, but also to psychological equality: to engaging with others as human beings, like ourselves. And it is also a commitment to respecting, and engaging with, all of our different parts. This is, perhaps, a relatively novel description of what it means to be progressive. However, I hope to have shown, in this chapter, how it is aligned to, and builds on, established progressive principles; and how it also draws on what we know best about how systems work. The following chapter now looks at concrete initiatives that can take such principles forward.

# 7

# Making it happen: concrete strategies for a psychology-informed progressivism

So what can we do, concretely, to help take forward the psychology-informed progressive principles developed in the previous chapter? Without doubt, much progressive activism – and, when in power, policymaking and implementation – is already oriented towards such goals. As discussed in the previous chapter, for instance, a society that maximises benefit for all needs equality of opportunity, and progressives already fight for this on many fronts. There is, for instance, the promotion of equality for minoritised and disempowered groups (such as people of colour, women, children, people with disabilities, refugees, people of minoritised sexual orientations, and animals), and the promotion of financial equality (by, for instance, fairer systems of taxation, tackling poverty, and the establishment of a universal basic income). Similarly, promotion of universally owned public services (in, for instance, health, education, housing, and social care) helps to ensure that resources are shared equally across citizens; while the decentralisation of decision-making to local groups helps to empower at the community level of organisation. International and overseas work – tackling, for instance, child poverty or disease – helps to promote greater equality across nations. There is also the critical work of tackling the climate emergency: building, for instance, renewable and low carbon energy sources that can help to ensure we thrive within our planetary doughnut.[1] At the same time, the establishment and dissemination of state-funded mental health services – such as England's Improving Access to Psychological Therapies service[2] and mental health services for children and young people[3] – can help to support greater psychological wellbeing for all.

This chapter focuses on five further areas for activism and policy work that may be key levers to the implementation of a psychology-informed progressivism: positive parenting, social and emotional learning, adopting a language of nonviolent communication, emotionally intelligent politics, and developing a wellbeing economy. These are concrete, psychology-based ways of implementing the intra- and interpersonal principles discussed in Chapter 6, such as 'communicate', 'be assertive', and 'trust'. This is not to suggest that these areas of activism and policy work are of greater importance to progressivism than the ones that progressives are already involved in. However, to date, such psychology-based practices have been less prominent on progressive agendas. Through mapping them out, therefore, and showing their importance to progressives, I hope to demonstrate what a rounded and integrated progressive agenda might look like: one that can support positive change in psychological as well as social and economic ways.

At the end of each section there are specific action points for progressives to consider. Some of these are directed at political activists, parties, policymakers, or other professionals. Others, however, are directed at lay-people – at all of us – in our everyday lives. Progressive principles and practices, from a psychology-informed stance, are not just 'out there', but about how we live our lives in relation to others. These are things we can all do personally, then, to help bring about a progressive vision: things that, by being aligned with progressive values and principles, should feel like a natural and helpful 'fit'.

## Positive parenting

### *Why positive parenting for progressives?*

There are three reasons why progressives should care enormously about parenting and care for children and young people (in this section, I will use the term 'parent' to refer to both parents and carers).

First, and most basically, we know that the way people are parented has a massive impact on their wellbeing: supporting, not only emotional and relational development, but also the development of cognitive and learning skills.[4] So, if we want to maximise wellbeing across society, parenting is no better place to start. As the 2021 report *Being bold: building budgets for children's wellbeing* states, 'we cannot begin to improve wellbeing across society … unless we begin with our youngest children and create the conditions for them to flourish from the outset'.[5]

Second, and perhaps most critically from a progressive perspective, a positive parenting experience is essential in helping children and young people develop the capacity to relate to others in cooperative, fair, and democratic ways. Philippa Perry, in her bestselling *The book you wish your parents had read (and your children will be glad that you did)* states: 'By having kind, genuine relationships with your children and each other and providing a safe human environment for them, you are nurturing human beings who are more likely to turn out to be loving, powerful, thoughtful and moral citizens, which is better for us all.'[6] This point, perhaps, can not be made strongly enough. To the extent that children and young people are brought up in authoritarian, controlling, and disempowering ways – or, at worse, manipulative, bullying, neglectful, and abusive – it will be very difficult to create a society of cooperatively minded, empathic citizens with a commitment to sharing and social justice, as described in previous chapters. Why? First, because children model the behaviours that they have seen around them. This is one of the best established facts in psychology,[7] and means that, if children have been parented in non-cooperative ways, it may be difficult for them to move out of this default style of relating in later life. Second, if children are frustrated in attaining, from their parents, the satisfaction of such highest-order needs and wants as safety, self-worth, and relatedness, then they may get 'stuck' there: that is, continuing to desperately battle to get these needs and wants met in later life.[8] Hence, along the lines of Maslow's hierarchy of needs (see Chapter 3, this volume), they may have less mental 'space' to look up to higher levels of organisation, and focus on more cooperative and synergetic actions. In addition, if children do not experience the satisfaction of these fundamental needs and wants in direct ways, then they may come to develop more indirect means of trying to get them met (see Chapter 3, this volume). They may, for instance, strive to elicit affection from others by being 'manipulative', or through 'attention-seeking' behaviours. As we have seen in Chapter 6 (this volume), however, maximally beneficial solutions tends to come through direct, honest, and open communication: indirect attempts to get needs and wants met are likely to lead to messy, and unsatisfying, results. The individual may also give up on trying to get these fundamental needs and wants met at all. The child who has poor parenting, then, is like a player entering the prisoner's dilemma game who, again, already feels that they have lost. Battered down in this way, their capacity to initiate, establish, or agree to cooperative solutions may be much reduced.

Third, research suggests that positive parenting may contribute to greater social mobility. Typically, there is a vicious cycle between low socioeconomic status and less positive parenting styles: limited resources can lead to increased stress in parents, which can then hinder parents' capacities to be sensitive and responsive to their children.[9] Of course, one way to break this cycle is through improving the material resources of those at the lowest rungs of society, but an additional approach (and by no means opposed) is to improve their parenting skills. Research shows, for instance, that positive parenting can improve the odds of children from disadvantaged backgrounds doing better at school.[10] Impoverished children who were securely attached at 18 months, for instance, were more than twice as likely to be positively adjusted at age eight, as compared with insecurely attached infants.[11] Indeed, the promotion of positive attachment relationships may be particularly important for children living in poverty because it can serve as an important protective factors against economic and social stressors.[12] As the Social Mobility Commission's report, *Helping parents to parent*, states:

> [T]o improve social mobility in the United Kingdom it is important that public policy does not shy away from the issue of parenting and what the Government could do to support families in the earliest years of a child's life to help all parents to be the best parents they can be.[13]

In terms of why focus on parenting, it is also important to note that public policy can make a real difference to parenting behaviours, including parenting style, the creation of a supportive home learning environment, relationships within the family, parental stress and mental health.[14] This means that parenting is not only an important area for progressive policies, but also one in which policy changes can make a real difference to social wellbeing. And, indeed, progressive governments are beginning to focus on the promotion of positive parenting programme as, for instance, with the Scottish Government's *Mental health strategy: 2017–2027*.[15] However, the issue of parenting remains a rare feature on most progressive agendas. Perhaps, at some unconscious level, this is because it is associated with the realm of the 'feminine' – that is, mothering, home, and nurturing – rather than the more dominant 'masculine' realms of world and work.

### *Principles of positive parenting*

*Positive parenting* is, to a great extent, a style of parenting consistent with the progressive principles of relating and communicating articulated in Chapter 6. It has been defined as a parenting style that 'includes a high level of warmth, low levels of harsh discipline, firmness in setting boundaries and engagement with the child in activities that foster learning and development'.[16] Across a range of research findings, it has been associated with improved outcomes for children;[17] and is closely aligned to contemporary evidence on brain, development, and psychology.[18] The concept of positive parenting reaches back to the work of the Austrian psychiatrist Alfred Adler in the 1920s; and is a parenting style advocated by numerous contemporary experts and researchers in the field.[19] It is synonymous with the concept of 'authoritative' (or 'collaborative') parenting; as opposed to 'authoritarian' (being strict) or 'permissive' (being lax).[20] While the concept of positive parenting comes from a different background to the theories discussed in Chapters 3–6 of this book, it is highly compatible. Essentially, as Eanes puts it, positive parenting is about trying to develop win–win relationships with children.[21] It is an approach to parenting children – including 'disciplining' them – that aims to help them realise their fundamental needs and wants, within the parameters of what other members of the family or wider system may also be directed towards.

Eanes describes five principles underlying positive parenting: attachment; respect; proactive parenting; empathic leadership; and positive discipline.

### *Attachment*

First is offering children secure attachment.[22] This can be taken to include the provision of love, care, soothing, encouragement, unconditional acceptance, and attention to children[23] – the prizing, niceness, and responsiveness articulated in Chapter 6 (this volume). These are all satisfiers of such fundamental human needs as relatedness, safety, and self-worth. Providing infants with secure attachment is also essential to the development of trust and connection:[24] a key foundation for a healthy process of development[25] and to the capacity to establish cooperative solutions (see Chapter 6, this volume). As already discussed in this book, satisfiers like attachment, love, and praise – unlike more material satisfiers – can be endless in supply: a limitless, non-zero-sum source of wellbeing.[26]

### *Respect*

Second, and closely related, positive parenting means treating children with respect – even if we are disciplining them. 'Children deserve the same consideration we afford to others', writes Rebecca Eanes, author of *Positive parenting: an essential guide*. 'Children need to be treated in a thoughtful, civil, and courteous manner, just as we treat other people.'[27] This means treating children and young people fairly and sensitively; respecting their opinions; and trying to see things from their perspective – a phenomenological gaze (Chapter 1, this volume) – rather than judging or analysing them from our own, external standpoint.[28] Perry suggests a very interesting exercise for trying to see things from a child's standpoint, inviting parents to write a letter to themselves from the child's point of view. This might read, for instance, 'I felt sad and scared when you came home late. I know it was annoying, but I kept pulling on your shirt while you were cooking to try and get you to give me a hug.' Through doing this, what may seem like deliberately irritating or provocative behaviour can come to be seen as intelligible. This does not mean treating children the same as adults or assuming, for instance, that they will know as much as we do. But Eanes suggests that we should see children as 'inexperienced' rather than 'inferior': different in what they understand or know – and in how much responsibility they can take for things – but equally worthy of respect.

Treating children with respect means extending the principle of psychological equality (Chapter 1) to even the youngest of infants. As Perry puts, it, 'babies and children are people too':[29] striving towards their own, intelligible needs and wants – albeit lacking, at times, the communication and coping skills to get themselves there. So psychological equality means refraining from seeing infants as manipulative, conniving, and full of malicious intentions; or naughty or bad; or monsters; or tyrants; or 'duplicitous masterminds'; or our enemies or adversaries.[30] However much we may feel tired, frustrated, or overstretched in a parenting role, it is important to remember the differences between intentions and effects (see Chapter 6, this volume): just because, for instance, we are on the verge of tears with exhaustion, it does not mean that a child has engineered things so that we feel this way. 'Look for the positive motives behind your child's behaviour', writes Eanes. 'If you believe and convey that you believe she's a good person, she'll believe she is too.'[31]

From a progressive standpoint, this point about treating children with fairness and respect is, perhaps, a particularly important one. Extending Dorothy Law Nolte's well-known poem, *Children learn what they live*,[32] we might add that if children live with respect, they learn to respect others; and if they live with fairness, they learn to give and share. Put conversely, if, as progressives, we want to build a society of people who can cooperate, love, and be generous and inclusive to others, then, surely, our most fundamental starting point should be to ensure that children experience this in their first and most formative relationships? How we do so is by no means easy; but finding ways to convey fairness and respect to our children should be as important to progressives as, for instance, establishing fairness in the workplace or in other public domains.

### *Proactive parenting*

The third principle of positive parenting, for Eanes, is being proactive: adopting an active and dialogic, rather than passive, parenting role. This is consistent with the principle of taking responsibility (Chapter 6, this volume); and means addressing problems as they develop, and before they become more serious. 'Whereas reactive parents act impulsively', writes Eanes, 'responsive parents are in control of themselves and able to execute the plan when a situation arises'.[33] This proactive stance can be considered a key different between an authoritative parenting style and one that is more permissive – the latter leaving the child more 'to their own devices'.[34] A.S. Neill, founder of Summerhill School, for instance, wrote that, '*I believe to impose anything by authority is wrong. The child should not do anything until he comes to the opinion – his own opinion – that it should be done.*'[35] Permissive parenting, however, has tended to fall out of favour today; with a recognition that children do need some direction, guidance, and boundaries from their parents (as well as space for self-exploration and self-leadership).

A proactive parenting style also means parents taking responsibility for developing their own self-awareness, in terms of how their own life experiences may have impacted their approach to parenting.[36] Parents can ask themselves, for instance, What was my own childhood like? What was successful and not successful in how I was parented? How might this impact on my own approach to parenting? Developing such self-awareness may help parents understand the assumptions and biases with which they come into parenting. For instance, if they experienced a very distanced and neglectful parenting style themselves, they may unconsciously assume this is what parents do. Through such self-awareness work, parents can also identify 'triggers': when their own, emotionally reactive behaviours kick in. For instance, I know that I can be quite obsessive about work, and therefore can get unreasonably anxious and frustrated if my children need things during 'work time'. Recognising this helps me to step back, and reflect on what might, actually, may be most helpful and appropriate in such situations. Whenever a parent has strong feelings towards their children, it is always worth them examining what these feelings are, what they are perceiving and thinking, and what their needs and wants behind these experiences may be. It is also worth them considering what was going on for them at a similar age to their child.[37] For instance, if a parent finds it hard to respond to their toddler's cries it may be because, at that age, they experienced withdrawal and neglect from a parent. Of course, this is not about being a 'good' or 'bad' parent – Perry suggests that we should ditch these labels altogether – but about recognising areas for development as well as strengths.

### *Empathic leadership*

Closely related to being proactive and taking responsibility, positive parenting means being 'leaders' for our children: guiding them on their developmental journeys.[38] Carolyn Webster-Stratton, founder of the *Incredible Years* parenting programme,[39] writes:

> In order to feel secure, children need their parents to provide behaviour control and clear decision-making in the early years. Children need to be taught the skills to share, wait, respect others, and accept responsibility for their behavior. Although limit setting may make children feel frustrated and resentful at times, clear and consistent limits and rules also help them feel safe, to learn self-control, and to balance their wishes against those of others.[40]

In contrast to the passivity of permissive parenting, then, positive parenting involves being assertive with children (Chapter 6, this volume): setting clear and consistent limits for them (even in the midst of a tantrum) – albeit the minimum necessary for the child's safe, healthy, and prosocial thriving. Commands like, 'Please don't put your fingers need the plug sockets' or 'I want you to turn off your phone for dinner' – delivered in calm, kind, but consistent and firm, ways[41] – are all quite appropriate elements of a positive parenting approach. This can also be described as a process of setting *boundaries*: a 'metaphorical line you draw in the sand that you won't allow the other to cross'.[42] Setting boundaries involves teaching children that they live within a relational context, and that others have needs and wants too. In this respect, setting boundaries to children like 'I don't want you to pinch me' and 'I want you to be really careful when crossing the road', is, effectively, a means of inducting them into genuine dialogue (Chapter 6, this volume): of helping them learn that their needs and wants must be considered against – and realised in the context of – the needs and wants of others.

From a positive parenting perspective, leadership is an empathic – rather than controlling – process: understanding the child's need, wants, and feelings; helping them to feel heard; and modelling for them constructive and prosocial ways of realising their directions. This closely corresponds to the facilitating, coordinating, leadership role discussed in Chapter 6: *in the service of* the other, rather than serving one's own needs and wants. Particularly important here, from the psychotherapy field, is the 'containment' of the child's feelings: including their strongest and most overwhelming emotions.[43] Containment, as with mentalisation (Chapter 6, this volume), is about being able to acknowledge and validate the child's mental and emotional state – staying in connection with the child – while also being able to maintain some distance from their emotions and not get overwhelmed, ourselves, in the situation. This means we can respond in constructive and rational – rather than emotionally reactive – ways. A child in 'meltdown', for instance, may trigger our own feelings of anger of being treated unfairly. Containing such feelings means being able to recognise – and put to one side – our own immediate felt-responses, so that we can empathically enter the child's inner world and lead them towards constructive resolutions of their difficulties.

In terms of teaching children skills, two particular types are emphasised in positive parenting. First, social skills: for instance, learning to share, take turns, and to consider how others may see things.[44] Critically, from a positive parenting perspective, social skills' development means helping children learn how to communicate effectively – as per the communication skills in Chapter 6 (this volume). This can include being able to listen attentively to another without interruptions, being polite and positive, using 'I-statements' (such as 'I'd like to do something different' rather than 'You're boring'), focusing on solutions rather than blame, and avoiding 'mind-reading' (that is, assuming we know what another's intentions are; see Chapter 6, this volume). From a positive parenting perspective, a particularly powerful way that parents can teach children these skills is through modelling. This means parents using the same communication skills when talking to their child – and, critically, with their partner or other adult members of the household. For instance, rather than saying to a child who is being insulting, 'You're being rude and nasty', a parent might say, 'I feel hurt and angry by how you are talking to me.' Children might also be taught social skills through prompting, through being encouraged to practice them with a parent, and through praising the child whenever the skill is demonstrated. The second type of skills, overlapping with the first, are emotional skills. This includes learning to recognise and label feelings; being able to share feelings with another; noticing if another child is hurt or upset; and learning to tolerate difficult feelings, such as frustration and boredom. Importantly, too, children can be taught to recognise the needs and wants behind their emotions, and to communicate these to others in assertive ways. Here, again, perhaps the best way children can learn these skills is through seeing them modelled by a parent, which requires the parent to develop their own emotional self-awareness.

### *Positive discipline*

A fifth principle of positive parenting, and a foci of many parent training programmes (see 'Social and emotional learning', this chapter), is the development of an assertive – as opposed to aggressive (or permissive) – approach to disciplining children. Positive discipline is a move away from punishment: making the child 'suffer enough to cause them to want to avoid that particular behavior again in the future'.[45] Spanking, threatening, criticising, blaming, or humiliating children are, therefore, all vehemently rejected. Rather, there is a focus on engaging with children in respectful and non-critical – albeit clearly boundaried – ways: working together to find positive solutions to problems rather than simply highlighting what the child is doing wrong.

Punishment, implicitly or explicitly, starts from the premise that the child is being 'bad'.[46] Positive discipline, in contrast, starts from the assumption that misbehaviour – or what Perry calls 'inconvenient behaviour' – is a signal for help: a way that the child is expressing their needs and wants.[47] The goal of positive discipline, therefore, is to teach the child 'to control impulses and behavior, to learn new skills, and to fix mistakes and find solutions'.[48] Positive discipline involves giving children a consistent message about limits and boundaries but also allowing time for them to comply, with warnings and reminders.[49]

Eanes, along the lines of other guidance, suggests three steps for positively disciplining children when there is problematic behaviour.[50] First, as already suggested, the parent should try to understand the child's underlying need or want: what is it that, at the most fundamental level, may be motivating the child's aggression or disrespect? This, suggests Eanes, may resolve the situation in itself. Second, parents should strive to calm their child (and themselves), so that subsequent actions come from a point of 'groundedness', rather than emotional reactivity. This may be particularly important if a child is having a tantrum: a state of high emotional dysregulation.[51] This calming could involve, for instance, deep breathing, reconnecting with the child through gently holding them, or sending the child to a 'calm-down' area in the home. Third is teaching and problem-solving: working together with the child to find cooperative solutions. One of Eanes's suggestions is to create a 'peace table', around which conflicts with children can be discussed and resolved. This search for cooperative solutions with children, then, is very much along the lines discussed in Chapters 5 and 6 (this volume) and, as well as helping to solve immediate difficulties, can help children develop essential problem-solving skills for later life. 'Young children usually react to their problems in ineffective ways', writes Webster-Stratton. 'Some cry, others hit, and still others tattle to their parents. These responses do little to help children find satisfying solutions to their problems. In fact, they create new ones.'[52] So parents can have a critical role here in helping children to learn effective problem-solving; and Webster-Stratton suggests we can do this by encouraging children to ask themselves such questions as:

- What is my problem? What am I feeling? (Which serves to define the problem)

- What are some solutions? (Brainstorming)
- What are the consequences? What is the best solution? (Evaluation of options)
- What is my plan? Am I using my plan? (Implementation)
- How did I do? (Evaluation)

Note, again, how similar this is to the problem-solving steps used between couples, communities or, indeed, between different parts of a person (Chapter 5, this volume).

For Webster-Stratton, some degree of sanctioning – used minimally and calmly – may also play an important role in positive parenting. Most basically, this may just involve allowing the child to experience the 'natural consequences' of their 'bad' behaviour: for instance, if they break a toy, they then do not have it to play with. Webster-Stratton also encourages the use of ignoring children, as a way of not reinforcing problematic behaviour; and 'time outs' to help children both calm down and recognise that certain behaviours are unacceptable. However, as with other approaches to positive parenting, the focus is more on rewarding good behaviour than punishing bad: for instance, incentivising children through small and inexpensive rewards like a sticker, a treat, or time with a parent.

### *Parent training programmes*

To support parents in developing such positive parenting skills, a range of training programmes have now been established. As Matthew Sanders, founder of the Triple-P parenting training programme writes, 'parents generally receive little preparation beyond the experience of having being parented themselves; with most learning, on the job and through trial and error'.[53] Programmes are available to support children and young people across the age ranges (from birth upwards); with some focusing on general parenting skills and others on more specific areas, such as problem behaviours, drug use, and health.[54] Encouragingly, programmes show robust, albeit modestly sized, positive effects on both parental outcomes (such as skills and self-efficacy) and child outcomes (such as anxiety, aggressive behaviour, and school grades).[55] This seems particularly the case for programmes that involve actual practising of parental skills, and teaching parents to communicate positively and consistently with their children.[56]

Alongside the Incredible Years – a parent training programme based directly on the principles in this section[57] – probably the most comprehensive, well-established, and well-evidenced positive parenting programme is Sanders's Triple-P (standing for 'Positive Parenting Program'). Triple-P, as with Incredible Years, is offered in a wide variety of format: from online modules for parents of babies, children, and young people; to community-based short courses and talks; to group-based trainings for health and social care professionals who work with parents.[58] Triple-P spans five levels of parenting and family support: from universal-level interventions (for instance, television shows and commercials that promote positive parenting practices); through to enhanced and individually tailored family-based interventions where children have severe and sustained behavioural problems (including, for instance, home visits and coping skills training). Evidence from over 100 studies supports the effectiveness of Triple-P – across levels, and both in the short- and long-term – in improving social, emotional, and behavioural outcomes for children, with benefits also for participating parents.[59]

An example of a much more specific parent training programme, right at the very youngest end of the age scale, is Minding the Baby.[60] This is described as a '[m]entalisation-based preventative parenting programme that incorporates nurse home-visiting and infant-parent psychotherapy models, developed explicitly to promote secure parent-child attachment relationships through engaging and enhancing parental reflective functioning. The programme is targeted at disadvantaged families, where the mother is under 25 years old with additional and complex needs'.[61] In Minding the Baby, visits are begun with the mother in the third trimester of her pregnancy, and then regular home visits are provided up until the baby is two years old. To enhance reflective functioning, the practitioners use a range of skills, such as expressing curiosity about the child's and parent's state of mind, and articulating some of the feelings that the mother and child may be experiencing. Health education, advice on child development, and help with any legal or court issues are also provided to the mothers. Preliminary research suggests that the programme has positive effects on both health and attachment outcomes.[62]

## *Action points*

Developing more cooperative, compassionate, and effective styles of parenting can, perhaps, make the most significant contribution to the realisation of a progressive vision for the future. Encouragingly, there are many ways in which, together, we can bring about this change. Some specific action points for progressives to consider are proposed in the following list, from the most macro level to the most personal and micro:

- Progressive parties should prioritise funding for positive parent training programmes. These should be programmes with evidence of effectiveness; and inclusive of universal-level programmes (that is, not just individual treatments) that can change the culture of parenting as a whole.
- Progressive parties should support the establishment of one-stop services for parents, such as the 'parenting shops' that were developed in Belgium.[63]
- Progressive parties, and progressives in the educational sector (for example, headteachers, school governors), should promote the inclusion of positive parenting skills in secondary school curricula (for example, during personal, social, health and economic education [PSHE] classes).
- Progressives in the mental health field, and who work with parents, should consider developing their skills and knowledge in positive parenting methods.
- Progressives who are parents should reflect on their own ways of parenting, and engage with the positive parenting literature (such as Philippa Perry's *The book you wish …*) or online resources (such as the Triple-P modules), to ensure that they are maximising their own children's opportunities to learn collaborative, dialogic, emotionally intelligent ways of relating.
- We should all be willing to challenge friends, family, or members of our communities who are parenting children in negative ways: such as bullying, intimidating, or using violence.

Just as we would not tolerate racist or sexist abuse, so we should not tolerate abusive or oppressive behaviours towards children.

## Social and emotional learning

Social and emotional learning (SEL) can be defined as the 'inter (e.g., social skills) and intrapersonal (e.g., self-regulation) competencies that enable children to effectively navigate their social environment'[64] (for the purposes of this chapter, the term 'children' is used for all 0–18-year-olds). This includes developing skills in such domains as recognising and managing emotions, appreciating the perspective of others, and establishing and maintaining positive relationships with others. SEL is known by a range of other names, such as 'social and emotional aspects of learning (SEAL)',[65] and 'life skills for psychosocial competences'.[66] SEL is also closely related to the concepts of 'emotional intelligence' or 'emotional literacy'.[67]

SEL can be provided in a wide range of settings – such as youth clubs, libraries, faith-based groups, and juvenile justice settings[68] – and from preschool children through to students in higher education.[69] However, the principal sites of delivery are schools, both primary (for children aged approximately 5–11 years) and secondary (for children aged approximately 12–18 years).[70] Schools are where most children spend most of their days; are accessible to nearly all children (aside from those excluded from school); and are a controlled, structured, and consistent environment in which SEL programmes have the potential to be systematically implemented.[71] In England, SEL is often delivered as part of the PSHE programme; but, as we will see, can vary from specific, classroom-based topic work (such as dealing with bullying), to school-wide attempts to transform an educational institution's culture and functioning. SEL, like positive parenting, is primarily delivered at the *universal* level (that is, to all pupils in a school or class); but can also be *targeted* (for children at risk of particular difficulties, such as taking up drugs or being bullied), or *indicated* (for children who are experiencing such problems).

The concept of SEL was developed in the early 1990s in the US, with the launch of the still-influential Collaborative for

Academic, Social, and Emotional Learning (CASEL).[72] Today, SEL is promoted through legislative and policy action in several US states.[73] SEL is disseminated all over the globe, with a significant upsurge in recent years.[74] In the UK, by 2010, a SEL programme was being implemented in 90 per cent of primary schools and 70 per cent of secondary schools.[75] However, its specific nature and quality of implementation in the UK remains unclear, with reports suggesting that it is 'patchy'.[76] PSHE remains non-statutory and often loses out on timetabling to 'core' subjects.

In the 2019 elections, some progressive parties did propose greater support for SEL. Most notably, the Liberal Democrats said that they would prioritise government spending on '[s]chools that build emotional resilience and properly prepare our children for both work and relationships'.[77] This included developing a 'curriculum for life' in all state-funded schools, which would broaden PSHE to include such areas as environmental awareness and mental health education. The Green Party also emphasised creativity, self-expression, and liberation in education; with properly funded training to support the delivery of PSHE.[78] However, across the world, 'SEL is marginalized in educational decision making by most educators and policymakers',[79] including by those on the left. Indeed, research suggests that even a majority of children feel that schools are not equipping them with key social competencies, such as empathy and conflict resolution skills;[80] and less than one-third of children feel that schools are a caring and encouraging environment.[81] In this section, I want to suggest that SEL, like positive parenting, should be at the forefront of a progressive agenda. This is, for three reasons, closely paralleling the reasons for developing, and promoting, positive parenting.

### *Why social and emotional learning for progressives?*

First, and most generally, if we want to create a society in which more people can thrive more of the time, then SEL may be one of the best ways of achieving that. In the most rigorous review to date – drawing on data from over 200 programmes and a quarter of a million children – universal, school-based SEL interventions were found to have significant positive effects on emotional distress, conduct problems, and positive social behaviour.[82] These effects, in statistical terms, were small, but sustained over time;[83] and there is also evidence that, economically, SEL interventions more than recoup their costs.[84] These skills may also be critical to our planet and our abilities to live with others and within our planetary means. 'I have no doubt', writes Linda Darling-Hammond, Professor of Education Emeritus at Stanford University and education advisor to Barack Obama's 2008 presidential campaign, 'that the survival of the human race depends at least as much on the cultivation of social and emotional intelligence as it does on the developmental of technical knowledge and skills'.[85]

In addition, what is clear from the research is that social and emotional competences, like parenting skills, can be taught. Intervention programmes lead to medium-sized improvements in social and emotional skills (such as perspective taking and interpersonal problem solving) that were sustained over time.[86] Importantly, SEL can be good for educators too. The development of these competences is associated with improved teacher wellbeing and reduced stress and burnout.[87]

Of relevance to schools, research demonstrates that SEL can also have significant and sustained benefits of academic outcomes.[88] However, for progressives, the development of intrapersonal and interpersonal skills should be considered important learnings in their own right, on a par with the development of cognitive skills.[89] Indeed, if aliens were to visit the Earth, they might find it bizarre that, while our children are required to develop skills and knowledge in all manner of subjects, such as geography and music, they are not taught skills and knowledge in the areas most directly relevant to living a full and rewarding life. Why is it, for instance, that our education system insist our children learn how to write and spell properly; but not how to recognise their emotions, find meaning in their lives, form friendships, or even love?[90] 'We have focused on everything else but the real core [of education]', write Timothy Shriver and Jennifer Buffett in the introduction to the US-based *Handbook of social and emotional learning*.[91] Maurice Elias and colleagues, later in the handbook, add, 'The answer is not to provide students for a life of tests but rather to prepare them for the tests of life.'[92]

As with positive parenting, a second, critical, reason why progressives should be prioritising SEL is because it can play a vital role in developing citizens who are capable of the skills detailed in Chapters 5 and 6 of this book. This includes the capacity for cooperation, communication, taking responsibility, seeing the bigger picture, and recognising what one's highest-order needs and wants are. Indeed, as we will see, the competence domains for SEL, as it has evolved over the previous decades, map closely on to the common principles of positive change discussed in Chapter 6. A report by the US-based Aspen Institute claims that the basis of SEL is 'not ideological at all'.[93] However, to the extent that SEL focuses on competences in such areas as empathy and compassion – rather than, for instance, competition, one-upmanship, or control of others – it very much aligns with a progressive (rather than conservative, neoliberal, or authoritarian) worldview.

Third, and again as with positive parenting, there is evidence that SEL may particularly benefit children from low-income communities.[94] That is, skills in establishing nurturing, loving, and emotionally stable relationships may be particularly important for children who have experienced trauma and adversity as a consequence of insecure and inadequate access to resources (such as housing, food, shelter, and safety). As the Aspen Institute report starts, 'Ensuring access to high-quality, equitable learning environments that respond to each child's needs, assets, culture, and stage of development can help mitigate some of these stresses and provide a pathway to a more equitable future.'[95] Of course, SEL is no substitute for real economic transformation, but it may be one means of breaking the cycle whereby being born into a disadvantaged environment leads to behaviours (or a lack of behaviours) that then compound that disadvantage.

### *Principles of social and emotional learning*

SEL draws on a wide range of psychological and educational theories, including humanistic understandings of people's needs and wants such as Maslow's hierarchy of needs.[96] As with positive parenting, however, it is particularly influenced by the very well-established and well-evidenced social learning theory,[97] which understands development as a directional and active process, based on what we learn from – and see modelled by – those around us (Chapter 3, this volume).

CASEL identifies five competence domains for SEL,[98] each covered to a relatively similar extent in actual classroom activities.[99] The following, brief review of them shows their alignment with the common principles of positive change (Chapter 6, this volume) – albeit from a different perspective and tradition – and also illustrates how such principles might be concretely applied in an educational setting.

### *Self-awareness*

The first of CASEL's five competence domains is *self-awareness*. This is closely aligned to mentalisation (Chapter 6, this volume), which involves children being able to recognise and understand their emotions; as well as other aspects of self, such as personal goals, strengths, needs, and values. Emotional awareness is a particular important feature here: helping children recognise, for instance, when they feel angry, sad, or happy; and being able to understand what the underlying need or want is (see Chapter 3, this volume). A typical classroom exercise might start by asking children to brainstorm all the feelings they can think of, and then discuss and classify them (for instance, as 'mild' versus 'strong', 'positive' versus 'negative').[100] The children might then be asked to mark down which of the feelings they have experienced and which they have not. Subsequent stages might then involve looking at pictures (for instance, of a girl waving goodbye as a bus leaves), watching films, or reading short stories, and trying to describe what the characters might be feeling. Children might also be asked to mime feelings for others to guess, or role-play situations to explore how feelings may affect how people behave. Self-awareness may also involve helping children develop a positive and optimistic sense of self – that they are capable and worthy of love; the ability to recognise interconnections between thoughts, feelings, and behaviours; and an understanding of mental wellbeing and forms of mental distress (such as stress, depression, and eating disorders).[101]

### *Self-management*

Building on self-awareness is the second CASEL competence domain of *self-management*. This involves teaching children to regulate emotions, and to express them and other thoughts and behaviours in constructive ways (the development of 'executive functioning'[102]). This, then, is the other side of the emotional literacy coin: not just being able to recognise and understand what we feel, but also being able to 'contain' our feelings, take responsibility, and express and communicate them in constructive ways.[103] As such, self-management includes 'the ability to delay gratification, manage stress, control impulses, and persevere through challenges in order to achieve personal and educational goals'.[104] These latter competencies can also be termed 'resilience'.[105] Self-management involves helping children to learn when the 'chimp part of the brain' has taken over (that is, the primitive, emotion-driven part that seeks immediate satisfaction; see 'rogue goals', Chapter 4, this volume), and being able to act, instead, with respect to longer-term goals. One common way children may be taught this is through the metaphor of a 'traffic light': 'red' for when they feel very powerful emotions (like anger or worry) and need to stop and relax; 'orange' to weigh up their options and make a plan; and 'green' for putting their plan into action.[106] Children may also be taught specific skills to support this process of self-management, such as deep breathing or mindfulness.

### *Social awareness*

The third CASEL domain of SEL is *social awareness*. This involves the capacity to mentalise different perspectives – including those of people from different backgrounds and cultures, or who are stigmatised and ostracised – and to be able to empathise and feel compassion for them. A common SEL method for developing empathic skills is 'circle time', where children are invited to sit down with each other and spend some time listening to each other's experiences and feelings. To develop this, children might then be asked to describe how they think others are feeling.[107] An alternative empathy exercise might be to show children a picture or a short film about someone (for instance, of a migrant crossing the seas), and then asked to describe how they think the person might be feeling, or write a story from their perspective.

### *Relationship skills*

*Relationship skills* is CASEL's fourth domain of SEL. Of particular centrality here are the kinds of communication skills discussed in Chapter 6 (this volume), such as being able to express one's needs and wants assertively, being able to listen to the needs and wants of others, and being able to negotiate conflict and find constructive solutions. As a classroom-based exercise to develop communication skills, children might be invited to discuss what 'communication' is, and what makes it good and bad. They could then be asked to role-play a situation in which miscommunications happen, and to explore how people could go about communicating in clearer and more effective ways.[108] Assertiveness training can also be conducted with older children:[109] helping them to learn direct, rather than aggressive or passive-aggressive, ways of asking for their needs and wants to be met. Communication skills training can also involve learning about – and developing competences in – such areas as eye contact, personal space, and the use of nonverbal communication. Developing knowledge and competences in establishing friendships is another critical skill that all children can be helped to learn: for instance, children can be invited to discuss, 'What makes a good friend?' and practice positive ways of approaching other children. These kinds of skills are essential in being able to realise, more effectively, a highest-order need for relatedness.

### *Responsible decision making*

The final CASEL domain for SEL is *responsible decision-making*. Building on the four previous domains, this involves the capacity to make constructive and prosocial choices across diverse settings: Again, to take responsibility for one's actions. Responsible decision making here involves having the capacity to consider longer-term goals as well as shorter-term ones – the kinds of effective choices described in Chapter 4, this volume – and being able to act with respect to relevant ethical standards, safety concerns, and with the wellbeing of others in mind. Central to this domain is the capacity to problem-solve effectively, using creative and critical thinking skills.[110] A classroom-based activity might involve presenting children with particular scenarios – for instance, the child's friendship group are being homophobic, or they are encouraging the child to take a drug – and then encouraging the child to discuss, and explore, how they would weigh up the situation and make choices about actions.

### *Implementing social and emotional learning*

As indicated earlier, SEL can be delivered as specific programmes (generally at the universal level), or as more school-wide changes to the institution's culture and values.

#### ***Specific programmes of social and emotional learning***

Research indicates that school staff can be as effective at delivered SEL programmes as non-school personnel (for example, researchers or consultants). However, SEL programmes tend to be more effective when they are delivered in a way that is 'SAFE'.[111] 'SAFE' stands for *s*equenced (that is, structured, step-by-step), *a*ctive (that is, involving the children as active, experiential learners), *f*ocused (that is, with sufficient time dedicated to skills development), and *e*xplicit (with clear learning goals, targeted at specific SEL objectives).

Over the last few decades, a number of such SAFE programmes have been developed for children of various age ranges, all of which aim to help children develop some – or all – of the SEL competences described earlier.[112] One of the best evidenced, for instance, is the 'PATHS' programme (Promoting Alternative THinking Strategies) for primary school age children. This consists of 33 brief (15- to 20-minute) lessons – insertable into a school curriculum during circle time – that use stories, pictures, and puppets to provide SEL skills instruction to the children.[113] PATHS focuses on SEL skills in four areas – friendship skills, emotional knowledge, self-control, and social problem-solving – closely overlapping the five CASEL domains. One of the best-known elements of PATHS is the 'turtle technique' for mentally distancing from strong emotions. Using the analogy of a turtle, children are taught to imagine 'tucking themselves inside their shell' when they feel upset, angry, or scared; taking some deep breaths, and then 'coming out' when they feel calmer and have a solution to the problem. In addition, as part of the PATHS programme, teachers are trained in strategies to help children generalise these SEL skills across the school day. Another well-evidenced programme, 'Merrell's Strong Kids', has around ten lessons of 30–75 minutes each, focusing on such topics as 'Understanding your feelings', 'Dealing with anger', and 'Letting go of stress'.[114] In each lesson, key concepts are introduced and defined, children's books relevant to the key content are discussed, and there is time to practice key skills.

Within the SEL field, it is recognised that specific programmes may need to be adapted to particular cultural, national, and socioeconomic contexts.[115] For instance, the skills that a programme teaches, or the scenarios or metaphors that a programme uses, may need to be revised to represent the particular cultural realities of the children taking part. An example here is eye contact: in the Western world, making eye contact during communication is generally perceived as expressing interest and engagement, but in some cultures (for instance, Native Americans) direct eye contact with those of higher status may be considered disrespectful.[116] Involving children, here, as consultants on – or co-developers of – a programme (also known as 'Patient and Public Involvement') may help to optimise the cultural relevance of such adaptations; as well as teaching children important interpersonal and organisational skills. There are also specific SEL programmes that have been developed for members of minoritised groups. For instance, the 'Sisters of Nia' is a 15-session programme that was developed to foster the cultural and ethnic identity of young African American females.[117] Lessons include learning about Africa, analysing media messages, and African American female leadership. Sessions begin with a libation: an African ritual of pouring water onto a plant to remember one's ancestors. African proverbs and principles – such as *ujima* (collective work and responsibility) and *nia* (purpose) – are then discussed. Pilot data suggests the programme is associated with improvements in racial identity, social strengths, and scholastic competence.

### *Whole-school approach*

'Unfortunately', write Roger Weissberg and colleagues in the *Handbook of social and emotional learning*, most SEL programmes 'are introduced into schools as a succession of fragmented fads, isolated from other programs, and the school becomes a hodgepodge of prevention and youth development initiatives, with little direction, coordination, sustainability, or impact'.[118] Specific SEL programmes, then, are only likely to have a positive benefit if they are embedded within a school-wide commitment to the development of social and emotional skills. Here, then, the focus broadens out from specific child-focused programmes of learning to the development of a coherent, integrated school-wide culture in which children can optimise their SEL. These approaches are important as large-scale research reviews have, 'concluded unequivocally that whole-school approaches are essential when attempting to tackle emotional and social issues in schools'.[119] That is, if children are participating in class-based SEL lessons, but then going out into a school that is authoritarian, punitive, and disrespectful of individual children's needs and wants, much of the SEL is likely to go to waste.

As with positive parenting, whole-school SEL means creating a school culture, community, and set of values and policies that are child-centred, friendly, caring, and safe.[120] Here, positive relationships between children and school staff – and also with parents and other members of the wider community – are prioritised;[121] children feel 'connected, safe, and supported' to learn.[122] In such a school, difference and diversity among pupils and school staff are celebrated; with active steps taken to prevent bullying, violence, discrimination, and racism.[123] Here, disciplinary procedure may still be strong but, as with authoritative parenting, based on clear, consistent, and collaborative guidelines; with an avoidance of punitive and counterproductive disciplinary strategies.

A whole-school approach to SEL may also involve drawing out SEL content across the full curriculum.[124] For instance, in English literature classes, students might be encouraged to imagine themselves in the shoes of the key protagonists: How might it feel, for instance, to be Shylock? What might he, or his daughter

Jessica, need and want? Or, in drama classes, students might be encouraged to role-play various inter- and intrapersonal situations, such as challenging homophobia or positive self-talk. In addition, where a whole-school approach to SEL is adopted, classes are likely to be delivered in a child-centred way, with lessons that are active and engaging and opportunities for children to shape their own learning activities.[125]

As with specific SEL programmes for children, there are a range of specific SAFE programmes to develop a whole-school SEL culture. These are typically oriented towards teachers and other members of the school staff. An example here is the Incredible Years Teacher Training Program, based on similar principles to the Incredible Years positive parenting programme (see 'Positive parenting', this chapter). This typically consists of monthly workshops for teachers, in which certified trainers – using such teaching methods as video demonstrations and moderated group discussion – help teachers develop such skills as structuring the classroom effectively to avoid behavioural problems, strengthening positive teacher–child relationships, and using incentives to motivate learning.[126] Another programme is 'Responsive Classroom', which aims to help teachers model and educate children about SEL through workshops, resources, and on-site professional development consultancy.[127]

As such programmes highlight, the development of whole-school SEL is dependent, perhaps more than anything else, on school staff who are socially and emotionally literate themselves: 'high on self-regard, self-knowledge, emotional awareness and the ability to manage their own emotions'.[128] This means teachers who, themselves, understand common principles of positive change (Chapter 6, this volume): who are able to communicate to pupils – as well as parents and other members of the school community – in warm, caring, facilitative, and transparent ways; using proactive strategies, rather than punitive ones, to address misbehaviour.[129] Certainly, in my own experience as a parent, such competences cannot be taken for granted. While, without doubt, there are many brilliantly caring and compassionate teachers, there are also some school staff who seem limited in key communication skills, such as the capacity to engage in dialogue. From my children's accounts, there are also some stories of teachers 'acting out' their anger, irritation, or stress on pupils; or responding to pupils in ways that severely dampen the child's self-worth, creativity, and initiative. The day of 'the slipper' may be gone; but authoritarian, controlling, and critical teacher–pupil relationships still seem to be evident, particularly in secondary schools. How, it might be asked, can we expect our young people to grow into cooperative, compassionate, and democratically minded citizens when, in some cases, what they see modelled by their teachers is so very different?

Gueldner and colleagues give an example of what SEL competences in a teacher might look like, with the teacher beginning a class by modelling self-knowledge, emotional awareness, and the capacity for managing their emotions:

Teacher [*saying aloud to the class*]: I am feeling a little more stressed than usual. I wonder if this is because … testing is coming up and we have had to make sure we get a lot done. I can tell I'm feeling stressed because I have a little less patience, feel rushed, and my heart is beating faster. I also want to do everything I can in preparing you for the state test. … Next I am going to take a few deep breaths. … I'm pretty sure this is a good step in helping my body and mind feel calmer.[130]

In another example, they show how a teacher could demonstrate empathy and understanding, rather than criticism, to a child who is refusing to cooperate with testing procedures:

Teacher: Hey, Munir, I wonder if you're really frustrated right now. I'm wondering because your face looks a little mad, you're crossing your arms, and you've stopped talking. What's going on?

Munir: I don't want to take the test. It's stupid.

Teacher: I get it. You don't want to take the test and think it's stupid. What else? [Teacher's body language conveys attention via eye contact, a relaxed face, and a calm voice. … The teacher encourages the student to express himself and accepts all emotions as valid by not interrupting, offering advice, or trying to convince the student that he doesn't feel that way. The teacher views the situation as an opportunity to connect, support, and teach.]

Teacher: This is a really tough situation. It must seem like an impossible one because everybody has to take the test. I remember taking state tests – it felt like a waste of time sometimes and I got kind of nervous because math was really hard for me. Of course you feel irritated! I'd like to help. Let's think of some options.[131]

Of course, such conversations are, to a great extent, dependent on teachers having sufficient time to engage empathically and sensitively with their students. As stated throughout this book, therefore, progress requires change at multiple levels: at the socioeconomic level, in terms of increased resourcing, as well as at the interpersonal level of developing communication skills.

As with all people, the development of SEL skills in teachers requires training, and SEL for teachers is available as a component of several SEL programmes.[132] This can include developing skills in self-care, stress management, mindfulness, and resilience. A crucial site for the development of these skills is teacher training institutes, where SEL can, and should, be an essential element of the curriculum. Not only can training in these skills support students in developing their social and emotional competences, but they can also improve teacher wellbeing, and reduce stress, burnout, and teacher turnover.[133] Supervision and consultation for teachers – or the development of professional learning communities where groups of teachers can dialogue together – may also support the development of reflective practice.

In most cases, though, it is the headteacher in a school that plays the key role in establishing the school climate: 'setting priorities and goals, providing human and material resources, and establishing and sustaining programs and practices that support social, emotional, and academic development'.[134] The development of emotionally literate schools, therefore, requires headteachers who appreciate the key role that SEL can play in children's healthy development, are committed to prioritising the learning of these skills, and, themselves, have SEL skills. Having a designated 'implementer' at the school (for instance, the pastoral care lead, head of year, or school counsellor), who leads on the development and dissemination of SEL, may also be a critical element of embedding SEL in the school culture.[135] This was a central plank of the Department of Health in England's *Future in mind* report on 'Promoting, protecting and improving our children and young people's mental health and wellbeing'.[136] It proposed that all schools should have a 'named mental health lead': 'A specific individual responsible for mental health in schools, to provide a link to expertise and support to discuss concerns about individual children and young people, identify issues and make effective referrals. This individual would make an important contribution to leading and developing whole school approaches.'[137] This is currently being trialled across a range of sites in England.

Ultimately, 'A dream is where all children love school; where all children meet teachers who understand them, believe in them, challenge them, and unlock them; and where the heart of learning is at the centre of what is learned.'[138] This, in my own experience – and those of my children – still seems some way off. I remember school, and particularly secondary school (albeit 40 years ago), as a place of stress, boredom, and enforced uniformity. Bullying and hurtful interactions – not least with teachers – were rife. In my first year of secondary school (Year 7), probably the thing that most occupied my mind was how to avoid getting my head plunged down the school loos by the older pupils. If we want our children to learn to feel good about themselves, and to develop the capacity to work cooperatively and fairly with others, this is not a good start. As with positive parenting, progressives need to radically review how we think about schooling in our societies – to look at the cultures in which we are cultivating our children – and to consider much more nurturing and caring alternatives.

## *Action points*

Alongside positive parenting, SEL may be an enormously valuable means towards the realisation of a progressive vision for society. It is no quick fix; it may take a generation or more; but, over time, it has the potential to sow the seeds for deep and profound change: citizens who emerge into adulthood with the psychological maturity to communicate effectively, to cooperate with each other, and to embody the principles detailed in Chapter 6 of this book. Specific action points for progressives are:

- Progressive parties should promote and prioritise funding for SEL in schools, and revision of school curricula so that SEL is central to students' teaching and learning. For instance, progressive parties might consider creating an SEL GCSE, akin to the 'Nature GCSE' proposed by the Green Party.[139] This, of course, also requires the prioritisation of funding for education.
- Progressive parties should support the establishment of named mental wellbeing leads in schools, who can serve to develop, prioritise, and sustain SEL initiatives.
- Progressives based at teacher training institutes should explore how their programmes can optimally prepare teachers for SEL. Teacher training curricula, for instance, might include research on attachment and adverse childhood experiences (as increasingly happens now), as well as specific input on SEL methods and SEL-supportive styles of teaching.[140] Teachers should be expected to demonstrate high levels of social and emotional competences prior to graduating in the field (such as the capacity to listen, empathise, and communicate assertively); and potential to demonstrate and support SEL should be key criteria for selection into training programmes, teaching posts, and senior school roles.
- Progressives in the educational sector (including teachers, headteachers, and school governors), should familiarise themselves with SEL and consider how it might be implemented – or implemented more fully – in their institutes. Here, it will be important to remember that SEL development is a 'journey' not a 'sprint',[141] and works best as a whole-school transformation of culture and values, rather than the piecemeal introduction of one-off programmes. 'It's not a matter of tinkering around the edges', says the Aspen Report. 'It requires fundamentally changing how we teach children so that the

social, emotional, and cognitive dimensions of learning are recognized to be mutually reinforcing rather than distinct.'[142]

- Progressive school staff, including teachers and headteachers, should consider the development of their own SEL skills. This could be through established SEL programmes, supervision and consultancy, or through personal development-related activities such as mindfulness and peer development groups.
- Progressive parents should talk to their children's schools about the role of SEL in the school curriculum, encouraging headteachers and teachers to maximise its presence. Children and young people can also play a role in encouraging their schools to take SEL seriously.

### *Nonviolent communication for all*

*Nonviolent communication* (NVC) is a set of principles for cooperative communication with others – adults as well as children – that distils and codifies many of the interpersonal principles and practices promoted in positive parenting and SEL, as well as in the 'communication' and 'be assertive' sections of Chapter 6 of this book. NVC was heavily informed by the research and theory of the humanistic psychologist Carl Rogers (see Chapter 1, this volume); and, as such, is closely aligned to the psychology-informed progressivism developed in this book: a commitment, for instance, to psychological equality, and a view of human beings as 'always acting in the service of needs and values'.[143] The approach is called 'nonviolent' in reference to Ghandi's use of this term: 'our natural state of compassion when violence has subsided from the heart';[144] though terms like 'cooperative communication', 'compassionate communication', or 'respectful communication' might better convey what the approach is about (it is not really about dealing with 'violence', as that term is generally understood). However, the name NVC has stuck and it is widely known as such, and applied, across the globe.[145]

NVC was articulated by American psychologist Marshall B. Rosenberg in the 1960s and 1970s. As we shall see, it conceptualises cooperative communication in terms of four components: 'observations', 'feelings', 'needs', and 'requests'.[146]

The beauty of this formula is that it provides a simple, easy-to-follow rubric for communicating cooperatively across a multitude of settings. NVC has been, and can be, used in such situations as conflict resolution, politics, parenting, relationships, and the workplace – as well as being a staple for much individual and couples therapy. As such, it provides a general framework for communicating that progressives can advocate across a wide variety of settings. More than that, it provides a framework for communicating that, as progressives, we can adopt and enact in our lives: being the change that we want to see.

### *Basic principles of communicating to others*

The essence of NVC is to use the following format when communicating to others, particularly in situations of disagreement or conflict: 'When *a*, I feel *b*, because I am needing *c*. Therefore I would now like *d*'.[147] For instance, 'When you throw a party when everyone else is in lockdown, I feel really furious, because I believe passionately that we should all be equal and people in positions of authority shouldn't exploit their power. Therefore I would like you to reflect on what you did, apologise, and think about what you might do differently in the future.' As can be seen in this example, NVC involves communicating phenomenologically: in terms of subjective feelings, senses, and perceptions; rather than claiming some objective, universal, or moral truth (Chapter 1, this volume). As with other forms of conflict resolution, then, it is about getting beyond arguments over who is right and who is wrong – and blame – to a stance of mutual respect, in which both parties work together to try and find cooperative solutions to their needs and wants.[148] As with couples therapy, 'perception is everything. Don't focus on 'the facts''.[149]

#### ***Observations***

The first component of NVC is communicating to the other what the situation is that is affecting our wellbeing. This is the 'when *a* …'. For instance, 'When I feel you are ignoring the threat of climate catastrophe …', 'When you use the term "Jew" …', 'When you smear jam all over my iPad …'. To avoid getting into unproductive arguments about what did, or did not, happen, observations should be stated as clearly and specifically as possible, avoiding any statements that may be factually incorrect. For instance, if there is jam on the iPad and your child obviously smeared it there, it is reasonable to start with that as an observation. But if we were to start a conversation with a statement like, 'When you ignore climate change …', we might be making an assumption about what someone is thinking and experiencing that is not factually correct (that is, 'mind-reading', see Chapter 6, this volume). What we can do in these cases, however, is to present it as our subjective perception: 'When *I feel* you are ignoring …'. This is not something that someone can argue with us over: 'No, you don't feel I'm ignoring climate change.' We do feel that, we can state it as a truth (albeit a subjective truth), and then we can use it as the basis for dialogue. Critically, too, observations should be free of evaluation, expressed either directly (for example, 'You're a bad child for getting jam on my iPad') or indirectly ('You shouldn't use the term "Jew"'). From an NVC standpoint, it is just not necessary, and it introduces into the dialogue a right versus wrong focus that is unlikely to be constructive. No one – the other as well as us – is likely to want to conclude a disagreement with being shown to be wrong.

### *Feelings*

Second is feelings: the *b* that happens to us in situation *a*. For instance, 'When I feel you are ignoring the threat of climate catastrophe, *I feel really scared*,' 'When you use the term "Jew," *I feel uncomfortable*,' 'When you smear jam all over my iPad, *I feel angry*.' Stating feelings, again, gets away from arguments about who is right or wrong because it not something that the other can disagree with. They cannot say, for instance, 'No, you don't feel scared,' because we know we do. At the same time, as 'I-statements',[150] feelings are not an articulation of how the world *is*, or what someone has intended to do, but a factual statement about its effect on us. For instance, when we state, 'I feel uncomfortable when you use the word "Jew",' we are not claiming that someone else used the word to make us feel uncomfortable, or that it is a bad word to use, or that they are morally and politically bankrupt in some way. We are simply stating, clearly and succinctly, what impact it has on us. In this sense, statements of feelings do not try and bring about change by making demands on the other. Rather, they try and do this by calling on the humanity and compassion of the other to recognise the impact that their behaviours are having. That is, not changing because they *should*; but because, as with all human beings, they will not want to hurt or upset others unnecessarily.

### *Needs*

The third component of NVC is acknowledging the 'need, desire, expectation, hope, or values' at the roots of our feelings: the *c*. I feel scared about climate change, for instance, 'because I want my kids to grow up in a healthy environment'; I feel uncomfortable when you use the term 'Jew', 'because it makes me feel exposed and unsafe'. Expressing such needs and wants helps to convey to the other the intelligibility behind our feelings – to explain why we are feeling that way. Hopefully, this will help them be more receptive to our perspective. Also, it may help them to see our humanity more clearly. Rosenberg writes, 'the more we are able to connect our feelings to our own needs, the easier it is for others to respond compassionately'.[151] Rosenberg goes on to state that this is because, 'When we settle our attention on other people's feelings and needs, we experience our common humanity.'[152] For instance, if I say that being called a 'Jew' makes me feel unsafe, the other can see that my feelings are driven by the same needs and wants – in this instance, for safety – as they also have. In addition, communicating our needs and wants may reduce defensiveness in the other because, rather than communicating to them blame – 'You have made me feel *b*' – we are taking responsibility for our feelings. Also, as argued in Chapter 5 (this volume) and throughout this book, the first step towards the generation of cooperative solutions – whether intrapersonally or interpersonally – is the explication of underlying, higher-order needs and wants. Rosenberg says something identical when he writes, 'It has been my experience over and over again that from the moment people begin talking about what they need rather than what's wrong with one another, the possibility of finding ways to meet everybody's needs is greatly increased.'[153]

Despite the centrality of underlying needs and wants to the theory developed in NVC, and many other perspectives discussed in this book, it may be worth noting that their explicit expression is, perhaps, the least essential element of NVC. In the couples therapy literature, for instance, it has been suggested that 'master relaters' generally communicate using the form, 'I feel *b* because of *a*, and I would like it if we could *d*'.[154] Here, *c* is an optional extra. Perhaps this is because *c* (the needs and wants) is so often implicit in *b* (the feelings) and, potentially, also in *d* (the 'do different'). If I say to my partner, for instance, 'I feel really hurt when you don't text me in the mornings,' I do not really need to add to it, '… and I do not want to feel hurt'. Hopefully, she will have worked that bit out. And if I am asking her to text me more, then I am also, implicitly, communicating that I want to have more connection with her.

### *Requests*

Finally, and critically, we have the 'do differents', *d*. These are the specific, concrete changes that we would like to see in the other's behaviour. For instance, 'I would like you to … listen to me carefully when I talk about climate change/use the word "Jewish" rather than "Jew"/not eat food when you are using my iPad'. Expressing the specifics of what we want differently not only means we are more likely to get it, but it means that the other does not just hear complaints. Rather, we are being proactive and positive in proposing solutions. Importantly, too, we are not making demands on the other – provoking, potentially, a self-defensive response – but making requests: validating and, again, appealing to, their humanity.

## *Receiving the other*

How we communicate our observations, feelings, needs, and requests to the other is, of course, only half of NVC. The other side is being willing and able to receive what the other says to us. NVC, then, can be considered as a basis for genuine dialogue (Chapter 6): a two-way, interactive exchange in which both parties are honestly expressive to the other, and also able to receive the other in deep and meaningful ways. Receptivity, in NVC terms, means listening to the other's perception and experiences of a situation, the feelings that may have been evoked in them, the needs and wants they may have behind those feelings (whether those are explicitly or implicitly stated), and the things that they would like differently. In this respect, NVC means being empathic to the other: and not just intellectually, but with an emotional, embodied attunement.[155] It also means being non-critical: engaging with all the other has to say in a respectful, validating manner. That does not mean we cannot challenge the other, but *challenge* can be differentiated from *criticism* – the former questioning a person's behaviour (and the effect it may have), while the latter questions the person, per se.

The following is an example of NVC challenge in practice. Lennox, a male student who supports feminism, is walking home after a night at the pub with other young men from his college. It is dark and the streets are quiet. Walking ahead of them is a young woman they do not know. One of Lennox's acquaintances, Jasper, shouts out to the woman, 'Hey, hold up, let's have a chat.'

| | |
|---|---|
| Lennox: | Jasper, please! Can you stop that straight away. That makes me feel really uncomfortable. Let's just stop walking and cross over the street until she's gone. |
| Jasper: | What? |
| Lennox: | Jasper, you're shouting at that woman. Seriously, I really want you to stop that. |
| Jasper: | What? |
| Lennox: | Jasper, you might not mean this, but that could feel really threatening. |
| Jasper: | What? I'm just flirting with her. I just want to have a bit of a chat before we go back to halls. |
| Lennox: | I know. You might be doing it because you think it's fun. But it could be really different for her. You don't know. So just stop, please. |

In this vignette, Lennox's expression of his observations, feelings, needs, and requests are all intertwined, and not in the order of *a–d*; but it demonstrates how Lennox can very strongly challenge

Jasper's behaviour, without ever accusing Jasper of being a bad or malevolent person. In this way, Lennox focuses on challenging – and, hopefully, changing – Jasper's behaviour, and sidesteps any argument over the kind of person Jasper might be. Indeed, alongside Lennox's very firm request to Jasper to stop behaving like this, he still manages to show empathy. That is, he accepts, and reflects back to Jasper, Jasper's expressed intention, while concomitantly making it clear to Jasper that his behaviour has the potential to be really damaging to another (see Chapter 6).

### *Limitations of nonviolent communication*

But what happens, as may often be the case, that we intend to practice NVC with the other, but the other does not want, or does not know how to, communicate in NVC ways with us? Supposing, for instance, that the conversation between Lennox and Jasper goes like this:

| | |
|---|---|
| Lennox: | Jasper, please! Can you stop that straight away. That makes me feel really uncomfortable. |
| Jasper: | What? |
| Lennox: | Jasper, you're shouting at that woman. Seriously, I really want you to stop that. |
| Jasper: | What? Chill out, man, I'm just having some fun. |
| Lennox: | Jasper, you might not mean this, but that could feel really threatening. |
| Jasper: | Ah, Jeezus, 'Woke Brigade' coming down the line. Get a life, man, that's ridiculous. She's fine with it. Look, she's not bothered. |

A third friend, Paul, joins in:

| | |
|---|---|
| Paul: | C'mon Lennox, loosen up. You're so uptight. Seriously. What are you making a big fuss for? |

So what does Lennox do in this situation? Faced with such a response, Lennox might be tempted to shift into either passivity (silencing himself), aggressiveness (for instance, 'F*** off, you idiots'), or a passive-aggressive stance (for instance, 'You guys just do what you want, it doesn't bother me' [storms off]). A consistently maintained NVC stance (that is, assertiveness), however, might ultimately be most helpful for him, the woman, and for society more generally: bringing his acquaintances around to a more compassionate and empathic way of relating to others. For instance, 'I know you guys think I am uptight or being an uncool, but this is really important to me: I don't want you to behave in ways that might be experienced as threatening.' In addition, it is important to remember that responding in an NVC way does not preclude Lennox from taking other actions. If Jasper, for instance, ignored Lennox and tried to run towards the woman, Lennox could still choose to try and physically stop him, or to call the police, all the while engaging in an NVC way. To a great extent, then, NVC is a no-lose strategy: there are no real downsides to it (other than, perhaps, making ourselves somewhat more vulnerable through self-disclosure), and the potential benefits are immense. As with other cooperative stances presented in this book, then, NVC is not a 'soft option', or one that stands opposed to more radical actions. Indeed, it could take a lot of courage for a young man to try and maintain NVC, as Lennox might attempt to do in the scenario described.

A second criticism of NVC could be that, as with all humanistic approaches, it tends to emphasise – and aggrandise – individual needs and wants, at the expense of more community-, social-, or cultural-level processes and structures. Does everything, really, come down to meeting individual needs and wants; and is this not a very Western way of seeing the world? This is a fair criticism for NVC, when taken in isolation. In the present text, however, such an individual-level analysis is presented as just one possibility among a range of activities at higher and lower levels of organisation. So while the expression and negotiation of individual-level wants and needs is emphasised in this section, this does not preclude the possibility of additional levels of analysis and action: for instance, supporting women's aid organisations or public policies that help women feel safer on the streets. The aim of this book is to 'fill in' the psychological side of progressive thought and action, but this needs to be embedded in, and run alongside, other forms of analysis: 'both/and' rather than 'either/or'.

A similar response can be made to the charge that NVC does not take sociocultural power differentials, such as structural racism, into account. A Black person who feels that a White panel has discriminated against them at a job interview, for instance, may have little impact if adopting NVC. Indeed, to simply send an NVC email to the interview panel might seem absurd: 'When that job was given to a White person of less ability than me, I felt upset …'. Such a NVC communication may be simply ignored or dismissed by the White panel members because they have so much more power in that situation to impose their own will. This is true but, as discussed, NVC communication does not mean that the applicant cannot, for instance, also seek legal redress, or initiate a social media campaign to boycott the company. And, indeed, minoritised groups speaking honestly and openly about the effects that minoritisation can have on them, and what they want instead – as, for instance, Frantz Fanon's *Black skin, white masks*,[156] or Eddo-Lodge's *Why I'm no longer talking to white people about race* – can be a valuable part of any wider set of political actions.

Finally, it should be noted that research on the effects of NVC, to date, are limited. However, it does show promise:[157] with NVC training increasing empathy levels in, for instance, medical students[158] and people suffering from alcoholism.[159]

### *Action points*

NVC is popular around the world because it provides a concrete, easy-to-learn set of guidelines for how to communicate cooperatively with others – applicable across a wide range of situations. As human beings, we cannot always communicate in NVC ways. If we are feeling overwhelmed with hurt or anger, for instance, we may find ourselves blaming, criticising, or acting manipulatively. NVC, however, provides progressives with a valuable 'benchmark' for how cooperative communication can be done, and a standard towards which we can strive – and encourage others to strive. Action points, therefore, are that:

- All progressives should familiarise themselves with the principles of NVC. A good starting place is the website for the Centre for Nonviolent Communication,[160] or Rosenberg's text *Nonviolent communication: A language of life*.

- All progressives, in all of their interactions, should strive to practice NVC – just as we would strive to talk in, for instance, non-racist or non-homophobic ways. This includes communication and work in such spheres as political dialogue, activism, and governance; parenting; teaching; employment; relationships with family, friends, and partners. Although changing communication patterns can feel strange at first, the principles can be integrated into everyday discourse in natural and fluent ways.
- As part of positive parenting, parents can teach and encourage their children to communicate in NVC ways; just as teachers and education policymakers, as part of SEL, can encourage pupils to adopt it.

### *Emotionally literate politics*

What might political debate and activity look like if progressives were to engage with others – including our political opponents – according to the principles of NVC, and of cooperative communication and relating more broadly (Chapter 6)? The aim of this section is to describe such a form of *emotionally literate politics* (as also advocated by the UK campaigning organisation, Compassion in Politics[161]). As an articulation of what it means to relate to others from a position of psychological equality, such a politics has the possibility of forming the heart of a psychology-informed progressivism.

### *From a politics of blame to a politics of understanding*

If the aforementioned aliens were to visit the Earth, something else that they might be quite amazed by is that the political leaders of our countries – supposedly among the brightest and most able of our citizens, and including those that profess values of cooperation and respect – seem to talk to each other like six-year-olds in a school playground:

> 'You did this!'
> 'No, you did this!'

> 'Well, you're stupid and you lie!'
> 'No, you're stupid and you lie, I'm telling everyone.'
> 'I don't care.'
> 'Well, I don't care either …'

As with squabbling six-year-olds, political rhetoric is full of blame, insults, insinuations, and put-downs: the other construed as either idiotic, or as deliberately trying to act in malevolent and dishonest ways. Direct, honest communication is often entirely absent. This, for instance, is the exchange (abridged) between the Prime Minister (Boris Johnson) and the Leader of the Opposition (Keir Starmer) (at the time of writing) in the UK Government on the 7 July 2021 (Prime Minster's Questions, PMQs). It regards strategies for 'opening up' the country, following the COVID-19 crisis. I have added in what the intended communication might be.

| | |
|---|---|
| Keir Starmer: | [I]f infections reach that level of 100,000 per day what does the Prime Minister expect the number of hospitalisations and deaths and the number of people with long covid will be in that eventuality? [*I want the public to see you as a dangerous maverick.*] |
| The Prime Minister: | There are a number of projections, and they are available from the Scientific Pandemic Influenza Group on Modelling graphs. … I think what people would like to hear from the Labour party, because I was not quite clear from that opening question, is whether or not it will support the progress that this country is intending to make on 19 July [removing COVID-19 restrictions]. The right hon. and learned Gentleman says it is reckless to go ahead; does that mean he is opposing it? [*I want to make sure you say that you oppose opening up, which I know will make you unpopular.*] |

Keir Starmer: We know that the link between infection rates and deaths has been weakened but it hasn't been broken, and the Prime Minister must, and certainly should, know the answer to the question I asked him. That he will not answer it here in the House hardly inspires confidence in his plan. … Knowing all that, is the Prime Minister really comfortable with a plan that means 100,000 people catching this virus every day and everything that that entails? [*I'm going to reinforce the point that you are a dangerous maverick.*]

The Prime Minister: I really think we need to hear from the right hon. and learned Gentleman what he actually supports [… *and I'm going to force you into a position of either saying something which will make you unpopular, or else make you look indecisive and weak*]. We will continue with a balanced and reasonable approach, and I have given the reasons. This country has rolled out the fastest vaccination programme anywhere in Europe. … Last week, or earlier this week, the right hon. and learned Gentleman seemed to support opening up and getting rid of the 1 metre rule – he seemed to support getting back into nightclubs and getting back into pubs without masks – but if he does not support it, perhaps he could clear that up now: is it reckless or not? … The right hon. and learned Gentleman cannot have it both ways. He says it is reckless to open up, yet he attacks self-isolation, which is one of the key protections that this country has. Let me ask him again. On

| | |
|---|---|
| | Monday, he seemed to say he was in favour of opening up on 19 July; now he is saying it is reckless. Which is it, Mr Speaker? [*What you say is completely contradictory – you're an idiot.*] |
| Keir Starmer: | The question was simply how many people are going to be asked to self-isolate if there are 100,000 infections a day, and the Prime Minister will not answer it. We know why he will not answer it and pretends I am asking a different question. [*No, you're an idiot.*] |
| The Prime Minister: | It is still not clear – I think this is about the fourth or fifth time, Mr Speaker – whether the right hon. and learned Gentleman is actually in favour of this country moving forward to step 4 [removing restrictions] on the basis of the massive roll-out of vaccines. [*No, really, you're the idiot.*] |
| Mr Speaker: | Once again, it is Prime Minister's questions and the Prime Minister answers questions. [*You're both idiots.*] |
| Keir Starmer: | If the Prime Minister stopped mumbling and listened, he would have heard the answer the first time. [*You can't even hold a proper conversation.*] We want to open in a controlled way and keep baseline protections that can keep down infections, such as mandatory face masks on public transport. We know that that will protect people, reduce the speed of the virus and the spread of the virus, and it will not harm the economy. It is common sense. Why can the Prime Minister not see that? |
| The Prime Minister: | Of course we can see that it is common sense for people in confined spaces to wear a face mask out of respect and |

> courtesy to others, such as on the tube, but what we are doing is cautiously, prudently moving from legal diktat to allowing people to take personal responsibility for their actions. … We are getting on with taking the tough decisions to take this country forward. We vaccinate, they vacillate. We inoculate, while they are invertebrate. [*Actually, really, we are the best.*][162]

Wow, 'invertebrate'! I actually had to re-check the Hansard transcript and the definition of that last word to really believe that the most powerful political figure in the UK, at the time of writing, would describe the leader of another political party in such a way.

As a progressive, reading an exchange like this, I by no means find it easy to be unpartisan. Rather, what I am thinking and feeling is, 'Go Keir … I hate that bloody f****** Johnson and his Tories.' And I would love nothing better than to see Johnson humiliated, stumbling, crumbling apart to reveal an incoherent, self-serving core at the heart of Tory ideology. I want to be there, in the school playground, jeering and laughing at Johnson as he and Starmer fight: 'Come on Keir, Kick him up the bum, get him on the ground.'

When you stand back and look at this from a more mentalised perspective, however, or think about it in terms of the four 'horsemen' of interpersonal relating – blame, contempt, defensiveness, and stonewalling[163] – the reality is, such a dialogue is setting an appalling example of how human beings should talk to each other. This is not genuine dialogue, being assertive, or taking responsibility – and it is definitely not trusting the other (Chapter 6, this volume). Granted, this is PMQs, and it is not necessarily representative of how politicians always talk to each other (for instance, in cross-party committees). But when the highest profile political exchanges take this blaming, combative, and competitive format, it models a form of political interchange – from dyadic, to local, to national level – that is more about demonisation, egos, and the avoidance of shame then any genuinely cooperative attempt to find mutually agreeable solutions.

If we really want to change the views of those on the right (as well as of other progressives) – and for them to take our viewpoints seriously – we need to move beyond such a politics of blame. If such an approach was even remotely helpful, specialists in negotiation and mediation would have adopted it long ago – yet, as we see (Chapter 6), they do the very opposite. Blame does not persuade the other because it threatens their sense of self-worth, and is therefore likely to make them want to protect themselves and 'shut down'. Rosenberg writes:

> [W]hen our heads are filled with judgments and analyses that others are bad, greedy, irresponsible, lying, cheating, polluting the environment, valuing profit more than life, or behaving in other ways they shouldn't, very few of them will be interested in our needs. … The more people hear blame and judgment, the more defensive and aggressive they become.[164]

This politics of blame also just reinforces a black-and-white way of seeing the world: 'We're good, they're bad.' And, as cognitive psychology teaches us, while black-and-white thinking may be highly satisfying in the short term, it generally fails to bring long-term benefits (Chapter 4, this volume).[165] This is because it just is not matched to the complex reality of how the world is, and therefore how it can be changed. Personally, for instance, I found it deeply satisfying to demonise Johnson and his Tory 'cronies': 'self-serving morons whose only real concerns were to boost the interests of themselves and their class'. But was that really true? *Yes*, every pore of my body wants to say 'yes'; but, no, the complex, nuanced, rationally assessed reality is almost certainly not. Johnson, I am guessing, did not wake up every morning and think, 'Right, how can I screw over the working classes?' More likely, he woke up, gave his partner a cuddle, brushed his teeth, thought about the things he dreaded that day, talked to people, wondered what's fair, tried to do good things for people from his class, tried to do good things for others, felt over-confident, struggled to know what is right, felt vulnerable, got angry, felt ashamed, felt like he had to defend himself, got overwhelmed, worried, kissed his son and his partner goodnight.

However much it might pain me to think it, Johnson was a human being like the rest of us; and, as a fellow human being, would be most likely to be changed if he felt that others were genuinely trying to understand how he is thinking, feeling, and seeing his world.

Alongside parliamentary exchanges, this politics of blame is blatant across party manifestos. Take the following statement from the 2019 Labour Party manifesto: 'Tory cuts … have been deliberately targeted at the poorest areas of the country.'[166] At one level, of course, I want to believe this; but 'deliberately'? Why? This is not just saying that what the other does has a negative effect but that, phenomenologically, the other is downright evil. But do the Conservatives really sit down and think, 'Right, how can we make cuts to the poorest people?' This is the kind of 'mind-reading' that, as we saw in Chapter 6 (this volume), is detrimental to any kind of genuine dialogue. Of course, Labour is not the only progressive party to demonise the other. Here is an extract, for instance, from the 2019 manifesto of the Liberal Democrats: 'Labour and the Conservatives are looking to the past for answers that will not work today: Labour want to hike up income tax in a way that will not even ensure that more tax is paid.'[167] So what is this saying: that the Labour Party are just willy-nilly trying to increase taxation, all the while knowing (or being too stupid to realise) that it will not be to any benefit? And what kind of people does that, then, make Labour: ignorant, closed-minded, uncaring? The Labour Party, the Liberal Democrats go on to state, have failed in ways that are 'morally indefensible' and 'economically illiterate',[168] failing entirely to 'stand up to hatred or combat entrenched inequalities'.[169] I mean, come on, is this really a way to talk about other intelligent and intelligible adults? And according to the Scottish National Party, the Labour Party are trying to 'bribe' the electorate[170] – what terrible human beings they are!

In all this, of course, it is only 'ourselves' that are willing or able to do good things. 'Only Labour has a plan to fix the housing crisis', write the Labour Party;[171] 'Liberal Democrats are the only party capable of building a criminal justice system that can effectively prevent crime', write the Liberal Democrats;[172] 'we are the only party you can trust to act in time to tackle the Climate Emergency and rapidly reduce social and economic inequality', write the Green Party.[173] One of the worst example of this posturing is the following statement in the Liberal Democrats' manifesto: 'Liberal Democrats are the only party forward-looking enough to do what it takes to foster high quality public debate.'[174] Seriously? Initiating 'high quality public debate' by belittling one's adversaries? 'We are good/competent/right, they are bad/incompetent/wrong' – while the pull towards such black-and-white posturing is entirely human (and, perhaps, effective on some segments of the electorate), it seems to set a really unhelpful example for how human beings should communicate with each other.

## *Action points towards a politics of understanding*

Of course, for me to criticise and demonise other progressives for criticising and demonising other progressives is just as bad. Much more useful is to understand where that frustration and anger comes from. In addition, building on NVC and the principles in Chapter 6 of this book, what follows is eight action points that all progressives – politicians and laypeople alike – can take towards developing emotionally-literate political exchanges with others: both within, and outside of, progressive circles. These are similar to the principles developed by Compassion in Politics, who are working with UK parliamentarians to 'call out' hostile, toxic, and shaming styles of interaction between politicians; and instead foster respectful, cooperative, and constructive dialogue.[175]

### *Take the first step*

I have no doubt that those on the right could do much to develop their emotional literacy too. Calling people 'invertebrates'! And I'm sure, if you went through Conservative Party manifestos, you could also find numerous examples of blame, demonisation, and self-aggrandisement – perhaps many more. But focusing on 'the enemy' just gets us back into the politics of, 'We're right, you're wrong', or 'You're as bad as us.' Besides which, it locks us into a right-wing mindset: because the whole basis of conservative ideology is that people are naturally competitive and adversarial, so when we bicker like that, we are just proving them correct. So let us, for now, just forget how the right are doing politics, and instead take the first step ourselves towards a more constructive, dialogic, and understanding way of being political ourselves. This is taking the lead, as discussed in Chapter 6 – because someone has to do it. And we should do it because, ultimately, it is only going to be through that attitude of openness and respect that we can bring about positive change. As Martin Luther King put it in his sermon 'Loving your enemies': 'Darkness cannot drive out darkness; only light can do that. Hate cannot drive out hate; only love can do that.'[176] This is also about embodying in our politics, and modelling, our vision of a better world. Lerner writes, 'we need to engage in tactics that embody the kind of society we want to build – namely, tactics that are unfailingly living, kind, compassionate, generous, and empathic'.[177]

### *Accept and value the other*

As emphasised throughout this book, acceptance is not about condoning all forms of behaviour, and neither does it require us to eschew the use of force – if needed – to protect the rights of minoritised and oppressed peoples. Acceptance is about recognising the humanity of the other: that they are directional beings, striving towards the things that they need and want in, probably, the best ways that they know how. Moreover, at those highest orders, many of the things that they need and want are probably pretty similar to our own: feeling safe and secure (a big one for Conservatives, I am sure); experiencing pleasure; and wanting relatedness and self-worth (Chapter 3, this volume).

In practical terms, then, acceptance does not mean refraining from challenging the ideas or actions of our political opponents. We can challenge these as vigorously as we like. What it does mean, though, is trying to refrain from imputing malevolent motivations behind their thoughts and actions. So this involves trying not to see them, or talk to them, as if they are 'bad' or 'evil' – separating intentions from effects (Chapter 6, this volume). 'Mind-reading' of any sort is unlikely to be of much help. So while we might say, for instance, that we are incredibly concerned about the way Tory policy is impacting on the poor, or that we are angry at the effects we are seeing, let's refrain from the kind of 'You are deliberately trying to harm people' demonisations. We do not know that. It is probably not true. And it is only likely to get our political opponents' backs up: as Rosenberg said, no one likes to be told that they are bad, greedy, and cheating – when, in their own eyes, they are probably trying to do their best in challenging and difficult circumstances.[178]

Moreover, where possible, let us go beyond tolerating our political opponents to actually valuing what they have to say. Again, this does not mean refraining from challenging them, or feeling some obligation to see things how they do. But what it does mean is being willing and able to see the value and legitimacy of what they are wanting to contribute. Ultimately, what we want – for ourselves, for our communities – is the best possible outcomes; and that is unlikely to come from any one single set of ideas. Being genuinely open to the other and what they might know and be able to contribute is likely to be the best way to achieve that. Politics should not be about what makes us right – it should be about what makes people fulfilled.

### *Try to understand the other*

As stated earlier, if we want to change something, we need to know how it works. If my car breaks down, my first response might be to get out and kick it, because I have no idea how cars work, but that is not going to fix it. Rather, it needs someone who understands cars to examine it, diagnose the problem, and then use that knowledge to work out what to do. And while maybe that is not as satisfying, in the short term, as just kicking the car, it is ultimately what is needed to resolve the problem. In the same way, then, if we want to have any hope of changing the political views of those around us, we need to understand why they see things in that way: to empathise with the other – irrespective of whether the other tries to empathise with us. And this is not asking why they see things as 'flawed', 'misguided', and/or 'malevolent' human beings – that's easy to characterise – but why meaning-oriented, sense-making, well-intended human beings might come to act or see things in the ways that they do. Let us imagine ourselves in their shoes: what might we need to have experienced, learnt, or felt – or what might our history or living context need to have been – to adopt a similar stance? And what might their highest-order needs and wants be in it all: What are they, ultimately, striving for?

When we enter into the world of another, what we nearly always see is that there is a lot more vulnerability and fear than was initially visible. What seemed like arrogance, toughness, or disinterest so often turns out to be a desire for self-protection: a fear, by that person themselves, that they will get hurt or something will be taken from them. So, as progressives, when we look at people in positions of privilege in this way (such as the ruling class, White people, men, citizens of the global North) we are going to see that they are also vulnerable and hurting too.[179] Does that mean we should feel sorry for them, focus our attention on how to make them feel better, or withhold our challenges? No, no, and no – there's a lot of other people hurting a lot more right now, and things need to change. But we can do all that without demonising those who were born into positions of privilege. As Lerner writes:

> Being aware of the suffering dimension of the lives of many of the most brutal and uncaring of the rich and powerful may make us more effective and not one ounce less committed to stopping them from hurting anyone more than they, as well as those who do their bidding and the global capitalistic and patriarchal systems they serve, already have done.[180]

Similarly, in contrast to the socialist humanist position outlined in Chapter 2, it does little for progressive parties to see the 'man on the street' as an inane robot, blindly following the whims of the ruling classes and the media magnates. 'We need to see their humanity', writes Lerner, 'understand what is motivating them to vote against their own needs and interests, and treat them and speak to them with respect and dignity.'[181] Without doing so, as discussed in Chapter 2, progressives can come across as elitist, and seeing themselves as 'smarter' and more knowing than those whose support they hope to win.

As Lerner summarises, then, this empathy:

> does not entail the uncritical acceptance of hateful ideas. Rather, it is asking all of us to be genuinely curious about what might lead someone who is not yet with us to choose a particular behaviour, promote a particular

> policy, or support a particular candidate. … Empathy requires the ability to imagine that someone who voted for a candidate we know to be pursing hurtful or even evil programs may only have a superficial commitment to that candidate's actual policies, and to explore with genuine curiosity what it is that underlies a person's identification with such candidates and programs – for example, how fears about one's personal well-being and security may get manipulated into fear of the Other.[182]

### *Engage in genuine dialogue*

Accepting, understanding, and valuing the other leads on to a willingness to engage in genuine political dialogue. This, as we saw in Chapter 6, involves both a willingness to receive the views of the other, and then an expressivity: a willingness to be open and transparent in the encounter. Genuine dialogue, as Buber writes, is a risk: we cannot wholly control the encounter, and we cannot know how we may be changed by it,[183] but it provides a means for real socioeconomic change, because it provides an opportunity to engage with the views of an other in a deep and meaningful way. 'There is no dichotomy between dialogue and revolutionary action', writes Freire, 'On the contrary, *dialogue is the essence of revolutionary action*.'[184] This is as true for dialogues within progressive perspectives as it is with people who are outside of it. Take, for instance, the following example of what genuine dialogue might look like over the issue of antisemitism in the Labour Party:

Jewish Labour Party Member: It just really breaks my heart, as a Jew and as a socialist, that I don't feel safe in the Labour Party.

Pro-Palestinian Labour Party Member: I'm really sorry to hear that. Tell me more about 'not safe'?

Jewish Labour Party Member: I feel like, at any point, I could walk into something really antisemitic. I don't feel people have got my backs. After centuries of persecution, it feels as bad here as it is 'out there'. I just hoped for so much more from the Labour Party.

Pro-Palestinian Labour Party Member: That sounds really awful. I wouldn't want anyone to feel excluded. Labour should be about all of us feeling safe. I guess, the thing is, we also want it to be a place that Palestinians can feel really safe too, and we need to be able to criticise the state of Israel.

Jewish Labour Party Member: I agree. But sometimes when you criticise Israel it feels like you are criticising Jews. There's a sensitivity there – I'm sure you understand why.

Pro-Palestinian Labour Party Member: Of course. But maybe I hadn't quite understood how deep that runs, and how, because of that history, things can easily be interpreted as against you.

Jewish Labour Party Member: Thank you. Yes, I think that's right. It would really help to hear, within the Party, some really positive, pro-Jewish stuff for instance. And some willingness to acknowledge that antisemitism can and does exist, like other forms of racism. I think that would really free me up much more to support Palestinian perspectives and rights. I totally agree that Palestinian people should have there own nation and freedom and I really want to find a way of supporting that.

This is an entirely fictional conversational, but it demonstrates how, within progressivism itself, a combination of receptivity (listening, trying to understand) and expressivity (being honest, open, vulnerable) may help us move forward towards more mutually agreeable, synergetic understandings and actions.

### *Be honest*

Genuine dialogue requires us to express ourselves honestly, and this truthfulness is also essential for the development of trust (Chapter 6). Yet political debate, today, seems a million miles from being an exchange in which two people are simply genuine with each other. Let's imagine how that PMQ debate might go if Johnson and Starmer were actually being honest:

| | |
|---|---|
| Keir Starmer: | Look, I've got to say, I'm really worried about what's happening with COVID-19 and all the hospitalisations, deaths, and the number of people with long COVID. Do you have any idea where all of this is going? |
| The Prime Minister: | Well, there's are a number of projections, but to be honest we're not totally sure. It's scary, isn't it. |
| Keir Starmer: | Yeah, really. And, you know, everyone is looking to us politicians for answers. |
| The Prime Minister: | Yeah, I know. Really scary – it keeps me up at night. Are you sleeping OK? |
| Keir Starmer: | Yeah, most nights, but I do get some really bad dreams. |
| The Prime Minister: | Oh, sorry to hear that. Look, we've been doing a lot of thinking and planning this side but it'd be good to hear what you think. |
| Keir Starmer: | Well, we think you're right to try and open things up a bit more, but we also think it's important to be really cautious for now. So how about … |

Less dramatic and entertaining, perhaps, but at least it cuts through the bluster and posturing, and means that politicians and parties can get down to constructive dialogues about the best ways forward. And it models, for everyone else, a mature and constructive way for two people to engage with each other. If we want our young people to develop social and emotional competences – many of which are centred around the capacity to communicate in open and cooperative ways – it would seem essential that these are modelled 'from the very top'.

### *Show vulnerability*

Being honest means being willing to show all aspects of ourselves, including our vulnerabilities; and that is something that politicians seem loathe to express. Perhaps there is a fear that, if the electorate sees their vulnerabilities, they will see them as weak, indecisive, and unable to govern. Perhaps, too, there is a residue here of the male sex-role demand – for many female, as well as male, politicians – where vulnerability is the very antithesis of what it means to be a 'real man'. This is the challenge, as Lerner puts it, of being seen as 'weak or girly'[185] – a 'snowflake'[186] – vulnerable, as all humans are, to emotional hurt and pain. But the reality is, we can show our vulnerabilities *and* be strong at the same time: after all, for the vast majority of us, that is the reality of our lives. We feel worries, feel hurt, feel insecure – but also get on with living our lives in the best ways we know how.

Showing our vulnerabilities, in political thought and action, means being able to acknowledge our fears and worries. It means being able to express uncertainty and tentativeness: 'I think X is the right policy, and we've decided it on the best evidence we have, but the reality is that we don't know for sure'; and it means acknowledging our complexity and multifacetedness (just, as Mason points out, like snowflakes). It also means being able to acknowledge when we have got things wrong and, where appropriate, apologising. In this way, vulnerability can help to keep progressive perspectives away from the kind of dogmatism that, as the socialist humanists pointed out (Chapter 2), have been their ruin. And, of course, being able to show our vulnerabilities is anything but weakness or cowardice, it requires the greatest courage and strength.

### *Develop self-awareness*

These last steps all require self-awareness. To be able to engage in genuine dialogue, to be honest, and particularly to be able to show vulnerability, we need to be able to mentalise (Chapter 6) – and know – ourselves. We need to know what our values are, we need to know what we need and want, and we need to know what we are feeling. No doubt, much political behaviour is driven by such 'personal' factors, and when they act unconsciously – rather than with our awareness and acknowledgement – they are much more likely to subvert constructive conversations.

Developing self-awareness is not about 'psychologising away' political views and actions. It is not about saying, for instance, that a person's commitment to social justice just comes down to them feeling treated unfairly as a child. It is also not about blaming people for having their political behaviours influenced by personal needs, wants, and emotions – that will happen to us all. Rather, it is about recognising how these personal elements may be mixed up in how we are politically, and then seeing if there is anything we might want to change. We might recognise, for instance, that, in political arguments, our tendency is to present ourselves as extremely confident and sure, particularly when we cannot fully understand the other person's argument. We do not want to appear stupid, so we tend to overcompensate. Noticing this, we may then choose to communicate in more open-minded and questioning ways. Understanding some of the drivers behind our behaviours then also gives us the option of sharing this with others, leading to potentially more honest and constructive dialogue. Acknowledging to someone, for instance, that we are really struggling to follow their argument, rather than simply lobbing back something we can be confident in saying, may ultimately lead to a more constructive and clarifying conversation.

### *Develop self-compassion and self-care*

It is a cliché but, ultimately, to be able to feel compassion and care to others – including those we disagree with – we also, generally, need to feel it towards ourselves. Rosenberg puts this boldly when he states, 'It is impossible for us to give something to another if we don't have it ourselves.'[187] Why? First, because it requires energy and resources to reach out to others, and if we cannot nurture ourselves, then we are less likely to have resources to give to others. Rosenberg adds here, 'If we find ourselves unable or unwilling to empathize despite our efforts, it is usually a sign that we are too starved for empathy to be able to offer it to others.' Second, if we try and be caring and compassionate to others without feeling it to ourselves, then we are likely to end up feeling resentful and frustrated: why do they get to be accepted when we do not? Third, it is the same skills that we need to feel care and compassion to others as it is to ourselves. So if we can cultivate that mindset 'inwards', it will help us be able to express it outwards – and vice versa. Put conversely, if our default stance towards ourselves is primarily one of criticism, contempt, and blame, there may be a greater likelihood that that will also be our default stance towards others. As we saw in Chapter 5 (this volume), however, the relationship between the realisation of needs and wants across different levels of organisation is a complex one: an exclusive focus on self-care, for instance, could take our attention away from caring for others. Most likely, there is some optimum level of self-care – different for each individual – that maximises their ability to care for self and care for others in synergetic ways.

## Developing a wellbeing economy

The fifth area of activity to be discussed in this chapter, again with the potential to make a major concrete contribution to a psychology-informed progressive vision, is one of the most exciting new developments in international politics today: *wellbeing economics*. This approach is, again, at the psychology–politics interface, and closely aligned to the principles and theory developed in this book. However, whereas the proceeding four sections have primarily focused on intra- and interpersonal agenda issues that can contribute towards progressive social change, wellbeing economics focuses on the use of psychological (as well as community- and environmental-level) benchmarks to guide political policy. As argued in the Introduction, psychology can be useful to progressive politics because it can help us understand what it is that people really need and want; and wellbeing economics gives a compelling example of how such a politics might look. In reviewing the field of wellbeing economics, then, I aim to show how progressive political agendas can take improved wellbeing as their principal focus: at the individual level, the community level, and all within the global limits within which human beings need to function.

Much of the wellbeing economic agenda has been spurred, and coordinated, by an organisation called the Wellbeing Economy Alliance (WEAll), which was established in 2018 and now comprises of more than 200 organisations.[188] WEAll is 'a prominent cross-sectoral collaboration hub for academics, businesses, citizens, and networks, with the mission of spreading knowledge and policy tools working towards a Wellbeing Economy'.[189] Most impressively, perhaps, WEAll has sparked the development of a Wellbeing Economy Governments partnership (WEGo), which (at the time of writing) comprises the national governments of Scotland, New Zealand, Iceland, Wales, and Finland. 'WEGo is a collaboration of national and regional governments promoting sharing of expertise and transferable policy practices, with the aim to deeper their understanding and advance their shared ambition of building Wellbeing Economies.'[190]

Although WEAll does not have a stated political affiliation, its politics are generally aligned with progressive parties and policies: advocating, for instance, higher taxation to support the development of wellbeing practices.[191] WEGo governments also tend to be left of centre (and, interestingly, almost exclusively led by young women): Jacinda Ardern, for instance, leading New Zealand's Labour Party; and Sanna Marin heading the centre-left Social Democratic Party in Finland.

In England, Caroline Lucas, former leader of the Green Party and MP for Brighton Pavilion, has been closely aligned with WEAll. In February 2020, she tabled an Early Day Motion to the UK Parliament, making proposals for a 'sustainable and inclusive wellbeing economy',[192] with a debate on a Wellbeing Economy approach to meeting climate goals held on 30 November 2021.[193] Lucas's motion received support from a range of MPs, including from the Labour Party, Scottish National Party, and the Social Democratic and Labour Party of Northern Ireland (SDLP). In line with a wellbeing economics perspectives, the Green Party manifesto also made a 'quality of life' guarantee, 'unleashing the potential for everyone to live happier, more secure lives – and making this the central purpose of government'.[194] Most directly, the 2019 manifesto of the Liberal Democrats committed to introducing a New Zealand-style wellbeing budget; and, uniquely, also proposed the appointment of a 'Minster for Wellbeing', who would 'make an annual statement to Parliament on the main measures of wellbeing and the effects of government policies on them'.[195] In the 2021 London mayoral elections, the Women's Equality Party also proposed a wellbeing budget for the city.[196]

## *What is a wellbeing economy?*

The concept of a wellbeing economy is best understood in terms of what it opposes: a fixation on gross domestic product (GDP) as the principle indicator of a nation's wealth and progress.[197] GDP can be defined as 'the market value of goods and services produced with a nation's borders in a year'.[198] GDP is one of the most prominent economic statistics and is typically used to assess the size and health of a country's economy over time.[199] As Robert Kennedy famously quipped, however, GDP 'measures everything … except that which makes life worthwhile'.[200] Indeed, we could consider an exclusive focus on GDP as a rogue goal (Chapter 3, this volume): a positively reinforcing objective that hijacks a societal system at the expense of numerous other psychological, social, and environmental directions. Here, growth, de facto, becomes 'good', without anyone asking, 'growth of what, and why, and for whom, and who pays the cost, and how long can it last, and what's the cost to the planet, and how much is enough'?[201] As an example of this, in the 2021 Early Day Motion Debate, Rebecca Long Bailey of the Labour Party noted that an increase in the number of car crashes would lead to greater GDP (with, for instance, more money spent on car repairs), but at a terrible human cost. Similarly, Claire Hanna of the SDLP stated, 'It is very clear that a system that accounts for tobacco sales and bets placed by gambling addicts, but does not find any way to capture time spend raising children or the value of clean air, is no longer fit for purpose.'[202] In fact, as Raworth points out, our addiction to GDP has taken us into extremely dangerous territory: 'caught in the twin dynamics of growing social inequality and deepening ecological degradation'.[203] Raworth argues, then, that we should be 'growth agnostic': open to the possibilities of GDP growth, but not prioritising it as the be-all and end-all of nation-level progress.

In this sense, a wellbeing economy has been termed a 'beyond-GDP-approach'.[204] It can be defined as '[a]n economy that is designed with the purpose of serving the wellbeing of people and the planet first and foremost', and hence, 'delivers social justice on a healthy planet'.[205] Here, the economy is 'in service of wellbeing goals, not a goal in and of itself'.[206] Lerner proposes something similar when he calls on our global societies:

> [T]o embrace a new bottom line so that every economic, political, societal, and cultural institution is considered efficient, rationale, and/or productive – not according to the old bottom line of how much these institutions maximized money, power, or ego but rather how much they maximize love and generosity, kindness and forgiveness, ethical and environmental sustainable behavior, social and economic justice.[207]

While different wellbeing economics frameworks define and operationalise wellbeing in different ways, WEAll describes five universally identified needs: to live a dignified life; a safe and restored natural world for all beings; connections to people and institutions; fairness and justice; and participation in communities.[208] This shares many similarity to the set of highest-order needs and wants identified in Chapter 3 (for example, dignity as self-worth, and connection as relatedness); but also includes community-, nation-, and global-level indicators of wellbeing, as well as those at the individual level. In the terms of this book, then, wellbeing economies are fundamentally about putting the realisation of highest-order needs and wants – at the individual, community, and national level – at the heart of economic and government policy. Rather than starting with long-standing economic theories, this is about starting with humanity's long-term goals – the things that make life truly worthwhile – and then seeking out the economics that would get us there.[209] Economic growth, from this perspective, can be part of that wellbeing agenda, but it needs to be considered within the system as a whole; and as a lower-order means to specific ends, rather than a highest-order end in itself.

### *Wellbeing metrics and their application*

Developing a wellbeing economy, by necessity, needs to start with the establishment of metrics and tools that are 'capable of capturing and assessing human wellbeing'.[210] These indicators may be 'subjective' (that is, non-material): drawing, for instance, on data from self-report surveys; or 'objective' (that is, material), using 'hard data' such as mortality rates. Hundreds of different 'beyond GDP' measures now exist[211] – the UN's Sustainable Development Goals being a prime example (see Chapter 5, this volume) – often combining individual-, community-, and environmental-level measures of wellbeing; and with a focus on equitability of distribution as well as averages. As an example, the Organisation for Economic Co-Operation and Development (OECD) has established 11 dimensions along which wellbeing can be assessed (on a 0–10 scale): safety, housing, life satisfaction, access to services, civic engagement, education, jobs, community, environment, income, and health.[212] Most of these are assessed through objective indicators (for instance, 'safety' by homicide rates, and 'education' by share of labour force with at least secondary education), but subjective indicators are also used for some dimensions (for instance, 'life satisfaction' by average scores on a self-report satisfaction question, and 'community' by perceived social support network). In some instances, such indicators are then combined into a single score of wellbeing, such as the Gross National Happiness Index of Bhutan established in 2008.[213] Through complex statistical procedures, such indicators and indexes can also be converted into standardised metrics, such as 'wellbeing adjusted life years'. These can then be used to highlight areas of concern, conduct cost–benefit analyses, and steer policy decisions towards the greatest wellbeing return on investment.[214] For instance, in Denmark (one of the happiest countries in the world), it is estimated that 75,000 good years of life are lost to loneliness annually in the adult population.[215] Wellbeing has also been 'monetised' for the purposes of embedding it in economic and policy decision-making. For instance, in New Zealand, 'Feeling lonelier' has been allocated a monetary cost of $17,543 (equivalent to about £9,000), and 'Living in a colder home' has been allocated a cost of $6,681 (equivalent to about £3,500).[216]

At the most basic level, wellbeing metrics can then be used by governments, policymakers, or statistical offices to monitor citizens' wellbeing. They might be employed, for instance, to compare across nations or regions within nations, and they can also be used to analyse change over time. In addition, they can be employed to identify subgroups of the population that are at different levels of wellbeing. For instance, in Bhutan, the Gross National Happiness Index is used to categorise citizens in 'deeply happy', 'extensively happy', 'narrowly happy', and 'unhappy' groups (8.3 per cent, 32.6 per cent, 48.7 per cent, and 10.4 per cent of the population, respectively, as of 2011[217]). Dashboards and indexes of wellbeing are also, typically, available to members of the general public. For example, OECD wellbeing data can be accessed at an interactive online dashboard.[218] Here, for instance, it is possible to compare life satisfaction, health, and environment in Greater London (currently 5.9, 8.7, and 6.5, respectively) against other regions in the UK like Scotland (currently 7.4, 4.9, and 8.2, respectively), or other parts of the world, like Eastern Anatolia in Turkey (currently 1.5, 4.6, and 0.2, respectively). An interactive dashboard of wellbeing across nations, with the possibility to weight different dimensions, is also available through the OECD Better Life Index.[219] Another publicly available site is the Happy Planet Index (HPI), which combines data on life expectancy, wellbeing (self-reported satisfaction), and ecological footprint (average impact per resident on the environment, as hectares of land needed, per person) to produce an overall HPI score, with Costa Rica, Vanuata, and Colombia heading the table in 2019.[220]

By definition, however, a wellbeing economy needs to go beyond the monitoring of societal wellbeing. In addition, it needs to use this data to *prioritise*: to inform 'government priorities, wellbeing budgets, and/or concrete agendas'.[221] Beyond this, there is then the active use of wellbeing metrics in *policymaking*: providing a systematic impact – for instance, through cost–benefit analysis – of what is expected, and achieved, by different policies; and then implementing the most wellbeing-efficient.

### *Wellbeing economies in action*

'The concept of "Wellbeing Economy" is increasingly being implemented by governments all over the world with New Zealand's Wellbeing Budget the most prominent example.'[222] This budget, handed down on 30 May 2019, was the first in which a nation's entire financial planning was designed around wellbeing priorities. Grant Robertson, New Zealand Minister of Finance, described the budget as a new approach to how government works, placing the wellbeing of New Zealanders at the heart of what government did. In line with the philosophy behind wellbeing economics, he states:

> This approach represents a significant departure from the status quo. Budgets have traditionally focused on a limited set of economic data. Success has been declared on the basis of a narrow range of indicators, like GDP growth. But New Zealanders have questioned that claim of success when they have seen other things that we hold dear – child wellbeing, a warm, dry home, or being able to swim in our rivers and lakes – getting steadily worse. The old ways have left too many people behind. It is time to change.
>
> New Zealanders want us to measure our success in line with their values – the importance of fairness, the protection of the environment, the strength of our communities. That is what this Wellbeing Budget sets out to do.[223]

This 2019 Wellbeing Budget had five priorities, including taking mental health seriously; improving child wellbeing; and supporting Māori and Pasifika aspirations. This led to a range of concrete financial commitments. For instance, as part of 'taking mental health seriously', the New Zealand Government established a new frontline service for mental health with a \$455 million programme (approximately £250 million), gave suicide prevention services a \$40 million boost (approximately £20 million), and sought to tackle homelessness with over 1,000 new places in a housing programme. To weigh up different budgetary proposals, New Zealand's ministries undertook economic analyses using standardised, monetised values of wellbeing, as detailed in the previous subsection. Trebeck and Baker explain:

> Individual departments are instructed that their budget proposals will be assessed against 12 wellbeing outcomes and four capitals (natural, human, physical/financial and social), including a wellbeing analysis (who is affected?) and intervention logic. Any bids for the wellbeing budget funds that are aligned with

> one or more of the five budget priorities and which demonstrate collaboration between departments are prioritised.[224]

This commitment to wellbeing economies has subsequently been enshrined in New Zealand's 2020 Public Finance (Wellbeing) Amendment Bill.[225] This requires all government budget policy statement to 'explain how wellbeing objectives have guided the Government's Budget decisions',[226] and 'explain how the wellbeing objectives are intended to support long-term wellbeing in New Zealand'.[227]

New Zealand is just one of numerous examples where wellbeing economies are now being implemented at the national or regional level. Iceland, for instance, as another of the WEGo nations, has established its own wellbeing indicators, linked to the UN's Sustainable Development Goals – in this case divided into society (for example, health, security), environment (for example, air quality, land use), and economy (for example, employment, housing) – which are now being used to inform government policy formation.[228] As a more local example, the city of Canoas, part of the Porto Alegre conurbation in Brazil, has experimented with innovative means of involving citizens in policy design and implementation.[229] This includes, for instance, the mayor and municipal secretaries setting up a weekly street stall to discuss policies and issues with their citizens, and participatory budgeting, in which '[c]itizens determine priority policies and services for their neighbourhoods through an annual vote'.[230]

### *Action points*

- Progressive parties should consider making the development of wellbeing economies a central plank of their manifestos: committing to establish robust, transparent, and evidence-based wellbeing indicators, and using these to prioritise and to guide policy.
- Progressive politicians in power – at the local as well as the national level – should focus, explicitly, on the development of their citizens' wellbeing. Clear guidance on developing a wellbeing vision has been provided by WEAll, for

instance: establishing wellbeing priorities and goals, engaging in meaningful public participation, and giving extra weight to the wellbeing priorities of marginalised communities.[231]
- Progressive individuals should familiarise themselves with the principles of wellbeing economics (through, for instance, the numerous resources on the WEAll website) and consider becoming members of WEAll – one of the most dynamic, innovative, and influential political movements at the present time.

## Summing up

This chapter details five concrete strategies that can support movement towards a psychology-informed progressive society. Positive parenting and SEL can help us raise children who are able to develop cooperative solutions with others, and NVC skills can help us consolidate – and practice that – as adults. An emotionally literate politics takes this cooperative stance into the political arena, modelling positive and progressive ways of relating for all. Wellbeing economics gives us a goal and a pathway ahead: to assess, and steer, a society by the wellbeing of its citizens, rather than a country's economic productivity. These strategies are not proposed as alternatives to established progressive agendas. Equally, however, they are not proposed simply as 'add ons'. Rather, they are proposed as integral ingredients to developing a world in which people can genuinely work together in more cooperative, democratic, and egalitarian ways. That is, just as such a world needs people who are committed to caring for the planet, for animals, and to tackling social injustices; so such a world needs people who have learnt to communicate with each other – from the earliest ages – in respectful, valuing, and humanising ways.

These five strategies, however, are just some of the ways in which we might use psychology ideas and practices to support progressive social change. Developing compassionate institutions – as proposed by Compassion in Politics – might be another much-needed area for growth: for instance, compassionate prisons, compassionate hospitals, and compassionate immigration systems. What would all such public institutions look like if we put caring, empathic, and NVC ways of relating to others at their forefront?

There is also, of course, the role of psychological interventions in alleviating distress, as well as helping to develop people's capacities to relate in compassionate and cooperative ways. Mental health problems such as depression or anxiety not only create misery for millions of people but, in many instances, may make it more difficult for people to focus on caring and contributing to others. When we are locked in our own fears or obsessions, the wellbeing of others can seem a distant concern. Another recent development with considerable potential for progressivism is the researching and articulation, as noted in Chapter 5, of 'Inner Development Goals': individual-level skills and qualities that can support the establishment of a more socially just, thriving globe (as defined by the UN's Sustainable Development Goals).[232] These map closely on to the common principles of positive change detailed in Chapter 6 (this volume), with 23 skills and qualities organised into five categories: relationship to self (for example, inner compass, self-awareness); cognitive skills (for example, critical thinking, long-term orientation and visioning); caring for others and the world (for example, connectedness, empathy and compassion); social skills (for example, communication skills, trust); and driving change (for example, courage, creativity).

In the next chapter, I want to take this analysis a step forward by asking what a psychology-informed progressive society might look like decades, or even centuries, ahead. This is a move away from the concrete strategising of the present chapter towards a more utopian vision of how things might, one day, be. Idealistic and fantastical perhaps, but from the directional perspective adopted in this book, where we are going is always part of who we—and our communities and nations—are. Hence, the question is not whether we have a vision for the long-term future or not. Rather, it is whether we make that vision explicit; and doing so may enable us to examine, discuss, and improve upon it as far as possible.

8

# The further future: envisioning a progressive utopia

As a child, I often wondered what the communist paradise would look like. For some reason, despite my family's atheism, I imagined lots of people wandering around on clouds (and eating lots of sweets) – clearly my religious education lessons had seeped in somewhere. But what did people actually do in this better world? How did they live? And what was it about this world that gave people more satisfying and fulfilling lives? Communism, it seemed to me, was all about making a better world, but what I wanted to understand was what that better world might actually be like. And indeed, as introduced in Chapter 1, progressives have been accused of spending much more time focusing on what they see as wrong as opposed to articulating what 'right' would look like. Socialism, writes Bregman, has become little more than a force for resisting and reigning in the opposition: 'Anti-privitazation, anti-establishment, anti-austerity. Given everything they're against, one is left to wonder, what are underdog socialists actually *for*?'[1]

So what kind of society would need to exist for the full development and thriving of each individual, each community, and the planet as a whole? That is the subject matter of the present chapter, which critically explores the nature of a far future progressive utopia, based on the psychological principles outlined in Chapters 3 and 4, the system-wide principles of cooperative organisation set out in Chapters 5 and 6, and then the practical steps of Chapter 7. The chapter begins by setting out why utopian thinking may be so important for progressives, and then defines utopias in terms of the realisation of highest-order needs and wants. On this basis, the chapter uses the eight fundamental directions, set out in Chapter 3 – as well as directionality itself – as the basis for considering what an ideal society might look like. Key here is the creation of synergies (Chapter 4): to maximise benefit in a society, we need to find ways in which multiple highest-order needs and wants can be realised together, rather than in opposition to each other. Of course, along the lines of previous chapters, the aim here is not to pin down – definitively – what a progressive utopia should look like. Rather, it is to stimulate reflection and consideration on this question: to help us, as progressives, create a vision for the future that is coherent and meaningful, and compelling for others as well as ourselves.

## Utopian thinking in progressive politics

No doubt, there are good reasons why progressives have been wary of presenting positive visions of society, particularly in their most utopian forms. Against the backdrop of worldwide inequality, discrimination, and struggle, it can seem something of a luxury – indeed, somewhat unempathic and gauche – to talk of how things might be: bourgeois, abstract, global North fantasies to indulge in while the rest of the world suffers. Marx and Engels were certainly no fans of utopian thinking.[2] In fact, in writings such as the *Manifesto of the Communist Party*, their anger and derision is as much directed to the early utopian socialists – such as Henri de Saint-Simon, Joseph Fourier, and Robert Owen – as it was to the ruling classes. For Marx and Engels, such reformist thinking threatened to deaden, rather than stoke, the real (class) struggles.[3] Moreover, in contrast to the technological determinism of Marx's later work, utopian thinking could be seen as placing too great an emphasis on the agency of individual human beings and their capacities to bring about change.[4]

Progressives may also have been wary of utopian thinking because of the materialist, rationalist roots of progressive politics – away from idealism, mysticism, and fantastical thinking.[5] Zygunt Bauman, a Polish-born social theorist, wrote:

> One can only suppose that the disrepute into which utopian thinking has fallen is that shared by magic,

> religion, and alchemy – all those slushy paths of the errant human mind which modern science set about eliminating once and for all from the map of human action. Having been defined from the outset as an idle, unrealistic blueprint without much basis in reality, utopia was irretrievably cast among the false ideas which in fact hinder human progress by diverting human effort from the ways of reason and rationality.[6]

From a broader perspective, the Austrian-British philosopher Karl Popper argued that utopian visions can lead to authoritarianism and violence.[7] For Popper, there is an inherent pluralism to human beings' highest-order needs and wants (as discussed in Chapter 3, this volume), such that we will all have different views of what an ideal society might look like. Popper argued, therefore, that one utopian vision can only come to the fore by dominating and eliminating others.

As I intuited as a child, however, utopian elements can also be considered at the very heart of progressive thought and action.[8] 'The Left', writes Kolakowski, 'gives forth utopias just as the pancreas discharges insulin'.[9] Indeed, for Kolakowski, it is this utopianism that distinguishes progressive perspectives from conservative ones: the latter idealising 'what is', while the former – by its very definition – reaches forward to 'what may be'. Despite Marx's anti-utopianism, his historical analysis is based on the assumption that society is progressing towards an ideal of social organisation – communism – in which the 'riddle of history' is solved. In his early writings, Marx also gives glimpses of what life, here, might be like: for instance, extensive leisure time, people adopting a multiplicity of social and occupational roles, and labour in which people express their individuality and community with others.[10] Similarly, the early socialist utopians did, indeed, try to envision ideal forms of social organisation and, to some extent, put these into practice. At his cotton mills in New Lanark, for instance, Robert Owen built a 'model community' from 1800 to 1825 in which workers could have free education and healthcare, leisure and recreation activities, and the world's first infant schools. Feminist, postcolonial, green, anarchist, and other progressive perspectives also – either implicitly or explicitly – have put forward a vision of what a 'viable, free, and humane post-capitalist order', as Chomsky puts it, might look like.[11] In this sense, utopian thinking is inherently aligned with a progressive desire to improve the human condition: we cannot have one without the other.

For progressives such as Buber (*Paths in utopia*, 1949), Bauman (*Socialism: The active utopia*, 1976), and Bregman (*Utopia for realists*, 2017), utopian visions are not only at the heat of progressive social change, but capable of determining and directing it. 'Without the utopian of other times', writes Bauman, 'men would still live in caves, miserable and naked'.[12] Why might this be the case?

First, utopian ideas can serve to negate, critique, and dispel the illusion – fostered by conservatives – that the present social configuration is the only one possible.[13] Utopian thinking lays out possibilities for what might be, and hence subverts our reification of what currently is. In psychological terms, utopian thinking invites us to mentalise (Chapter 6, this volume): to stand back from our current reality and to consider it as one among numerous possibilities. A powerful example of this is the 1915 novel *Herland*, by first wave feminist Charlotte Perkin Gilman, which envisages a female-only society: devoid of such 'male' qualities as competition, hierarchies, and personal pride.[14] For the early 20th-century reader, this novel presented a radical challenge to the assumption that male domination was inevitable. And, even if such possibilities are just possibilities – outlandish, unrealistic, impractical – it 'cuts loose our thinking' and 'throws open the windows of the mind'.[15] If you have ever taken part in a 'brainstorming' exercise to solve a problem – generating multiple possibilities in a non-critical environment – you will know the value of simply being allowed to 'let go' and think openly and creatively.[16] Nine out of every ten ideas may be highly impractical, but by creating a context in which people feel free to generate possibilities, the tenth idea may be brilliant. Indeed, across multiple models of cooperative problem-solving (see Chapters 5–7, this volume), the free and creative generation of multiple possible solutions is consistently advocated as a key stage towards success.

In recent years, the horizons of possibilities opened up by utopian thinking has been strongly emphasised by José Esteban Muñoz, the late Cuban American academic, in *Cruising utopia: The then and there of queer futurity*. 'The present is not enough' writes Muñoz, 'It is impoverished and toxic for queers and other people who do not feel the privilege of majoritarian belonging, normative tastes, and "rational" expectations.'[17] For Muñoz, utopian thinking was a way of standing back from a heteronormative world (which, for instance, assumed straight marriage and reproduction), as well as from a 'neoliberal gay agenda' (which, for instance, campaigned for gay marriages or the rights of gays to serve in the military). Instead it allowed for the collective consideration of other, more experimental forms of love, sex, and relationships. 'Queerness is essentially about the rejection of a here and now', wrote Muñoz, 'and an insistence on potentiality or concrete possibility for another world'.[18] In this respect, for Muñoz, queerness and utopian fantasising were fundamentally intertwined: he saw utopianism as having the same potential function for other liberationist struggles.

Utopian thinking, then, can also be invaluable to the development of a more progressive society because it creates a new 'lodestar' – albeit a 'distant, uncharted continent'[19] – of where we want to be. When we know what we are striving for, we can be more focused and more persistent; we are also reminded of our own agency in being able to bring change about.[20] In these ways, the visioning of a new society can energise and motivate people: inspiring them towards new, progressive possibilities.[21] As Lerner points out, Martin Luther King, in one of the most inspiring and oft-quoted speeches of all time, did not say 'I have a ... complaint'.[22] It was his dream, his positive vision for the future that galvanised people into action. Here, utopian visions can also 'keep hope alive' at times when more reactionary ideologies may dominate.[23]

Indeed, in these respects, utopian visions can be considered the social-level equivalent of personal goals: 'Subjectively desirable states of affairs that the individual intends to attain through action'.[24] And, as is clear from the psychological literature, goal setting (and monitoring of goal progress) is associated with greater progress towards our objectives.[25] This is particularly the case when our goals are approach goals (that is, what we want), rather than avoidance goals (that is, what we do not want).[26] More broadly, in terms of the psychological model outlined in Chapter 3 (this volume), utopian ideas can be seen as a social-level expression of our directionality: our inherent on-the-way-to-somewhereness. 'The essence of utopia seems to be desire', writes Ruth Levitas, author of *The concept of utopia*, 'the desire for a different, better way of being'.[27] From this standpoint, then, human beings are, by definition, utopian;[28] with utopian thought expressing the 'inner aim' of our existences.[29] Hence, it may not be a question of whether individuals – and societies – have utopian visions or not. Rather, it may more be a question of whether those visions are explicitly articulated; or whether they are left to wither beneath layers of cynicism, anti-idealism, and negativity.

There is a third reason, however, why utopian thinking may be so important to progressives: we actually, genuinely, need to work out what a better, fairer society might look like. Without doubt, some elements may be straightforward, like reduced poverty or increased care for the environment. But what about the nature of work (if any), or leisure; and how might we balance the need for collectivisation against a need for personal autonomy? Of course, these questions cannot just be answered in a theoretical vacuum, but they do need to be considered, discussed, and debated. We cannot create a better world without knowing what that is; and, perhaps, most of us progressives do not have a clear, detailed vision of what that better world would be. Indeed, perhaps part of the reason that progressives have tended to dismiss utopian thinking is that, at heart, it is just very difficult to envisage what a better world would look like. Far easier to criticise the current state of affairs than to take on the challenging and complex task of articulating what it is we are actually wanting.

## What is a utopia?

Bauman defines a utopia as 'an image of a future and better world' with four characteristics: (a) it is desirable; (b) it is, as of yet, unfulfilled; (c) it requires effort to be brought about; and (d) it is a critical response to the existing social configuration.[30] The term was coined by Thomas More in his 1516 book of that name, 'ou' meaning no or not in Greek, and 'topia' meaning place.[31] However, More also refers to his mystical island as 'Eutopia', 'eu' meaning good or well. So Utopia can be interpreted as 'no place', 'good place', or both. Notions of an ideal future society, however, stretch far back before More in both time and place: from the ashrams of India as early as 1500 BCE, to Plato's philosophy, to Christian conceptualisations of the 'Kingdom of Heaven', to contemporary African literature.[32]

Sargent, in his *Short introduction to utopianism*, describes three different kinds of utopianism.[33] First there are *literary utopias*: narrative descriptions of a future, better way of being, as in More's Utopia or in the works of Ursula le Guin. Second are *utopian practices*, in particular 'intentional communities' or communes, such as kibbutzim, in which individuals attempt to live out particular, idealised forms of social organisation. Third is *utopian social theory*, which includes both political visions of a preferred future society – as in Marx's communism – but also critical analyses of utopian ideas and the roles that they have played in social and political processes.

Literary utopias are, perhaps, where the boundaries of human imagination and possibility have been most fully extended. More's Utopia, for instance, is a land of communal ownership, and with an 'equal' distribution of goods (though 'equal' meaning across un-enslaved males only). There is a six-hour working day, with free time to cultivate the mind, and an emphasis on 'higher' mental and physical pleasures, such as music and healthy living.

American journalist Edward Bellamy presents another classic utopian vision in his widely read 1888 text, *Looking backward*.[34] Here, foreshadowing elements of the Soviet state, Bellamy describes a highly mechanised and industrialised socialist society – controlled by the workers – where even dinners are produced and consumed collectively. In Bellamy's Boston of the year 2000, buying and selling – along with money – have been abolished. Equality (this time a real equality, across genders and without slaves) is rigorously maintained. Each person contributes to society what they can, based on their 'natural aptitude'. The greatest achievement in this society, write Bellamy, is not wealth, property, or power, but simple 'red ribbons', awarded by the people to the greatest artists, engineers, and workers of their generation.

A very different utopia is described by English textile designer and socialist activist William Morris in his *News from nowhere* – partly in response to the urbanised state socialism of Bellamy, which Morris abhorred.[35] Morris, instead, describes a pastoral idyll that his future self journeys through as he travels up the Thames: clean, beautiful, and natural – a world devoid of technology, machinery, and large urban sprawls. Small-scale farming, collectives, and craft activities dominate; free love rather than the institution of marriage. And, unlike Bellamy, Morris describes a world in which government no longer exists: 'because the whole people is our parliament'.[36]

Gilman's *Herland* is another kind of ecological paradise, but this time hidden among the dense forests of some 'savage' land. In this women-only world, children are cared for collectively, there are no wars, no punishments, and no capitalist incentivisation. The women live in harmony with their environment, respectful to the animals and the natural world around them.

For centuries, literary utopias have provided progressives with a forum in which they can articulate, explore, and debate their visions for a better society. Experimental, indeed, but they also allow for some very serious examination of the direction in which progress should be oriented, and the principles on which that should be based.

## Utopia as the realisation of needs and wants

Utopian views of a future, better world are closely connected to an understanding of what it means to be, and thrive as, a human being; that is, what human beings most fundamentally need and want (Chapter 3, this volume). In the medieval poem *The Land of Cockaigne*, for instance, paradise is presented as a world of endless pleasures with rivers of milk and wine – representing, no doubt, what was foremost in the medieval peasant's mind.[37] Similarly, in the voices of the Utopians, More articulates his beliefs that human beings are most fulfilled when they experience 'pleasure', defined as 'any state of activity, physical or mental, which is *naturally* enjoyable'.[38] By this More particularly means the 'higher' forms of enjoyment such as learning and the arts; while 'unnatural' joys – such as fashionable clothes, jewellery, or hunting – are derided as idiotic (note the parallel with Fromm's 'true' and 'false' needs, Chapter 2). Similarly, Bellamy's utopia is designed to 'give free play to every instinct of human nature which does not aim at dominating others or living on the fruit of others' labour'.[39] And what are these instincts? Here, Bellamy takes a more pluralistic view than More, holding that, while some may desire artistic, scientific, and scholarly pursuits, for others, it may be enjoyment, travel, and 'every imaginable form of recreation'.[40] 'If bread is the first necessity of life', writes Bellamy, 'recreation is a close second, and the nation caters for both'. For Marx, too, the essence of a utopian society was the manifestation – and satisfaction of – multiple human needs, in contrast with capitalism's sole focus on acquiring wealth.[41]

So what might a future utopia look like if we (a) started with a contemporary, evidence-based understanding of human beings' highest-order needs and wants, as summarised in Chapter 3; and (b) took into account the principles of, and concrete strategies for, maximising the realisation of these needs and wants, as detailed in Chapters 5 to 7? This is the challenge taken up in the following sections: to describe what a psychology-informed progressive utopia might look like. To achieve this, the sections focus, in part, on how each different directions could be realised as fully as possible. However, given the potential for synergies and dysergies between different needs and wants, the chapter also considers which directions might be most important to prioritise. As with Raworth's doughnut, the starting point for this analysis is also that we have to live within our planetary resources. However, like Mason[42] and Bastani,[43] I am assuming a future of technological abundance: with, for instance, limitless power generation, asteroid mining, and massive increases in computing power.

## Physiological needs

At the most basic level, a progressive utopian society would need to ensure that everyone's essential physiological needs are met: for instance, for food, drink, sleep, physical warmth, and health. Equality of access to such satisfiers would be particularly important because, as Maslow suggests, these physiological requirements may be right at the very base of a hierarchy of needs, 'the most prepotent of all'.[44] Hence, if some members of society did not have these basic needs met, they may struggle to actualise any higher-order directions at all. This means that, at the most basic level, our progressive utopia would need to be a society free of hunger; where there is good housing and excellent healthcare available for all. To ensure this, a progressive utopia would need policies, institutions, and services in place. This means, for instance, well-funded healthcare, housing, and social services; and a basic income for all.[45] As argued in Chapter 6, this would require coordinating agencies – local, national, and international governments – that can support the fair distribution of resources.

## Safety

Safety from threat is, in many respects, an extension of physiological needs. Indeed, by guaranteeing the realisation of physiological needs, a society would go a long way to reducing the anxieties that people might experience: for instance, of being homeless, unemployed, or going hungry. Safety, again, would mean that everyone would have adequate housing, and a welfare state that cared for people throughout their lives.[46] Needless to say, the fulfilment of people's desires for safety would require the ending of intra- and international conflict, and the protection of the environment: we cannot feel safe in a world that is dying. In addition, there would need to be safety from psychological and interpersonal threats, for instance bullying, abuse, ridicule, rejection; emotional and interpersonal hurts. Such challenges may not feature in many political or economic models of ideal social functioning but, from a psychology-informed perspective, would be essential to a utopian future.

Absolute safety, of course, cannot be guaranteed – except, perhaps, with a massive compromise in autonomy and the potential for growth. We cannot stop people in relationships, for instance, getting hurt, and probably would never want to eradicate this: friends will reject us, lovers will leave, parents will get things wrong. But, in our progressive utopia, there would be a profound appreciation for the needs that each of us have to feel physical, emotionally, and interpersonally safe. As with social and emotional learning (SEL; Chapter 7), citizens would be educated to see the sensitivity of others; to see beneath (or perhaps get rid of) the masks of invulnerability that each of us presents to the world, so that we would relate to others authentically; and with sensitivity, care, and compassion. Hurt would not be dispensed with, but surplus hurt would be minimised: hurt that comes from misunderstandings, miscommunications, or damaging interpersonal relationships.

## Pleasure

Central to the socialist dream, as with the capitalist one, is a world of 'uncurbed and untarnished human happiness'.[47] For progressives, however, this is a happiness available *for all* – and for the 'underdog above all' – not only for the 'strong and successful'.[48] Progressives have described a world that is 'light, pretty, playful';[49] where people 'feel good' and have fun.[50] To this, perhaps, we would add that in a progressive utopia people will not take themselves too seriously: we would have the mentalising ability to stand back from ourselves and always know there are other ways of being. This would be a lightness of spirit: an ability to see our flaws as well as our strengths.

For Marx, as with other progressives, this move towards more pleasurable living comes through the elimination of alienated labour. The worker is no longer impelled to carry out boring, mechanised, meaningless labour: *bullshit jobs*, 'a form of paid employment that is so completely pointless, unnecessary, or pernicious that even the employee cannot justify its existence'.[51] Other utopians, too, have emphasised the need to overcome the drudgery of work. 'Can anyone doubt that an absolute minimum of unpleasant labor is part of the good life', writes the behavioural psychologist B.F. Skinner in his utopian novel, *Walden two*.[52] For Bastani, this reduction in alienated labour will be an inevitable consequence of increased automation and the availability of resources, with robots undertaking the most boring, repetitive, and unskilled of tasks.[53]

In this progressive utopia, a reduction in alienated labour would likely correspond to a significant increase in leisure and recreational time. Shorter working days or working weeks, for instance, have been proposed which would give people opportunities to do the things that they genuinely enjoy: such as reading, sport, cinema, or walking.[54] Here, 'free time', as well as 'work time', might become a measure of a society's wealth.[55] A reduction in alienated labour, however, could also correspond to greater synergies between working activity and activities that are pleasurable and/or purposeful: that is, people working in jobs that they genuinely enjoy and/or find meaningful. In Morris's utopia, for instance, 'All work which would be irksome to do by hand is done by immensely improved machinery; and in all work which is it a pleasure to do by hand machinery is done without.'[56] This is the core of Morris's utopia: that work and happiness become synonymous. In addition, where difficult, unpleasant, or hazardous tasks need to be undertaken in a society, progressive utopians have suggested that these jobs should have the greatest rewards (in the form, for instance, of 'credits', or shorter working hours).[57] Hence, greater equality can be assured across pain and pleasure.

In our progressive utopia, more enjoyable living might also come through a total de-shaming of pleasurable activities. In a capitalist world – or perhaps in any world of limited resources – shame over pleasurable activities can be seen as serving a function: ensuring that people attend to 'productive' activities.[58] But in a world that no longer requires people to compete or produce, such shame is simply surplus: unnecessarily undermining a highest-order desire for pleasure (as well as self-worth). In a progressive utopia, then, the desire to engage in pleasurable activities may be seen as legitimate as any other desire. No shame, for instance, about wanting to relax, or wanting to play. And, as with Marcuse, no shame for desiring and having sex (assuming full consensuality, of course). In this progressive utopia, sexual activity may feature prominently. This is partly because it can be such an intense satisfier for pleasure (though not for everyone), partly because it can synergise the direction for pleasure and the direction for relatedness, and partly because it has the potential to synergise the direction for pleasure in one person with this direction in another.

## Growth

It is important to acknowledge, however, that the direction towards pleasure also has a dysergetic potential. As we saw in the Marshmallow Test (Chapter 3), for instance, it can undermine our orientation towards more reasoned, longer-term goals; and it may also keep us focused on our own, individual-level directions rather than looking up towards the wellbeing of others and our planet.

Most importantly, perhaps, a society that focused exclusively on the satisfaction of pleasure might not allow people to realise their highest-order directions towards growth, change, and personal development: those 'higher activities' that utopian writers have often pointed to.[59]

In part, growth might involve the adoption of multiple roles: Marx's hunting in the morning, fishing in the afternoon, rearing cattle in the evening, and criticising after dinner.[60] This desire for growth could also be met through extensive opportunities for learning and education – a feature of many literary utopias, from More onwards. Consistent with this, continued learning is known to be one of the five most important routes to wellbeing.[61] This learning could be general: discovering and understanding in a wide range of areas. However, contra Marx, it may also include specialisation: to know, not just everything, but to know, deeply, in certain areas. That is, to have understandings and skills that are unique to that individual or that community.

Closely related to this, a progressive utopia might be expected to have creativity – through, for instance, the arts, imagination, and crafts – at its core. Marx writes, 'What is wealth if not the absolute unfolding of man's creative abilities [through which man] produces his totality.'[62] More prosaically, Sunkara writes, 'The deluge of bad poetry, strange philosophical blog posts, and terrible art will be a sure sign of progress.'[63] Everything, here, could become an opportunity for creative activity: from the design of computers and running shoes to the furnishing of a house or public spaces. Indeed, even the radical behaviourist, Skinner, wrote, 'a world which has been made beautiful and exciting by artists, composers, writers, and performers is as important for survival as one which satisfied biological needs'.[64] Arts, crafts, music … creativity is an expression of each of our directions towards growth and differentiation (Chapter 3, this volume), and a society that can facilitate that can allow each of us to feel fulfilled and satisfied. More than that, creativity is a profoundly synergetic activity, in that one person's joy in being creative is, so often, another person's joy in 'consuming' their creative outputs: the musician on stage, for instance, immersed in their performance; and the audience, mesmerised by the musician's skills. Or the artist who, through the creative act, connects powerfully to their deepest-yet-intangible feelings, and the viewers who are able to grow and evolve through engaging with their work. Of course, not all creativity inspires, and its production can be torturous. But creativity is one of those activities that, like sex, has an enormously synergetic potential. It is therefore likely to be at the heart of any progressive utopia (see Chapter 9, this volume, for a narrative illustration of how this might be).

Based on the present framework, creative activities may also be core to a progressive utopia because they allow for the existence of a wide range of 'goods' (Chapter 6). That is, creativity, by its very nature, takes on numerous forms; and therefore creates a vast range of channels through which people can grow and realise their potential. It also creates a vast range of channels through which people can find meaning and feel good about themselves. Of course, to some extent, we already have a range of legitimate creative pursuits in our society: people have the potential to be artists, musicians, or writers. But creativity begets creativity: in a world that prizes and prioritises creative acts, more and more opportunities for growth are opened up. Like fractal patterns, an emphasis on creativity establishes ever-increasing levels of detail, complexity, and possibility to be explored. A general principal for a progressive utopia would be to expand the number of satisfiers that are available – from music to sport to scholarly activity – and emphasising creative goals would be one of the primary ways in which that might happen.[65]

Hence, as with Morris, specialist craft activities – like furniture-making, brewing, or gardening – produced locally, and individually or in small collectives, might have a central place in a progressive utopia.[66] In Morris's utopia, 'there are so many, indeed by far the greatest number among us, who would be unhappy if they were not engaged in actually making things, and things which turn out beautiful under their hands'.[67] This means a move away from monopolies and towards smaller-scale specialised producers.[68] Such a development would allow for a number of valuable synergies. Here, not only can the creator realise their specialised abilities and the consumer experience their craftsmanship, but the product can also serves as a satisfier for more practical needs and wants: for instance, a multifunctional chair, or a beautiful garden to look on to. In addition, a move away from monopolies would make an important contribution towards a more egalitarian society.

Art, at its contemporary, cutting edge, can also catalyse developments for society as a whole: as with, for instance, artistic modernism, Afrofuturism, or, indeed, humanism itself (during the Renaissance). A progressive utopia, by definition, cannot be a fixed and static thing: it needs to grow and evolve, just like the people within it. Art has the capacity to be at the very forefront of new ideas, concepts, and practices: critiquing society and pushing the limits of who and how we might be.

A focus on growth also means that a progressive utopian society, without doubt, would put enormous emphasis on the prizing of differences and diversity. A valuing of heterogeneity provides a means whereby each person can realise their highest-order needs and wants as a unique and distinctive person; and, as discussed in Chapter 6, is inherently synergetic. In a progressive utopia, this prizing of difference and diversity would be at a community level as well as at an individual one. This would allow people to tap into deep veins of culture, tradition, and wisdom; but in a way that contributes to – rather than detracts from – the wisdom of others. Cultures and communities, like the threads of a tapestry, would be distinctive but making an essential contribution to the richness and beauty of the whole. Such cultures and communities may be based around ethnicities, but there may also be communities centred on particular genders, sexualities, or other dimension. In recent years, for instance, there has been a flourishing of trans and gender variant identities beyond the traditional bifurcated norm: from agendered to bigendered to genderfluid to genderqueer. All these – and numerous more – have the potential to help people express their unique needs, wants, and ways of being; but in a way that makes for a richer, fuller, and more stimulating world for all. For Muñoz, this world of the 'incommensurable' and 'incalculable' – 'a world that exceeds equivalence' – is a world of 'queerness'.[69] In this sense, a prizing of queerness might be another way of describing the essential qualities of a psychology-informed progressive utopia.

## Relatedness

As we saw in Chapter 3, relatedness with others is identified as a fundamental direction in nearly all contemporary psychological models, and an abundance of research shows the links between relatedness and wellbeing. We can imagine, then, that good relationships with others would be at the heart of a progressive utopia. Based on the evidence, this would be, first, a *quality* of connections, so that everyone would have the potential for at least some close, intimate, relationships with others. Indeed, it is interesting to note that, in many of the utopian novels – such as *News from nowhere*, *Walden two*, and *Looking backwards* – there is a subplot involving the protagonist finding love in the utopian world. Love, for many of us, is such an exquisite experience that it is hard to imagine a utopian world that is not, to a large extent, centred around it. Second, it would be a *quantity* of connections, with people having the potential to embed themselves within a broad, diverse, and supportive network of social relationships and communities. This would be at a range of different levels of intimacy: from colleagues, to friends, to lovers.

No doubt, relatedness in a progressive utopia would include close and numerous relationships with nonhuman organisms too,[70] as well as the natural world. Indeed, given the current climate crisis – with, for instance, a 1.1°C increase in global surface temperature over the last century and a 0.2m rise in the oceans[71] – the issue of our relationship with our environment is a critical one for almost all our needs and wants. Learning to flourish within our planetary boundaries will be a major challenge for a progressive utopia; yet there is potential here for important synergies between experiencing closeness to nature and an economy of care and conservation.[72] Morris's pastoral idyll in *News from nowhere* is an example of this, where 'the fulfilment of man is at the same time the fulfilment, without violence, of nature'.[73]

Given people's needs for safety, attachment, and to be loved, it seems likely that relationships with others in this progressive utopia would be characterised by high levels of warmth, affiliation, and care. For the Care Collective, this can be considered the very essence of a radical egalitarian politic, whether feminist, queer, or anti-racist.[74] Here, social activity involves 'the nurturing of all that is necessary for the welfare and flourishing of life', whatever a person's identity or characteristics.

The Women's Equality Party, campaigning in the 2021 London elections, refer to this as a 'care revolution'.[75] Furthermore, as we have seen in Chapter 6 (this volume), being nice to others and being trustworthy can be considered important ingredients for the development of synergetic relationships between people, per se.

At the same time, assertiveness would have an important role in this progressive utopia, ensuring that people articulated, and were able to realise, their needs and wants. Others, however kind, will not always know what we want or where we are trying to get to; and there are times in which they will, inevitably, transgress or block our own directions. As with the TIT FOR TAT strategy, then, the default mode of relating in this progressive utopia may be warmth and kindness; but with the capacity to stand up for ourselves if need be (see Chapter 6, this volume). In addition, expressing warmth and kindness to others is only likely to increase social utility to the extent that it is genuine: if it is a phony, Pollyanna-ish glaze, then we do not grow, the other does not grow, and our sense of competence (that we, as the genuine people that we are, have something to offer), is not enhanced. Interestingly, in fact, while love, intimacy, and affection play a central role in Skinner's *Walden two*; praise, thanks, and interpersonal gratitude are all prohibited. This is on the grounds that people should do things through their own self-motivation, and not to please others. It may be, then, that a progressive utopia would do away with niceties, with people feeling less of a need to express warmth and friendliness unless they genuinely feel it.

Certainly, communication in this progressive utopia is likely to be more direct and transparent, as per nonviolent communication (NVC, Chapter 7). Here, people would feel free to express what they need and want: for instance, 'I'd like us to spend time together going to the beach,' 'I'd like some time on my own,' 'I'd like us to talk through our relationship.' Direct communication, as we have seen, allows for more trust to emerge and more potential to find cooperative solutions, without any immediate losses. At the same time, as with NVC, this direct *expression* of our needs and wants would not be conflated, in any way, with the *demand* that our needs and wants be met. 'I'd like us to spend some time together going to the beach,' then, would be absolutely accompanied by, 'and I want to know what you'd like to do so we can decide on this together'.

Relatedness, of course, is not just at the one-to-one level, but also in terms of the development of *communities*: groups of people who, not only care for each other, but *care* that they care for each other.[76] For Lucien Goldmann, the Jewish-Romanian Marxist humanist, 'authentic communities' are radically different from the faceless, anonymised groupings that characterise capitalist society. For Goldmann, communities are characterised by the free, self-determined effort of its members towards larger, common goals – by its very definition, a synergetic configuration. Goldmann states that the very essence of philosophy is the realisation of community: the establishment of the 'we', the 'transindividual subject'.

Relatedness would also feature prominently in a progressive utopia because, of all the highest-order needs and wants, it is probably the most synergetic between people. Relatedness, by definition, is a mutual act; and it requires, and supports the realisation of, the same want in another. When we love someone, or cherish them, or experience deep relational contact with them, we support their potential to experience the same feelings towards us. Love begets love, friendship fosters friendship, community draws out communal feelings in others. And this synergetic potential extends to many other relational-type wants and needs. For instance, the desire to be compassionate to others, to care for others, or to live a life of virtue all have the potential to contribute to the wellbeing of others, as well as the self. As the Care Collective write, 'all our lives are improved when we care and are cared for, and when we care together'.[77]

Our deep need for relatedness would be well-supported by the development of the crafts-, arts-, and creativity-oriented society discussed in the previous section, as small-scale, local, and potentially community-based activities, arts and craft production open up the possibility for much more personal connections between producers. Compare this, for instance, against the isolation and alienation of contemporary call centre workers, of workers in Amazon's mega-warehouses (as depicted, for instance, in Chloé Zhao's *Nomadland*), or of delivery drivers (as shown, for instance, in Ken Loach's *Sorry we missed you*). Small-scale production also opens up opportunities for greater relatedness between producers and consumers. Think, for instance, of the browser at a craft fair who talks to the craft-maker about their work, or the diners at a local restaurant who can chat to the chef about their meal. The president and chief executive officer of McDonald's does not talk to us; none of the McDonald's servers have time to talk to us. But the chef in the local restaurant who has made a delicious paella might; and, even if they do not, we have a personal relationship to them and their food. Small-scale, creative, diverse … there are numerous reasons why, from a psychological perspective, this would be the face of a progressive utopia.

## Autonomy

Given a fundamental human desire for freedom, autonomy, and self-control, a progressive utopia must also have space for people to be free. Here, however, it may be useful to introduce Berlin's distinction between 'freedom from' (*negative freedom*) and 'freedom to' (*positive freedom*).[78] Negative freedom refers to freedom from oppression, obstruction, and interference; and would be a sine qua non of a progressive utopia. Not only do we know, from the research, the amount of psychological distress that oppression causes (see Chapter 4, this volume); but the blocking of such needs as to feel safe, to be creative, or to express our sexuality would come at high personal cost without any meaningful gains to others.

Positive freedom, in the sense of freedom to do whatever we want, is more complex, as it has the potential to run against the needs and wants of others. For instance, our freedom may mean that others feel less safe and secure as our behaviours are not entirely predictable. Our freedom may also undermine relatedness: doing our own thing rather than acting collectively with others. And positive freedom may also pull against a basic, progressive desire for equality. If people, for instance, enact the freedom to accumulate vast sums of money, then (within a zero-sum context) they may concomitantly restrict the freedom of others to be financially sufficient. In addition, in contrast to relatedness, positive freedom has little synergy at the interpersonal level: greater freedom for one person does not necessarily lead to greater freedom for others.

Indeed, for Sartre, our interactions with others are essentially a battle of freedoms: through enacting our subjective freedom, we inevitably impinge on the freedom of the other.[79]

The positive freedom of one person, then, has the potential to reduce the negative freedom of another. Berlin writes, 'Freedom for the pike [a positive freedom] is death for the minnows [a negative freedom].'[80] We encountered this in the fictional neighbours' dispute being mediated in Chapter 5 (this volume): If no one can obstruct me from listening to my music at full volume then what of my neighbour's freedom to sleep soundly? Likely, a progressive utopia would need to balance, on an ongoing basis, the positive freedoms of some individuals or communities against the freedoms of others. Perhaps that would be a key role of state or government: to find ways of maximising freedoms for all, in the knowledge that freedoms are not always compatible.

In attempting to address – and resolve – such complexities, one important consideration may be the extent to which a person's, or community's, highest-order needs and wants can be met in alternative, but equally fulfilling, ways. For instance, let us consider a conflict between Person A's freedom to identify themselves as transgendered, and Person B's freedom to live in a world where only a simple gender binary – 'male' and 'female' – exists. Here, both desires may be rooted in legitimate, higher-order directions: Person A's to feel free to express their genuine sense of self, Person B's to experience safety and security. But the difference is, Person A may only be able to experience an authentic sense of self by identifying as transgendered, while Person B is likely to have multiple other ways in which they can find safety and security. In this example, then, the freedom of Person A would deserve priority over the freedom of Person B, because it allows for a greater overall optimisation of benefit. Another way to put this might be that Person A's freedom would deserve greater priority because it is a highest-order 'freedom from', whereas Person B's freedom is a lower-order, more context-related and contingent 'freedom to'. Prioritising more synergetic, and more effective, ways of fulfilling higher-order needs and wants may also make sense for a progressive utopia. Should people have the freedom, for instance, to smoke cigarettes in a restaurant, or should others have the freedom to dine smoke-free? A person's smoking may give them some pleasure; but given that it cuts across their own health needs, as well as the health and pleasure needs of other people, it may be an appropriate place for state intervention and guidance.

Freedom must also include the freedom to decide what kind of world we want to live in; including, for instance, the freedom to entirely reject the progressive utopia being described here. This means that a progressive utopia can never be enforced on people – however much such a society might allow for the realisation of other fundamental needs and wants. Rather, there must always be opportunities for people to struggle against, change, and decide together on the nature of their society; otherwise it is no utopia at all. So a key feature of a progressive utopia may be that it is always unfinished, always evolving, never reaching a place where it says, 'This is how it must be.' It is a direction rather than an endpoint: in the terminology of motivation psychology, a 'process goal' rather than an 'outcome goal'.[81]

## Self-worth

In a progressive utopia, society also needs to be configured in such a way that people, as far as possible, feel good about who they are. An obvious starting point here would be through positive parenting and SEL (Chapter 7, this volume), which could communicate to children that they are worthy of deep love and acceptance, however different and diverse they might be.

As with autonomy, however, supporting a direction towards self-worth may be quite complex. This is because, at the interpersonal level, people's needs for self-worth may be dysergetic: with feelings of competence defined *in contrast to* others, rather than *alongside* others.[82] A student who receives mainly '7s' at GCSE (a key academic qualification in England, Wales, and Northern Ireland), for instance, is likely to feel very different if their peers received all 9s, as opposed to their peers receiving 4s and 5s. The reality is that if we see others doing well in something we want to do well in, it can make us feel worse about ourselves; and, if we see others doing badly in that field, it can boost our relative sense of self-worth. As Gore Vidal cynically puts it, 'It is not enough to succeed, others must fail.'[83]

In the utopias of Morris, Skinner, and Gilman, competition between people has been transcended. However, Corning writes that there is:

> a congenital naivete among the utopians about the role of competition in human societies. All the evidence we have about human nature indicates that reordering society without regard to the competitive aspect of our evolutionary heritage is biologically unsound. Our egoistic, competitive impulses are hardly confined to capitalist societies and are certainly not a capitalist invention. Indeed, over the centuries there have been a great many failed attempts to establish and sustain small cooperative communities, perhaps in response to some deep urge to reincarnate the tribal societies of our ancient past. All these experiments have failed, save a few exceptions that don't disprove the rule.[84]

In contrast to Corning, in the present psychological framework, competitiveness is not seen as a core human characteristic. Rather, what is seen as core is a human desire to feel of value; and also to strive and move forward (that is, directionality), which can often take the form of competitiveness against others. Hence, through positive parenting and SEL, a progressive utopia could encourage people to develop self-esteem by setting goals that are for themselves, rather than against others. This might mean, for instance, that a potter's objectives are to create vases that, for them, are distinctive and beautiful; rather than ones that are *more* distinctive and *more* beautiful than those of other potters.

An emphasis on multiple goods, as discussed in Chapter 6, might also be a way of facilitating the development of self-worth in non-competitive ways. By creating a wide range of fields in which people can accomplish and be recognised, more people may be able to experience more of a sense of achievement more of the time. As Richard Layard, the influential economist and author of *Happiness: Lessons from a new science* writes, 'A different way to deal with the status race is to increase the respect that is given to other things.'[85] So, for instance, people would not just be venerated for being rich; but equally for being loyal friends, or skilled baristas, or safe bus drivers. Every walk of life has the potential to have areas in which people can excel and can be recognised for excelling. This is closely aligned to the development of an arts-, craft-, and creativity-oriented society, as discussed earlier in this chapter. Here, as with Morris's utopia, 'Each man is free to exercise his special faculty to the utmost, and everyone encourages him in doing so.'[86] This means that, as noted in this chapter, a progressive utopia may have some degree of 'positive' division of labour, in the form of specialisation. While some people may choose towards a life of varied activities, others may dedicate themselves to unique and specific expertise.

Paradoxically, another means of creating a society that optimises feelings of self-worth may be to encourage people to communicate more openly about their vulnerabilities, fears, and failures: the expressivity and willingness to trust discussed in Chapter 6. Our sense of success may be relative, but it is often in comparison to what we *see* others as presenting, rather than against how they may *genuinely* feel inside. Presenting a veneer of success to others – whether in everyday talk or social media – is like a lose–lose arms race: we present the positive side of what we are doing, forcing the other to 'up the ante'. More genuine disclosure of vulnerabilities and weaknesses, then, could help all of us feel that what we are doing is, relatively, good enough. And it would help build feelings of relatedness: that we are like the other, struggling along with trying to do something good, rather than alone in our failures.

Lerner suggests a third strategy for harnessing a tendency towards competitiveness in people: orientate competitive activities towards prosocial outcomes, such as being generous and caring for other human beings, animals, and the planet.[87] In this way, the desire for self-esteem – even relative to others – can become synergetic with other prosocial activities and outcomes. Might there be, for instance, an 'Olympics' of caring, or loving, or peace-keeping work?

## Meaning and values

A progressive utopia that supports, for all, the attainment of our most fundamental needs and wants may still count for little unless those directions feel *meaningful*. That is, people feel that they are things worth living for. It is possible to conceive, perhaps, of a future society in which people have many of their most fundamental needs and wants met, and yet have a profound sense of existential emptiness: they experience pleasure, feel free, have closeness with others … yet feel that it is all, ultimately, pointless: that there is no intrinsic value in anything that they do.

If people, as described earlier in this chapter, are engaged in work and other activities that are creative, unique to them, and in which they can actualise their potentialities, then it seems more likely that they will experience a sense of meaning. Meaning comes – in the form of significance – because only *they* can do the work that they do: they are irreplaceable and unexchangeable. As the socialist humanists argue (Chapter 2, this volume), being part of a mass production process is not likely to feel meaningful, because the assembly line worker or the shelf-stacker in an Amazon warehouse knows that they are fundamentally replaceable. But small-scale, creative, arts and crafts work can be meaningful – because without that person or community, that product would never exist. Moreover, here, the person or community have chosen what they want to create, so that the process of making it is more likely to feel of worth and value. In addition, in a future of increased mechanisation and automation, creativity is an area where humans can 'beat robots hands-down'.[88] This may be an important criterion for establishing areas of meaningful work for the future: pointing towards the centrality of empathy-, relating-, and insight-oriented activities for humans in a further future society.

Work and other activities, in this progressive utopia, might also be supported to feel meaningful through an emphasis on contributing towards a greater whole: reaching beyond our individual selves towards something larger and more enduring. As Bregman writes, meaningful jobs are not only valuable for self, but also for the wider community: enhancing overall wealth and wellbeing rather than just shifting it around.[89] Too much submergence in the greater whole, however, and our sense of individual significance may start to falter. A progressive utopia, then, would need to support people to find a balance between an individual sense of significance, and integration into wider groups and communities.

From the perspective developed in this book, values might also be at the forefront of a progressive utopia: as guiding lights to which people orientate their activities. These values might be such things as truth, discovery, tradition, or spirituality. Values that were consistent with other highest-order wants and needs – both of the self and others – would be most synergetic overall: for instance, 'It is good for people to experience safety and pleasure' or 'We should care for others.' As before, values that focused on wellbeing at higher levels of organisation would also be highly synergetic: such as 'We need to create a planet that can flourish and thrive.' Across orders and levels, 'relatedness values' – for instance, caring, humanising, and acting cooperatively – are likely to be among the most synergetic. To maximise synergies across directions, the establishment of synergies, itself, could also become a principle value and direction.

Given, however, that meanings and values are only meanings and values to the extent that they are freely chosen, there would need to be a great deal of openness and indeterminacy in the meanings and values that a progressive utopia supported. Community-oriented values, for instance, could not be mandated over individualistic ones. Rather, a progressive utopia would need to help people explore, identify, and establish values for themselves. Indeed, by its very nature, a progressive utopia could never get to a point where a final and finite set of values would be established. Rather, at best, the issue of values and meanings would be a topic of ongoing social dialogue: 'Who are we, as a community?' 'Where do we want to go?' 'What is important to us?'

## Directionality, itself

Closely related to meaning and values, and drawing many earlier points together, a progressive utopia needs to support the process of realising needs and wants, themselves. That is, it needs to help people have objectives to orientate towards, to feel that these are attainable, to experience progress in attaining them, to be able to achieve them, and then to be able to appreciate their achievement. Hence, to be truly utopian, a progressive society needs to give people the opportunity to lead dynamic lives: where there is striving, movement, and change. This is why, as suggested earlier, capitalism may be so durable. Despite all its faults, capitalism 'succeeds' because it offers people the hope – however rogue – that they can achieve something, get somewhere. To be compelling, a progressive vision also needs to offer such hope, possibilities, and dynamism – with the difference that it can actually fulfil that promise, by supporting the realisation of directions for all. In this way, a progressive utopia needs to offer more than stagnation at the individual, community, or national level. It needs to provide opportunities for challenge, struggle, and striving, even if that means that people may experience failure and despair, as well as hope and success. A progressive utopia, like capitalism, also needs to have some degree of indeterminacy: it needs space for uncertainty, unpredictability, and change. Too fixed and certain, and it becomes a structure that can cater for only our most basic needs.

## Summing up

In this chapter, I have tried to describe some underlying principles of a progressive utopia, based on the psychological framework developed in this book. To summarise: equality of opportunity is a sine qua non, meaning that each citizen is supported to realise their own, highest-order needs and wants, to the maximum extent. This is a society that protects and cares for its citizens, and puts relatedness and love at the heart of its structures and values. Creativity and the valuing of diversity are central: an 'approach' mindset, with constant opportunities for new learnings, new possibilities, challenge, and change. This community orientation, however, is balanced against individual freedoms: here, as far as possible, people are supported to strive and set values in their own particular way. This progressive utopia is not a fixed, stagnant society but one that is constantly evolving: questioning and challenging itself, finding ever more synergetic and effective ways of helping its citizens and communities get more of what they need and want. To the extent that this is how progressives, already, envision an ideal future society, this chapter shows that it is based on robust psychological principles.

In maximising the realisation of directions across society, this chapter has particularly focused on forging synergies across non-material, 'softer' needs and wants – as opposed to the 'harder', more material ones. Material satisfiers, such as food and housing, are relatively zero-sum: if one person has more, another has less – there is not much room for synergies. But non-material needs and satisfiers – like relatedness, creativity, and meaning – are all non-zero-sum: more for one person can mean more for another person too. Non-material satisfiers, being relatively abstract and conceptual, are also more malleable than material satisfiers, offering greater scope for development. For example, changing a society's values – for instance, through SEL or intercommunity dialogue – may be more possible than changing the availability of food or energy resources. Hence, while progressive politics, quite rightly, has tended to focus on material satisfiers and their equitable distribution; an analysis of non-material satisfiers – and the potential synergies between them – also has considerable value for a progressive politics. Lerner writes, 'Liberal and progressive movements need to move beyond a focus on economic entitlements and political rights to embrace a new discourse of love, kindness, generosity, and awe.'[90] This focus on such non-material needs as relatedness, self-worth, and meaning opens up enormous possibilities for generating creative, synergetic visions for a better society.

Of course, life in this progressive utopia would not be perfect. As Sunkara, for instance, states, 'Even under socialism life would still be filled with plenty of lows. It will still sometimes feel overwhelming, you'll probably get your heart broken, and people will still die tragically from accidents and suffer bad luck.'[91] Indeed, by its very nature, the present framework must allow for experiences of disappointment, worry, and loss – as well as pleasure, joy, and satisfaction. Furthermore, whatever the emphasis on collaboration, it is likely that conflictual interpersonal relationships will always exist.[92] But, as Sunkara goes on to state (along the lines of Freud), 'even if we can't solve the human condition, we can turn a world filled with excruciating misery into one where ordinary unhappiness reigns'. Surplus suffering can be minimised, and we can work to ensure that optimal levels of wellbeing are available to all.

Of course, too, the progressive utopian vision presented in this chapter (and the following one) is just one sketch: with, no doubt, many flaws and limitations. But the point, here, is less to say what a progressive utopia needs to be, and more to add to an exploration of possibilities and alternatives. Indeed, as Bregman points out, the development of multiple utopian visions is the very lifeblood of a democracy.[93] So, here, the questions being asked, and the methodology used to try and answer them, may be more important than the specific answers given: What kind of world do we, as progressives, want to see? What would it look like if we took the organising principle of care seriously?[94] What kind of principles should we found our progressive visions on? For progressives to progress, as Buber writes, 'the catchword "Utopian" must be cracked open and examined for its true content'.[95] To conclude this chapter with the words of Oscar Wilde:

> [A] map of the world that does not include Utopia is not worth even glancing at, for it leaves out the one country at which Humanity is always landing. And when Humanity lands there, it looks out, and seeing a better country, sets sail. *Progress is the realisation of utopias.*[96]

9

# A day in utopia

The previous chapter envisioned, conceptually, what a psychology-informed progressive society might look like. In this chapter, following the tradition of literary utopias, I want to take this description one step further by switching in to a narrative, fictional account of what it might be like to experience such a world. This chapter feels risky: I am not a fictional writer, and this is the first time I have included an entirely fictional section in any of my books. But I wanted to give as concrete and vivid as possible a sense of what that better world might look like – and *feel* like: How it might really be to be in this world. Because it is one thing to conceptualise a progressive utopia of creativity, relatedness, and care; and another to really explicate how people might actually live and coexist in such a world. This is particularly in the face of some of the fundamental psychological, social, and environmental challenges of existence. We cannot, for instance, always get our needs and wants met; we do not always get on with others; and we have to find ways of living within our environmental limits. What is more, if people are fundamentally directional, how do you create a world in which people can strive and struggle for things – with the potential for disappointment as well as achievement and success – while at the same time coexisting together in a safe, secure, and generally pleasurable way?

What follows, then, is a narrative account of how the principles laid out in the previous chapter of this book – and throughout it – might play out in practice. The focus is particularly on a world in which people are able to realise their creative and relational directions, with the skills to communicate honestly, warmly, and effectively with each other – and their world. As with the literary utopia genre, I have also used this narrative format to flesh out, in more detail, what the philosophy and principles of a psychology-informed progressive utopia might be. To emphasise, this is an entirely personal vision: I showed a draft of this chapter to one of my elder sisters, for instance, and she said she envisioned a progressive utopia entirely differently – a lot less drugs and a lot more vegetable allotments! But see what you think. And, of course, the point of this chapter, as with the previous one, is not to prescribe how an ideal progressive society should be; but to stimulate thinking, creativity, and dialogue on this question. What, for you, would an ideal society really look like? How would it be to exist in it? And, how would it relate to your view of human beings (and society)? By asking ourselves these questions, we can develop a clearer and more coherent sense of what it is we are striving for: and, in doing so, enhance our prospects of sailing there.

★★★

Dalya was staring, intensely, at a large monitor-like screen. It was hollow, and a 3D rectangular wireframe – purple and flickering – was protruding out of it. Dalya was manipulating the wireframe with her hands.

I walked over to her and peered over her shoulder. 'Um, Dalya?' She didn't respond. I continued watching as she kneaded the wireframe: pushing, pulling, and then pinching it carefully with her fingers. 'Dalya?' Again, no response. 'Dalya, I was just wondering …' Finally she turned to me and smiled. 'Oh', she said, somewhat distractedly, 'How are things going? Discovered anything new?'

'I've … Can I ask you about a few things?'

'Mick', she said softly, smiling. 'I'm really focused here. I'd prefer it if we can talk later.'

'Is it OK to watch?'

'Sure', she said, smiling again. Dalya's face tightened in concentration. Her left hand was now reaching through the screen, pressing very softly on the left back corner of the wireframe. Then gently, very gently, she was tapping it. I could see that the wireframe was slowly curving inwards, moulding to her touch. Then her right hand, too, reaching inwards into the screen, tapping and shaping the right side of the wireframe.

'Damn.' Dalya suddenly let go of the wireframe and sat back. 'It won't …' She scrunched up her face, leaned forward, and pulled the wireframe towards her, rotating in with her hands. 'It's …' Dalya turned to me, her face darkening. I smiled awkwardly – fully aware there was nothing I could do to help. Dalya grunted and turned back to the screen. On its right hand side was a virtual slider and Dalya nudged it down. The wireframe turned from purple to a dark red.

'José, the frame, it's not – how do I get the fractals?' Dalya seemed to be talking into the air. Then there was a pause as she concentrated, quietly. 'No, but it's not – I know, I'm turning it but it's just bending in.' Another pause. 'Red, yes, red. No. … Oh.' Dalya grasped the slider in her right hand and this time turned it slightly clockwise. The wireframe flickered more intensely. 'Hm …' Dalya murmured to herself, 'Cheers José.' She went back to tapping the corner of the edge with her left hand.

I walked back to my chair, a few feet away. I was just about to sit down when I heard Dalya's tapping was getting louder. I turned around and saw that Dalya's tapping and the flickering of the wireframe were now synchronising. The taps were longer apart, and the frame was now a deep blue each time Dalya tapped it, then disappearing. 'Yes, just …' said Dalya, 'it's …'. Dalya turned to me and smiled. Just as she did, a multicoloured swirl of blue light burst from the screen, pouring out into the room. It was accompanied by a deep, resonant wave of sound. The light and the sound swirled around me, over me, and then through me. All the tension seemed to dissipate from my body. My legs gave way and I slumped down into the chair. I could see Dalya's face through the lights and she was beaming. 'Huh, that's ...' She turned back to the screen and nudged the slider up a little. 'Just go with it, Mick,' Dalya said. My insides seemed to be resonating with the light and sound. At first, a gentle throbbing, then more defined – with a focus that was moving: first in the centre of my chest, then down to my stomach. I lay back in the chair. My body felt like it was opening out to the swirls of light and sound: deep pleasure … deepening, deepening, deepening …

I must have fallen asleep, and awoke to see Dalya sitting opposite from me on a sofa. Next to her, snuggled up tight, was a tall, dark green-skinned person – to my 21st-century eyes of indeterminate gender. They were wearing a shiny green catsuit, from ankles to a high halter neck; swashes of light green make-up on their chiselled face, gold hair rising in spikes. 'So looks like Dalya got her piece going!' they said to me, grinning.

'It was– wow, was it supposed to do that?'

'Sort of', said Dalya. I'm still working on it. 'Did you feel the ripples?'

'Uh huh. I think. In my chest, yes, definitely, down to my stomach.'

'And …?' asked Dalya.

'I don't know. I must have fallen asleep. It was amazing … amazing pleasure.' Dalya looked at me, her face beginning to wrinkle with disappointment. The person snuggling in to her gave her a playful squeeze around her middle.

'Stop it Drake. Don't …'

'You gotta nail it, you gotta …' Drake grinned, their shoulders wiggling with pleasure.

Dalya looked at me and shrugged. 'It's OK. It's not your fault. I've just– I'm just feeling the time pressures. I want to get it right.'

'Ripples to the core, lover', said Drake to Dalya, 'ripples to the core'.

'I know you're teasing me', Dalya replied to Drake, 'But can you stop now please. I'm actually really frustrated.'

'Sorry.' Drake stopped grinning and stilled. They gave Dalya a hug. 'Why don't you talk to Leviticus? She's always good on these things.'

Later that afternoon, when Drake had gone, Dalya told me what she was working on. She explained that she was a 'somatic artist'. She had been working in that area since her early 20s and was part of a small group called the Post-Hedonists. Their focus was to evoke feelings of absolute bliss and absolute nihilism at the same time. It was, she explained, both an expression of hedonism but also a step beyond it. 'When you touch those moments', said Dalya, 'it's like the core of everything just opens out: The Great Unfolding'.

Dalya was showcasing her piece in two weeks' time at her city's largest community arcade, and was worried that the nihilistic elements were still not coming through strongly enough. 'I'd really like to go and see Leviticus', she said, 'I could really do with her advice'.

***

We walked down the stairs of Dalya's apartment, opened the door, and stepped out on to the street. 'Leviticus is just down at the community local', Dalya said.

It was warm and bright. The sun was high in the cloudless sky, geese flying overhead. 'The weather', I asked Dalya, 'is that something you control?'

'They learnt to do that decades ago', replied Dalya, 'but then we realised it was better letting Earth do what it wanted to. When they took the control off they remembered how magical and mystical that unpredictability was. And, in any case, you just couldn't do it. They wouldn't let you.'

'Who?'

Dalya burst out laughing, shaking her head.

'So … wait', I said, 'You haven't explained to me yet: How do you make decisions here? How does government work?'

Dalya clipped a blue, shell-like device off from behind her ear and held it up to me. 'It's all Network. When we've got big decisions, it comes through to all of us and we get to input and decide. The little decisions they just get on with. We agree on Facilitators who do all that.'

'Who are the Facilitators?'

'I mean, it's amazing people want to do it, but they do. I'm full of gratefulness to them, just can't think how or why anyone would want to do that role. But, yes, they love it. Most of them, anyway. Some see it as their calling. I had this friend, Max. He loved order. Putting things in boxes. Always wanted to be a Facilitator. He's there, sitting in his hut over the Hindu Kush, sipping his chai, working out who goes where and who does what on his screen.'

'So does he have control?' I asked.

'I mean, not really. They organise things, put the big decisions out for Consultations. Explain what's going on. But, no, it's a really tough training and, it's years of learning about impartiality. Working out what decisions need to go out.'

I looked back up at the warm sun. 'So, with things like the weather, it's all the people who've decided not to alter it?'

Dalya turned to me and grinned.

'Uh?'

'So do you think the whales or the ants are going to be OK if we started messing around with the weather?'

'You've got to protect them?'

'It's not protecting, Mick. When you've got millions of whales networked in, and billions of spiders and pigeons, and all the microbes and trees, you can't just do what you want.' Dalya took my hand and pressed her fingers, gently, into my palm.

'What, they talk to you?'

'Well, not exactly talk. But the Network taps into what they want. You feel them. It's a force, a weight, a direction, a presence – it's always there. A few decades ago some people tried to move into the Borneo forests – there was such a screaming in the Network they had to stop.' Dalya's finger made playful circles on my palm.

'I'm surprised all the animals and plants don't decide just to kill off the humans. They'd probably have a better world without us.'

'Actually', smiled Dalya, 'they did try. It was massive for years. The cats were the worst: and not the lions or tigers but those little pussies who you used to think were cuddling up to you. Their ferocity was just intense. But you'd be amazed at how caring and prosocial most of the animal world is. Even the plants. They think network. It's natural to them.'

Feeling the warm sun on my face, I imagined the world alive. A vibrant system of animals, plants, and humans all linked together. I watched the geese and wondered what their force might be like: where they would be trying to move the Network? Or the ants and spiders: How would it be to feel their directions?

Dalya kissed the palm of my hand and then hugged me. 'Mm', she said, 'It's good to be here with you Mick.' She put her hands on my shoulder and gave me a friendly push. Then around me again, a kiss on the other cheek. 'So what do you think?' she said, standing back, 'Here you are.'

★★★

I looked out onto the road: a wide strip of wood-like material curving off into the distance, gleaning under the sun. On either side of the road were small bushes, and beyond them rolling fields. I was struck by how quiet it was, aside from the faint honking of the geese and some bird song: no cars, just some bicycle-like vehicles.

Further down the road I could see some people coming and going: a beautiful, colourful array, different clothes, different shapes and sizes. Towards us walked a group of three people, all arm in arm, with a large dog walking alongside them. On the left was a boy in a bright yellow jumpsuit, coloured circular hoops spinning around his waist. Next to him was a man whose clothing looked familiar: jeans and a white shirt. The third man was naked except for blue metallic hoops on each leg that slid up and down as he walked. The dog was without a leash and intently sniffing the road. Dalya smiled at them as we walked past and I smiled too – slightly nervous given the size of the unleashed dog.

In the distance I could see some buildings on either side of the road. As we came closer, I could see that they were of various shapes, sizes, and colours; clad in brightly lit 3D signs. The first we passed on the left was covered in vines, with a wide open door leading inwards. 'Rainforest' it said above the passageway. I could hear jungle sounds emanating from inside it, and the smell of damp plants and rain. I asked Dalya what the building was. 'These are Portals', she said. 'I love that one. Me and Drake spent three days going out on a canoe.' To our right was a large, pyramid-shaped building: 'Siberian Desert'. 'That's too hot for me', said Dalya, 'but Drake and Leviticus love it. They go back there every year, digging for fossils.' We walked past a few more portals on the left and right, each decorated as their name might suggest: 'Alps Meadow', 'Stratosphere', 'Inside the Volcano'.

Beyond the volcano building was a two-storey yellow brick saloon, decked out with a veranda as if it was from a Western movie. Dalya took me by the arm. 'Come here, I'll show you this.' Just to the side of the entrance was a small, shiny red plaque. *White Elephant Saloon, Fort Worth, 1890*. 'They moved it here', said Dalya, 'I love this place.'

We walked in through the batwing doors. Inside was smoky, with sand on the floor. A few of the patrons were dressed in 19th-century 'wild west' outfits, others in more modern clothes.

'Leviticus', Dalya shouted across the saloon. By the far wall, there was a woman sitting alone at a table. She turned around and smiled at us. Dalya pulled me to where Leviticus was sitting and gently pushed me down into a chair. She kissed the top of her head, then my head, and then sat in the third chair.

'You are *so* noisy', said Leviticus to Dalya, smiling. 'And this is, I guess, Mick. I heard from Drake. Part of the Project.'

I smiled at Leviticus. She had a broad, dark-skinned face, wide-set eyes, and short cropped white hair. In her 50s perhaps. She wore a plain white collarless shirt, buttoned to the top. Leviticus smiled at me, cautiously. Her eyes slightly glazed.

Dalya picked up Leviticus's glass. 'Is that your second or third Joy? I could do with some.'

'Jeez, you think I'd have just Joy?'

'What are you mixing?'

'I spent 20 minutes at the bar', said Leviticus. 'They've got some new Ochre Melancholy. I've been trying that and Arctic Joy. Then mixing in some new Nostalgia they've got from China: "Oriental Nostalgia". Really strong.'

Dalya grabbed Leviticus's glass and raised it. 'OK?' she asked.

'Sure, but leave me a bit.'

Dalya took a sip, and then another. 'Mm. Feels good.'

'It's got a half-life of five.'

Dalya smiled at me and then at Leviticus. 'Is it OK to ask you some things', she said to Leviticus, 'about the technology for my latest piece?'

'I'm free for 30 minutes, then I've got to get off to a group.'

Dalya rested back in her chair and closed her eyes. 'Mm, that's great', she said, 'I'm just going to let the Joy kick in for a bit.'

We sat there quietly for a few minutes, watching Dalya slope deeper into her chair. 'So', Leviticus said to me, 'How are you finding it all?'

At the bar, two people were laughing loudly, cuddling and caressing each other. They were dressed in furry brown onesies. Leviticus looked up at them, irritated: 'Hang on', she said to me. Leviticus stood up from her chair and walked over to the pair. To my surprise, Leviticus kissed them both, several times, on either cheek. She spent a few minutes talking to them, gave them warm hugs, and then returned. 'Cuddlebunnies', Leviticus grinned, 'They drive me crazy, they're so effin' happy. I tried to talk them in to taking some Melancholy!'

Dalya laughed and sat up in her chair, slowly opening her eyes. 'Mm, that is good', she said, 'I love the Melancholy and Nostalgia combo. Had me back with my great-grandmother, on her boat. What does the Ochre do?'

'I couldn't quite work it out', said Leviticus, 'but it's something on the 5-$HT_2$ receptors – switches them around in some way'.

'Leviticus's an alchemist', said Dalya.

Leviticus smiled. 'I'm trying to be. Third career. First a philosopher, then a dancer. Now I've turned to drugs.'

'Where do you two know each other from?' I asked.

'Back in the New Hedonists', said Dalya. 'We were all going out together. Leviticus had started off in the Nihilists and we seemed to just catch her on a wave.'

'Ultra-Nihilists', Leviticus corrected her, smiling. 'The extremists. I'd basically given up on everything.'

'She did a piece that we all loved', said Dalya, '*Abyss and Absolution*, I've still got the poem on my wall: "Freedom through nihilism".'

'I went through nihilism and came out the other side', said Leviticus. 'It just seemed to burst alive in my body: into dance. Dalya, Drake, and the others were coming from the other direction: technical hedonism, hedonism in art. And just ... Bang!'

Behind me, I heard the sound of raucous laughter. I turned around and could see a group of five or six cuddlebunnies. They were sitting around a table, with two of the cuddlebunnies play-wrestling on the floor.

'We had some great shows', continued Dalya. 'Berlin, do you remember Berlin?'

'With the Primitivists. That night swordfighting through the arcade.' Leviticus and Dalya both rolled their eyes and laughed.

'Huh, it's the nostalgia', said Leviticus, after a few moments. 'But look, I need to go soon. How can I help?' Leviticus picked up a sparkling red tote bag that was besides the table, rummaged around in it, then put it down.

I struggled to understand much of the conversation that followed. Dalya wanted some advice from Leviticus on how she could deepen the nihilistic element of her work. They talked back and forwards about technical, biochemical, and poetic options. Leviticus had been developing some new variant of cortisol that evoked intense, but short-lived, feelings of intense dread. There was an aerosol system at the installation place that could, potentially, be used; but Dalya needed to check whether it could distribute enough droplets at an exact time.

'Here's an idea', said Leviticus, 'Why don't you put Mick right into the middle of the installation and he can talk about how fantastic everything is in our world. You can't get much more nihilistic than that!'

Dalya smiled. 'I think', she said to me, 'we'd better check out the installation space'.

★★★

Dalya and I walked out of the saloon and into the light. 'Let's take a lift', she said. We walked down the street for a few minutes and then descended some stairs. At the bottom, a door opened into a small glass compartment. We walked inside and sat down. The door closed and we started moving forward: slowly at first, then at a pace. I looked at the glass walls of the compartment and could see the underground tunnels of earth and rocks as we sped through them.

'Leviticus and me – we were lovers for several years', Dalya said. 'On and off – but we were always very close.'

'So how do relationships work here?' I asked.

'There's no one way', said Dalya, 'people are really different. So some people find a partner when they're young and stay together for life. Others have loads of partners throughout their lives. And people can really change. Like all of us in the New Hedonists were incredibly promiscuous, and then I got into a monogamous relationship with a person called Chi for several years. Now I'm back to blending multiple friendships and sexual relationships – I don't really draw any lines between them. But that's just me. When I was with Chi, I could really see why some people choose monogamy.'

'What happened with Chi?' I said. 'I hope that's OK to ask?'

'Sure. But it was so painful. We loved each other incredibly. But Chi was getting more and more involved in an animistic spiritual community and was reaching out for something I just couldn't see. We talked and talked but in the end we both knew that Chi had to move on and I had to let go. It totally broke my heart. Chi moved to New Guinea to join the community. Still there I guess: there's a Vow of Disconnection so I never heard after that.'

'I'm sorry.'

'Thanks. It was my gorgeous Chi. I loved them to bits.'

We sat silently for a few moments as the compartment rushed through the dark earth.

'I probably know the answer to this', I said to Dalya, 'but I'm guessing that there's loads of different sexualities here. Right?'

Dalya smiled at me.

'So I'm thinking', I said, 'that it's "no one way" again: you've got people who are heterosexual, and then homosexual, and then bisexual, and then pansexual, and just about any configuration and combination you can think of. And people change over time if they want to. And I'm guessing you've also got a plethora of different genders: male and female if people want to stay that way, but then transgendered and pangendered and demigendered …'

'… and that's just a start', said Dalya. 'People do get born mostly male or female, but then what they want to do after that is entirely up to them, and they can change it at any time. I went male for most of the time I was with Chi, and before that I was pangendered, but I'm currently staying mostly female.'

'It was such a big issue at my time.'

'To be honest, when people can have multicoloured skin, and tattoos, and body mods of any type, gender is just one of those things that changes. Do you know the slogan, "Gender is art?"'

'No.'

'Oh, maybe after your time. That was years ago, but we still have gender artists now. There's Mishka, who's created some of the most amazing genders. They did an ultrafeminine that was just sublime.'

'And I'm guessing everyone is OK with however anyone else is?'

'Did anyone think you were a better or worse person for wearing a blue shirt or a green one? It did take a long time for those prejudices to go, but today there would just be no point making those judgements. Why would you? Who gains?'

'I guess people were scared', I said, 'they like to know where they stand'.

'And what we try and do today is make people feel safe, and happy, and confident, and feel good about who they are – without treating others badly. And, of course, people still look at others and think, "That looks weird", or "I don't like that" or "I wouldn't want to be that myself." But they have the self-awareness to know that that's their judgment, and not a universal truth.'

I watched as the glass compartment continued to speed through the earth. I noticed how smooth and quiet the movement was.

'What about sex?' I asked Dalya gingerly. 'In my day there was still a lot of shame and secrecy around it.'

'One of my body artist friends has really got into sex art. You should see their show. They've got this piece which uses deep crimson to take you into multiple orgasms. It's lovely. You wouldn't believe how many times I came.'

I shifted uncomfortably in my seat, flushing with embarrassment.

'Oh Mick', said Dalya grinning. 'It's sex. Sex. Orgasms. I came. Multiple times. You lot were just so funny about sex?' Dalya paused, 'Look at me.'

I tried to look into Dalya's eyes but felt too uncomfortable and turned away.

'I'm sorry', said Dalya, 'I know sex was different for you then. And it is complicated, even now. There's sex art, and a whole load of sex craft industries and sex recreation. The erogenous zones are just amazing if you're into pleasure. And, of course, people don't think there's anything bad about it. But there's others that see it much more spiritually. You've got communities that literally worship sex: treat it as a sacred energy. That's what Chi got into. And then you've got the Monogamists and other Relationalists who see sex in terms of making – and deepening – love.'

'And you?' I asked.

'Kind of in between and changing, like most things. I was facilitating a spiritual sex group for a while with Chi, but he got more and more into it and it just wasn't quite right for me. Something didn't click.'

The glass compartment was slowing down and eventually came to a halt. We exited and walked up some stairs. On our way up, it occurred to me that I had not seen any people operating anything. 'Is it all automated here', I asked Dalya. 'The train and the lifts?'

'You do sometimes get people wanting to do that work, but for most of us it's just too monotonous, so we just leave it for the automatons. Leviticus did ride the lifts for a few months, but that was off her face on Joy, so I'm not sure it really counts!'

★★★

At the top of the stairs, Dalya announced 'Centre Park'. Around us in each direction were green lawns, cut through by narrow channels of water and bounded by hedges. 'This way', said Dalya. We walked alongside one of the water channels, taking in the sun, the fresh air, and the bird song. I could see rabbits, mice, and rats on the lawns. To my surprise, they did not dart away as we drew close.

In the distance was a long, tall glass-domed building. We walked up to it and went inside. On either side of the central passageway were stalls with various goods. One had a selection of curved wooden figurines, another multicoloured hoops like I had seen on the people earlier that day. Many seemed to be food or drink stalls, with people standing around them, trying the various delicacies. 'You'll love this', said Dalya, pulling me over to one of the stalls. The stall had strips of a jerky-like food, in various shades of reddy-brown. 'Try this one.' Dalya picked up one of the strips, smiling at the short, naked woman standing behind the stall. I took it from Dalya's hands and bit into it. I had been expecting something chewy; but the texture was much softer, with a fishy, rancid taste. Dalya and the stall holder looked at me, expectantly. 'Mm', I said.

'Oh, you think it's disgusting, don't you', said Dalya, smiling at the stall holder. 'Just say it, no one minds.' Dalya pushed me affectionately on my shoulder. 'He's from the Project', she said to the woman.

'Di-hydroxy hyacinth', the woman said. 'It's not to everyone's taste.'

'I love this', said Dalya, picking up a few strips and stuffing them into her mouth. 'It's that mixture of salty and nasty. Just sublime.' The stall holder smiled.

'I guess I was just expecting something more meaty, like steak or something.'

For the first time during my visit, I saw a sternness moved across Dalya's face – the stall holder's too. They looked at each other, an awkward pause. 'I know this might be hard to hear, Mick', Dalya said eventually, 'and I know it was of a particular time, but for us it's just so upsetting to think that you ate animals back then. If I'm honest, I do struggle to understand how you could all be cannibals.' Dalya looked over at the stall owner who nodded softly.

'I was mostly vegetarian – most of the time', I said defensively. Dalya and the stall holder looked at me. Another uncomfortable pause.

'And angry', said Dalya. 'How could you do that?'

I looked away. 'I guess your Network wouldn't like me too much', I said half-joking.

'No they fucking wouldn't', replied Dalya, her face still serious. 'No wonder the cats wanted to wipe you lot out.'

'Well they're just as …'

'Mick, just think about it', Dalya interrupted. 'Take it in.'

I breathed deeply, resisting the urge to defend myself further. 'Yes, OK.'

'Perhaps, with the Project', said the stall holder, 'there'd be a way of feeding something back into the Network. Something apologetic, some real contrition from the past.'

'Maybe', said Dalya, 'maybe'.

Dalya smiled at the stall holder, took a few more strips from the stall, and said goodbye. We walked on in silence. After a couple of minutes, Dalya stopped, turned to me, and hugged me. 'Let's let it go', she said, 'for another time'.

'I'm sorry. I could have done better.'

'It's just so painful to imagine.' I could see that Dalya's eyes were watering. She wiped them with her fingers. 'For another time.'

As we walked past the stalls, Dalya stopped at various places, trying and offering me the food, drink, or various other sensory delights. There was a stall with golden orbs. Dalya picked up a small one and held it against the back of my neck. I could feel a warm shudder of pleasure run down my spine. We tried a bright yellow liquid, reminiscent of a banana milkshake. There was a stall with iris flowers of all colours and sizes. Dalya looked over them and picked a tall one with white and purple petals, edged in orange. She smiled at the stall owner. 'Can I take this?'

'No', said the stall holder, smiling warmly. 'It's reserved already, but you might like this one.' Dalya took the grey and silver iris she was offered, thanked the stall holder, and we walked on.

At the end of the passageway was a stairway. Dalya and I went up several floors. We exited into a large, circular sun-lit room, the glass panels overhead. 'This is the space', she said.

★★★

In the corner of the room was a panel. Dalya walked over to it, switched it on, and started moving the virtual buttons and levers. 'Hm', she said. 'Mick, I just need to focus on this for now. We can talk more later.' I walked over to the windows and looked out onto the park below me. From there I could see how large it was, herds of deer in the distance and a large moon-shaped lake.

Dalya was inspecting, now, the corners of the ceiling. 'Mm', she said. She took a vial out of her pocket, went back to the panel, and placed it inside. Suddenly, out of nowhere, I felt the most intense sense of despair, like every morsel of hope had drained out of me. I sat down on the floor. Dalya looked at me. 'Perfect', she said.

Just as the feeling of despair had come, so it left me. 'Ooh, that was awful', I said to Dalya. 'Do you really want that?'

'You can see it, can't you? Just imagine that despair with the deep blue swirl. It'll be amazing.'

'Powerful for sure. Intense. Is that what you really want? Isn't it going to really upset people?'

'It needs it', said Dalya. 'It's the evocation. The intensity. The body memory. It's the absolutely, utterly most powerful. Driving through pleasure to the emptiness underneath. There's nothing beyond.'

At that moment there was a knock on the door. 'Yeah, what', shouted Dalya. 'I'm busy. Can you hang on?'

Another knock.

'OK, OK', said Dalya, irritatedly, 'just come in'.

The door opened. A person walked in, their skin a deep, golden brown; a soft, handsome face. 'Leviticus said I'd find you here' they said gently.

'Oh my freaking world', said Dalya, her eyes wide with amazement and excitement. 'Chi?'

# 10

# In conclusion ...

As Katherine Trebeck of the Wellbeing Economy Alliance (WEAll) writes, 'COVID-19 has revealed that enormous shifts in policy are possible. ... Policies previously dismissed as unrealistic are being seriously discussed and levels of government intervention that would have been baulked at in many countries [like compulsory mask-wearing] are now being rolled out.'[1] The proposal made in this book for a more cooperative, compassionate, progressive society —with empathy and radical acceptance at its heart—are, without doubt, radical; but they are also within reach. The rollout, for instance, of social and emotional learning (SEL) and positive parenting programmes, and the establishment of wellbeing economies through the Wellbeing Economy Governments (WEGo) alliance, shows that psychology-informed agendas and understandings can be integrated into contemporary political practices.

To conclude the book, this chapter focuses on specific political strategies by which a psychology-informed progressive programme might be developed. It then goes on to summarise together the principal thesis of this book – that we can develop a more comprehensive, coherent, and compelling progressivism through the integration of psychology – before summing up with some final thoughts.

## Political collaboration

Chapter 7 proposed a range of concrete strategies that could be adopted by separate progressive parties with the aim of creating a world more conducive to cooperation. As the Care Collective write, however, a more effective approach – and one more consistent with the progressive principles being articulated – would be an alliance of progressive parties, integrating these intra- and interpersonal concerns alongside a wider range social, economic, and ecological agendas.[2] Despite our differences, perhaps progressives can recognise that we are all on the 'same team'. If we believe passionately in a cooperative world, we should be able to develop the skills to cooperate with each other and overcome party partisanship – the emotionally literate politics discussed in Chapter 7 (this volume) and promoted by Compassion in Politics. Reading, for instance, in the Labour 2019 manifesto that 'Only Labour' can rebuild Britain's leadership on climate democracy seems deeply counterproductive and just plain wrong.[3] Have they really not heard of the Green Party, or Caroline Lucas, or the Liberal Democrats' commitment to a Green society and a Green economy? So often, when people think of the left, what comes to mind is the classic meme from *Monty Python's Life of Brian*: 'Judean People's Front?' 'Fuck off! We're the People's Front of Judea.' As progressives, we need to do our own psychological work – and nonviolent communication (NVC) is a great start – where we can get over the 'narcissism of small differences'[4] and dialogue cooperatively, together, for the greater good.

Encouragingly, various organisation are now beginning to emerge that can foster such collaboration. WEAll is one (Chapter 7), another is the cross-party organisation Compassion in Politics. A third is Progressive International, founded in 2018 by the Democracy in Europe Movement and the Sanders Institute to form a 'common front' for all progressive forces.[5] Its vision is a world that is – among other aspirations – decolonised, egalitarian, sustainable, and plural. From the perspective developed in this book, we might add to this as core progressive principles:

- *Fulfilling*, where all people are supported to realise their personal needs and wants.
- *Cooperative*, that people know how to work together to find mutually beneficial solutions.
- *Compassionate*, where all beings – and our planet – are treated with empathy, care, and understanding.

Another global progressive organisation is openDemocracy, a UK-based political website which 'seeks to challenge power and encourage democratic debate around the world'.[6] Alongside articles on a wide range of topics – from economics to migration to sex workers' rights – the website hosts live discussions and aims to inform and influence media outlets globally.

## A 'wellbeing' party?

In developing a psychology-informed progressive agenda, another strategy might be to develop a political organisation, or even party, with that focus. This could be something that sat under a broad progressive umbrella but with a particular focus on developing wellbeing and cooperative functioning at the individual and interpersonal level. In Australia, something was developed along these lines – the 'Australian Mental Health Party', which operated from 2014 to 2020 and put up parliamentary candidates, primarily on a platform to improve publicly funded mental health services. Lerner also describes plans for the future establishment of a Love and Justice Party – a 'Tea Party of the Left' – which would bring together a social justice agenda with a psychological commitment to care and understanding.[7]

The development of a wellbeing party would have the advantage of being able to focus, in depth, on psychological issues and processes. It could also act as a coordinating point for, or ally to, other political movements and parties. There is a danger, though, that it would become just one more fragmented voice of the left, with all the tribalism that that can entail. There is also the question of whether it would be seen as credible by the general public. Is society ready for a political party that would explicitly promote cooperation, wellbeing, and psychological health? As the furore over the introduction of measures of personal wellbeing by the Office of National Statistics in 2011 suggests, happiness and life satisfaction are still seen by many as soft, self-indulgent, and effete concerns. '[A] futile attempt to measure things that cannot be counted, and a waste of money when the state has none to spare', as *The Daily Mail* reports.[8]

Such scepticism, however, should not be grounds for political inactivity. Perhaps a wellbeing pressure group or campaigning group, however small, could create a space in which psychological issues could be considered more seriously on the political plane. As with Greenpeace or Amnesty International, members of such an organisation could be involved in a wide array of other political groupings.[9] Campaigning organisations like Mind,[10] Schizophrenia and Psychosis Action Alliance,[11] and Young Minds[12] do already exist, but such a group would be less focused on the rights of people with particular mental health challenges, and more on the centrality of mental wellbeing for us all (through, for instance, positive parenting, SEL and NVC). It could also be a group that aimed to bring emotional literacy to the political domain itself (Chapter 7, this volume): encouraging a politics of understanding rather than one of blame. In all of this, the key would be collaboration: to work with other progressive political voices to embed psychological insights within the context of wider socioeconomic and cultural concerns.

## A moral arc

In addition to such developments, we might hope that there is a natural, historical tendency for human beings to come together in more cooperative – and more socially just – ways. As Martin Luther King famously stated: 'The moral arc of the universe is long, but it bends towards justice.'[13] Wilkinson and Pickett, in *The spirit level*, also write of 'an almost unstoppable historical trend towards greater equality'.[14] Certainly, it does not always seem that way, but viewed over the long term (comparing, for instance, our society against medieval feudalism), we are, perhaps, moving in a less hierarchical, less unequal, more empathic direction.

Maybe this movement towards greater cooperative functioning is a general principle of systems.[15] In the evolutionary domain, for instance, as discussed in Chapter 4, species came together into mutualistic relationships with each other, or sexes evolved that required each other for reproduction. Historically, communities and nations came to trade and exchange with each other: dependent on the other for resources and goods. At the intrapersonal level, too, Rogers argues that we have a natural tendency towards self-integration.[16] Why might the arc bend in such a way? Perhaps because, as we saw in Chapter 4, cooperative, win–win relationships create greater overall benefit and therefore, over time, have greater 'stickability'. As we saw in the prisoner's dilemma game, nice strategies can 'invade' a world of nastiness and even come to dominate because, ultimately, they have the greatest hardiness. They are most fit for purpose.

## Towards a more comprehensive, coherent, compelling progressivism

The principal aim of this book has been to show how, through the integration of psychology, we can develop a progressivism that is more comprehensive, coherent, and compelling. To summarise, building on the insights of the socialist humanists, this framework starts with an understanding of human beings as directional: striving to fulfil highest-order needs and wants. Wellbeing, here, is the realisation of these directions, and this can be achieved through both socioeconomic and psychological mechanisms. This means that a progressive approach, which wants to help all individuals thrive, needs to support people on both psychological and socioeconomic fronts. In addition, what we discover, when we look across intrapersonal and interpersonal levels of organisation, is that the core strategy for achieving benefit – within the same set of resources – is actually very similar. This is the principle of cooperative relating; and, when we look at how such cooperation can be achieved, there are a common set of principles across different levels of organisation. This, then, gives us a set of system-wide principles on which a psychology-informed progressivism can be based, such as trusting, taking responsibility, and being fair. In recent years, a number of concrete strategies have been developed that can help people learn, and act in accordance with, these principles (such as SEL and NVC); and there is also the wellbeing economy agenda that puts psychological thriving right at the heart of public policy. From a directional standpoint, thinking further into the future can support, and orientate, progressive thought and action; and we can use psychological insights into people's highest-order needs and wants – as well as system-wide principles, such as the value of synergetic relationships – to envision what an ideal progressive society might look like.

This would be a world oriented around relatedness, care, and creativity; where each person would have the chance to realise their own individual strivings, but in a context of community and of physical and emotional safety.

As stated in the Introduction, part of the rationale for developing this analysis was to demonstrate the robustness and legitimacy of progressive thought and action, as it currently stands. Progressives believe in cooperation, favour state intervention to ensure equality and justice, prize inclusivity, want to see each individual develop themselves to their full potential, and have concerns for our wider planetary context. An analysis of wellbeing and functioning at the psychological level of organisation shows how such values are not just specific to the socioeconomic domain, but are more general, system-wide principles for creating greater overall benefit. When you synergise, when you work cooperatively, there is the possibility for overcoming the destructive conflicts that plague any system – psychological, interpersonal, international – and achieving win–win outcomes that are better for us all. Progressivism, then, is not just an emotional oversentimentality, or a faddish wokeness, but a logical and rigorous system for creating the greatest benefit overall, supported by complex theoretical modelling and evidence.

At the same time, this book has tried to take progressive thought and action forward by articulating a specific, psychology-informed approach. One key feature of this is an emphasis on radical acceptance. This means that, even with our political opponents and those we see behaving destructively, there is an emphasis on understanding and engaging with their perspectives. This does not mean kowtowing or accepting what is unacceptable, but holding a position of psychological equality: assuming that others, like ourselves, are intelligible beings striving to realise highest-order needs and wants. Here, cooperation means cooperation throughout. It means eschewing blame and demonisation. It is a stance of treating others, everyone, with dignity and respect. The development of an emotionally literate politics is a key consequence of this: a radical new style of political engagement that can help us overcome the divisiveness, contemptuousness, and counter-productiveness of much political 'dialogue'. With its emphasis on – and bridging to – more micro psychological and relational concerns, this psychology-informed approach also introduces to progressivism a range of relatively new agenda items: positive parenting, SEL, NVC, and the centring of policy around wellbeing concerns. Through consideration of a progressive utopia, this psychology-informed approach also puts relatedness, creativity, and personal strivings at the heart of a progressive vision.

The integrated psychological–political framework developed in this book also allows for a smoother movement between – and joining of – intrapersonal and interpersonal realms of understanding and action. When we try and address issues of human misery we do not want to be jumping between dissonant and disconnected psychological and socioeconomic frames. This sets up an unhelpful 'either/or' dynamic when, so often, the reality is 'both/and'. People suffer for psychological reasons *and* they suffer for socioeconomic reasons: having both sets of factors in one framework makes this easier to see. Moreover, this makes it more possible to see the interactions across different levels: how, for instance, psychological-level SEL interventions can lead to more social justice and, conversely, how greater social justice can lead to improved mental health. By aligning these levels of organisation into one framework, with common principles of positive change, it also becomes more possible to learn from each other about the best means of creating more benefit for all.

Such a psychology-informed progressivism may be comprehensive and coherent, but would it be compelling? As indicated earlier, at the present time, there is a good chance that many voters would consider a psychology- or wellbeing-oriented approach indulgent or soft. Psychological research into minority influence, however, shows that a coherent and committed minority position, however much initially dismissed, can ultimately sway a majority.[17] Key here is that it is consistent: the same message, over time. In this case it would be that psychology matters, that how you feel is a legitimate focus for government. Just as many members of the public now recognise the importance of environmental concerns, a calm, steady focus on wellbeing could be equally persuasive.

Similarly, if progressives were to stop denouncing their political opponents, and instead to engage and challenge them in emotionally literate ways, the immediate effect could be to worsen their standing in many voters' eyes: have they gone soft, uncertain, 'lost their balls'? To many experienced politicians, no doubt – left as well as right – the idea of showing one's vulnerabilities and uncertainties would amount to political suicide. But, over time, a consistent position of respect, valuing, and reaching out – however barbed the challenges of opponents – could be highly appealing. When children are bullied, we do not tell them to bully back; rather, we tell them to talk to adults about it, act mindfully, and, ideally, ignore the bullies. So if others are insulting or ridiculing us in the political arena, do we really need to stoop down to this level too? Ultimately, a stance of acting mindfully and constructively – despite provocation – may be the most compelling to voters. What voters would also see here is progressives leading by example: having the integrity, transparency, and openness that can help to build up trust – something voters so often call for. An emotionally literate politics could also help voters feel like they are being talked to as adults, rather than as simpletons to be coaxed into seeing 'the truth'.[18] Here, the political 'tactic' would be to have no tactics. No strategies. No bullshit. No manipulation. Just honest, authentic communication.

> You can win by telling *the* truth, by avoiding engaging in personal attacks, trusting the intelligence of voters – and even by showing goodwill! You can win, above all, if you put forward a positive, exciting programme, one which touches the citizens' heartfelt expectations and is not limited to denouncing the madness of populists, or opportunistically wielding together mere fragments of the electorate.[19]

## Summing up

'Hope must be recovered', writes Ruth Levitas in her book, *The concept of utopia*, 'hope that we may collectively build a world of peace, justice, cooperation and equality in which human creativity can find its full expression'.[20] The aim of this book is to contribute towards that hope. The psychology-informed progressivism being described here is revolutionary; but it is not a revolution of antagonism, conflict, or violence. Rather, as with a growing number of contemporary voices[21] it is a revolution of compassion, cooperation, and openness. This is a revolution that goes against the old order of things, not through hating it, but through striving to understand it and to progressing, collectively, with it. In many ways, this is a revolutionary strategy that is even harder. Mahatma Ghandi writes, 'Non-violence is not a cover for cowardice, but it is the supreme virtue of the brave. Exercise of non-violence requires far greater bravery than that of swordsmanship.'[22] In the same way, accepting our vulnerabilities and uncertainties and bringing them into our public dialogues requires enormous courage. But if we are committed to a genuinely more equal and cooperative world, it is a step that we may have to take. We cannot meet the other – cannot dialogue or cooperate with them – from a place of absolute certainty and conviction. This does not mean repressing our passion, commitment, and values; but, rather, deepening them. Taking a step forward to really challenge ourselves to 'be the change that we want to see'. This is a progressivism that truly embraces humanity (both ours and that of others) – as well as our planet – as a diverse, creative, and beautiful whole.

'Either we learn a new language of empathy and compassion, or the fire this time will consume us all', writes West.[23] He goes on to conclude:

> We simply cannot enter the twenty-first century at each other's throats, even as we acknowledge the weighty forces of racism, patriarchy, economic inequality, homophobia, and ecological abuse on our necks. We are at a crucial crossroads … and we either hang together by combatting those forces that divide and degrade us or we hang separately. Do we have the intelligence, humor, imagination, courage, tolerance, love, respect, and will to meet the challenge? Time will tell. None of us along can save the nation or the world. But each of us can make a positive difference if we commit ourselves to do so.[24]

# Notes

## Chapter 1

1. Mason, P., *Clear bright future: A radical defense of the human being* (Penguin, 2019).
2. https://twitter.com/terfnonsense/status/1528131150304235522
3. https://twitter.com/owenjones84/status/1511726196219858951?lang=en
4. Amiel, D. and Emelien, I., *The new progressivism: A grassroots alternative to the populism of our times*, trans A. Brown (Polity, 2020).
5. Bregman, R., *Utopia for realists: And how we can get there*, trans E. Manton (Bloomsbury, 2016).
6. Nandy, L., Lucas, C. and Bowers, C, 'Editors' introduction', in *The alternative: Towards a new progressive politics*, ed L. Nandy, C. Lucas and C. Bowers (Biteback, 2016).
7. Bastani, A., *Fully automated luxury communism: A manifesto* (Verso, 2019).
8. Varoufakis, Y., *Another now* (Vintage, 2020).
9. Nandy, L. et al, *The alternative*.
10. Lerner, M., *Revolutionary love* (University of California Press, 2019), p 16.
11. Saleem, R., Morrill, Z. and Karter, J.M., 'Introduction to the special issue on radical humanism, critical consciousness, and social change', *Journal of Humanistic Psychology* 61, no 6 (2021); Segal, L., *Radical happiness: Moments of collective joy* (Verso, 2017).
12. Care Collective, *The care manifesto* (Verso, 2020), p 2.
13. Mason, P., *Clear bright future*, p 294.
14. Cooper, M., 'Searching for the anti-sexist man: A history of the men's movement', *Achilles Heel* (1991), https://mick-cooper.squarespace.com/s/1991-Mens-movement-AH.pdf
15. Segal, L., *Radical happiness*.
16. Layard, R., *Happiness: Lessons from a new science* (Penguin, 2006); Kirsch, J.A., Love, G.D., Radler, B.T. and Ryff C.D., 'Scientific imperatives vis-à-vis growing inequality in America', *American Psychologist* 74, no 7 (2019).
17. Saleem, R. et al, 'Introduction'.
18. Friedli, L. and Stearn, R., 'Positive affect as coercive strategy: Conditionality, activation and the role of psychology in UK government workfare programmes', *Medical Humanities* 41, no 1 (2015).
19. Saleem, R. et al, 'Introduction'.
20. Ibid, p 852.
21. Layard, R., *Happiness*.

22 Rowson, J., 'Rediscovering the soul of progressive politics', in *The alternative: Towards a new progressive politics*, ed L. Nandy, C. Lucas and C. Bowers (Biteback, 2016), p 158.
23 *The Labour Party manifesto 2017: For the many not the few* (The Labour Party, 2017).
24 Green Party, *Green Party manifesto 2019: If not now, when?* (Green Party, 2019).
25 Galtung, J., 'The basic needs approach', in *Human needs: A contribution to the current debate*, ed K. Lederer (Oelgeschlager, Gunn & Hain, 1980), p 57.
26 Lerner, M., *Revolutionary love*.
27 Ibid, p 131.
28 Bregman, R., *Humankind: A hopeful history*, trans E. Manton and E. Moore (Bloomsbury, 2020), p 2.
29 https://www.compassioninpolitics.com/
30 hooks, b. *All about love: new visions* (William Morrow, 2001).
31 Lerner, M., *Revolutionary love*, p 39.
32 Sunkara, B., *The socialist manifesto: The case for radical politics in an era of extreme inequality* (Verso, 2019), p 26.
33 Taylor, C., 'The diversity of goods', in *Utiliarianism and beyond*, ed A. Sen and B. Williams (Cambridge University Press, 1982), p 130.
34 In Fromm, E., *Marx's concept of man* (Continuum, 1961), p 198.
35 Bregman, R., *Humankind*, p 2.
36 Raworth, K., *Doughnut economics: Seven ways to think like a 21st century economist* (Random House, 2017).
37 Cain, D.J., Keenan, K. and Rubin, S., 'Introduction', in *Humanistic psychotherapies: Handbook of research and practice*, ed D.J. Cain, K. Keenan and S. Rubin (American Psychological Association, 2016), p 4.
38 See, for instance, Rogers, C.R., *On becoming a person: A therapist's view of therapy* (Constable, 1961).
39 Rogers, C.R., 'The necessary and sufficient conditions of therapeutic personality change', *Journal of Consulting Psychology* 21, no 2 (1957).
40 Said, E.W., *Humanism and democratic criticism* (Columbia University Press, 2004), p x.
41 In Fromm, E., 'Introduction', in *Socialist humanism*, ed E. Fromm (Penguin, 1965), p ix.
42 Spencer, R., 'Postcolonialism is a humanism', in *For humanism: Explorations in theory and politics*, ed D. Alderson and R. Spencer (Pluto, 2017); Fromm, E., 'Introduction'; Said, E.W., *Humanism and democratic criticism*; Fisher, R.J., 'Needs theory, social identity and an eclectic model of conflict', in *Human needs theory*, ed J. Burton (Macmillan, 1990).
43 Spencer, R., 'Postcolonialism is a humanism', p 151.
44 Said, E.W., *Humanism and democratic criticism*, p 22.
45 Spencer, R., 'Postcolonialism is a humanism', p 151.
46 Brennan, T., 'Introduction: Humanism's other story', *For humanism: Explorations in theory and politics*, ed D. Alderson and R. Spencer (Pluto, 2017)
47 Butler, J., *Gender trouble* (Routledge, 1990).
48 Said, E.W., *Humanism and democratic criticism*.

49 Althusser, L., *For Marx* (Verso, 2005).
50 Buber, M., *I and thou*, trans R.G. Smith, 2nd edn (T & T Clark, 1958).
51 Husserl, E., *Cartesian meditations: An introduction to phenomenology* (Martinus Nijhoff, 1960).
52 Gupta, N., 'Harnessing phenomenological research to facilitate *conscientização* about oppressive lived experience', *Journal of Humanistic Psychology* 61, no 6 (2018).
53 Freire, P., *Pedagogy of the oppressed*, trans M.B. Ramos (Penguin, 1993).
54 Laing, R.D., *The politics of experience and the bird of paradise* (Penguin, 1967).
55 Laing, R.D., *The divided self: An existential study in sanity and madness* (Penguin, 1965).
56 Crossley, N., *Intersubjectivity: The fabric of social becoming* (SAGE, 1996).
57 Heidegger, M., *Being and time*, trans J. Stambaugh (State University of New York Press, 1996).
58 See, for instance, Rowan, J. and Cooper, M., eds, *The plural self: Multiplicity in everyday life* (SAGE, 1999); Schwartz, R.C., *No bad parts: Healing trauma and restoring wholeness with the internal family systems model* (sounds true, 2021).
59 Greenberg, L.S. and Dompierre, L.M., 'Specific effects of gestalt 2-chair dialog on intrapsychic conflict in counseling', *Journal of Counseling Psychology* 28, no 4 (1981).
60 Nandy, L. et al, 'Editors' introduction', pp xix–xx.
61 Amiel, D. and Emelien, I., *The new progressivism*.
62 Ibid.
63 Burke, E., *Reflections on the revolution in France* (Amazon, 1789), p 104.
64 Ibid, p 40.
65 Ibid, p 51.
66 Mason, P., *Clear bright future*; Amiel, D. and Emelien, I., *The new progressivism*.
67 Rowson, J., 'Rediscovering the soul of progressive politics'; Simms, A., 'Reimagining Britain: A new approach to environmental issues' in *The alternative: Towards a new progressive politics*, ed L. Nandy, C. Lucas and C. Bowers (Biteback, 2016).
68 Cooper, Mick, *Integrating Counselling and Psychotherapy: Directionality, Synergy, and Social Change* (London: Sage, 2019).
69 See, for instance, Totton, N., *Psychotherapy and politics* (SAGE, 2000); Proctor, G. et al, eds, *Politicising the person-centred approach: An agenda for social change* (PCCS Books, 2006); Hoffman, L., Cleare-Hoffman, H., Granger Jr., N. and St. John, D., *Humanistic approaches to multiculturalism and diversity: Perspectives on existence and difference* (Routledge, 2020).
70 Johnstone, L., Boyle, M., Cromby, J., Dillon, J., Harper, D., Kinderman, P. et al, *The power threat meaning framework* (British Psychological Society, 2018).
71 See, for instance, Solomonov, N. and Barber, J.P., 'Conducting psychotherapy in the Trump era: Therapists' perspectives on political self-disclosure, the therapeutic alliance, and politics in the therapy room', *Journal of Clinical Psychology* 75, no 9 (2019).

72 Solomonov, N. and Barber, J.P., 'Patients' perspectives on political self-disclosure, the therapeutic alliance, and the infiltration of politics into the therapy room in the Trump era', *Journal of Clinical Psychology* 74, no 5 (2018).
73 Morris, W., *News from nowhere* (CreateSpace Independent, 2016), p 49.
74 Bregman, R., *Utopia for realists*.

## Chapter 2

1 Mason, P., *Clear bright future*.
2 Epstein, B., 'The rise, decline and possible revival of socialist humanism', in *For humanism: Explorations in theory and politics*, ed D. Alderson and R. Spencer (Pluto, 2017).
3 Mason, P., *Clear bright future*; Anderson, K., 'Marxist humanism after structuralism and post-structuralism: The case for renewal', in *For humanism: Explorations in theory and politics*, ed D. Alderson and R. Spencer (Pluto, 2017); Alderson, D. and Spencer, R., 'Conclusion', in *For humanism: Explorations in theory and politics*, ed D. Alderson and R. Spencer (Pluto, 2017).
4 See Marcuse in Dunayevskaya, R., *Marxism and freedom: From 1776 until today* (Humanity, 2000).
5 Marx, K., *Economic and philosophical manuscripts*, trans M. Milligan (Prometheus Books, 1988), p 102 (subsequently *EPM*).
6 Fromm, E., 'The application of humanist psycho-analysis and Marx's thought'. In E. Fromm (Ed.), *Socialist Humanism* (Penguin, 1965).
7 Holloway, J., 'The tradition of scientific Marxism', in *Change the world without taking power: The meaning of revolution today*, ed J. Holloway (Pluto, 2002); Engels, F., *Socialism: Utopian and scientific* (First Rate, 2014).
8 Marcuse in Dunayevskaya, R., *Marxism and freedom*.
9 Dunayevskaya, R., 'Marx's humanism today,' in *Socialist humanism*, ed E. Fromm (Penguin, 1965).
10 Epstein, B., 'Socialist humanism'.
11 Alderson, D. and Spencer, R., eds, *For humanism: Explorations in theory and politics* (Pluto, 2017).
12 Dunayevskaya, R., *Marxism and freedom*.
13 Fromm, E., *Marx's concept of man*, p 4.
14 Dunayevskaya, R., *Marxism and freedom*.
15 Bauman, Z., *Socialism: The active utopia* (Routledge, 1976).
16 Thompson, E.P., 'Socialist humanism: An epistle to the Philistines', *The New Reasoner* 1, no 2 (1957), p 109.
17 Ibid, p 116.
18 Kolakowski, L., *Towards a Marxist humanism: Essays on the left today*, trans J.Z. Peel (Grove, 1968), p 165.
19 Mason, P., *Clear bright future*, p 140.
20 Ibid, p 141.
21 Marx, K. and Engels, F., *The German ideology* (Prometheus, 1998), p 42.
22 Lukács, G., *History and class consciousness* (Bibliotech, 2017); Epstein, B., 'Socialist humanism'.

[23] Cohen, M., *The wager of Lucien Goldman: Tragedy, dialectics, and a hidden god* (Princeton University Press, 1994).
[24] Fromm, E., 'Application of humanist psycho-analysis'.
[25] Alderson, D., 'Queer theory, solidarity, and bodies political', in *For humanism: Explorations in theory and politics*, ed D. Alderson and R. Spencer (Pluto, 2017).
[26] Epstein, B., 'Socialist humanism'.
[27] In Dunayevskaya, R., *Marxism and freedom*; Epstein, B., 'Socialist humanism'.
[28] Kolakowski, L., *Marxist humanism*; de Beauvoir, S., *The ethics of ambiguity* (Citadel, 1948); Sartre, J.-P., *Being and nothingness: An essay on phenomenological ontology*, trans H. Barnes (Routledge, 1958).
[29] West, C., *Race matters*, 25th anniversary edn (Beacon, 2017), p 14.
[30] Epstein, B., 'Socialist humanism'; Chomsky, N., *On anarchism* (Penguin, 2013).
[31] Galtung, J., 'Basic needs', p 100.
[32] Roy, R., 'Human needs and freedom: Liberal, Marxist, and Ghandian perspectives' in Human needs: A contribution to the current debate, ed K. Lederer (Oelgeschlager, Gunn & Hain, 1980).
[33] Alderson, D., 'Queer theory'; Epstein, B., 'Socialist humanism'; Chomsky, N., *On anarchism*.
[34] Chomsky, N., *On anarchism*, pp 34–35.
[35] Marx in Dunayevskaya, R., *Marxism and freedom*, p 124.
[36] Marx, K., *EPM*.
[37] Fromm, E., *Marx's concept of man*; Epstein, B., 'Socialist humanism'.
[38] Marx, K., *EPM*; Brennan, T., 'Introduction: Humanism's other story'.
[39] Marx, K., *EPM*, p 24.
[40] Ibid, p 86, original emphasis.
[41] Laing, R.D., *The politics of experience and the bird of paradise*, p 22.
[42] Lukács, G., *History and class consciousness*.
[43] Ibid, p 71.
[44] Fromm, E., *Marx's concept of man*.
[45] Marx, K., *EPM*, p 78, original emphasis.
[46] Marcuse, H., *One-dimensional man* (Routledge, 1964).
[47] Avruch, K. and Mitchell, C., 'Basic human needs in theory and practice', in *Conflict resolution and human needs: Linking theory and practice*, ed K. Avruch and C. Mitchell (Routledge, 2013).
[48] Fromm, E., *Marx's concept of man*, p 24.
[49] Marcuse, H., *One-dimensional man*, p 7.
[50] Ibid.
[51] Fromm, E., 'Application of humanist psycho-analysis'.
[52] Ibid, p 214.
[53] Ibid, p 215.
[54] Chomsky, N., *Profit over people: Neoliberalism and the global order* (Seven Stories, 1999).
[55] Fromm, E., *The fear of freedom* (Routledge, 2001), p 162.
[56] Lukács, G., *History and class consciousness*.
[57] Bastani, A., *Fully automated communism*, p 17.

58 Lukács, G., *History and class consciousness.*
59 Marcuse, H., *One-dimensional man.*
60 Ibid, p 35.
61 Ibid, p 250.
62 Ibid.
63 Ibid.
64 Fromm, E., *Marx's concept of man*; Fritzhand, M., 'Marx's ideal of man', in *Socialist humanism*, ed E. Fromm (Penguin, 1965).
65 Marx, K., *EPM*, p 102, original emphasis.
66 Marx, K. and Engels, F., *The German ideology*, p 53.
67 Fritzhand, M., 'Marx's ideal of man'.
68 Ibid, p 165.
69 Fromm, E., 'Application of humanist psycho-analysis', p 213.
70 May, R. and Rogers, C.R., 'Rollo May', in *The Carl Rogers Dialogues*, ed H. Kirschenbaum and V. Henderson (Constable, 1990), p 244.
71 In Fromm, E., *The sane society*, 2nd edn (Routledge, 1991), p xlvi.
72 Jones, O., *Chavs* (Verso, 2020).
73 In Fromm, E., *The sane society*, p xlvi.
74 Heller, A., 'Can "true" and "false" needs be posited?', in *Human needs: A contribution to the current debate*, ed K. Lederer (Oelgeschlager, Gunn & Hain, 1980).
75 Dahl, R.A., *Democracy and its critics* (Yale University Press, 1989), p 105.
76 Chomsky, N., *On anarchism*, p 140.
77 Heller, A., '"True" and "false" needs', p 213.
78 Ibid, p 214.
79 Lukes, S., *Power: A radical view*, 3rd edn (Red Globe, 2021).
80 Ibid, p 2.
81 Hay, C., 'Divided by a common language: Political theory and the concept of power', *Politics* 17, no 1 (1997), pp 47–48.
82 Cooper, M., 'The intrinsic foundations of extrinsic motivations and goals: Towards a unified humanistic theory of wellbeing', *Journal of Humanistic Psychology* 53, no 2 (2013).
83 Levitas, R., *The concept of utopia* (Peter Lang, 2011).
84 Leiss, in ibid, p 167.
85 Ryan, R.M. and Deci, E.L., 'Self-determination theory and the facilitation of intrinsic motivation, social development, and well-being', *American Psychologist* 55, no 1 (2000).
86 Office for National Statistics, 'Employment by sector 2021' (31 May 2022), https://www.ethnicity-facts-figures.service.gov.uk/work-pay-and-benefits/employment/employment-by-sector/latest
87 Epstein, B., 'Socialist humanism', p 20.
88 Ibid, p 18.
89 Firestone, S., *The dialectic of sex: The case for feminist revolution* (Verso, 2015).
90 Anderson, K., 'Marxist humanism', p 89.
91 Epstein, B., 'Socialist humanism'; Mason, P., *Clear bright future.*

## Chapter 3

1 Cooper, M., *Integrating counselling and psychotherapy: Directionality, synergy, and social change* (SAGE, 2019).
2 For example, Watson, J.B., *Behaviourism* (Norton, 1925).
3 Bandura, A., *Social learning theory* (General Learning Press, 1971), p 27.
4 Ibid.
5 For example, Bloch, E., *Natural law and human dignity*, trans D.J. Schmidt (MIT Press, 1986).
6 Woodfield, A., *Telology* (Cambridge University Press, 1976).
7 Mason, P., *Clear bright future.*
8 Perugini, M. and Bagozzi, R.P., 'The role of desires and anticipated emotions in goal-directed behaviours: Broadening and deepening the theory of planned behaviour', *British Journal of Social Psychology* 40, no 1 (2001); Bagozzi, R.P. and Kimmel, S.K., 'A comparison of leading theories for the prediction of goal-directed behaviours', *British Journal of Social Psychology* 34, no 4 (1995).
9 Wellman, H.W. and Phillips, A.T., 'Developing intentional understandings', in *Intentions and intentionality: Foundations of social cognition*, ed B.F. Malle, L.J. Moses and D.A. Baldwin (MIT Press, 2001).
10 Cooper, M., *Existential psychotherapy and counselling: Contributions to a pluralistic practice* (SAGE, 2015), p 58.
11 For example, Bargh, J.A. and Ferguson, M.J., 'Beyond behaviorism: On the automaticity of higher mental processes', *Psychological Bulletin* 126, no 6 (2000).
12 Holland, R.W., Hendriks, M. and Aarts, H., 'Smells like clean spirit: Nonconscious effects of scent on cognition and behavior', *Psychological Science* 16, no 9 (2005).
13 Shotton, G. and Burton, S., *Emotional wellbeing: An introductory handbook for schools* (Routledge, 2019); Sandole, D.J.D., 'The biological basis of needs in world society: The ultimate micro-macro nexus', in *Human needs theory*, ed J. Burton (Macmillan, 1990).
14 Friedman, Y., 'About implicit limitations on satisfiers', in *Human needs: A contribution to the current debate*, ed K. Lederer (Oelgeschlager, Gunn & Hain, 1980), p 151.
15 Marx, K., *EPM*, p 154, original italics.
16 Marx, K. and Engels, F., *The German ideology*, pp 49–50.
17 For example, Caspar, F., *Plan analysis: Towards optimizing psychotherapy* (Hogrefe & Huber, 1995); Woodfield, A., *Telology*; Powers, W.T., *Behaviour: The control of perception* (Aldine, 1973).
18 Mansell, W., Carey, T.A. and Tai, S.J., *A transdiagnostic approach to CBT using methods of levels therapy* (Routledge, 2013).
19 Powers, W.T., *Behavior*; Mansell, W. et al, *A transdiagnostic approach to CBT using methods of levels therapy*.
20 For example, Mitchell, C., 'Necessitous man and conflict resolution', in *Human needs theory*, ed J. Burton (Macmillan, 1990); Gilwald, K., 'Conflict

and needs research', in *Human needs theory*, ed J. Burton (Macmillan, 1990); Judge, A.N.J., 'Needs communication: Viable needs patterns and their identification', in *Human needs: A contribution to the current debate*, ed K. Lederer (Oelgeschlager, Gunn & Hain, 1980).

21 For example, Galtung, J., 'International development in human perspective', in *Human needs theory*, ed J. Burton (Macmillan, 1990); Rosenberg, M.B., *Nonviolent communication: A language of life*, 3rd edn (Puddledancer, 2015); Judge, A.N.J., 'Needs communication'; Reiss, S. and Wiltz, J., 'Why people watch reality TV', *Media psychology* 6, no 4 (2004).

22 Cooper, M., *Integrating counselling*.

23 Corning, P., *The fair society: And the pursuit of social justice* (University of Chicago Press, 2011); Maslow, A.H., *Motivation and personality*, 3rd edn (Dorling Kindersley, 1987).

24 Maslow, A.H., *Motivation and personality*.

25 Galtung, J., 'Basic needs'; Sites, P., 'Needs as analogues of emotions', in *Human needs theory*, ed J. Burton (Macmillan, 1990).

26 Eddo-Lodge, R., *Why I'm no longer talking to white people about race* (Bloomsbury, 2017).

27 Bentham, 1789, in Gregory, R.L., *The Oxford companion to the mind* (Oxford University Press, 1987), p 308, original emphasis.

28 Freud, S., 'The unconscious', in *General psychological theory: Papers on metapsychology*, ed S. Freud (Collier, 1963).

29 Skinner, B.F., *Walden two* (Hackett, 1948).

30 For example, Harsanyi, J.C., 'Morality and the theory of rational behaviour', in *Utiliarianism and beyond*, ed A. Sen and B. Williams (Cambridge University Press, 1982).

31 Dolan, P., *Happiness by design: Finding pleasure and purpose in everyday life* (Penguin, 2014).

32 For example, Ryff, C.D. and Singer, B.H., 'Know thyself and become what you are: A eudaimonic approach to psychological well-being', *Journal of Happiness Studies* 9, no 1 (2008).

33 Rogers, C.R., 'A theory of therapy, personality and interpersonal relationships as developed in the client-centered framework', in *Psychology: A study of science*, ed S. Koch (McGraw-Hill, 1959).

34 Goldstein, K., *Human nature in the light of psychopathology* (Schocken Books, 1940); Rogers, C.R., 'Theory of therapy'; Maslow, A.H., *Towards a psychology of being*, 2nd edn (D. van Nostrand Co., Inc, 1968).

35 Sites, P., 'Needs as analogues of emotions'.

36 For example, Baumeister, R.F. and Leary, M.R., 'The need to belong: Desire for interpersonal attachments as a fundamental human-motivation', *Psychological Bulletin* 117, no 3 (May 1995); Bowlby, J., *The making and breaking of affectional bonds* (Routledge, 1979); Stern, D.N., *The present moment in psychotherapy and everyday life* (W.W. Norton, 2004); McClelland, D.C. and Burnham, D.H., *Power is the great motivator* (Harvard Business Review Press, 2008).

37 Pohlmann, K., 'Agency- and communion-orientation in life goals: Impact on goal pursuit strategies and psychological well-being', in *Life goals and well-being: Towards a positive psychology of human striving*, ed P. Schmuck and K.M. Sheldon (Hogrefe & Huber, 2001).

38 Clark, M.E., 'Meaningful social bonding as a universal human need', in *Human needs theory*, ed J. Burton (Macmillan, 1990).

39 See Mearns, D. and Cooper, M., *Working at relational depth in counselling and psychotherapy*, 2nd edn (SAGE, 2018).

40 Pohlmann, K., 'Agency- and communion-orientation in life goals'.

41 Corning, P., *The fair society*.

42 Clark, M.E., 'Meaningful social bonding as a universal human need', p 39, italics added.

43 Rosenberg, M.B., *Nonviolent communication*, p 1.

44 Aked, J., Marks, N., Cordon, C. and Thompson, S., *Five ways to wellbeing: The evidence* (New Economics Foundation, 2008).

45 For example, Angyal, A., *Foundations for a science of personality* (Commonwealth Fund, 1941); Powers, W.T., *Living control systems II* (Control Systems Group, 1992); Sites, P., 'Needs as analogues of emotions'.

46 Brickell, J. and Wubbolding, R., 'Reality therapy', in *Introduction to counselling and psychotherapy: The essential guide*, ed S. Palmer (SAGE, 2000), p 294.

47 In Dunayevskaya, R., *Marxism and freedom*, p 53.

48 Galtung, J., 'Basic needs'.

49 Sheldon, K.M., Ryan, R. and Reis, H.T., 'What makes for a good day? Competence and autonomy in the day and in the person', *Personality and Social Psychology Bulletin* 22, no 12 (1996); Reis, H.T., Sheldon, K.M., Gable, S.L., Roscoe, J. and Ryan, R.M. 'Daily well-being: The role of autonomy, competence, and relatedness', *Personality and Social Psychology Bulletin* 26, no 4 (2000).

50 For example, Brickell, J. and Wubbolding, R., 'Reality therapy'; Maslow, A.H., *Motivation and personality*; Mezulis, A.H., Abramson, L.Y., Hyde, J.S. and Hankin, B.L., 'Is there a universal positivity bias in attributions? A meta-analytic review of individual, developmental, and cultural differences in the self-serving attributional bias', *Psychological Bulletin* 130, no 5 (2004); Sites, P., 'Needs as analogues of emotions'.

51 Sheldon, K.M. et al, 'What makes for a good day?'; Reis, H.T. et al, 'Daily well-being'.

52 Ryan, R.M. and Deci, E.L., 'Overview of self-determination theory: An organismic-dialectical perspective', in *Handbook of self-determination research* ed E.L. Deci and R.M. Ryan (University of Rochester Press, 2002), p 7.

53 Sandole, D.J.D., 'Extending the reach of basic human needs: A comprehensive theory for the twenty-first century', in *Conflict resolution and human needs: Linking theory and practice*, ed K. Avruch and C. Mitchell (Routledge, 2013).

54 For example, Frankl, V.E., *Psychotherapy and existentialism: Selected papers on logotherapy* (Clarion Books, 1967); van Deurzen, E., *Psychotherapy and the quest for happiness* (SAGE, 2009).

55 Baumeister, R.F., *Meanings of life* (The Guilford Press, 1991), p 233.

56 Quoted in Frankl, V.E., *Man's search for meaning*, revised and updated edn (Washington Square Press, 1984), p 97, original emphasis.

57 Boorman, J., Morris, E. and Oliver, J., 'Acceptance and commitment therapy', in *The SAGE handbook of counselling and psychotherapy*, ed C. Feltham and I. Horton (SAGE, 2012); Harsanyi, J.C., 'Morality and the theory of rational behaviour'.

58 Sandole, D.J.D., 'Extending basic human needs', p 22.

59 Ryan, R.M. and Deci, E.L., 'Self-determination theory and the facilitation of intrinsic motivation, social development, and well-being'.

60 Galtung, J., 'International development in human perspective'.

61 Maslow, A.H., *The farther reaches of human nature* (Penguin, 1971).

62 Maslow, A.H., 'A theory of human motivation', *Psychological Review* 50 (1943).

63 See, for instance, Sandole, D.J.D., 'The biological basis of needs in world society'; Bouzenita, A.I. and Boulanouar, A.W., 'Maslow's hierarchy of needs: An Islamic critique', *Intellectual Discourse* 24, no 1 (2016).

64 Galtung, J., 'International development in human perspective'.

65 West, C., *Race matters*, p 13.

66 Rubenstein, R.E., 'Beyond natural law', in *Human needs theory*, ed J. Burton (Macmillan, 1990).

67 Simmons, S., 'From human needs to the moral imagination: The promise of post-Burtonian conflict resolution', in *Conflict resolution and human needs: Linking theory and practice*, ed K. Avruch and C. Mitchell (Routledge, 2013); Lederer, K., 'Introduction', in *Human needs: A contribution to the current debate*, ed K. Lederer (Oelgeschlager, Gunn & Hain, 1980); Butler, J., *Gender trouble*.

68 Galtung, J., 'Basic needs'.

69 Ibid.

70 Glaeser, B., 'Labor and leisure in conflict? Needs in developing and industrial societies', In *Human needs: A contribution to the current debate*, ed K. Lederer (Oelgeschlager, Gunn & Hain, 1980).

71 Jordan, J.V., Walker, M. and Hartling, L.M. eds, *The complexity of connection: Writing from the Stone Center's Jean Baker Miller Training Institute* (Guilford Press, 2004).

72 Sandole-Staroste, I., 'Through gender lenses: Human needs theory in conflict resolution', in *Conflict resolution and human needs: Linking theory and practice*, ed K. Avruch and C. Mitchell (Routledge, 2013).

73 Galtung, J., 'Basic needs'.

74 McClelland, D.C. and Burnham, D.H., *Power is the great motivator*.

75 Murray, H.A. and Kluchhohn, C., 'Personality in nature, society, and culture', in *Personality in nature, society, and culture*, ed C. Kluchhohn, H.A. Murray & D.M. Schneider (Knopf, 1953), p 53.

76 Kekes, J., *The morality of pluralism* (Princeton University Press, 1993), p 29.

77 Berlin, I., 'The pursuit of the ideal', in *The crooked timber of humanity: Chapters in the history of ideas*, ed H. Hardy (Random House, 2003); Kekes, J.,

*The morality of pluralism*; Rawls, J., 'Social unity and primary goods', in *Utiliarianism and beyond*, ed A. Sen and B. Williams (Cambridge University Press, 1982).

78 Rawls, J., 'Social unity and primary goods', p 183.

79 Galtung, J., 'International development in human perspective'.

80 Kekes, J., *The morality of pluralism*, p 12.

81 Ibid, p 30.

82 More, T., *Utopia*, trans P. Turner (Folio, 1965), p 82.

83 Rosenberg, M.B., *Nonviolent communication*.

## Chapter 4

1 Kasser, T. and Ryan, R.M., 'A dark side of the American dream: Correlates of financial success as a central life aspiration', *Journal of Personality and Social Psychology* 65, no 2 (1993); Kasser, T. and Ryan, R.M., 'Be careful what you wish for: Optimal functioning and the relative attainment of instrinsic and extrinsic goals', in *Life goals and well-being: Towards a positive psychology of human striving*, ed P. Schmuck and K.M. Sheldon (Hogrefe & Huber, 2001).

2 For example, Cooper, M., *Integrating counselling*; Grosse Holtforth, M. and Michalak, J., 'Motivation in psychotherapy', in *The Oxford handbook of human motivation*, ed R.M. Ryan (Oxford University Press, 2012); Freund, A.M., 'Differentiating and integrating levels of goal representation: A life-span perspective', in *Personal project pursuit: Goals, action, and human flourishing*, ed B.R. Little, K. Salmela-Aro and S.D. Phillips (Lawrence Erlbaum Associates Publishers, 2007); Wiese, B.S., 'Successful pursuit of personal goals and subjective well-being', in *Personal project pursuit: Goals, action, and human flourishing*, ed B.R. Little, K. Salmela-Aro and S.D. Phillips (Lawrence Erlbaum Associates Publishers, 2007); Bagozzi, R.P. and Pieters, R., 'Goal-directed emotions', *Cognition & Emotion* 12, no 1 (1998).

3 Steger, M.F., Frazier, P., Oishi, S. and Kaler, M., 'The meaning in life questionnaire: Assessing the presence of and search for meaning in life', *Journal of Counseling Psychology* 53, no 1 (2006).

4 Steger, M.F., 'Experiencing meaning in life', in *The human quest for meaning: Theories, research, and applications*, ed P.T.P. Wong (Routledge, 2013).

5 Bandura, A., 'Social cognitive theory: An agentic perspective', *Annual Review of Psychology* 52 (2001).

6 Galtung, J., 'Basic needs'.

7 Care Collective, *The care manifesto*.

8 Raworth, K., *Doughnut economics*, p 282.

9 Wikipedia, 'Poverty in the United States' (14 December 2021), https://en.wikipedia.org/wiki/Poverty_in_the_United_States

10 Sandole, D.J.D., 'Extending basic human needs'.

11 Clark, M.E., 'Meaningful social bonding as a universal human need'.

12 Galtung, J., 'Basic needs', p 96.

13 Bay, C., 'Taking the universality of human needs seriously', in *Human needs theory*, ed J. Burton (Macmillan, 1990).

[14] For example, Segal, L., *Radical happiness*; Clark, D.M., Layard, R., Smithies, R., Richards, D.A., Suckling, R. and Wright, B., 'Improving access to psychological therapy: Initial evaluation of two UK demonstration sites'; *Behaviour Research and Therapy* 47, no 11 (2009); Ryff, C.D., 'Eudaimonic well-being, inequality, and health: Recent findings and future directions', *International Review of Economics* 64, no 2 (2017); Wilkinson, R. and Pickett, K., *The inner level: How more equal societies reduce stress, restore sanity and improve everyone's well-being* (Allen Lane, 2018); Layard, R., *Happiness*; Owens, E.B. and Shaw, D.S., 'Poverty and early childhood adjustment', in *Resilience and vulnerability: Adaptation in the context of childhood adversities*, ed S.S. Luthar (Cambridge, 2003).

[15] Marcuse, H., *Eros and civilization* (Sphere, 1966), p 42.

[16] Bastani, A., *Fully automated communism*.

[17] Marcuse, H., *Eros and civilization*.

[18] Raworth, K., *Doughnut economics*, p 10.

[19] Cooper, M., *Integrating counselling*.

[20] Deutsch, M., *The resolution of conflict: Constructive and destructive processes* (Yale University Press, 1973); Kriesberg, L., 'Moral judgments, human needs, and conflict resoultion: Alternative approaches to ethical standards', in *Conflict resolution and human needs: Linking theory and practice*, ed K. Avruch and C. Mitchell (Routledge, 2013); Fisher, R., Ury, W. and Patton, B., *Getting to yes: Negotiating agreement without giving in*, 3rd edn (Penguin, 2011).

[21] Marx, K. and Engels, F., *Manifesto of the Communist Party* (Foreign Languages Publishing, 1953).

[22] Sandole, D.J.D., 'The biological basis of needs in world society'; van Deurzen, E., *Existential counselling and psychotherapy in practice*, 3rd edn (SAGE, 2012).

[23] Adapted from Deutsch, M., *Resolution of conflict*.

[24] Systems Innovation, *Systems modelling: A field guide* (Systems Innovation, 2020), https://www.systemsinnovation.io/post/system-modeling-guide

[25] Cooper, M., *Integrating counselling*.

[26] Ibid.

[27] Gottman, J.S. and Gottman, J.M., *10 principles for doing effective couples therapy* (W.W. Norton, 2015).

[28] Bargh, J.A. and Huang, J.Y., 'The selfish goal', in *The psychology of goals*, ed G.B. Moskowitz and H. Grant (Guilford Press, 2009), pp 131.

[29] Mischel, W., *The marshmallow test* (Penguin, 2014), p 78.

[30] Dryden, W., *Rational emotive behavioural counselling in action*, 2nd edn (SAGE, 1999), p 3.

[31] Mischel, W., *The marshmallow test*.

[32] Amlung, M., Marsden, E., Holshausen, K., Morris, V., Patel, H., Vedelago, L. et al, 'Delay discounting as a transdiagnostic process in psychiatric disorders: A meta-analysis', *JAMA Psychiatry* 76, no 11 (2019).

[33] Mischel, W., *The marshmallow test*.

[34] Ibid, p 220.

[35] Cooper, M., 'Socialist humanism: A progressive politics for the twenty-first century', in *Politicising the person-centred approach: An agenda for social change*,

ed G. Proctor, M. Cooper, P. Sanders and B. Malcolm(PCCS Books, 2006), p 88.
36 Boudreaux, M.J. and Ozer, D.J., 'Goal conflict, goal striving, and psychological well-being', *Motivation and Emotion* 37, no 3 (2013).
37 Bregman, R., *Utopia for realists*, p 57.
38 Ibid.
39 Marx, K., *EPM*, p 117, original emphasis.
40 Maslow, A.H., *Motivation and personality*.
41 Ryan, R.M. and Deci, E.L., 'Self-determination theory and the facilitation of intrinsic motivation, social development, and well-being', p 249.
42 Felitti, V.J., Anda, R.F., Nordenberg, D., Williamson, D.F., Spitz, A.M., Edwards, V. et al, 'Relationship of childhood abuse and household dysfunction to many of the leading causes of death in adults: The Adverse Childhood Experiences (ACE) study', *American Journal of Preventive Medicine* 14, no 4 (1998).
43 Jordan, J.V., 'The role of mutual empathy in relational/cultural therapy', *Journal of Clinical Psychology* 56, no 8 (2000).
44 Cooper, M., *Integrating counselling*.
45 Corning, P., *Nature's magic: Synergy in evolution and the fate of humankind* (Cambridge University Press, 2003).
46 Covey, S.R., *The 7 habits of highly effective people*, 25th anniversary edn (Simon & Schuster, 2004), p 274.
47 Ibid.
48 Ibid, p 275.
49 Fuller, R.B., *Synergetics: Explorations in the geometry of thinking* (Macmillan, 1975).
50 Bandura, A., *Social learning theory*.
51 Marks, I.M., *Living with fear: Understanding and coping with anxiety* (McGraw-Hill, 1978).
52 Bandura, *Social learning theory*.
53 For example, Gottman, J.S. and Gottman, J.M., *10 principles*; Williams, M., *Couples counselling* (Amazon, 2012).
54 Williams, M., *Couples counselling*.
55 Dolan, P., *Happiness by design*.
56 Armor, D.E. and Taylor, S.E., 'Situated optimism: Specific outcome expectancies and self-regulation', in *Advances in experimental social psychology*, ed M.P. Zanna (Academic Press, 1998).
57 'Body image survey results (2020), https://publications.parliament.uk/pa/cm5801/cmselect/cmwomeq/805/80502.htm
58 van Deurzen, E., *Existential counselling and psychotherapy in practice*, 2nd edn (SAGE, 2002); van Deurzen, E., *Psychotherapy and the quest for happiness*.
59 Schooler, J., D. Ariely and G. Loewenstein. 'The pursuit of happiness can be self defeating', in *The psychology of economic decisions* (vol 1: rationality and wellbeing) ed I Brocas and J.D. Carrillo (Oxford University Press, 2003), cited in Dolan, P., *Happiness by design*.
60 Raworth, K., *Doughnut economics*.

## Chapter 5

1 Cooper, M., 'Facilitating the expression of subpersonalities through the use of masks: An exploratory study' (DPhil, University of Sussex, 1995), https://mick-cooper.squarespace.com/articles.

2 Rowan, J., *Personification: Using the dialogical self in psychotherapy and counselling* (Routledge, 2009); Hermans, H.J.M., 'Voicing the self: From information processing to dialogical interchange', *Psychological Bulletin* 119, no 1 (1996); Herman, H.J.M. and Gieser, T., eds, *Handbook of dialogical self theory* (Cambridge University Press, 2012). For a highly accessible contemporary account, see Schwartz, R.C. *No bad parts.*

3 Greenberg, L.S. and Dompierre, L.M., 'Specific effects of gestalt 2-chair dialog on intrapsychic conflict in counseling'.

4 Amiel, D. and Emelien, I., *The new progressivism.*

5 Koestler, A., *The ghost in the machine* (Pan, 1967). Koestler is a controversial figure about whom a number of allegations have been made, for example in the biography of him written by David Cesarani, *Arthur Koestler: The homeless mind* (William Heinemann, 1998). See also https://www.theguardian.com/books/2010/feb/14/arthur-koestler-appreciation.

6 See, for instance, Systems Innovation, *Systems modelling: A field guide*; Fuller, R.B., *Synergetics: Explorations in the geometry of thinking*; Capra, F. and Luisi, P.L., *The systems view of life: A unifying vision* (Cambridge University Press, 2014).

7 Capra, F. and Luisi, P.L., *Systems view of life*, p 154.

8 Collins, P.H. and Bilge, S., *Intersectionality*, 2nd edn (Polity, 2020).

9 Eddo-Lodge, R., *Talking about race.*

10 Wallensteen, P., *Understanding conflict resolution*, 5th edn (SAGE, 2019).

11 Gibbs Jr, R.W., 'Intentions as emergent products of social interactions', in *Intentions and intentionality: Foundations of social cognition*, ed B.F. Malle, L.J. Moses and D.A. Baldwin (MIT Press, 2001).

12 'Pizza Hut mission statement, vision, values, and strategy' (2021), https://visionarybusinessperson.com/pizza-hut-mission-statement-vision-statement/

13 Segal, L., *Radical happiness.*

14 Cohen, M., *Lucien Goldman.*

15 United Nations General Assembly, *Transforming our world: The 2030 Agenda for Sustainable Development* (United Nations, 2015).

16 International Council for Science, *A guide to SDG interactions: From science to implementation* (International Council for Science, 2017), p 19, https://council.science/wp-content/uploads/2017/05/SDGs-Guide-to-Interactions.pdf

17 United Nations General Assembly, *Transforming our world: The 2030 Agenda for Sustainable Development*, 6/35.

18 Inner Development Goals, *Inner development goals: Background, methods and the IDG framework* (Inner Development Goals, 2021), https://www.innerdevelopmentgoals.org/s/211201_IDG_Report_Full.pdf

19 Sandole, D.J.D., 'Extending basic human needs'; Scimecca, J.A., 'Self-reflexivity and freedom: Toward a prescriptive theory of conflict resolution',

in *Human needs theory*, ed J. Burton (Macmillan, 1990); Avruch, K. and Mitchell, C., 'Basic human needs'; Fisher, R.J., 'Acknowledging basic human needs and adjusting the focus of the problem-solving workshop', in K. Avruch and C. Mitchell, *Conflict resolution and human needs: Linking theory and practice* (Routledge, 2013).; Rouhana, N.N., 'The dynamics of joint thinking between adversaries in international conflict: Phases of the continuing problem-solving workshop', *Political Psychology* 16, no 2 (1995).

20 Kriesberg, L., 'Moral judgments'.

21 Fisher, R.J., 'Acknowledging basic human needs and adjusting the focus of the problem-solving workshop', p 200.

22 Avruch, K. and Mitchell, C., 'Afterword', in K. Avruch and C. Mitchell, *Conflict resolution and human needs: Linking theory and practice* (Routledge, 2013).

23 Fisher, R.J., 'Needs theory, social identity and an eclectic model of conflict', p 103.

24 Sandole, D.J.D., 'Extending basic human needs'.

25 Avruch, K., 'Basic human needs and the dilemma of power in conflict resolution', in in K. Avruch and C. Mitchell, Conflict resolution and human needs: Linking theory and practice (Routledge, 2013).

26 Dukes, E.F., 'Human needs and conflict resolution in practice: Environment and community' in K. Avruch and C. Mitchell, Conflict resolution and human needs: Linking theory and practice (Routledge, 2013).

27 Scimecca, J.A., 'Self-reflexivity and freedom'; Abu-Nimer, M., 'Basic human needs: Bridging the gap between theory and practice', in *Conflict resolution and human needs: Linking theory and practice*, ed K. Avruch and C. Mitchell (Routledge, 2013).

28 Rader, V., 'Human needs and the modernization of poverty', in *Human needs theory*, ed J. Burton (Macmillan, 1990), p 228.

29 Fisher, R.J., 'Needs theory, social identity and an eclectic model of conflict'.

30 Simmons, S., 'From human needs to the moral imagination'.

31 Fisher, R.J., 'Acknowledging basic human needs and adjusting the focus of the problem-solving workshop'.

32 Avruch, K. and Mitchell, C., 'Basic human needs'.

33 Harsanyi, J.C., 'Morality and the theory of rational behaviour'.

34 Urmson, J.O. and Ree, J., *The concise encyclopedia of western philosophy and philosophers* (Routledge, 1989).

35 Roy, R., 'Human needs and freedom'; Hare, R.M., 'Ethical theory and utilitarianism', in *Utiliarianism and beyond*, ed A. Sen and B. Williams (Cambridge University Press, 1982).

36 Harsanyi, J.C., 'Morality and the theory of rational behaviour', p 55.

37 Rescher, N., *Pluralism: Against the demand for consensus* (Oxford University Press, 1993).

38 Kekes, J., *The morality of pluralism*, p 70.

39 Cooper, M., *Integrating counselling*; Hare, R.M., 'Ethical theory and utilitarianism'.

40 Harsanyi, J.C., 'Morality and the theory of rational behaviour', p 55, original emphasis.

41 Dahl, R.A., *Democracy and its critics*, pp 180, 307–308, original emphasis.
42 'Hedonistic vs. preference utilitarianism' (Centre on Long-Term Risk, 2017), https://longtermrisk.org/hedonistic-vs-preference-utilitarianism/
43 Amiel, D. and Emelien, I., *The new progressivism*, p 34.
44 Ibid, p 61.
45 Gottman, J.M., Coan, J., Carrere, S. and Swanson, C., 'Predicting marital happiness and stability from newlywed interactions', *Journal of Marriage and the Family* 60, no 1 (1998).
46 Segal, L., *Radical happiness*.
47 Mason, P., *Clear bright future*, p 39.
48 Ibid, p 67.
49 Segal, L., *Radical happiness*.
50 Layard, R., *Happiness*.
51 Wallensteen, P., *Understanding conflict resolution*.
52 Ibid.
53 Fisher, R.J., 'Needs theory, social identity and an eclectic model of conflict'.
54 Stewart, F., 'Root causes of violent conflict in developing countries', *BMJ* 324, no 7333 (2002).
55 Corning, P., *The fair society*; Sherif, M. and Sherif, C.W., *Groups in harmony and tension: An integration of studies of intergroup relations* (Harper, 1953).
56 Bellamy, E., *Looking backward* (Dover, 1996), pp 135–136.
57 Roy, R., 'Human needs and freedom'.
58 Fisher, R. et al, *Getting to yes*.
59 Baffoe, G., Zhou, X., Moinuddin, M., Somanje, A.N., Kuriyama, A., Mohan, G. et al, 'Urban–rural linkages: Effective solutions for achieving sustainable development in Ghana from an SDG interlinkage perspective,' *Sustainability Science* 16, no 4 (2021); International Council for Science, *A guide to SDG interactions: From science to implementation*; Pradhan, P., Costa, L., Rybski, D., Lucht, W. and Kropp, J.P., 'A systematic study of sustainable development goal (SDG) interactions', *Earth's Future* 5, no 11 (2017).
60 International Council for Science, *A guide to SDG interactions: From science to implementation*, p 7.
61 Pradhan, P. et al, 'A systematic study of sustainable development goal (SDG) interactions'.
62 https://sdginterlinkages.iges.jp/visualisationtool.html
63 'Synergy' (Lexico, 2021), https://www.lexico.com/definition/synergy
64 Roddy, M.K., Walsh, L.M., Rothman, K., Hatch, S.G. and Doss, B.D., 'Meta-analysis of couple therapy: Effects across outcomes, designs, timeframes, and other moderators', *Journal of Consulting and Clinical Psychology* 88, no 7 (2020); Rathgeber, M., Bürkner, P.C., Schiller, E.M. and Holling, H., 'The efficacy of emotionally focused couples therapy and behavioral couples therapy: A meta-analysis', *Journal of Marital and Family Therapy* 45, no 3 (2019).
65 Rathgeber, M. et al, 'Efficacy of emotionally focused couples therapy'.
66 Williams, M., *Couples counselling*, p 45.
67 Ibid.

68 Gottman, J.S. and Gottman, J.M., *10 principles*, p 204.
69 Williams, M., *Couples counselling*.
70 Gottman, J.S. and Gottman, J.M., *10 principles*.
71 Ibid.
72 Ibid, p 192.
73 Beer, J.E. and Packard, C.C., *The mediator's handbook* (New Society, 2012), p 105.
74 Ibid, p 147.
75 Ibid, p 145.
76 Ibid, p 9.
77 Ibid.
78 Fisher, R. et al, *Getting to yes*.
79 Ibid, p 43.
80 Ibid, p 44.
81 Ibid, p 4.
82 Ibid.
83 Beer, J.E. and Packard, C.C., *The mediator's handbook*.
84 Ibid.
85 Ibid, p 3.
86 Rouhana, N.N., 'The dynamics of joint thinking between adversaries in international conflict'.
87 Ibid, p 321.
88 Wallensteen, P., *Understanding conflict resolution*; Rouhana, N.N., 'The dynamics of joint thinking between adversaries in international conflict'.
89 Wallensteen, P., *Understanding conflict resolution*, p 41.
90 Ibid.
91 Kelman, H.C., 'Applying a human needs perspective to the practice of conflict resolution: The Israeli-Palestinian case', in *Human needs theory*, ed J. Burton (Macmillan, 1990), p 291.
92 Ibid, p 295.
93 Abu-Nimer, M., 'Basic human needs'; Rouhana, N.N., 'The dynamics of joint thinking between adversaries in international conflict'.
94 Abu-Nimer, M., 'Basic human needs'.
95 Fisher, R. et al, *Getting to yes*.
96 Mitchell, C., 'Necessitous man and conflict resolution'; Galtung, J., 'Human needs'.
97 In Covey, S.R., *7 habits*, p 50.
98 Spaniel, W., *Game theory 101: The complete textbook* (William Spaniel, 2015), p 1.
99 Wallensteen, P., *Understanding conflict resolution*.
100 Note, though, that they are not entirely synonymous: 'synergies' and 'cooperation' involve some interactions between parts; and, potentially, 'cooperative' or 'synergetic' solutions might not involve both parts 'winning' – one part, for instance, could gain a lot while the other part might lose just a little.

101 Wright, R., *Nonzero: The logic of human destiny* (Vintage Books, 2000); Axelrod, R., *The evolution of cooperation* (Basic, 1984).
102 'Prisoner's dilemma' (2021), https://en.wikipedia.org/wiki/Prisoner%27s_dilemma
103 Axelrod, R., *The evolution of cooperation*, p 9.
104 Rapoport, A., *Fights, games and debates* (University of Michigan Press, 1960).
105 Axelrod, R., *The evolution of cooperation*.
106 Covey, S.R., *7 habits*, p 18.

## Chapter 6

1 Cooper, M., *Integrating counselling*, Chapter 16.
2 Axelrod, R., *The evolution of cooperation*, p 15.
3 Rapoport, A., *Fights, games and debates*.
4 Bateman, A. and Fonagy, P., *Psychotherapy for borderline personality disorder: Mentalization-based treatment* (Oxford University Press, 2004).
5 Powers, W.T., *Behavior*; Mansell, W. et al, *A transdiagnostic approach to CBT using methods of levels therapy*.
6 Mischel, W., *The marshmallow test*.
7 NSPCC and UCL, *Minding the baby: Qualitative findings on implementation from the first UK service* (NSPCC, 2017), https://learning.nspcc.org.uk/research-resources/2017/minding-the-baby-qualitative-findings-implementation
8 Gottman, J.S. and Gottman, J.M., *10 principles*.
9 Fisher, R. et al, *Getting to yes*, p 25.
10 In Harsanyi, J.C., 'Morality and the theory of rational behaviour', p 39.
11 Ibid.
12 Rawls, J., *A theory of justice*, revised edn (Harvard University Press, 1971).
13 Fisher, R. et al, *Getting to yes*, p 38.
14 Ibid.
15 Fromm, E., *Marx's concept of man*, p 44, original emphasis.
16 Marx, K., *EPM*, p 116.
17 Walzer, M., *Spheres of justice* (Basic Books, 1983); Hudis, P., *Marx's concept of the alternative to capitalism* (Haymarket, 2012).
18 Mason, P., *Clear bright future*, p 66.
19 Kasser, T. and Ryan, R.M., 'A dark side of the American dream'; Kasser, T. and Ryan, R.M., 'Further examining the American dream: Differential correlates of intrinsic and extrinsic goals', *Personality and Social Psychology Bulletin* 22, no 3 (1996).
20 Fromm, E., *The fear of freedom*.
21 Mason, P., *Clear bright future*, p 21.
22 Prentice, H. and Rust, M.-J., 'The breast-milk of the Inuit mother: A tale of micro and macrocosm, shadow and light', in *The politics of psychotherapy: New perspectives*, ed N. Totton (Open University Press, 2005).
23 Ibid, p 46.
24 Burke, E., *Reflections on the revolution in France*, p 57.
25 Mischel, W., *The marshmallow test*.
26 Kahneman, D., *Thinking, fast and slow* (Penguin, 2011).

27 Powers, W.T., *Living control systems II.*
28 Cooper, M., *Essential research findings in counselling and psychotherapy: The facts are friendly* (SAGE, 2008).
29 Williams, M., *Couples counselling.*
30 Kahneman, D., *Thinking, fast and slow.*
31 Lukács, G., *History and class consciousness.*
32 Fisher, L., *Rock, paper, scissors: Game theory in everyday life* (Basic Books, 2008).
33 West, C., *Race matters*, p 7.
34 Covey, S.R., *7 habits.*
35 Segal, L., *Radical happiness*; Deutsch, M., *Resolution of conflict.*
36 Beer, J.E. and Packard, C.C., *The mediator's handbook*, p 96.
37 Ibid.
38 Corning, P., *The fair society*; Beer, J.E. and Packard, C.C., *The mediator's handbook.*
39 Williams, M., *Couples counselling.*
40 Lukes, S., *Power*, p 74.
41 Freeman, J., *The tyranny of structurelessness* (1972), http://www.cooperatives-wales.coop/wp-content/uploads/2013/01/The-Tyranny-of-Structurelessness-Jo-Freeman.pdf
42 Bay, C., 'Taking the universality of human needs seriously', p 248.
43 Beer, J.E. and Packard, C.C., *The mediator's handbook.*
44 Freeman, J., *The tyranny of structurelessness.*
45 Deutsch, M., *Resolution of conflict*; Wright, R., *Nonzero*; Alderson, D., 'Queer theory'; Covey, S.R., *7 habits.*
46 Fisher, L., *Rock, paper, scissors*, p 129.
47 'Trust (social science)' (2021), https://en.wikipedia.org/wiki/Trust_(social_science)#Types_of_social_trust
48 Schwartz, R.C., *No bad parts*, p 20.
49 Ibid, p 36.
50 Boszormenyi-Nagy, I., Grunebaum, J. and Ulrich, D., 'Contextual therapy', in *Handbook of family therapy*, ed A.S. Gurman and D. Kniskern (Brunner-Mazel, 1991), p 28.
51 Cooper, M., 'The fully functioning society: A humanistic-existential vision of an actualizing, socially-just future', *Journal of Humanistic Psychology* 56, no 6 (2016).
52 Axelrod, R., *The evolution of cooperation*, p 13.
53 Ibid, p 112.
54 Gottman, J.S. and Gottman, J.M., *10 principles.*
55 Ibid, p 129.
56 Williams, M., *Couples counselling.*
57 Beer, J.E. and Packard, C.C., *The mediator's handbook.*
58 Fisher, R. et al, *Getting to yes*, p 56.
59 Amiel, D. and Emelien, I., *The new progressivism*, p 119.
60 Axelrod, R., *The evolution of cooperation*, p 33, original italics.
61 Ibid, p 68.
62 Rosenberg, M.B., *Nonviolent communication.*

63 For example, Rogers, C.R., 'Theory of therapy'; Gilbert, P., *Compassion focused therapy* (Routledge, 2010).
64 Beer, J.E. and Packard, C.C., *The mediator's handbook.*
65 Williams, M., *Couples counselling.*
66 Abu-Nimer, M., 'Basic human needs', p 167.
67 Markey, P., Funder, D. and Ozer, D., 'Complementarity of interpersonal behaviors in dyadic interactions', *Personality & Social Psychology Bulletin* 29, no 9 (2003).
68 Cantor, N. and Sanderson, C.A., 'Life task participation and well-being: The importance of taking part in daily life', in *Well-being: The foundations of hedonic psychology*, ed D. Kahneman, E. Diener and N. Schwarz (Russell Sage Foundation, 1999).
69 Sheldon, K.M. and Schmuck, P., 'Suggestions for healthy goal striving', in *Life goals and well-being: Towards a positive psychology of human striving*, ed P. Schmuck and K.M. Sheldon (Hogrefe & Huber, 2001).
70 Seaford, C., Michaelson, J. and Stoll, L., *Well-being evidence for policy: A review* (New Economics Foundation, 2012), 29.
71 Aked, J. et al, *Five ways to wellbeing.*
72 Covey, S.R., *7 habits.*
73 In Sunkara, B., *Socialist manifesto*, p 144.
74 Covey, S.R., *7 habits*, p 289.
75 Ibid.
76 Schwartz, R.C., *No bad parts*, p 11.
77 Segal, L., *Radical happiness.*
78 Elliot, A.J. and Church, M.A., 'Client articulated avoidance goals in the therapy context', *Journal of Counseling Psychology* 49, no 2 (2002).
79 Marks, I.M., *Living with fear.*
80 Deutsch, M., *Resolution of conflict.*
81 Beer, J.E. and Packard, C.C., *The mediator's handbook.*
82 Grosse Holtforth, M. and Grawe, K., 'Bern inventory of treatment goals: Part 1. Development and first application of a taxonomy of treatment goal themes', *Psychotherapy Research* 12, no 1 (2002).
83 Dilk, M.N. and Bond, G.R., 'Meta-analytic evaluation of skills training research for individuals with severe mental illness', *Journal of Consulting and Clinical Psychology* 64, no 6 (1996).
84 Fisher, R. et al, *Getting to yes.*
85 Williams, M., *Couples counselling.*
86 Wallensteen, P., *Understanding conflict resolution.*
87 Mason, P., *Clear bright future*, p 300.
88 West, C., *Race matters*, pp xi–xii.
89 Rapoport, A., *Fights, games and debates*; Axelrod, R., *The evolution of cooperation.*
90 Fisher, R. et al, *Getting to yes.*
91 Beer, J.E. and Packard, C.C., *The mediator's handbook*, p 3.
92 Williams, M., *Couples counselling*, p 3.
93 Deutsch, M., *Resolution of conflict.*
94 Gottman, J.S. and Gottman, J.M., *10 principles.*

95 Depaulo, B.M., Hoover, C.W., Webb, W., Kenny, D.A. and Oliver, P.V., 'Accuracy of person perception: Do people know what kinds of impressions they convey', *Journal of Personality and Social Psychology* 52, no 2 (1987); Williams, M., *Couples counselling*.

96 Beer, J.E. and Packard, C.C., *The mediator's handbook*; Williams, M., *Couples counselling*; Wallensteen, P., *Understanding conflict resolution*; Deutsch, M., *Resolution of conflict*.

97 Williams, M., *Couples counselling*.

98 Fisher, R. et al, *Getting to yes*.

99 Rouhana, N.N., 'The dynamics of joint thinking between adversaries in international conflict'.

100 Katz, R. and Murphy-Shigematsu, S., eds, *Synergy, healing and empowerment: Insights from cultural diversity* (Brush, 2012).

101 Deutsch, M., *Resolution of conflict*.

102 Gottman, J.S. and Gottman, J.M., *10 principles*.

103 Williams, M., *Couples counselling*; Fisher, R.J., 'Acknowledging basic human needs and adjusting the focus of the problem-solving workshop'.

104 Buber, M., 'Dialogue', in *Between man and man* (Fontana, 1947); Bohm, D., *On dialogue* (Routledge, 1996); Cooper, M., Chak, A., Cornish, F. and Gillespie, A., 'Dialogue: Bridging personal, community and social transformation', *Journal of Humanistic Psychology* 53, no 1 (2012).

105 Gottman, J.S. and Gottman, J.M., *10 principles*.

106 Cooper, M., 'Welcoming the other: Actualising the humanistic ethic at the core of counselling psychology practice', *Counselling Psychology Review* 24, nos 3–4 (2009); Schmid, P.F., 'The challenge of the other: Towards dialogical person-centered psychotherapy and counseling', *Person-Centered and Experiential Psychotherapies* 5, no 4 (2006); Cooper, M. and Spinelli, E., 'A dialogue on dialogue', in *Existential psychotherapy: Vibrancy, legacy and dialogue*, ed L. Barnett and G. Madison (Routledge, 2012).

107 Beer, J.E. and Packard, C.C., *The mediator's handbook*; Fisher, R. et al, *Getting to yes*.

108 Buber, M., 'Dialogue'.

109 Deutsch, M., *Resolution of conflict*.

110 Williams, M., *Couples counselling*; Wallensteen, P., *Understanding conflict resolution*.

111 Beer, J.E. and Packard, C.C., *The mediator's handbook*.

112 Covey, S.R., *7 habits*.

113 Freeman, J., *The tyranny of structurelessness*.

114 Eddo-Lodge, R., *Talking about race*.

115 Ibid, p 218.

116 Ibid, p 92.

117 Ibid.

118 Ibid, p 108.

119 'Distribution of wealth' (2021), https://en.wikipedia.org/wiki/Distribution_of_wealth#Wealth_distribution_pyramid

120 Walzer, M., *Spheres of justice*, p xi.

121 For example, de Vries, D.A., Möller, A.M., Wieringa, M.S., Eigenraam, A.W. and Hamelink, K., 'Social comparison as the thief of joy: Emotional consequences of viewing strangers' Instagram posts', *Media Psychology* 21, no 2 (2018).
122 Wilkinson, R. and Pickett, K., *The spirit level: Why equality is better for everyone* (Penguin, 2010).
123 Ibid, p 29.
124 Ibid.
125 Kahneman, D., *Thinking, fast and slow.*
126 Corning, P., *The fair society*, p 5.
127 Cohen, G.A., *Why not socialism?* (Princeton University Press, 2009), pp 5–6.
128 Corning, P., *The fair society*; Wilkinson, R. and Pickett, K., *Inner level.*
129 Wilkinson, R. and Pickett, K., *Inner level*, pp 121–122.
130 Curtice, J., 'Is there a progressive majority?', in *The alternative: Towards a new progressive politics*, ed L. Nandy, C. Lucas and C. Bowers (Biteback, 2016)..
131 Dolan, P., *Happiness by design.*
132 Rabin, M., 'Incorporating fairness into game theory and economics', *The American Economic Review* 83, no 5 (1993).
133 Rilling, J.K., Gutman, D.A., Zeh, T.R., Pagnoni, G., Berns, G.S. and Kilts, C.D., 'A neural basis for social cooperation', *Neuron* 35, no 2 (2002).
134 Oosterbeek, H., Sloof, R. and Van De Kuilen, G., 'Cultural differences in ultimatum game experiments: Evidence from a meta-analysis', *Experimental Economics* 7, no 2 (2004).
135 Said, E.W., *Humanism and democratic criticism*, p 10.
136 Corning, P., *The fair society.*
137 Wilkinson, R. and Pickett, K., *Inner level*, p 134.
138 Corning, P., *The fair society.*
139 Wilkinson, R. and Pickett, K., *Inner level.*
140 Layard, R., *Happiness.*
141 Hare, R.M., 'Ethical theory and utilitarianism', p 27.
142 Kahneman, D., *Thinking, fast and slow.*
143 Layard, R., *Happiness*, p 52.
144 Walzer, M., *Spheres of justice.*
145 Ibid, p xiv.
146 Amiel, D. and Emelien, I., *The new progressivism.*
147 Galtung, J., 'Basic needs', p 101.
148 Rawls, J., 'Social unity and primary goods', p 3.
149 Walzer, M., *Spheres of justice.*
150 Žižek, S., *Living in end times* (Verso, 2011), p 41.
151 Wilkinson, R. and Pickett, K., *Inner level.*
152 Dunayevskaya, R., *Marxism and freedom.*
153 Wilkinson, R. and Pickett, K., *Inner level.*
154 Walzer, M., *Spheres of justice*, p 19.
155 Mitchell, C., 'Necessitous man and conflict resolution'.
156 Potapchuk, W.R., 'Processes of governance: Can governments truly respond to human needs?', in *Human needs theory*, ed J. Burton (Macmillan, 1990);

Sites, P., 'Needs as analogues of emotions'; Lukes, S., *Power*; Hay, C., 'Divided by a common language'.

157 West, C., *Race matters*.

158 Sites, P., 'Needs as analogues of emotions', p 27.

159 Powers, W.T., *Behavior*, pp 281–282, original emphasis.

160 Stone, H. and Winkelman, S., *Embracing Our Selves: The Voice Dialogue Manual* (Nataraj Publishing, 1989).

161 Deutsch, M., *Resolution of conflict*; Dimaggio, G., Hermans, H.J.M. and Lysaker, P.H., 'Health and adaptation in a multiple self: The role of absence of dialogue and poor metacognition in clinical populations', *Theory & Psychology* 20, no 3 (2010).

162 Mindell, A., *The leader as martial artist: An introduction to deep democracy* (Deep Democracy Exchange, 2014), p 42.

163 Boszormenyi-Nagy, I. et al, 'Contextual therapy'.

164 In Dahl, R.A., *Democracy and its critics*, p 86.

165 Ibid.

166 Ibid, p 322.

167 Ibid, p 104.

168 Ibid, p 141.

## Chapter 7

1 See Raworth, K., *Doughnut economics*.

2 Layard, R. and Clark, D.M., *Thrive: The power of psychological therapy* (Penguin, 2014).

3 Department of Health and Department for Education, *Transforming children and young people's mental health provision: Green paper* (Department of Health and Department for Education, 2017).

4 Clarke, B., Younas, F. and Project Team Family Kids and Youth, *Helping parents to parent* (Social Mobility Commission, 2017), https://www.researchgate.net/profile/Fatima-Younas-2/publication/331235246_Helping_Parent_to_Parent/links/5c73ca69299bf1268d232189/Helping-Parent-to-Parent.pdf

5 Trebeck, K. and Baker, A., *Being bold: Building budgets for children's wellbeing* (Children in Scotland, Cattanach, Carnegie Trust UK), p 4, https://www.carnegieuktrust.org.uk/publications/being-bold-building-budgets-for-childrens-wellbeing/

6 Perry, P., *The book that you wish your parents had read (and your children will be glad that you did)* (Penguin, 2019), p 249.

7 Bandura, A., *Social learning theory*.

8 Perry, P., *Book you wish*.

9 Clarke, B. et al, *Helping parents to parent*.

10 Kiernan, K.E. and Mensah, F.K., 'Poverty, family resources and children's early educational attainment: The mediating role of parenting', *British Educational Research Journal* 37, no 2 (2011).

11 Owens, E.B. and Shaw, D.S., 'Poverty and early childhood adjustment',

12 Ibid.

13 Clarke, B. et al, *Helping parents to parent*, p 4.

14 Ibid.
15 Scottish Government, *Mental health strategy: 2017–2027* (The Scottish Government, 2017), https://www.gov.scot/publications/mental-health-strategy-2017-2027/documents/
16 Clarke, B. et al, *Helping parents to parent*, p 11.
17 For example, Kiernan, K.E. and Mensah, F.K., 'Poverty, family resources and children's early educational attainment'.
18 Eanes, R., *Positive parenting: An essential guide* (TarcherPerigee, 2016).
19 For example, Perry, P., *Book you wish*; Webster-Stratton, C., *The incredible years: A trouble-shooting guide for parents of children aged 3–8 years* (Incredible Years, 2019).
20 Baumrind, D., 'Effects of authoritative parental control on child behavior', *Child Development* 37, no 4 (1966); Perry, P., *Book you wish*.
21 Eanes, R., *Positive parenting*.
22 Bowlby, J., *Attachment* (Basic Books, 1969).
23 Perry, P., *Book you wish*; Webster-Stratton, C., *Incredible years*.
24 Eanes, R., *Positive parenting*.
25 Erikson, E.H., *Childhood and society* (Penguin, 1950).
26 Webster-Stratton, C., *Incredible years*.
27 Eanes, R., *Positive parenting*, p 7.
28 Perry, P., *Book you wish*.
29 Ibid, p 144.
30 Eanes, R., *Positive parenting*.
31 Ibid, p 123.
32 https://childrenlearnwhattheylive.com/
33 Eanes, R., *Positive parenting*, p 8.
34 Baumrind, D., 'Effects of authoritative parental control on child behavior'.
35 Neill, A.S., *Summerhill: A radical approach to education* (Victor Gollancz, 1964), p 105, original emphasis.
36 Eanes, R., *Positive parenting*; Perry, P., *Book you wish*.
37 Perry, P., *Book you wish*.
38 Eanes, R., *Positive parenting*.
39 https://incredibleyears.com/
40 Webster-Stratton, C., *Incredible years*, p 24.
41 Perry, P., *Book you wish*.
42 Ibid, p 212.
43 Ibid.
44 Webster-Stratton, C., *Incredible years*; Perry, P., *Book you wish*; Eanes, R., *Positive parenting*.
45 Eanes, R., *Positive parenting*, p 9.
46 Ibid.
47 Perry, P., *Book you wish*; Eanes, R., *Positive parenting*.
48 Eanes, R., *Positive parenting*, p 9.
49 Kaminski, J.W., Valle, L.A., Filene, J.H. and Boyle, C.L, 'A meta-analytic review of components associated with parent training program effectiveness',

*Journal of Abnormal Child Psychology* 36, no 4 (2008); Webster-Stratton, C., *Incredible years*.

50 Eanes, R., *Positive parenting*.

51 Webster-Stratton, C., *Incredible years*.

52 Ibid, p 225.

53 Sanders, M.R., 'Triple P-Positive Parenting Program: Towards an empirically validated multilevel parenting and family support strategy for the prevention of behavior and emotional problems in children', *Clinical Child and Family Psychology Review* 2, no 2 (1999), p 72.

54 Clarke, B. et al, *Helping parents to parent*.

55 Kaminski, J.W. et al, 'A meta-analytic review of components associated with parent training program effectiveness'.

56 Ibid.

57 Webster-Stratton, C., *Incredible years*.

58 https://www.triplep.uk.net/uken/home/

59 Sanders, M.R., Kirby, J.N., Tellegen, C.L. and Day, J.J., 'The Triple P-Positive Parenting Program: A systematic review and meta-analysis of a multi-level system of parenting support', *Clinical Psychology Review* 34, no 4 (2014); De Graaf, I., Speetjens, P., Smit, F., De Wolff, M. and Tavecchio, L., 'Effectiveness of the Triple P Positive Parenting Program on parenting: A meta-analysis', *Family Relations* 57, no 5 (2008).

60 NSPCC and UCL, *Minding the baby*; Sadler, L.S., Slade, A., Close, N., Webb, D.L., Simpson, T., Fennie, K. et al, 'Minding the baby: Enhancing reflectiveness to improve early health and relationship outcomes in an interdisciplinary home-visiting program', *Infant Mental Health Journal* 34, no 5 (2013).

61 NSPCC and UCL, *Minding the baby*, p 7.

62 Sadler, L.S. et al, 'Minding the baby'.

63 Clarke, B. et al, *Helping parents to parent*.

64 Wigelsworth, M., Humphrey, N. and Lendrum, A., 'A national evaluation of the impact of the secondary social and emotional aspects of learning (SEAL) programme', *Educational Psychology* 32, no 2 (2012), p 219.

65 Ibid.

66 World Health Organization, *Life skills education for children and adolescents in schools* (World Health Organization, 1997).

67 Goleman, D., *Emotional intelligence: Why it can matter more than IQ* (Bloomsbury, 1996).

68 Aspen Institute, *From a nation at risk to a nation at hope* (The Aspen Institute, 2019), http://nationathope.org/

69 Bierman, K.L. and Motamedi, M., 'SEL programs for preschool children', in *Handbook of social and emotional learning: Research and practice*, ed J.A. Durlak, C.E. Domitrovich, R.P. Weissberg and T.P. Gullotta (Guilford Press, 2015); Conley, C.S., 'SEL in higher education', in *Handbook of social and emotional learning: Research and practice*, ed J.A. Durlak, C.E. Domitrovich, R.P. Weissberg and T.P. Gullotta (Guilford Press, 2015).

70 World Health Organization, *Life skills education*.

71 Gueldner, B.A., Feuerborn, L.L. and Merrell, K., *Social and emotional learning in the classroom*, 2nd edn (Guilford Press, 2020).

72 Weissberg, R.P., Durlak, J.A., Domitrovich, C.E. and Gullotta, T.P., 'Social and emotional learning: Past, present, and future', in *Handbook of social and emotional learning: Research and practice*, ed J.A. Durlak, C.E. Domitrovich, R.P. Weissberg and T.P. Gullotta (Guilford Press, 2015), https://casel.org/

73 See Gueldner, B.A. et al, *Social and emotional learning in the classroom*; Durlak, J.A, Domitrovich, C.E., Weissberg, R.P. and Gullotta, T.P. , eds, *Handbook of social and emotional learning: Research and practice* (Guilford Press, 2015).

74 See Elias, M.J., Leverett, L., Duffell, J.C., Humphreys, N., Stepney, C. and Ferrito, J., 'Integrating SEL with related prevention and youth development approaches', in *Handbook of social and emotional learning: Research and practice*, ed J.A. Durlak, C.E. Domitrovich, R.P. Weissberg and T.P. Gullotta (Guilford Press, 2015); Torrente, C., Alimchandani, A. and Aber, J.L., 'International perspectives on SEL', in *Handbook of social and emotional learning: Research and practice*, ed J.A. Durlak, C.E. Domitrovich, R.P. Weissberg and T.P. Gullotta (Guilford Press, 2015).

75 Gedikoglu, M., *Social and emotional learning: An evidence review and synthesis of key issues* (Education Policy Institute, 2021), https://epi.org.uk/publications-and-research/social-and-emotional-learning/

76 Ibid.

77 Liberal Democrats, *Liberal Democrats manifesto 2019: Stop BREXIT build a brighter future* (Liberal Democrats, 2019), p 27.

78 Green Party, *Manifesto 2019.*

79 Jones, D., Greenberg, M.T. and Crowley, N., 'The economic case for SEL', in *Handbook of social and emotional learning: Research and practice*, ed J.A. Durlak, C.E. Domitrovich, R.P. Weissberg and T.P. Gullotta (Guilford Press, 2015) , p 97.

80 Darling-Hammond, L., 'Social and emotional learning: Critical skills for building healthy schools', in *Handbook of social and emotional learning: Research and practice*, ed J.A. Durlak, C.E. Domitrovich, R.P. Weissberg and T.P. Gullotta (Guilford Press, 2015).

81 Durlak, J.A., Weissberg, R.P., Dymnicki, A.B., Taylor, R.D. and Schellinger, K. B., 'The impact of enhancing students' social and emotional learning: A meta-analysis of school-based universal interventions', *Child Development* 82, no 1 (2011).

82 Ibid.

83 Taylor, R.D., Oberle, E., Durlak, J.A. and Weissberg, R.P., 'Promoting positive youth development through school-based social and emotional learning interventions: A meta-analysis of follow-up effects', *Child Development* 88, no 4 (2017).

84 Jones, D. et al, 'The economic case for SEL'.

85 Darling-Hammond, L., 'Social and emotional learning', p xi.

86 World Health Organization, *Life skills education*; Durlak, J.A. et al, 'The impact of enhancing students' social and emotional learning'; Taylor, R.D. et al,

'Promoting positive youth development through school-based social and emotional learning interventions'.

87 Aspen Institute, *Nation at hope.*

88 Durlak, J.A. et al, 'The impact of enhancing students' social and emotional learning'; Taylor, R.D. et al, 'Promoting positive youth development through school-based social and emotional learning interventions'.

89 Aspen Institute, *Nation at hope*; Gueldner, B.A. et al, *Social and emotional learning in the classroom.*

90 hooks, b. *All about love.*

91 Shriver, T.P. and Buffett, J., 'The uncommon core', in *Handbook of social and emotional learning: Research and practice*, ed J.A. Durlak, C.E. Domitrovich, R.P. Weissberg and T.P. Gullotta (Guilford Press, 2015), p xv.

92 Elias, M.J. et al, 'Integrating SEL with related prevention and youth development approaches', p 36.

93 Aspen Institute, *Nation at hope*, p 6.

94 Franke, H.A., 'Toxic stress: Effects, prevention and treatment', *Children (Basel, Switzerland)* 1, no 3; Wilson, S.J. and Lipsey, M.W., 'School-based interventions for aggressive and disruptive behavior: Update of a meta-analysis', *American Journal of Preventive Medicine* 33, no 2 (2007).

95 Aspen Institute, *Nation at hope.*

96 Brackett, M.A. et al, 'Applying theory to the development of approaches to SEL', in *Handbook of social and emotional learning: Research and practice*, ed J.A. Durlak et al (Guilford Press, 2015); Shotton, G. and Burton, S., *Emotional wellbeing.*

97 Bandura, A., *Social learning theory.*

98 Weissberg, R.P. et al, 'Social and emotional learning'.

99 Wigelsworth, M., Verity, L., Mason, C., Humphrey, N., Qualter, P. and Troncoso, P., *Programmes to practices identifying effective, evidence-based social and emotional learning strategies for teachers and schools: Evidence review* (Education Endowment Foundation, 2020).

100 World Health Organization, *Life skills education.*

101 Weissberg, R.P. et al, 'Social and emotional learning'; Shotton, G. and Burton, S., *Emotional wellbeing.*

102 Shotton, G. and Burton, S., *Emotional wellbeing.*

103 Ibid.

104 Weissberg, R.P. et al, 'Social and emotional learning', p 6.

105 Shotton, G. and Burton, S., *Emotional wellbeing.*

106 Ibid.

107 Ibid.

108 World Health Organization, *Life skills education.*

109 For example, Çeçen-Eroğul, A.R. and Zengel, M., 'The effectiveness of an assertiveness training programme on adolescents' assertiveness level', *Ilkogretim Online* 8, no 2 (2009).

110 World Health Organization, *Life skills education.*

111 Durlak, J.A. et al, 'The impact of enhancing students' social and emotional learning'.

[112] Bierman, K.L. and Motamedi, M., 'SEL programs for preschool children'; Weare, K., *Developing the emotionally literate school* (Paul Chapman Publishing, 2004).
[113] Bierman, K.L. and Motamedi, M., 'SEL programs for preschool children'.
[114] Gueldner, B.A. et al, *Social and emotional learning in the classroom.*
[115] Ibid; Hecht, M.L. and Shin, Y., 'Culture and social and emotonal competencies', in *Handbook of social and emotional learning: Research and practice*, ed J.A. Durlak, C.E. Domitrovich, R.P. Weissberg and T.P. Gullotta (Guilford Press, 2015).
[116] Hecht, M.L. and Shin, Y., 'Culture and social and emotonal competencies'.
[117] Grimes, L.E., Haizlip, B., Rogers, T. and Brown, K.D., ' " Sisters of Nia": A social justice advocacy intervention for school counselors in their work with adolescent African American females', *Georgia School Counselors Association Journal* 20, no 1 (2013); Aston, C. and Graves Jr, S., 'Challenges and barriers to implementing a school-based Afrocentric intervention in urban schools: A pilot study of the Sisters of Nia cultural program', *School Psychology Forum* 10, no 2 (2016).
[118] Weissberg, R.P. et al, 'Social and emotional learning', p 11.
[119] Weare, K., *Developing the emotionally literate school*, p 53.
[120] Durlak, J.A. et al, 'The impact of enhancing students' social and emotional learning'.
[121] Weare, K., *Developing the emotionally literate school.*
[122] Gueldner, B.A. et al, *Social and emotional learning in the classroom*, p 79.
[123] Aspen Institute, *Nation at hope.*
[124] Weare, K., *Developing the emotionally literate school.*
[125] Gueldner, B.A. et al, *Social and emotional learning in the classroom.*
[126] Bierman, K.L. and Motamedi, M., 'SEL programs for preschool children'.
[127] https://www.responsiveclassroom.org/
[128] Weare, K., *Developing the emotionally literate school*, p 128.
[129] Gueldner, B.A. et al, *Social and emotional learning in the classroom*; Weare, K., *Developing the emotionally literate school.*
[130] Gueldner, B.A. et al, *Social and emotional learning in the classroom*, pp 122–123.
[131] Ibid, p 123.
[132] Ibid.
[133] Aspen Institute, *Nation at hope.*
[134] Weare, K., *Developing the emotionally literate school*, p 25.
[135] Gueldner, B.A. et al, *Social and emotional learning in the classroom.*
[136] Department of Health and NHS England, *Future in mind: Promoting, protecting and improving our children and young people's mental health and wellbeing* (Department of Health and NHS England, 2015).
[137] Ibid, p 42.
[138] Shriver, T.P. and Buffett, J., 'The uncommon core', p xvi.
[139] Green Party, *Manifesto 2019.*
[140] Aspen Institute, *Nation at hope.*
[141] Gueldner, B.A. et al, *Social and emotional learning in the classroom.*
[142] Aspen Institute, *Nation at hope*, p 30.

143 Rosenberg, M.B., *Nonviolent communication*, p 132.
144 Ibid, p 2.
145 Wikipedia, 'Nonviolent communication' (2021), https://en.wikipedia.org/wiki/Nonviolent_Communication
146 Rosenberg, M.B., *Nonviolent communication.*
147 Ibid, p 197.
148 Williams, M., *Couples counselling*; Rosenberg, M.B., *Nonviolent communication.*
149 Gottman, J.S. and Gottman, J.M., *10 principles.*
150 Williams, M., *Couples counselling.*
151 Rosenberg, M.B., *Nonviolent communication*, p 51.
152 Ibid, p 150.
153 Ibid, p 54.
154 Williams, M., *Couples counselling*; Gottman, J.S. and Gottman, J.M., *10 principles.*
155 Rosenberg, M.B., *Nonviolent communication.*
156 Fanon, F., *Black skin, white masks*, trans C.L. Markmann (Pluto, 1991).
157 Juncadella, C.M., 'What is the impact of the application of the nonviolent communication model on the development of empathy? Overview of research and outcomes' (MSc in Psychotherapy Studies, University of Sheffield, 2013), https://www.cnvc.org/sites/default/files/NVC_Research_Files/Carme_Mampel_Juncadella.pdf
158 Epinat-Duclos, J., Foncelle, A., Quesque, F., Chabanat, E., Duguet, A., Van der Henst, J.B. et al, 'Does nonviolent communication education improve empathy in French medical students?', *International Journal of Medical Education* 12 (2021).
159 Yang, J. and Kim, S., 'Effects of a nonviolent communication-based training program for inpatient alcoholics in South Korea', *Perspectives in Psychiatric Care* 57, no 3 (2021).
160 www.cvnc.org
161 https://www.compassioninpolitics.com/ and Hawkins, M. and Nadel, J. (eds) (2022) *How compassion can transform our politics, economy, and society*, London: Routledge.
162 'Engagements', Volume 698, debated on Wednesday 7 July 2021 (2021), https://hansard.parliament.uk/commons/2021-07-07/debates/1C736EA1-AB82-4BE4-81D6-9D2F284BEAB3/Engagements
163 Gottman, J.S. and Gottman, J.M., *10 principles.*
164 Rosenberg, M.B., *Nonviolent communication*, p 148.
165 Beck, A.T., Rush, A.J., Shaw, B.F. and Emery, G., *Cognitive therapy of depression* (Guilford Press, 1979); Kahneman, D., *Thinking, fast and slow.*
166 Labour Party, *It's time for real change: The Labour Party manifesto 2019* (Labour Party, 2019), p 49.
167 Liberal Democrats, *Manifesto 2019*, p 23.
168 Ibid, p 39.
169 Ibid, p 73.
170 Scottish National Party, *Stronger for Scotland: 2019 Scottish National Party manifesto* (Scottish National Party, 2019), p 16.

171 Labour Party, *Manifesto 2019*, p 78.
172 Liberal Democrats, *Manifesto 2019*, p 64.
173 Green Party, *Manifesto 2019*, p 6.
174 Liberal Democrats, *Manifesto 2019*, p 82.
175 Hawkins, M. (2022) Compassion in politics. In M. Hawkins (ed) *How compassion can transform our politics, economy, and society*, London: Routledge.
176 25 December 1957, Alabama, https://www.shmoop.com/quotes/darkness-cannot-drive-out-darkness.html, quoted in Lerner, M., *Revolutionary love*, p 144.
177 Ibid, p 123.
178 Rosenberg, M.B., *Nonviolent communication.*
179 Lerner, M., *Revolutionary love.*
180 Ibid, p 42.
181 Ibid, p 123.
182 Ibid, p 103.
183 Buber, M., 'Dialogue'; Buber, M., *I and thou.*
184 Freire, P., *Pedagogy of the oppressed*, p 116, emphasis added.
185 Lerner, M., *Revolutionary love.*
186 Mason, P., *Clear bright future.*
187 Rosenberg, M.B., *Nonviolent communication*, p 103.
188 weall.org
189 Nordic Council of Ministers, *Towards a Nordic wellbeing economy* (Nordic Council of Minsters, 2021), https://www.norden.org/en/publication/towards-nordic-wellbeing-economy
190 Wellbeing Economy Alliance, *Wellbeing economy policy design guide* (Wellbeing Economy Alliance, 2017), p 7, https://wellbeingeconomy.org/wp-content/uploads/Wellbeing-Economy-Policy-Design-Guide_Mar17_FINAL.pdf
191 Trebeck, K. and Baker, A., *Being bold.*
192 'Proposals for a sustainable and inclusive wellbeing economy', EDM (Early Day Motion) 196 (2020), https://edm.parliament.uk/early-day-motion/54654/proposals-for-a-sustainable-and-inclusive-wellbeing-economy
193 'Climate goals: Wellbeing economy', Volume 704, debated on Tuesday 30 November 2021 (2021), https://hansard.parliament.uk/commons/2021-11-30/debates/5159DD63-D112-4D03-AE68-57A6A63F8659/ClimateGoalsWellbeingEconomy
194 Green Party, *Manifesto 2019*, p 49.
195 Liberal Democrats, *Manifesto 2019*, p 27.
196 Women's Equality Party, *Manifesto: London elections 2021* (Women's Equality Party, 2021).
197 Raworth, K., *Doughnut economics.*
198 Ibid, p 31.
199 https://www.bankofengland.co.uk/knowledgebank/what-is-gdp
200 'Robert F. Kennedy's remarks at the University of Kansas' (2021), https://en.wikipedia.org/wiki/Robert_F._Kennedy%27s_remarks_at_the_University_of_Kansas
201 Meadows, in Raworth, K., *Doughnut economics*, p 40.

202 'Climate goals: Wellbeing economy'.
203 Raworth, K., *Doughnut economics*, p 154.
204 Nordic Council of Ministers, *Towards a Nordic wellbeing economy.*
205 Wellbeing Economy Alliance, *Wellbeing economy policy design guide*, p 6.
206 Trebeck, K. and Baker, A., *Being bold*, p 47.
207 Lerner, M., *Revolutionary love*, p 2.
208 Wellbeing Economy Alliance, *Wellbeing economy policy design guide.*
209 Raworth, K., *Doughnut economics.*
210 Nordic Council of Ministers, *Towards a Nordic wellbeing economy*, p 15.
211 Ibid.
212 Organisation for Economic Co-operation and Development, *OECD regional well-being: A user's guide* (OECD, 2018), www.oecdregionalwellbeing.org
213 Wikipedia, 'Gross national happiness' (2021), https://en.wikipedia.org/wiki/Gross_National_Happiness
214 Nordic Council of Ministers, *Towards a Nordic wellbeing economy.*
215 Ibid.
216 Ibid.
217 Wikipedia, 'Gross national happiness'.
218 www.oecdregionalwellbeing.org
219 www.oecdbetterlifeindex.org
220 https://happyplanetindex.org/
221 Nordic Council of Ministers, *Towards a Nordic wellbeing economy*, p 14.
222 Ibid, p 1.
223 Government of New Zealand, *The wellbeing budget 2019* (Government of New Zealand, 2019), p 3, treasury.govt.nz/publications/wellbeing-budget/wellbeing-budget-2019
224 Trebeck, K. and Baker, A., *Being bold*, p 44.
225 Government Bill, Public Finance (Wellbeing) Amendment Bill (Government of New Zealand, 2020).
226 Ibid (26KB(a)).
227 Ibid (26M(5)).
228 Government of Iceland, *Indicators for measuring well-being* (Government of Iceland, 2019), https://www.government.is/lisalib/getfile.aspx?itemid=fc981010-da09-11e9-944d-005056bc4d74
229 Wellbeing Economy Alliance, *Wellbeing economy policy design guide.*
230 Ibid, p 39.
231 Ibid.
232 Inner Development Goals, *Inner development goals.*

## Chapter 8

1 Bregman, R., *Utopia for realists*, p 257, original emphasis.
2 Segal, L., *Radical happiness*; Sunkara, B., *Socialist manifesto.*
3 Marx, K. and Engels, F., *Manifesto of the Communist Party.*
4 Buber, M., *Paths in utopia* (Syracuse University Press, 1996).
5 Engels, F., *Socialism*; Žižek, S., *Living in end times.*
6 Bauman, Z., *Socialism*, pp 9–10.

7 'Popper's critique of utopianism and defence of negative utilitarianism' (2018), https://philosophicaldisquisitions.blogspot.com/2018/01/poppers-critique-of-utopianism-and.html
8 Levitas, R., *Utopia*; Hudis, P., *Marx's alternative.*
9 Kolakowski, L., *Marxist humanism*, p 67.
10 Marx, K. and Engels, F., *Manifesto of the Communist Party*; Marx, K., *EPM*; Marx, K. and Engels, F., *The German ideology*; Marx, K., *Grundrisse: Foundations of the critique of political economy*, trans M. Nicolaus (Penguin, 1993); Hudis, P., *Marx's alternative.*
11 Chomsky, N., *Profit over people*, p 15.
12 Bauman, Z., *Socialism*, p 11.
13 Ibid; Kolakowski, L., *Marxist humanism.*
14 Gilman, C.P., *Herland* (Amazon, 1915).
15 Bregman, R., *Utopia for realists*, p 13.
16 Lerner, M., *Revolutionary love.*
17 Muñoz, J.E., *Cruising utopia: The then and there of queer futurity*, 10th anniversary edn (New York University Press, 2019), p 27.
18 Ibid, p 1.
19 Bregman, R., *Utopia for realists*, p 20.
20 Locke, E.A. and Latham, G.P., 'Building a practically useful theory of goal setting and task motivation: A 35-year odyssey', *American Psychologist* 57, no 9 (2002); Locke, E.A., Shaw, K.N., Saari, L.M. and Latham, G.P., 'Goal setting and task performance: 1969–1980', *Psychological Bulletin* 90, no 1 (1981); Di Malta, G.S., Oddli, H.W. and Cooper, M., 'From intention to action: A mixed methods study of clients' experiences of goal-oriented practices', *Journal of Clinical Psychology* 75, no 10 (2019); Cooper, M., *Integrating counselling.*
21 Lerner, M., *Revolutionary love.*
22 Ibid, p 141.
23 Segal, L., *Radical happiness.*
24 Kruglanski, A.W. and Kopetz, C., 'What is so special (and nonspecial) about goals? A view from the cognitive perspective', in *The psychology of goals*, ed G.B. Moskowitz and H. Grant (Guilford Press, 2009), p 29.
25 Harkin, B., Webb, T.L., Chang, B.P., Prestwich, A., Conner, M., Kellar, I. et al, 'Does monitoring goal progress promote goal attainment? A meta-analysis of the experimental evidence,' *Psychological Bulletin* 142, no 2 (2016); Epton, T., Currie, S. and Armitage, C.J., 'Unique effects of setting goals on behavior change: Systematic review and meta-analysis', *Journal of Consulting and Clinical Psychology* 85, no 12 (2017).
26 Elliot, A.J. and Church, M.A., 'Client articulated avoidance goals in the therapy context'.
27 Levitas, R., *Utopia*, p 209.
28 Sargent, L.T., *Utopianism: A very short introduction* (Oxford University Press, 2010); Levitas, R., *Utopia.*
29 Paul Tillich in Sargent, L.T., *Utopianism.*
30 Bauman, Z., *Socialism*, p 17.

31 More, T., *Utopia.*
32 Sargent, L.T., *Utopianism*; Segal, L., *Radical happiness.*
33 Sargent, L.T., *Utopianism.*
34 Bellamy, E., *Looking backward.*
35 Morris, W., *News from nowhere.*
36 Ibid, p 40.
37 See translation at http://wpwt.soton.ac.uk/trans/cockaygn/coctrans.htm
38 More, T., *Utopia*, p 94, italics added.
39 Bellamy, E., *Looking backward*, p 83.
40 Ibid, pp 95–96.
41 Hudis, P., *Marx's alternative.*
42 Mason, P., *Clear bright future.*
43 Bastani, A., *Fully automated communism.*
44 Maslow, A.H., *Motivation and personality*, p 58.
45 Bastani, A., *Fully automated communism*; Bregman, R., *Utopia for realists.*
46 Care Collective, *The care manifesto.*
47 Bauman, Z., *Socialism*, p 58.
48 Ibid.
49 Ibid, p 128.
50 'Mental health: Britain's biggest social problem' (2004), http://www.cabinetoffice.gov.uk/strategy/downloads/files/mh_layard.pdf
51 Graeber, D., *Bullshit jobs* (Penguin, 2019), pp 9–10.
52 Skinner, B.F., *Walden two.*
53 Bastani, A., *Fully automated communism.*
54 Dunayevskaya, R., *Marxism and freedom*; Bregman, R., *Utopia for realists.*
55 Marcuse in Dunayevskaya, R., *Marxism and freedom.*
56 Morris, W., *News from nowhere*, p 51.
57 Skinner, B.F., *Walden two*; Bellamy, E., *Looking backward*; Lerner, M., *Revolutionary love.*
58 Marcuse, H., *Eros and civilization.*
59 Levitas, R., *Utopia.*
60 Marx, K. and Engels, F., *The German ideology.*
61 Aked, J. et al, *Five ways to wellbeing.*
62 In Hudis, P., *Marx's alternative*, p 120.
63 Sunkara, B., *Socialist manifesto*, p 27.
64 Skinner, B.F., *Walden two*, p xiii.
65 Mitchell, C., 'Necessitous man and conflict resolution'.
66 Cooper, M., 'The fully functioning society'; Corning, P., *The fair society.*
67 Morris, W., *News from nowhere*, p 45.
68 Amiel, D. and Emelien, I., *The new progressivism.*
69 Muñoz, J.E., *Cruising utopia.*
70 Haraway, D.J., *Staying with the trouble: Making kin in the Chthulucene* (Duke University Press, 2016).
71 Intergovernmental Panel on Climate Change, *Climate change 2021: The physical science basis* (Cambridge University Press, 2021), https://www.ipcc.ch/report/ar6/wg1/downloads/report/IPCC_AR6_WGI_Full_Report.pdf.

72 Simms, A., 'Reimagining Britain'.
73 Marcuse, H., *Eros and civilization*, p 123.
74 Care Collective, *The care manifesto*, p 5.
75 Women's Equality Party, *Manifesto*.
76 Cohen, G.A., *Why not socialism?*
77 Care Collective, *The care manifesto*, p 44.
78 Berlin, I., 'Two concepts of liberty', in *Liberty*, ed H. Hardy (Oxford University Press, 1958).
79 Sartre, J.-P., *Being and nothingness*.
80 Berlin, I., 'Two concepts of liberty', p 171.
81 Austin, J.T. and Vancouver, J.B., 'Goal constructs in psychology: Structure, process, and content', *Psychological Bulletin* 120, no 3 (1996).
82 Maslow, A.H., *The farther reaches of human nature*; Morse, S. and Gergen, K., 'Social comparison, self-consistency, and the concept of the self', *Journal of Personality and Social Psychology* 16, no 1 (1970).
83 Layard, R., *Happiness*, p 151.
84 Corning, P., *The fair society*, p 140.
85 Layard, R., *Happiness*, p 156.
86 Morris, W., *News from nowhere*, p 43.
87 Lerner, M., *Revolutionary love*.
88 Raworth, K., *Doughnut economics*, p 194.
89 Bregman, R., *Utopia for realists*.
90 Lerner, M., *Revolutionary love*.
91 Sunkara, B., *Socialist manifesto*, p 29.
92 Deutsch, M., *Resolution of conflict*.
93 Bregman, R., *Utopia for realists*.
94 Care Collective, *The care manifesto*.
95 Buber, M., *Paths in utopia*, p 7.
96 Wilde, O., *The soul of man under socialism* (Penguin, 2001), p 141, emphasis added.

## Chapter 10

1 Trebeck, K., 'A wellbeing economy agenda to help shape the post-coronavirus economy', *Eurohealth* 26, no 3 (2020), p 6.
2 Care Collective, *The care manifesto*.
3 Labour Party, *Manifesto 2019*, p 98.
4 Freud, S., *Civilization, society and religion: Group psychology, civilization and its discontents and other works* (Penguin, 1991).
5 https://progressive.international/
6 https://www.opendemocracy.net/en/
7 Lerner, M., *Revolutionary love*; see https://www.tikkun.org/
8 Doughty, S., 'The 10 signs of happiness: How the Coalition plans to measure your well-being', *The Daily Mail* (2011), https://www.dailymail.co.uk/news/article-2055888/The-10-signs-happiness-How-Coalition-plans-measure-being.html
9 Amiel, D. and Emelien, I., *The new progressivism*.

10 https://www.mind.org.uk/
11 https://sczaction.org/
12 https://www.youngminds.org.uk/
13 In Wilkinson, R. and Pickett, K., *Spirit level*, p 270.
14 Ibid, p 267.
15 Corning, P., *Nature's magic.*
16 Rogers, C.R., *On becoming a person.*
17 Moscovici, S. et al, 'Influences of a consistent minority on the responses of a majority in a colour perception task', *Sociometry* 32, no 4 (1969).
18 Amiel, D. and Emelien, I., *The new progressivism.*
19 Ibid, p 5, original emphasis.
20 Levitas, R., *Utopia*, p 231.
21 For instance, Lerner, M., *Revolutionary love*; Bregman, R., *Humankind*; Care Collective, *The care manifesto.*
22 Ghandi, M., *Selected writings of Mahatma Ghandi* (Faber & Faber, 1971), p 55.
23 West, C., *Race matters*, p 8.
24 Ibid, p 109.

# Index

## G



## H

## P

## R

## S

## W



## Y



## Z

CPSIA information can be obtained
at www.ICGtesting.com
Printed in the USA
JSHW031239260123
36882JS00005B/26